FISK UNIVERSITY
JUBILEE
SINGERS

EX

LIBRIS

Unspeakable ShaXXXspeares

Unspeakable ShaXXXspeares

Queer Theory and American Kiddie Culture

Richard Burt

St. Martin's Press
New York

ISBN 0-312-21363-8

Library of Congress Cataloging-in-Publication Data

Burt, Richard, 1954-
    Unspeakable ShaXXXspeares : queer theory and American kiddie
culture / by Richard Burt.
    p. cm.
    Includes bibliographical references and index.
    ISBN 0-312-21363-8
    1. Shakespeare, William, 1564-1616—Appreciation—United States.
2. Homosexuality and literature—United States—History—20th
century. 3. Popular culture—United States—History—20th century.
4. United States—Civilization—English influences. 5. Shakespeare,
William, 1564-1616—Adaptations. 6. Youth—United States-
-Attitudes.   I. Title.
PR2971.U6B87   1998
822.3'3—dc21   98-6589
                                                                  CIP

Book design by Acme Art, Inc.

First edition: October, 1998
10 9 8 7 6 5 4 3 2 1

In memory of my brother,
David Maclay Burt

What are the noises of the waking morning that we draw into our dreams? The "ugliness," the "out-of-date," are only dissembled voices which speak from our childhood.
—Walter Benjamin, *Passagen-Werk,* V, 1214.

Anyone who presumes to speak about stupidity today runs the risk of coming to grief in a number of ways. It may be interpreted as insolence on his part; it may even be interpreted as disturbing the progress of our time. . . . And so a question gradually arises that refuses to be put off: Just what is stupidity? . . . when confronted with stupidity I would rather confess my Achilles' heel right away: I don't know what it is. I have not discovered any theory of stupidity with whose aid I could presume to save the world. . . .
—Robert Musil, "On Stupidity"

Contents

List of Illustrations

My Own Private ShaXXXspeares

Generation XXX Criticism

This book is necessarily addressed not only to readers interested in Shakespeare but also to readers interested in American popular culture; film, video, and queer theory; psychoanalysis; and cultural criticism. It offers both a series of queer readings of Shakespeare films and a reading of Shakespeare as queer symptom of America's national unconscious, a symptom registered in popular culture, primarily film, video, and television of the 1980s and 1990s. Shakespeare is cited again and again across a variety of popular American film and television genres including comedy, science fiction, action, gangster melodrama, situation comedy, cartoon series, and so on, only to be cancelled out in ways that range from simply not marking the adaptation of Shakespeare as such, as in Gus Van Sant's *My Own Private Idaho;* to drowning him out, as in Baz Luhrmann's *William Shakespeare's Romeo and Juliet;* to his wholesale destruction in films such as *The Naked Gun* and *Skyscraper.* Until recently, Shakespeare's citation has been read in terms of his status as an author of classical texts: his plays have been regarded as adaptable to successive generations and cultures because of his poetic genius, complexity, and transhistorical, transcultural wisdom.[1] By contrast, I maintain that Shakespeare's citation in American popular culture registers the way his "classic" texts resonate with deep, unconscious elements of the United States's cultural self-legitimation. To explore this idea, I will take up the following wide-ranging questions: Why is Shakespeare both invoked and disappeared in America? What does Shakespeare enable American popular culture to do and say that it couldn't otherwise do and say without him? When can Shakespeare *not* be cited in American popular culture? Can American popular culture function without Shakespeare? What happens to academic representations of Shakespeare when they are positioned in a popular context? How do extra-academic representations of Shakespeare and their reception conflict with the widespread academic desire to control and regulate how Shakespeare is received both inside and outside of academia?

In addressing these broad questions, among others, *Unspeakable ShaXXXspeares* focuses on some of the implications of Shakespeare's mediatization over the past two decades: films are now widely accessible on video, and CD-ROMs and the internet have expanded archival possibilities. While Shakespeare's mediatization has made a new database available, it has also had the unintended effect of making it clear just how much Shakespeare has not been archived, indeed, how much cannot be archived because of its pervasiveness and impermanence. Any attempt to assess Shakespeare's significance as a cultural icon in American culture has to address this paradoxical phenomenon: as Shakespeare is dispersed, he allows certain ideas to be spoken, but he also remains unspeakable in a number of ways, as he gets drowned out, displaced, even, as we shall see, "terminated." Though many of the films and television episodes I discuss have not been archived, the category of the unspeakable is by no means confined to the unarchived, the unconscious, or the closeted, but traverses every point at which Shakespeare is being articulated and mediatized. Similarly, while the unspeakable refers to the relative tastelessness and absence of formal complexity of many of the films and television replays I discuss, the unspeakable traverses all productions from avant-garde to the most cheaply made pornographic adaptations.

The point of attending to unspeakable ShaXXXspeares isn't, then, to move some adaptations or citations from the cultural margin to the center, from the national unconscious to the national conscious, and thereby make possible liberatory, queer resignifications of heterosexist norms, as if the margin or the unconscious constituted the "truth" rather than a site of contradiction and ambivalence. Instead, I wish to analyze the paradoxical ways Shakespeare remains unspeakable even as he is made to speak various national fantasies. To this end, I analyze unspeakable ShaXXXspeares in relation to figures such as the porn star, the transvestite, the virtuoso, and particularly the loser, all of whom occupy versions of the castrated subject-position of what I call "kiddie culture." Shakespeare's mediatization, I suggest, calls into question whether Shakespeare can still signify what Jacques Lacan (1966) calls "the phallus" or "*objet petit a*," the cause of desire, and thus can no longer serve either as a signifier of a national, paternal identity in American popular culture or as some remainder outside the symbolic in terms of which American national fantasy is organized.[2] This book is thus partly about mourning the displacement of not only Shakespeare but, more generally, the literary by the cultural, as the United States moves into a multicultural, postpatriarchal social formation. I should add that focusing on Shakespeare's citation and resignification in American kiddie culture necessarily involves a transnational critical approach since the plays, as they are represented in popular terms now more in movies than onstage, migrate between the United States (particularly Hollywood) and other countries, primarily England, of course, but Italy and Germany as well.[3] My primary focus is on films made in the United States, but I also take up transnationally produced films and videos made in England, Italy, and Japan but widely marketed in the United States.[4]

In addition to enlarging the Shakespeare archive, I provide a way of making unspeakable ShaXXXspeares, hitherto archived or not, an object of criticism. Much of what might be considered by many to be "unspeakable" has remained undiscussed because it has seemed inane or just plain stupid. Rather than try to reclaim such replays and citations by showing that they are actually intelligent (that is, politically subversive, as present cultural criticism typically understands popular culture), I have attempted to think through their production and consumption in the context of a youth culture that paradoxically defines intelligence as dumbing down, and for which matters of speed, the new, the cool, the trivial, the inane, the belated, and the obsolete are crucial. My aim in focusing on unspeakable ShaXXXspeares is partly, then, to rethink the terms by which Shakespeare and cultural studies in general have been debated over the past two decades. Conservatives might deplore "unspeakable" popular resignifications of Shakespeare as symptomatic of a national decline in cultural literacy, an erosion of standards; by contrast, progressive cultural critics might celebrate unspeakable ShaXXXspeares as expressions of a protopolitical youth culture. Yet both conservative and progressive critics believe that they (and, in the case of cultural critics, popular texts) are intelligent and that the critics they oppose are not; both sides share the same assumption, that is, that intelligence, culture, and criticism are all on the same side.

What demands consideration in the 1990s, however, is the way Shakespeare is being recoded for a kiddie culture in which "cool" losers transvalue stupidity, indeed, in which stupidity and politics are not easily opposed, either in popular culture or in criticism and theory. The present transvaluations of stupidity and loserdom have significant implications both for pedagogy and for the way we think of the academic intellectual: If cultural critics now eschew an older model of the academic intellectual as vanguard reformer of politically incorrect popular culture, what, if any, possibilities remain for a newer model of the intellectual as a student who learns from popular culture, essentially now co-extensive with youth culture, once that culture announces itself as dumb and dumber?[5]

I hope it is clear, then, that *Unspeakable ShaXXXspeares* does not cover the much-traveled territory of Shakespeare films and adaptations. It is in no sense a performance history or filmography.[6] Instead, I focus on a series of replays of Shakespeare that are often so far from their "originals" they no longer count as interpretations of the plays at all. Thus, I do not generally offer new interpretations of Shakespeare's plays (on film and video), not because of space constraints but as a consequence of the post-textual parameters of the electronic archive and its modes of access. The focus of this book is on what I call "post-hermeneutic" ShaXXXspeares insofar as Shakespeare's texts in the brave new world of mediatization are no longer the symbolic source of a history of ongoing interpretations that respond to each other in a meaningful dialectic. (By the same token, I would not claim that Shakespeare's texts offer us any special access to this world.) "ShaXXX-speare" functions instead as an imaginary icon that inspires a series of decontextualized, disembodied, unmoored, even hallucinatory references and recreations. In a psychoanalytic register, one could say that the imaginary productions of psychosis and perversion have replaced symbolic chains of obsession and hysteria in the postmodern reception of Shakespeare.

In reading replays of Shakespeare in American popular culture through the lenses of film and queer theory and Lacanian psychoanalysis, I aim not merely to legitimate readings of popular culture by contextualizing them in the usual theoretically reflexive way (that is framing them in relation to recognizable theoretical discourses and debates) but to use Shakespeare to critique the American brand, as it were, of cultural studies—particularly the dominant academic fantasies about fandom, stardom, pedagogy, and the role of the academic intellectual—that he typically articulates. This book is a study of Shakespeare as a symptom of the American national unconscious, but it is also a study of Shakespeare as a symptom of the American academic unconscious.[7] I am interested in examining what can't be recycled rather than in recycling cultural trash. Thus, I do not follow out the work of Michel de Certeau and Pierre Bourdieu (see Cartnell 1997) and define myself as a critic who, as a fan of popular culture, can speak what is in unspeakably bad taste in a bourgeois sense about the ShaXXXspeare replays I discuss. Instead, I examine the ways in which this strategy inadvertently attempts to get rid of the academic unconscious. It (unknowingly) evades an inquiry into the now-dominant academic fantasies about popular culture, about politics as the license for attention to culture (high and low), about the desire of the critic/fan—the desire to keep desiring to do criticism, the will to will Will. Analysis of popular culture and celebrations of fandom have been enabled through a narrow conception of politics, a conception that comes at the expense of an analysis of the academic unconscious, even when, perhaps especially when, that criticism has drawn explicitly on psychoanalysis.

Parts of this book have already seen print. A much shorter version of chapter 1, "The Love That Dare Not Speak Shakespeare's Name: New Shakesqueer Cinema," appeared in *Shakespeare, the Movie: Popularizing the Plays on Film, TV, and Video,* edited by Lynda E. Boose and Richard Burt. I would like to thank Lynda Boose for encouraging me to write the original article. Parts of the Introduction come from my contributions to an essay in the same collection that I co-authored with Lynda, entitled "Totally Clueless: Shakespeare Goes Hollywood in the 1990s."

I have been particularly fortunate to have Maura Burnett of St. Martin's Press as my editor. From the very start, she had a great sense of what I wanted to do in this book and helped me to do it throughout the production process. The two readers of the manuscript, Laurie Osborne and Julia Reinhard-Lupton made many excellent suggestions for revision. Laurie also graciously shared with me her fine, as yet unpublished, work on Shakespeare and the internet and CD-ROMs. Time for research was greatly enabled by a Fulbright scholarship to Berlin, where I was able to spend a valuable year as a guest of the Humboldt University of Berlin and the Free University. Ulrike Unfug generously took me deep inside East Berlin in ways I continue to treasure. My good friend Manfred Pfister of the Institute for English Philology at the Free University and my colleagues at Humboldt, Annette Schlichter, Klaus Milich, and Gunther Lenz, provided very warm departments-away-from-my-department. Indira Ghose of the Free University remains an exceptional friend and colleague, and Nadja Geer offered me wonderful guided tours through the Berlin pop and academic scenes.

I would also like to thank the chair at the University of Jena, Jim Mendelson of the University of Tübingen, Bill Carroll, chair of the Shakespeare Seminar at Harvard University's Center for Literary and Cultural Studies, and Manfred Pfister for inviting me to deliver parts of this book. My gratitude is also owed to Laurence Rickels, who helped me think through issues about academic stardom by inviting me to organize and chair a panel on academic fantasy for the annual meeting of the Semiotic Society of America. This book has also benefited from my being able to circulate informally chapters of the book in a seminar entitled "Citing Shakespeare in American Popular Culture" I co-directed with Lynda Boose at the 1998 annual meeting of the Shakespeare Association of America. In addition, I have been exceptionally lucky in having particularly receptive, interested, often gifted students in my Shakespeare, Film, Video, and Popular Culture seminars at the Free University, Berlin, and at the University of Massachusetts, Amherst, particularly Alexander Wichmann, Mathias Schneider, Kristin Brenna (who, among other things, alerted me to the wonderful film, *Skyscraper*), Kate Lemons, Ignacio Lopez, Elizabeth MacDuffie, Kristine Ring, Josh Ruddy, Becky Kershman, and Noah Blaustein. Amy Kaplan provided valuable comments on chapter 3, and my colleague Wally Kerrigan did the same for the second chapter. Rebecca Schneider offered challenging readings of much of the book, as did Donald Cheney, Michael Schoenfeldt, and Stuart Culver. I would also like to express my appreciation to John Rogers and Jeffrey Wallen for their many conversations and their sensitive, careful, and often provocative comments on earlier drafts of several chapters. My friend and colleague Don Levine put his enormous knowledge of film at my disposal. It was a pleasure to discuss with him his ideas about "the cinematic ga(y)ze." Stephen Orgel generously gave me a copy of *Carnival in Venice* and Doug Lanier was kind enough to supply me with a copy of the *Ozzie and Harriet* episode, "An Evening with Hamlet." I am very grateful to Patrick Cassidy of Troma Entertainment for supplying me with a copy of *Tromeo and Juliet* as well as numerous slides and publicity stills, two of which are reproduced in this book. I am especially indebted to Betty Wilda, who was super helpful in obtaining almost all of the stills for this book.

My deepest appreciation goes to Elizabeth Power, whose own work on "dumb love" and the loser in American cinema has been an inspiration, and who, with her spacious heart, bright and shiny intellect, and quirky, wonderfully funny "loser" sensibility, has provided me with the most sustaining, engaging, and encouraging reader I could ever hope to expect or imagine.

Richard Burt
Northampton, MA

Dumb and Dumber Shakespeares: Academic Fantasy, the Electronic Archive, Loser Criticism, and Other Diminished Critical Capacities

Hello Shakespeare Kitty

At the end of 1996, a conservative Washington, D.C., think tank called the National Alumni Forum released a tabloidlike exposé ominously entitled *The Shakespeare File: What English Majors Are Really Studying,* that received national coverage (see Magner 1997, Yardley 1997). Taking the dropping of Shakespeare as a requirement of English majors at Georgetown University as its point of departure, the *File* denounced what it maintained was a widespread displacement of Shakespeare courses at major colleges and universities by courses on popular culture and (mostly queer) sex. "Shakespeare Out, Pop Culture 'In,'" ran the press release. The authors of the *File* insisted that intelligent life as we know it was to be found only in Shakespeare and other "great" authors:

> Concern about the "dumbing down" of America is widespread and well-justified. This country cannot expect a generation raised on gangster films and sex studies to maintain its leadership in the world, or even its unity as a nation. Shakespeare has shaped our language and our culture. His works provide a common frame of reference that helps us into a single community of discourse. (1996, 8)

While the authors decry the displacement of Shakespeare by popular culture and sex, ironically they end by praising Hollywood for popularizing Shakespeare in recent films directed by Franco Zeffirelli and Kenneth Branagh:

> Hollywood is doing more for cultural literacy than trendy English departments. . . . From Mel Gibson's "Hamlet" [sic] to Kenneth Branagh's "Henry V," audiences respond to the rich language, human drama, and enduring themes that touch their lives. It is sad to think that such achievements of the human spirit may be lost on future English majors. (1996, 8)

The conservatives' fear about dropping a Shakespeare requirement seems misplaced, however, since it depends on an opposition between popular culture and Shakespeare (understood as high culture) that clearly no longer holds.[1] It's not so much that Shakespeare is "out" in universities as that he has "popped" in, as it were.

I will return to the question of Shakespeare and pedagogy at length in chapter 5. For now, I simply wish to point out that pedagogy offers a crucial context in which to understand the ways in which Shakespeare is presently Americanized. Shakespeare is cited in a popular culture that is now co-extensive with a youth culture. This youth culture is not simply dumbed down but transvalues dumbing down. In animated cartoons such as *Beavis and Butt-Head*, films such as *Beavis and Butt-Head Do America* (dir. Mike Judge, 1996); *Romy and Michele's High School Reunion* (dir. David Mirkin, 1997); *Airheads* (dir. Michael Lehmann, 1994); *Dumb and Dumber* (dir. Peter Farrelly, 1994); *Tapeheads* (dir. Bill Fishman, 1988); *Forrest Gump* (dir. Robert Zemeckis, 1994); and *Slacker* (dir. Richard Linklater, 1993), television game shows such as MTV's *Idiot Savants,* with its tag line "There are no dumb answers. Well, maybe not"; and popular songs such as Beck's 1994 hit "Loser" and New Bad Things' 1995 "I Suck" to be stupid is to be cool. Shakespeare films have been directed at a youth market at least since Franco Zeffirelli's *Romeo and Juliet* (1968), and recent films continue to be. Like Keanu Reeves being lifted out of the teen movie *Bill and Ted's Excellent Adventure* (dir. Stephen Herek, 1989) to play Van Sant's modern Prince Hal in *My Own Private Idaho* (1993) and Don

John in Kenneth Branagh's *Much Ado About Nothing* (1993), actors chosen to participate in this contemporary Shakespearorama are now often American teen idols.[2] Animated movies such as the Disney *Hamlet* spin-off *The Lion King* (dir. Roger Allers and Ron Mikoff, 1994); television cartoon series such as *Animaniacs;* and children's shows like *Sesame Street* and *Wishbone* that do Shakespeare versions, or, in the case of the Saturday-morning cartoon *Gargoyles,* have characters named after Shakespearean characters (Puck, Titania, the witches, and so on), are only the most literal version of Shakespeare's entry into American 1990s youth culture.[3] All four of the so-called "big" Shakespeare tragedies have recently been reproduced in sophisticated comic book form, appropriate for college students; in 1990, Shakespeare began to appear in episodes of the comic book *The Sandman;* in 1995, English translations of the widely popular Japanese comic books *Ranma 1/2* and *Oh, My Goddess!* using *Romeo and Juliet* and *A Midsummer Night's Dream,* respectively, appeared; and in 1997, four plays in the *Classics Illustrated* comic book series of the 1950s were republished in booklet form (up from fifteen cents to five dollars) with a study guide at the back.[4] Even Adrian Noble's film version of his Royal Shakespeare Company theatrical production of *A Midsummer Night's Dream* (1996) was influenced by American popular film culture in this regard. The film begins in an early twentieth-century child's room with a McCauley Culkin–like child who is the dreamer of a Shakespearean "home alone" dream.

The production that has gone the furthest in enunciating itself as a teen film was the 1996 production *William Shakespeare's Romeo and Juliet,* orchestrated by Australian director Baz Luhrmann (whose claim to fame rested on his previous direction of *Strictly Ballroom* [1992]) and starring Leonardo DiCaprio as Romeo and Claire Danes as Juliet. The week before its U.S. release, the film sponsored the TV show in which Danes starred, *My So-Called Life,* with ads for the film blaring forth tracks from the first soundtrack CD performed by bands such as Garbage, Radiohead, Everclear, and Butthole Surfers (a second volume was released in April 1997). That same week MTV itself aired a half-hour Special on the film three times. The Special included segments that were introduced with semi-naked male and female bodies inscribed with the words "Family," "Honor," "Love," "Hate," and

"Revenge" tattooed in Gothic script, and clips of the film were intercut with interviews of local high school and college students conducted by Chris Connelly (who previously hosted MTV's "The Big Picture" when it aired weekly from 1989 to 1993). Moreover, as has become standard for all films, a website was announced. At this site a link for "Author" brought up the Chandos portrait modified such that Shakespeare wore a baseball cap backwards with "Bill" written on it.[5]

What is interesting about the MTV Special is the way it tries to reposition Shakespeare as something cool instead of something silly, feminine, or distasteful. The MTV Special fears kids don't or won't like Shakespeare, openly asking whether the students and their friends like Shakespeare, or ". . . if you say Shakespeare, they go 'Ooh, Shakespeare. Do I have to?'" The special indulges the latter attitude by gently mocking the standard ways of appreciating Shakespeare.[6] It shows an old clip of actors in period costume as a male voice-over, whose mannerisms obviously date him, announces "Shakespeare . . . as filled with meaning for today as ever in the past." Clips from a *Brady Bunch* episode (entitled "Juliet is the Sun") provide an even more mocking pedagogical context: Marcia's "Romeo, O Romeo" is followed by a clip from an old silent film of a man shaking his head in disapproval; at a later point, Marcia huffs, "These kids have no regard for Shakespeare," as she interrupts her rehearsal of Juliet's conversation with Romeo at the Capulet ball. The MTV Special overcomes the assumption that Shakespeare is "old" by having students say semi-articulate things such as "[the Luhrmann film] illustrates Shakespeare and how timeless it is. And that it can take place two hundred years ago or in today's, and you can see how it can relate to today's time." The students agree that anyone can quickly get past the play's "thees" and "thous." There is no critical response to the film itself or to the play. Instead the focus is on how the stars DiCaprio and Danes felt when they performed particular scenes (such as those in which they kissed each other, of course).[7]

The MTV *Romeo and Juliet* Special is not some pop ruse, however, to get students to read seriously an "authentic" Shakespeare. A 1990s American popular Shakespeare is precisely a dumbed down Shakespeare. The stress in recent Shakespeare film adaptations is on the performative rather than the rhetorical. *William Shakespeare's Romeo and Juliet's* editing is MTV-inflected. Two journalists (Maslin 1996, C12; Corliss 1996, 89-90) compared the film to an MTV rock video. The film is indeed framed with a television set at the beginning and end. Moreover, the video of the film was released in 1997 with a music video trailer put at the beginning, suggesting that the entire film following is one long music video. It was hardly a surprise when the 1997 MTV video awards did a parody of the balcony scene with Jenny McCarthy and Mike Meyers (reprising his film character Austin Powers) before cutting to presenter Claire Danes.[8]

The style and promotion of Luhrmann's film is not an aberration. Film technology is going in the direction of video. Since the 1980s, films have mostly been made with VCR viewing in mind. And of course the internet has become a major site for research and advertising. Even Al Pacino follows the lead of youth culture in his documentary *Looking for Richard* (1996), wearing a black baseball cap backward, and, at one point, smiling at the camera as he holds up his copy of *Cliffs Notes* for *Richard III.* Moreover, Pacino ironizes its own failings with a younger audience. Kevin Kline tells a story about his own disinterest in Shakespeare; in high school, "an English teacher brought us to a local production of *King Lear,* and after ten minutes of people doing 'Shakespearean acting,' I tuned out and started making out with my girlfriend in the back row. We left at intermission." A subsequent scene in which Pacino talks to high school students comically shows two students also making out.[9]

Of course, there's nothing terribly new about a dumbed down Shakespeare in America or student resistance to reading his plays.[10] As Lawrence Levine (1988, 54-56) has shown, since the late nineteenth century "knowledge" of Shakespeare's works has been reduced to stock phrases from a few plays,[11] typically *Julius Caesar, Hamlet,* and *Romeo and Juliet,* and even the producer of the earliest "quality" Shakespeare on silent film laughed off his thirty-minute versions of the plays.[12] Similarly, in the 1952 movie *She's Working Her Way Through College* (dir. H. Bruce Humberstone), Ronald Reagan played an English professor who stages a Shakespeare play every year in his Theater Arts class until a showgirl turned student (Virginia Mayo) urges him to "forget Shakespeare" and put on a musical she's written instead; after a vote in class in her favor, he consents and the musical is a big hit. And in an *Ozzie and Harriet* episode involving *Hamlet,* Ricky Nelson says that the play is "corny" and not "commercial." Ozzie and Harriet note that young people have a problem appreciating Shakespeare, and Ozzie, though initially appreciative of Shakespeare, later tries to get out of a family reading of the play so he can play poker at his neighbor's.[13] In what is to my knowledge the earliest instance of Shakespeare in American kiddie culture, "Shivering Shakespeare" (dir. Anthony Mack, 1929), the Little Rascals' performance of a school play based on *Quo Vadis* turns into a pie-throwing fest.[14]

So what's different about the 1990s American "kiddie" Shakespeare? The difference cannot be measured in terms of a (mythic) decline from a familiar Shakespeare (an assumed good) to a less familiar Shakespeare (an assumed evil). What is in question is less how much Shakespeare an American audience knows as it is how Shakespeare signifies as cultural token.[15] As William Uricchio and Roberta Pearson show in their study of the pre-Hollywood Vitagraph silent Shakespeare films, it was precisely a reduced Shakespeare that enabled him to take on a broad cultural function across classes:

> The consensus established through the reductionist approach [silent films were thirty minutes long] valorized the bard as cultural icon and referenced the plays, but it did not necessarily demand widespread and intimate familiarity with Shakespeare's texts. Members of all social formations, recognizing key social phrases and scenes, could participate in the overarching appropriation of Shakespeare for the purposes of consensus building. (1993, 67)

Until recently, the young person who hadn't learned to love Shakespeare would be thought to have made an imperfect adjustment to our culture. What's different about the way Shakespeare signifies in 1990s America, however, is that his status is contradictory in youth culture: he is both cool and uncool, both a signifier of elite and of popular culture, in part because of the way he is now positioned inside and outside of academia.[16]

This new contradiction can be grasped more fully if we contrast Shakespeare's appearance in two different pedagogical contexts, the 1971 *Brady Bunch* episode "Juliet is the Sun" and a short sequence about a *Hamlet* citation in the 1995 summer comedy *Clueless* (dir. Amy Heckerling). In *The Brady Bunch* (dir. Jack Arnold, 1972) episode, Shakespeare remains a signifier of authentic high culture. Marcia tries out for the role of the Nurse in a high school production of *Romeo and Juliet* but gets the part of Juliet instead. Initially miffed because she thinks her success is really due to nepotism, Marcia is encouraged by her family to think of herself as a beautiful actress. Her head quickly swells and she starts rewriting the play at will. Mike, her stepfather, reigns her in, however, patronizingly cautioning her that "no one could improve on Shakespeare." Marcia doesn't listen to his advice, however, and proceeds to ignore her high school teacher's stage directions as well. In a kind of feminist backlash moment, Carol, Marcia's mother, seeks out the high school teacher (also a woman) directing the production, and they agree that Marcia has to be cut for the play to go forward. The episode ends happily, however, when the student playing Lady Capulet drops out due to illness, and Marcia asks and is allowed to take over the part.

As a signifier of authentic high culture, Shakespeare can perform a patriarchal function in the context of the "blended" family. "First the part was too big for her," Mike says to Carol in his typical "we know best" tone, "and now she's too big for the part." Marcia's alternately inadequate and excessive relation to Shakespeare—she is either too small or too big—exposes a gendered symptom of a more general Brady family pathology, namely, a lack of fit. Marcia registers the return of the series' repressed origins, namely, the fact that the family isn't nuclear, as had hitherto been the case in series such as *The Donna Reed Show, Ozzie and Harriet,* and *Leave It to Beaver.* (The Brady family is the product of two remarriages; Carol and Mike are widow and widower. This fact is mentioned only in the second episode of the series.) If Shakespeare is a symptom of the family's unconventional origins, he is also a means of integrating Marcia into the family by recoding her adaptation of Shakespeare as the insubordination of a willful prima donna wanna-be. The heavily moralistic series makes sure Marcia learns her lesson, a lesson that has pointedly conservative political effects: as she moves from the role of Juliet to the role of Lady Capulet, she is repositioned from rebellious (soon to be sexually active?) teenager to traditional mother and housewife.

The opposition this *Brady Bunch* episode put in place between the original Shakespeare, coded as good, and a teenage girl's adaptation, coded as bad, no longer holds, however, in *Clueless*. Here Shakespeare is accessible not only through academia but through youth-driven, Hollywood, star-studded film adaptations of Shakespeare. Based on Jane Austen's *Emma, Clueless* narrates an ingenue's coming of age in a Beverly Hills high school.[17] Apparently an airhead (who likes to talk to her friend on a portable telephone, for example, while walking next to her), Cher Hamilton (Alicia Silverstone) gradually begins to take an interest in Josh (Paul Rudd), her college student step-brother (with whom she hooks up at the film's close).[18] At one point, she gets into a contest with Josh's girlfriend Heather (Susan Mohun), a nerd from Harvard, who tries to win a disagreement with Josh by citing *Hamlet:*

> HEATHER: It's just like Hamlet said: "To thine ownself be true."
> CHER: Uh, no. Hamlet didn't say that.
> HEATHER. [smiles condescendingly] I think that I remember *Hamlet* accurately.
> CHER: Well, I remember Mel Gibson accurately and he didn't say that. That Polonius guy did.

Point, set, and match. Josh smiles approvingly at Cher's victory, and his face falls only when Heather glares at him. Like Josh, the film sides with Cher, the cool loser (a term the full resonance of which I will examine shortly) over the more academically successful but nerdy Heather.

The contest is made possible in part because Shakespeare is now positioned both in academia and outside it, in popular film. In *Clueless,* the extra-academic Shakespeare can trump the academic one because it is cooler. Cher is hipper than Josh's Harvard girlfriend because she is a pragmatist without a program; she knows only what she needs to know about Shakespeare. The point of being hip in this case is not to be able to discuss *Hamlet* (whether the Shakespeare original or the Zeffirelli version) in depth but to win a victory of the moment, one that enables Cher to win a larger sexual and romantic victory. As a cool pragmatist/hipster, Cher is thus both brighter and dumber than the nerdy Harvard girlfriend she defeats. On the one hand, Cher poses as the loser, waiting for her potential competitors to put her down because they mistakenly assume that she is clueless; Cher can then seize the moment and win. But on the other hand, Cher is a clueless loser, possibly able to do a cultural critique of *Hamlet* but too cool, too easily bored, actually to bother to do so.

Being a loser is not just about cool indifference, then. Dumbing down is paradoxical: it is about setting, even raising standards as well as ignoring them. *Clueless* doesn't merely relocate high culture from a high to a low site (from London to Los Angeles). On the contrary, it regards Los Angeles as the present site of high culture, thereby comically calling into question the distinction between low and high. This is Shakespeare as received in Beverly Hills, not a Valley Shakespeare, not "Bill and Cher's Excellent Adventure." With their high-tech accessories and designer clothes, Cher Hamilton and her friends *are* the cultural elite, the snobs who want to "maintain standards" and to save fellow students from making the supreme mistake of doing or saying something *tasteless*.

This paradox may be understood as an overdetermined symptom of American culture of the 1980s and 90s. Youth culture has been redefined as what I call "kiddie culture."[19] Some twenty-somethings, for example, consume products designed for children, such as *Betty Boop* products; San Rio products such as *Hello Kitty, Kariope Frog,* and *Badtz • Maru; Josie and the Pussycats* and *Superman* T-shirts; and cat stickers, sometimes as part of a (punk) *grrrlie* look. Members of this generation also watch re-runs of child-oriented television programs such as *The Brady Bunch, Scooby Doo, The Jetsons, The Adams Family, Wonder Woman, The Pink Panther,* and consume their movie and comic book remakes (such as *The Flintstones* [dir. Brian Levant, 1994]). Whereas in the 60s, youth culture was valued for being purer, more advanced, and wiser than the existing, corrupt adult culture, kiddie culture emerges as childish, regressive, immature, and infantile in the 1990s context of diminishing expectations.[20] In response to having nowhere to go, some members of a younger generation no longer try to get ahead by knowing as much as possible but instead, in a kind of defiant resignation, give up on mastery in favor of knowing something about a few things, and may even choose to know about things others openly regard as childish, trivial, and stupid, or, as Beavis and Butthead might put it, things that willfully "suck."

A second central determination of a dumbed down 90s Shakespeare is the creation of electronic and video Shakespeare and popular culture archives. The ramifications of this mediatization are just now beginning to be theorized. As Jacques Derrida (1996) points out in a recent discussion of Freud, an archive not only includes media but is itself a form of mediatization. Had Freud been able to write via email and fax rather than letters, these technologies, according to Derrida,

> would have transformed this history from top to bottom and in the most initial inside of its production, in its very *events*. This is another way of saying that the archive, as printing, writing, prosthesis, or hypomnesic technique in general is not only the place for stocking and for conserving archivable content *of the past* which would exist in any case, such as, without the archive, one still believes it was or will have been. No, the technical structure of the archiving archive also determines the structure of the *archivable* content even in its very coming into existence and in its relationship to the future. The archivization produces as much as it records the event. . . . [A]rchival knowledge no longer determines, will never have determined, merely the moment of conservational recording, but rather the very institution of the archivable event. . . . To put it more trivially: what is no longer archived in the same way is no longer lived in the same way. Archivable meaning is also and in advance codetermined by the structure that it archives. (1996, 17)

The production of cheap, easily accessible video versions of many of Shakespeare's plays, of popular television sitcoms or melodramas, and pornography, along with the production of electronic archives for Shakespeare and popular films and shows (as of March 1998, over 40,000 matches for the words "William Shakespeare" were listed on Yahoo) has effectively enlarged and radically dispersed the Shakespeare archive, a point I will pursue momentarily. It has also called into question the degree to which Shakespeare functions as a signifier of intelligence, or whether Shakespeare as signifier of book culture lags behind postbook "smart" technology.[21] It's no coincidence that anxieties about declining educational standards and dumbing down have arisen at the moment when smartness is attributed to things ranging from weapons to drugs to cars to money (Ross 1994).

The citation of Shakespeare as paradoxically cool and uncool is also symptomatic of America's own doubts about its own status as an imperial power. Shakespeare appears in American kiddie culture not as unmarked, universal, but as marked, colonial, British. He is thus a symptom of an unconscious and vestigial American postcolonial identification with British colonial culture. In *Clueless,* for example, Shakespeare is cited in the context of a Hollywood film adaptation of Austen's *Emma.* Similarly, during the finale of MTV's *Idiot Savants,* an image of Shakespeare always appeared in the lower righthand corner of the screen when the first question was asked.[22] As if echoing Mark Twain's *A Connecticut Yankee in King Arthur's Court,* considered by some the beginning of American cultural imperialism and the end of American postcolonialism, Al Pacino in *Looking for Richard* moves from the Cloisters in New York to the then nearly reconstructed Globe theater in London; Pacino interviews English academics and actors, and he ends up performing before a dismayed Shakespeare sitting in the audience. Yet Shakespeare and British culture in general have also gone Hollywood (Boose and Burt, 1997).[23] On the one hand, then, Shakespeare remains the measure of American culture and intelligence; on the other, Mel Gibson and Hollywood are the measure of an intelligent Shakespeare.

In reading Shakespeare as a symptom of America's national unconscious, I draw on the psychoanalytic work of Jacques Lacan and queer and feminist film theory.[24] These theories do not, however, stand outside of stupidity and diminished critical capacity. I suggest, rather, that psychoanalytic notions of disavowal, repression, resistance, the phallus, castration, and so on all have to be recontextualized in relation to the dumbing down of culture in 1990s America, and more particularly, in relation to the current transvaluation of stupidity (and abjection as well) in American youth culture. For the 1990s intellectual does not stand apart from this transvaluation but instead seeks to dumb down and be a cultural channel surfer too. Major Shakespeare critics, for example, are turning their talents to readings of MTV videos. At least one critic has appeared in hip-hop garb on MTV and the pages of *New York* magazine, has held a conference on youth culture on his campus (Powers 1993), and professes to read glossy magazines rather than books (Mead 1994).[25]

I Want (to Know) It All!

In reading the Shakespeare symptom within the context of a dumbed down American kiddie culture, a culture in which the loser is now a paradoxically "cool" figure, I want to rethink the role of the intellectual as it has concerned some dominant academic fantasies, particularly those relating to fandom and queer theory. Much of what I am calling "unspeakable ShaXXXspeares" is unknown to many Shakespeareans. While all of it may be absorbed into the Shakespeare canon and discussed under the rubric of a "Shakespeare" author-function, it is in fact constructed out of a variety of academic and extra-academic rubrics in an electronic archive. Much of it appears in the context of other critical activities, particularly internet websites and chat groups. I obtained copies of *The Brady Bunch* and *Gilligan's Island* episodes, for example, through internet fan clubs. Similarly, I came across Shakespeare porn on an internet website (while looking, to be sure, for something other than Shakespeare). The category of the unspeakable emerges, then, as the critic crosses over from the domain of academic Shakespeare to multiple, mediatized popular culture sites in which Shakespeare may happen to show up.

In writing about unspeakable ShaXXXspeares, I want in part to contribute to enlarging the Shakespeare on film and video archive (Rothwell 1990; MacKernan 1994). There is currently no record, for example, of queer moments in Shakespeare, nor have any of the existing reference books on Shakespeare and film included instances of Shakespeare porn. I make no claim, however, to have provided a complete archive of unspeakable ShaXXXspeares, nor do I provide an exhaustive survey of the material of which I am aware. The unspeakable is not reducible in any case to the unknown or relatively obscure case. There is always something that remains unspoken, something unconscious, to put the point in psychoanalytic terms. As Michel Foucault (1969) maintains, the archive is about what can or cannot be spoken, under what conditions. The internet also radically complicates any archival project because websites are frequently short-lived, disappearing without a trace.

Some of the films and videos I discuss may not be familiar to many Shakespeareans and Americanists. And once made familiar, many of these films and videos might strike some critics as too stupid to be worth attending to critically. A reading of a *Gilligan's Island* episode (that deals with Shakespeare) through the lens of Frederic Jameson's (1981) notion of the political unconscious, for example, might strike some as critical overkill, probably not a good return on one's investment. Moreover, many of the examples I look at involve gay and pornographic sexuality, and I make no claim for their importance or interest on the grounds of their politically marginalized status. Indeed, most of them can lay no claim to being politically subversive or advancing a political agenda affirming the human rights of marginalized groups. Attention to unspeakable ShaXXXspeares may seem problematic, then, because it does not rely on the usual justifications and rationales for reading "politically incorrect" popular texts.

Why, then, should we attend critically to these unspeakable (re)productions? And why read them through the lenses of queer theory and what I call "loser criticism"? While I see in the unspeakable the possibility of a critique of what queer theorists call "heteronormativity" (Butler 1992; Warner 1993), I want to resist the temptation to align a sense of the unspeakable as tasteless with a sense of it as taboo. The dream of cultural criticism is to make these senses equivalent such that cultural trash is by definition the politically subversive. Harnessing trashy Shakespeare films (and possibly online cultural criticism of them) to fanzines and popular print and electronic discursive sites might seem to some cultural critics to be a way of countering neoconservative attacks on popular culture and its study in universities precisely by challenging the (mistaken) notion that Shakespeare and popular culture can be separated as high versus low culture. The fan of popular culture (including, I suppose, Shakespeare in popular culture) isn't a loser in this account, but an oppressed, unjustly maligned victim of the dominant culture who nevertheless manages to "win" by discursive acts of rewriting: "fandom," one critic writes, "is a way of appropriating media texts and rereading them in a fashion that serves different interests, a way of transforming mass culture into popular culture" (Jenkins 1991, 172 and 174; see also Jenkins 1992).

Yet the dispersal and mediatization of the popular (and elite) sites in which unspeakable ShaXXXspeares appear undermines this dream of anarchic transgression; indeed, that dispersal and mediatization shows that the dream is really about escaping an academic unconscious altogether. And it is here that I depart from recent attempts to recuperate popular culture fandom by interpreting fan discourses as expressions of dissident subcultures. Both popular culture and fan practices of receiving it in fanzines pose a threat to cultural criticism by implicitly demonstrating that such criticism cannot entirely be recuperated by being called political. The political, in the view of cultural critics, is also the intelligent. As Avital Ronell comments in an essay tracing the history of stupidity's place within the history of Western philosophy, "stupidity precisely cannot be seen as belonging to the domain of the political because it indicates that which lacks politics: it is being-outside-the-political" (1996, 6). Whereas for cultural critics politics operates as the phallus, that which guarantees the significance of their criticism by establishing distinctions between intelligence and stupidity, knowledge and trivia, and so on, the category of unspeakable ShaXXXspeare calls these distinctions into question and thereby calls into question the notion that cultural criticism's avowedly political status legitimates it as criticism. The cultural critic as an intellectual (and pedagogue) who is a fan or, in the more usual variant, a fan of fans, is, I will argue, necessarily a version of the dynamic, highly mobile, and paradoxical figure of the loser.

Before characterizing the loser, I want first to examine the academic fantasies underlying recent attempts to reconstruct an anti-authoritarian model of the intellectual in terms of fandom and popular culture, in order to show how they fail to redeem and legitimate both popular culture and cultural criticism. In a review of *Cultural Studies* (Grossberg 1992) Frederic Jameson notes: "Surely the most innovative treatment of the intellectual at this conference lies in the new model of the intellectual as 'fan'" (1993). Jameson goes on to cite Andrew Ross's comment in a discussion printed in the volume: "Some of the most exciting work being done in cultural studies . . . positions the intellectual in some respects as a 'fan.' . . . The new fan is something like a fan of fans"

(Grossberg 1992, 553; Jameson 1993, 43).[26] According to Jameson, "groupies are . . . already . . . potential or proto-intellectuals" (1993). The core of this fantasy is that the academic and the popular are identical, that critics are also fans, and that both are rational and intelligent, as Constance Penley (1992) and Andrew Ross (1993) have suggested. In conflating the critic and fan, cultural critics fantasize that the academic can cross over and adopt the extra-academic, popular position, indeed, can occupy all the positions even though they may be contradictory. In her essay "Feminism, Psychoanalysis, and the Study of Popular Culture" (1992), Constance Penley celebrates fans (who happen to be almost exclusively women) of *Star Trek* who rewrite or "slash" the show in terms of gay male porn. Fantasy is a crucial term in her analysis. She draws on psychoanalysis to criticize a too narrow understanding of gendered subjectivity and thereby to account for the fact that women rewrite *Star Trek* in terms of gay male porn fantasies. Yet Penley also worries that the fans' fantasies are not feminist enough; indeed, that they may not be feminist at all.[27] The perceived lack of political consciousness in *Star Trek* slash fandom leads critics such as Penley and Andrew Ross who want to deconstruct the distinction between the fan and the intellectual also want to keep that distinction at least faintly in place.[28] Penley wants to distance herself so that she doesn't merely appear to be "completely ga ga" (491) over the fans and describes herself as "a fan of [*Star Trek*] fandom" (491).[29] Similarly, Ross uses the qualifier "in some respects" to describe the similarities between intellectuals and fans (Grossberg 1992, 553).[30]

The academic fantasy here, untheorized as such, is that the cultural critic can occupy all positions, be the virtuoso, the one who can cross over, do it all. Penley's view of her fans, at once adoring and critical, arises from her position as a fan of fans rather than as just another fan of *Star Trek*. This position puts her in excess of the fans' relation to the television series. As Penley writes: "Where did I fit in to all this? Was I going to the conference as a fan, even a potential writer of K/S stories, a voyeur of fascinating subculture, or a feminist academic critic? . . . I finally decided I was all three, a fan, a feminist critic, and perhaps inescapably, a voyeur. . . ." (1993, 484). Though the fan may be lacking political consciousness in some ways (by not being feminist, or not feminist enough), the academic fan lacks nothing.

The identification of the critic with the fan enables a related academic fantasy about popular culture. As a fan, the intellectual no longer has to take a vanguard position politically, but instead can dumb down. The study of popular culture is authorized in the name of what Andrew Ross (1989) calls a "liberatory" non–politically correct criticism. In a discussion of pornography, Ross offers a model of the intellectual as the one who learns from mass culture rather than attempting to reform it. After rehearsing Janice Radway's positive assessment of romance fiction as porn for women and noting that "the 'problem' for feminism remains one of converting . . . dissatisfaction into real actions and consciousness that would be regarded as feminist and progressive" (1989, 193), Ross asks two crucial questions: "[W]hat if the popularity of such cultural forms as pornography, for men, and romance, for women, speak to desires that cannot be described according to the articulate forms and categories of an intellectual's conception of 'politics'? What if the pleasures of pornography and romance, however complicit with patriarchal logic, prove to be resistant to direct pressure from a reformist agenda?" (1989, 193). According to Ross:

> We must take into account the possibility that a large part of pornography's popularity lies in its refusal to be educated; it therefore has a large stake in celebrating delinquency and wayward and unauthorized behavior, and in this respect is akin to cultural forms like heavy metal music whose definitive, utopian theme, after all, is "school's out forever." To refuse to be educated: to refuse to be taught lessons about maturity and adult responsibility, let alone about sexism and racism: to be naughty, even bad, but mostly naughty; to be on your worst behavior—all this may be a ruse of patriarchy, a ruse of capitalism, but it also has something to do with a resistance to education, institutional or otherwise. It has something to do with a resistance to those whose patronizing power and missionary ardor are the privileges bestowed upon and instilled in them by a legitimate education. Surely there is a warning here for intellectuals who are committed today, as always, to "improving" the sentimental education of the populace. (1989, 201)

Ross concludes:

> For intellectuals, what is at stake specifically in an inquiry of this kind is a cultural politics which seeks to *learn from* the forms and discourses of popular pleasure, rather than adopting or supporting a legislative posture in the name of the popular. What intellectuals need to learn most from this are lessons in self-criticism, especially with respect to their habitually recruitist or instructional posture in the field of political correctness. (1989, 207)

Rather than try to reform popular taste, Ross suggests, the intellectual can learn from it instead. Fandom allows the intellectual to dumb down to learn (that one has nothing to teach). The cultural critic is here the poseur who goes slumming in trashy popular culture.

These academic fantasies rest on the following uncritically held assumptions, among others: (1) all other critical perspectives can be read from the master perspective of the academic insofar as the academic is defined as the political; (2) the deconstruction of the opposition between fan and critic works exclusively to legitimate both fan and critic (both produce knowledge); and (3) binary oppositions between politics and stupidity, knowledge and trivia, intelligent, progressive cultural criticism and dumb liberal or neoconservative criticism, and so on, do not self-deconstruct. Rather than attempt to secure these distinctions and the fantasies which they enable, I want to insist on the ways in which the critic's position as loser inevitably disturbs them.[31] My understanding of the term "loser" is by no means limited to the negative, insulting sense of it. The loser is a highly self-conscious, paradoxical figure whose practices deconstruct oppositions between the creative and (self-)destructive, intelligent and stupid, neurotically fixated and intellectually mobile, between success and failure, fan and celebrity, active and passive, productive and wasteful, narcissistic and self-hating, elitist and democratic. The loser may not be able to complete a project such as a work of criticism, much less see it published, for example, destroying successive drafts along the way, but he (or she) will produce a record of these failures. This record may in turn be regarded by others, if not by the loser, either as a work of art or as garbage. Moreover, the failure to complete the project may even be seen by the loser as a positive outcome. A published work, after all, would be full of mistakes, infelicities of style, and other inadequacies only too glaring to the loser's eyes. The loser is always both universal ("everyone is a loser, even me, at least in relation to the superior person who has done what I haven't, never will, never could") and an exception ("I am not really a loser, the other guy is"; or, in a more nuanced variant, "I may be a loser, but at least I'm not as big a loser as he is").

The loser also tends to be self-absorbed, caught up in private fantasies of (usually failed) self-transformation and self-legitimation: the loser in this way displaces and absorbs the fan since he or she identifies not only as a fan but also thinks he or she will one day become famous and have fans of his or her own.[32] Loser criticism emerges out of a fierce ambivalence about the famous person or text the loser discusses or rewrites. Loserdom, like fandom, is not merely celebratory or reformist. There is something destructive about it as well, as Nathaniel West's *Day of the Locust* (1939) and Martin Scorsese's *King of Comedy* (1983) make clear. In her essay "The Loser Thing," Rhonda Lieberman describes a typical version of fan aggression:

> The fan is, by nature, split off from this organ of real imaginary plenitude; the glamour industry institutionalizes the lack-in-being when it swerves back and attacks you with accusations that you're not someone else. . . . Abjection means cast off, existing in or resigned to a low state—dumped by yourself, as you psychotically misrecognize yourself in ideals. To counteract this condition, you can ferret through biographies and letters of famous people, remembering not their noble moments, which are to be expected, but the petty chinks in character that one can truly share. By bonding with them in moments of smallness, one experiences strange sublime relief. On a collective level, this need is served by the *National Inquirer*. (1993, 78)

But reading for smallness doesn't produce relief or bonding so much as it involves a constant, anxious, obsessive repositioning: I'm not as good as, I'm better than; I could have been, I could never be. The loser may concede he or she is a loser in some respects; the loser also thinks (at least some of the time) he or she is cool, even if others do not. The combination of endless resourcefulness and merciless ironization of every performance (or lack thereof) makes it impossible, I suggest, to sort the loser's contradictions out into a stable figure (either a loser in the negative, insulting sense of the word, or a "cool" figure who manages to transcend loserdom), one who might fall squarely either on the side of the political and intelligent or on the side of the apolitical and stupid.

The loser's desire to criticize arises precisely out of his or her highly defensive position. Loserdom necessarily involves moments of silence and privacy precisely because giving voice to the personal means one risks criticism not only from outsiders but, more crucially, from other insiders.[33] As Wayne Koestenbaum writes ironically about opera queens who watch and listen for camp:

> Experiencing the camp glow is a way of reversing one's abjection, and, by witnessing the depletion of cultural monuments, experiencing one's own power to fill degraded artifacts with meanings. When we experience the camp rush, the delight, the savor, we are making a private airlift of lost cultural matter, fragments held hostage by everyone else's indifference. No one else lived for this gesture, this pattern, this figure, before: only I know it's sublime. When I watch divas . . . I feel . . . that I've witnessed something tremendous and boundary-shattering, but that no one else around me realizes its significance and luminousness. I'm grateful, however, for the world's silence, for the privacy in which I study. . . . It's more sublime and more camp to keep quiet about joy and then rescue the story later, once everyone else has abandoned it. (1993, 69)

At certain moments, the personal has to remain private, unspoken, because making it public would expose one to competition, to the judgments of others. One's fantasy could be punctured, one could be ridiculed, since one person's sublime is another's gush and bad taste. As Koestenbaum notes, "the most illustrious and poignant fan clubs have only one member" (1993, 23).

The defensiveness of the loser also arises from his or her ambivalent relation to mainstream visual culture: the loser is disenchanted with it yet cannot fully break with it either. What the loser can't do is go out and make a movie, work in the medium that is drowning out his or her own chosen print medium (fanzines or literature), thereby making him or her an even bigger loser. Losers tend to write books. They may not write anything anyone else or even they themselves think is good, but pen and paper are always readily available. Yet the loser can't reject movie culture either since the fantasies the loser settles for, say, becoming the stripper instead of the star, will have been drawn at least as much from movies and television as from books. Precisely because the loser depends on movie and television culture for his or her fantasies yet can't make movies or television shows, the loser has become a kind of cultural critic of visual culture. Beavis and Butt-Head, for example, sit around and talk, quite stupidly, of course, at MTV video clips.[34] Yet they (and we) also get to see videos from some good loser bands like Psycho Sluts from Hell and Superchunk who never made it onto "heavy rotation" on MTV. Criticism of movies and other forms of visual popular culture is a way to avoid numbing out on what might otherwise be a multimedia overload.[35] The loser moves quickly and constantly to master her or his chosen media in an (often futile) effort to ward off hostile, dismissive criticism.

This very effort at mastery paradoxically fails even as it succeeds, however, insofar as distinctions between knowledge and trivia, the political and the apolitical, and so on begin to deconstruct. Consider, for example, the archivist of Shakespeare performances. Though the production of a new Shakespeare version or citation tends to imagine itself as breaking with the old, with tradition, it also always creates an archive making it continuous with past versions (Groys 1991). The screenplay of Luhrmann's *William Shakespeare's Romeo and Juliet* tries to do both, marketed as "the contemporary film, the classic play" (Pearce 1996). But the archive can never be mastered from a position that believes itself able to occupy all positions. Even like-minded, similarly positioned viewers will receive versions others will not; some frequencies may be too low or too high to be audible. The range of what the fan hears or doesn't hear is the effect of not only the dispersal of sites of fan criticism but of the fan's multiple, excessive positioning, a positioning that can never be fully rationalized, explained, or excused by being defined as the site of legitimate criticism, as knowledge.[36] Thus, a *Moonlighting* episode involving Shakespeare may show up in an article on *The Taming of the Shrew*, but similar episodes of *Gilligan's Island, The Brady Bunch, Happy Days, Mr. Magoo, 3rd Rock from the Sun, Star Trek, Star Trek: The Next Generation, Wishbone, Columbo, Family Matters, The Flintstones, Hawaii Five-O, Beverly Hills, 90210, Frasier,* or *Martin* will not appear in articles on other Shakespeare plays because the critic happens to be a fan of the one series and not the others. One could of course know about all these shows, but it is likely that still others would escape any given critic's notice. (It is noteworthy that the two leading reference works for Shakespeare on screen do not include references to Shakespeare in television programs.) Even if a critic were able to track down every reference, to know about unarchived films such as *Soapdish* (dir. Michael Hoffman, 1991), *In Like Flint* (dir. Gordon Douglas, 1967), *The Tall Guy* (dir. Mel Smith, 1989), *The Playboys* (dir. Gillies MacKinnon, 1992), *Bram Stoker's Dracula* (dir. Francis Ford Coppola, 1992), *Buffy the Vampire Slayer* (dir. Fran Rubel Kuzui, 1992), *Four Weddings and a Funeral* (dir. Mike Newell, 1995), *A Thousand Acres* (dir. Jocelyn Moorhouse, 1997), *Eve's Bayou* (dir. Kasi Lemmons, 1997), *Afterglow* (dir. Alan Rudolph, 1997), *Good Will Hunting* (dir. Gus Van Sant, 1997), *The Avengers* (dir. Jeremiah S. Chechik, 1998), *Love and Death on Long Island* (dir. Richard Kwietniowski, 1998), and *The Big Lebowski* (dir. Joel Coen, 1998), among others, that critic is as likely to be lauded for his or her archival mastery as he or she is to be mocked as an uncritical popular culture junkie, a loser who will watch anything to get his or her fix. The loser's will to knowledge is always already a willfulness to knowledge.

Some (loser) critics may have the phallus or what Lieberman calls "special stuff" (1993, 78) in the eyes of other critics, but their attempts at mastery (even by disavowing ownership) will always fail. The taste or tastelessness of their reception can be buttressed or subverted by other fans. The more one masters the archive, the more one appears to have the phallus, the more one is likely to be regarded as a loser (though one can be regarded as a cool loser through a certain self-ironizing self-consciousness that falls short of self-assurance, displays one's own insecurities by voicing all possible criticisms before they can be made by others). The fan is the one who wants to know it all, whose encyclopedic will to knowledge yields at worst an obnoxious, obsessive bore, at best an academic such as the professor in the 1993 Robert Redford film *Quiz Show* who simply gives the answers written by the show's producers. Loserdom reveals the stupidity and uncoolness of adopting the position of the one who knows. No one, queer or straight, will hear every unspeakable version of Shakespeare. One's knowledge can always be trumped by someone else. Loserdom is inescapable.

Loser criticism, I hope it is now clear, deconstructs the oppositions between the stupid and the intelligent, the political and the apolitical, by means of which cultural criticism presently legitimates itself, and it therefore does not arrive at what some cultural critics might consider to be a more fully political critical practice. For it is precisely the move to arrive at the "truly" political practice that turns out to be, well, kind of stupid in that it simply reproduces the problem it appears to resolve. A critic such as Andrew Ross can feel good about dumbing down because he does so in the name of the political. For Ross, a film such as *Terminator* (dir. James Cameron, 1988) or a CD by Ice Cube are more important than the complete works of John Dewey or John Stuart Mill because they teach us more about contemporary politics and economics (1992, 263). Ross can always afford to look dumb because his attention to what some might call trash, the grotesque, or cultural waste and his conflation of "real" politics with cultural politics can always be read by like-minded academics as a politically transgressive or oppositional "intervention" in the present scene of cultural criticism. From another point of view, however, this kind of cultural politics isn't real politics; rather, it's only academic politics. According to Richard Rorty (1991), Ross is engaged in trivial pursuits, having left traditional, extra-academic, activist politics behind. Even if one agrees with Ross that academic politics are always already part of the public sphere, there's not much of a difference between Ross's two models of the intellectual as authoritarian, hectoring vanguard teacher and as anti-authoritarian, liberatory student of popular culture. Both kinds of intellectuals aim to make our society more democratic, both claim that their account of politics is in fact "real" politics. All that's really different is where democracy is located: if a given text can't be read as subversive, then its audience can; and if the fan audience turns out not to be subversive enough, the academic who identifies with the fans critically can perform as transgressive. The political is equally unexamined as the phallus in both models of the intellectual.[37]

What happens if we examine the uncritically assumed ability of politics to trump not only all other modes of criticism, but to be the master mode of criticism that establishes what does or does not count as legitimate criticism as well? In calling attention to the dispersal of sites of fan discourses in electronic Shakespeare and popular culture archives, I want to suggest that cultural critics have managed to reclaim fandom, trivia, and cultural trash as dissident subcultural critical practices only by foreclosing the question of stupidity that arises out of the critic's / fan's position as loser. I do not mean merely that intelligence and stupidity may be relative to one's political or subject position, that what might look stupid to non-fans might be regarded by fans themselves as a kind of fanatic, know-it-all, critical intelligence that puts academic critics to shame. My point is that the difference between political knowledge and apolitical stupidity will always be blurred, no matter what social or subject position one occupies.[38] As Avital Ronell writes:

> when stupidity asserts itself without remorse, it paradoxically plays on the side of truth or at least poses as the replica of knowledge. Achieving closure, knowing its ground and meaning, stupidity is accomplice to the narcissisms of systems which close in on themselves as truth. . . . The resemblance [between truth and stupidity] is striking. Stupidity never admits to fault or error; it is dependent upon prejudicial entanglements and epistemological illusions. (1996, 7)

The distinction between apolitical stupidity and political intelligence is further blurred by the various speeds of knowledge production. Technology is always on fast forward. It's never the case that a slower car is being built. If, on the one hand, critics want to go at their own slow pace to read closely, on the other hand, they also desire to be current, to publish as soon as possible. Thus, criticism has come more and more to resemble the magazine, trading a shorter shelf-life and the prestige of a university press for the glamour and greater distribution of a trade press.[39]

Yet technological advances always outstrip academia such that academia may always be positioned, particularly by the youth (or now "kiddie") culture it primarily addresses, as obsolete, out of date. What forces an absorption of a psychoanalytic notion of mastery in which one could say that someone else is an imbecile (as Lacan did with his disciples) in a more historically specific context of a transvalued dumbing down in American popular culture is that hipness and progressive politics don't necessarily go together. If hipness mediates political opposition, then cultural critics remain in a difficult position. For the hip is both where the cultural critic wants to be and where she or he fears to be, namely, in the new. The new can be regarded as the innovative, the cutting edge, the really political, but it can also be regarded, even by cultural critics, as the trendy, the trivial, the fashionable, the not really political or the insufficiently political. The self-identity of hip cultural criticism is disturbed by the turbulent relation between critical intelligence and hipness: hipness can seem both intelligent and stupid. We arrive at the cultural critic as a loser of the cool sort for perhaps other like-minded cultural critics, a loser of the not-so-cool sort for everyone else.

What I WWWill.com

This book uses Shakespeare to advance a critique both of Shakespeare's citation and resignification in contemporary American popular culture and of contemporary American cultural criticism. Each chapter reads a particular instance of Shakespeare's citation or adaptation to triangulate explicitly or implicitly the relation between American culture and American cultural criticism. The first two chapters attend to the circulation of Shakespeare as the phallus in relation to the straight male Shakespeare actor or director. Chapter 1, "The Love That Dare Not Speak Shakespeare's Name: New Shakesqueer Cinema," focuses on Shakespeare as signifier of gay sexuality in order to contrast a gay and a queer hermeneutics of popular culture. I focus on what I call "eruptions" of gay sexuality in straight, mallhouse films such as *Porky's 2* (dir. Bob Clark, 1986), *The Goodbye Girl* (dir. Herbert Ross, 1977), *Dead Poet's Society* (dir. Peter Wier, 1986), *So Fine* (dir. Andrew

Bergman, 1981), and *In and Out* (dir. Frank Oz, 1997) to show that the least overtly gay films may nevertheless end up being the most queer.

In the second chapter, "Deep Inside William Shakespeare: Film and Video 'Classics' and the Castrated Gaze," I consider pornographic Shakespeare adaptations of the 1980s and 1990s in relation to what I call a castrated male gaze, one fractured by the heterogeneity of film production in which Shakespeare and director (as author and auteur, respectively) never participate in the sex. I suggest that an analogy between academic stardom and porn stardom (both are known very well by a very small number of people) troubles current attempts to legitimate cultural studies by viewing it as a recycler of transgressive cultural trash.

The third chapter, "Terminating Shakespeare with Extreme Prejudice: Postcolonial Cultural Cannibalism, Serial Quotation, and the Cinematic Spectacle of 1990s American Cultural Imperialism," pursues the analysis of stardom in the context of the production of homosocial, generic, serialized action pictures and their parodies, such as *Last Action Hero* (dir. John McTiernan, 1991), *The Naked Gun* (dir. David Zucker, 1988), *Star Trek VI: The Undiscovered Country* (dir. Nicholas Meyer, 1992), and *Skyscraper* (dir. Raymond Martino, 1995). Shakespeare's citation in these films enables them to produce a number of contradictory critiques, including critiques of American cultural imperialism, the Hollywood film industry, and the films themselves, particularly their leading stars. As in the case of the porn star who is restricted to performing a series of routine scenes, the star of the action picture is infantilized, reduced to performing the same part over and over in sequel after sequel. I clarify Shakespeare's status as symptom of America's postcolonial anxiety about its secondary relation to British culture by contrasting two other films, *Independence Day* (dir. Roland Emmerich, 1996), which cites other science fiction films extensively but does not literally cite Shakespeare, and *The Postman* (dir. Kevin Costner, 1997), which defines itself as a nonsequel and fully thematizes Shakespeare's citation.

Chapter 4, "When Our Lips Synch Together: The Transvestite Voice, the Virtuoso, Speed, and Pumped Up-Volume in Some *Overheard Shakespeares*," elaborates on the relation between nationalism and sexuality in the previous chapter by rearticulating the issues of stardom and castration in the context of what I call the transvestite voice. Drawing on recent queer operatic criticism and on feminist film criticism of film synchronization, I discuss Baz Luhrmann's *William Shakespeare's Romeo and Juliet;* Trevor Nunn's *Twelfth Night* (1996); an episode of *Gilligan's Island* entitled "The Producer" (dir. Ida Lupino and George M. Cahan, 1964) in which *Hamlet* is performed as a musical; *Kiss Me Kate* (dir. George Sidney II, 1953); *Porky's 2; Prospero's Books* (dir. Peter Greenaway, 1991); *The Dresser* (dir. Peter Yates, 1983); and, in an excursus, Derek Jarman's *Edward II* (1991) in relation to a popular film about transvestism, *Mrs. Doubtfire* (dir. Chris Columbus, 1994). I suggest that transvestism is really about being a virtuoso, the one who can cross over, perform any role, occupy any position. The male transvestite lip-syncher has or is the phallus insofar as he is a kind of castrato, a virtuoso performer whose ability to pass as the opposite gender perhaps depends on a loss of literal virility. Unlike the star, who can cover an older tune and still appear to be an author because of his or her singing signature, the transvestite voice is at best a DJ, a poseur whose authorship is limited to remixing and sampling codes already enunciated by others (though in a brazenly open manner, to be sure). To compensate for a potential loss of virility, physical penis size gets displaced onto vocal size as male performers pump up the volume, as it were, and pick up the tempo. I focus on both American and English examples here to focus on the way that accent marks competing claims for the virtuoso's transnational viability.

In chapter 5, "My So-Called Shakespeare: Mourning the Canon in the Age of Postpatriarchal Multiculturalism, or the Shakespeare Pedagogue as Loser," I return to the question of pedagogy and youth culture broached in this introduction and read cultural criticism's identification with youth culture in terms of popular representations of the American pedagogue as loser. I examine a range of films and television shows, including *She's Working Her Way Through College; Harry and Tonto* (dir. Paul Mazursky, 1977); *Quiz Show; Renaissance Man* (dir. Penny Marshall, 1994); *High School High* (dir. Hart Bochner, 1996); *My Bodyguard* (dir. Tony Bill, 1986); *Last Action Hero; Clueless; Looking for Richard; So Fine;* and episodes from the television situation comedies *Ozzie and Harriet, The Cosby Show,* and *3rd Rock from the Sun* as well as episodes from children's programs such as *Wishbone* (adapting *Romeo and Juliet* and *The Tempest*); *Sesame Street* (with Mel Gibson as Hamlet); *The Muppet Show* and *Muppets Tonight* (spoofing the balcony scene from *Romeo and Juliet,* with Miss Piggy as Juliet); and episodes of *Animaniacs* (spoofing scenes from *A Midsummer Night's Dream, Hamlet,* and *Macbeth*).

Far from being the star or the virtuoso, the Shakespeare pedagogue is typically portrayed as a loser, obsolete, already behind his or her more innovative students. Shakespeare appears in popular representations of pedagogy as "Shakes-tears," as it were, a melancholic symptom of the impossibility of mourning the passing of patriarchy, and with it, an earlier cultural moment. Taking mourning to be a model for interpretation, the broad question I pose in this chapter is whether, in a post-hermeneutic, mediatized world of quiz shows, space aliens, and virtual Valley girls, the plays are as "unteachable" as they are "unspeakable."

In the conclusion, "Spectres of ShaXXXspeare: Loser Criticism, Part Duh," I again consider the possibility that the unspokenness or what I here call spectralization of ShaXXXspeare replays demands a displacement of the academic intellectual as fan by the academic intellectual as loser. The question remains whether or not this displacement is a losing proposition for the academic intellectual.

As I hope it is now clear from this summary of *Unspeakable ShaXXXspeares,* my critical focus is Shakespeare in film rather than Shakespeare in television (or in other popular media such as comic books, detective and romance fiction, rock music, advertising, and so on). This is partly in an attempt to eliminate redundancy. Cultural criticism is not medium specific: the same kinds of issues raised by one kind of popular culture are raised by another (see Mellencamp 1990, 14; Ulmer 1989, 6). Nevertheless, I am concerned with the way television as a social institution, and increasingly music video, mediates the reception of Shakespeare on film. That said, it has also to be conceded that there is not a lot of unspeakable ShaXXXspeare to be found on television. When cited in television programs, Shakespeare is likely to be enlisted seriously as sacred icon in a drama such as *Star Trek* (or its spin-offs) or as a preachy parody in any number of situation comedies. The absence of many examples of unspeakable

ShaXXXspeares on television is of course largely due to the way the medium is constrained by federal broadcast legislation and network agencies that both actively censor programming and, since 1996, have regulated it with a ratings system. Syndication and reruns, including the wholesale recycling of the 1950s situation comedy form in the late 1980s, might be adduced as more evidence of television's conservatism. I have discussed some examples from television, however, to give a sharper sense of the historical development by which Shakespeare has become associated with the loser. Some critics, believing that television is a more conservative medium than film, might conclude that my account of Shakespeare and loser pedagogy has its limits: television citations of Shakespeare, particularly children's programming, where one would hardly expect to find anything remotely XXX about Shakespeare, might constitute something of a counter-example since Shakespeare tends to have an unambiguously upbeat status.[40] While children's programming might seem to be an exception to the rule of loser pedagogy, it is in fact, I maintain, the master example. Children's shows primarily produce a kiddie Shakespeare for adult audiences. The children's shows I examine are geared at two audiences, children and adults (who may or may not watch along with the children), and the latter is the one, in my view, that really counts. Many of the jokes and parodies can only be appreciated by adults. As I demonstrate in the conclusion, episodes of *Wishbone* and other children's television programs are yet more examples of loser kiddie culture. In what I take to be a new form of Bowdlerism, adult audiences act as censors by a paradoxically utopian imagining of childhood and children's entertainment as uncensored. I situate these examples in relation to other 90s movies such as *Hook* (dir. Stephen Spielberg, 1991) that even more overtly reconstruct childhood from an adult loser perspective.

I offer no further explanation for this book. In suggesting that the political is less the phallus than a signifier of the critic's paradoxical status as loser, I forego the usual moral justification for attending to the films I do. Consequently, whether the conjunction of "high" theory and "low" culture in this book produces heavy thinking or thinking lite I leave to readers to decide for themselves, if they feel so inclined. Whatever.

CHAPTER ONE

The Love That Dare Not Speak Shakespeare's Name: New Shakesqueer Cinema

Looking for William (in All the Wrong Places)

In 1977, Herbert Ross's film of Neil Simon's *The Goodbye Girl* showed a parodic New York theatrical production of *Richard III* with Richard Dreyfuss playing a straight actor being directed to play Richard III as a gay character. The production's director explains his interpretation to the assembled cast as follows:

> Richard III was a flaming homosexual. So was Shakespeare for that matter. But the angry mob at the Globe theater wasn't going to plunk down two shillings to see a bunch of pansies jumping about on the stage. It was society that crippled Richard, not childbirth. I mean read your text. He sent those two cute little boys up to the tower and we never saw them again. Oh, we know why, don't we? See, what I want to do here is to strip Richard bare, metaphorically. Let's get rid of the hump. Let's get rid of the twisted extremities and show him the way he would be today: the queen who wanted to be king.

In 1995, Ian McKellen, an openly gay actor who has fought Britain's homophobic Clause 28, played Richard straight in Richard Loncraine's film of *Richard III*.[1]

I open with this juxtaposition to foreground what I take to be the nonidentity of gay politics, a nonidentity I take to be insurmountable and that complicates any Whiggish narrative of progress about gay representations in popular film. Some critics might wish to see a progression from the jokey *The Goodbye Girl* to the serious Loncraine *Richard III*, the end point of which would be a unified, noncontradictory, gay-saturated *Richard III*: a gay actor playing a gay Richard, filmed by a gay director, produced by the gay head of a major film studio, all of whom would uncloset a gay Shakespeare. It seems to me that such a narrative forecloses the queering of Shakespeare rather than proliferates a queer utopia (in which everyone, even the audiences, would turn out to be gay, and in which a gay Shakespeare would no longer be a joke but a source of joy). This foreclosure of what might count as Shakesqueer cinema occurs precisely in a literal-minded attention to gay content and an attendant policing of particular films in terms of their positive or phobic representations of gay sexuality; moreover, this foreclosure often issues in contrasts between different means of film production and distribution: realist film, studio-financed, mall-distributed, easily available on video versus avant-garde film, independent, art house–distributed, perhaps unavailable or barely available on video. To be sure, such contrasts are significant. Lindsay Kemp's gay-affirmative adaptation of *A Midsummer Night's Dream* (dir. Celestino Coronado, 1984), with what at first sight appears to be an all-male cast (everyone is made up like drag queens, including women who could have just stepped out of *Pumping Iron II*) and in which Demetrius and Lysander, and Helena and Hermia, pair up as gay male and lesbian couples, is available on video through only one distributor in England.[2] Similarly, the lesbian-saturated *Playboy Twelfth Night* (1972), which gained a second life when aired on *Showtime* in 1991 and which has an explicit lesbian scene between Caesario and Olivia, circulates now only among an academic underground of Shakespeare scholars. Neither film is widely known, even to many professional Shakespeareans. Moreover, cinematic popularizations of Shakespeare can take a clearly homophobic turn. The film *Rosencrantz and Guildenstern Are Dead* (dir. Tom Stoppard, 1991), for example, eliminates almost all of the gay references to the players in Stoppard's play (particularly to the character Alfred, a boy actor who acts the part of the Player "Queen"), apparently in the belief that a censored film would be more widely receiveable.[3]

Figure 1.1: Ken-doll Branagh laments "another fall of man" in Branagh's *Henry V.*

What is interesting about the late 1990s, however, is the convergence of a mainstreaming of Shakespeare into popular film and of a gayed Shakespeare produced by straight and gay directors and actors whose very cinematic range begins to call into question what it means to do a gay Shakespeare. In 1987, Aki Kaurismaki, often called the gay Fassbinder, released his noir *Hamlet Goes Business,* which he defined explicitly as an expression of an alternative, prole subculture, not as an art film (1991, 94-95). In his 1989 *Henry V,* Kenneth Branagh foregrounds the fact that the traitor Lord Scroop was Henry's "bedfellow," using a number of shots of Henry on top of Scroop and close-ups of Henry's face on the verge of tears, nearly touching Scroop's, as he exposes what he clearly feels is a personal betrayal (see figure 1.1). In his *Much Ado About Nothing,* Branagh plays up a gay sadomasochistic relationship between Don John (Keanu Reeves in black leather pants) and Conrade (who serves as Don John's masseur). Similarly, in Oliver Parker's 1995 Snoop-Doggy-Dog-style *Othello,* Branagh plays Iago as a gay man who loves Othello but cannot admit it and so destroys him and his wife. (When speaking to Roderigo of Desdemona's "foul lust" for Cassio, Iago places his face immediately next to his and then gropes his genitals ["lechery, by this hand?"], while a heterosexual couple has vigorous intercourse on a cart above them; later, Emilia demands sex in return for the handkerchief and Iago turns her over on her stomach before having what appears to be anal sex with her; finally, after Othello kills himself, Iago crawls onto the bed and lies at Othello's feet.)[4] 1991 saw the premiere of Gus Van Sant's *My Own Private Idaho*, as well as Peter Greenaway's *Prospero's Books*, in which a gay dancer plays Caliban.[5] The same year Oliver Stone opposed gay conspirators to the Shakespeare-citing prosecutor Jim Garrison in *JFK*. Sally Potter's *Orlando*, the film adaptation of Virginia Woolf's novel that in turn queers *As You Like It* by making Orlando a transsexual character, appeared in 1992 and included a Jacobean-like performance of part of the final act of *Othello* with Desdemona played by a man in drag.[6] The gay character whose death occasions the funeral of *Four Weddings and a Funeral* (dir. Mike Newell, 1995) cites Sir Andrew Aguecheek's line, "I was adored once, too" (*Twelfth Night* 2.3.160). In Trevor Nunn's 1996 *Twelfth Night*, Orsino's diminished interest in the revealed Viola suggested that he preferred her when she was a he; and the Baz Luhrmann 1996 *William Shakespeare's Romeo and Juliet* portrayed Mercutio as a bisexual, gun-toting cross-dresser who "consorts" with Romeo[7] (see figure 1. 2). And 1996 also saw the release of Troma Entertainment's *Tromeo and Juliet* (dir. Lloyd Kaufman), in which Juliet and the Nurse also have a lesbian relationship (made clear in a softcore porn sequence) (see figure 1.3). A character declares "Murray was a fag" with amused astonishment upon witnessing Murray Martini, a character based on Mercutio, ask Tromeo for a kiss after being mortally wounded by Tyrone (Tybalt's equivalent). Adrian Noble's 1996 *A Midsummer Night's Dream* flirts with a gay relationship between Oberon and Puck, as well as between Oberon and the changeling "boy."[8] In 1997, the comedy *In and Out* (dir. Frank Oz) represented the outing of a high school English teacher who discovers he's gay and who recites Shakespeare (and whose jilted bride-to-be also trades quotations from *Romeo and Juliet* with an ex-student turned movie star). And in the 1998 comedy *Love and Death on Long Island* (dir. Richard Kwietniowski), a film based on the novel of the same name that rewrites Thomas Mann's *Death in Venice*, John Hurt played a gay,

Figure 1.2: Star-crossed buns at the Capulet ball in Baz Luhrmann's *William Shakespeare's Romeo and Juliet.*

recently widowed English novelist and scholar fond of Shakespeare, Giles De'Ath, who falls for a young, heterosexual, B-movie actor/teen idol named Ronnie Bostock (Jason Priestly) after seeing him, by mistake, in *Hotpants College II*.[9] "If Shakespeare were writing today," the surprised Bostock asks De'Ath, "you mean he'd be writing *Hotpants College 2?*"[10] In addition, there are two hardcore, gay male pornographic adaptations of *Romeo and Juliet* (1986; 1993), and several hardcore, heterosexual pornographic adaptations of *Romeo and Juliet, Hamlet, Taming of the Shrew,* and *A Midsummer Night's Dream* released in the late 1980s and mid-1990s contain lesbian scenes.[11] (I will examine these films and video in the next chapter.)

Making sense of the present moment of a gay and popular Shakespeare requires, I believe, that we contextualize it within the present struggle over gay representation in general and gay cinematic representations in particular. In recent English and American legal controversies over gay rights, the issue has often been less about actual gay sex than it is about the mainstreaming of representations of it.

Figure 1.3: Juliet and her nurse (Ness) as lesbian lovers in Lloyd Kaufman's *Tromeo and Juliet*.

Homophobes tend to legislate against representations that view gays in a positive light. Within this historical context, debates over gay cinema tend to be framed by those who favor films that are assimilationist, sentimental, fairly widely distributed, nonsexual, and practically non-gay such as *Philadelphia* (dir. Jonathan Demme, 1994), *It's My Party* (dir. Randall Kleiser, 1995), and *The Birdcage* (dir. Mike Nichols, 1996), on the one hand, and those who favor the new queer cinema of sexually explicit, anti-assimilationist, narrowly distributed films such as *Swoon* (dir. Tom Kalin, 1991), *Edward II* (dir. Derek Jarman, 1991), *Poison* (dir. Todd Haynes, 1991), *The Living End* (dir. Greg Araki, 1992), *Totally F***ed Up* (dir. Greg Araki, 1993), and *Heavenly Creatures* (dir. Peter Jacks, 1994), on the other.

What happens to this opposition when Shakespeare (who, at least in the United States until recently might well have lost his high cultural status approval if his plays were construed as gay precisely because he would stand for decadent high art) becomes a mainstream signifier of queer sex *and* of popular culture? How do the horizons of the elite, the contemporary popular American reproductions of Shakespeare, and gayness, all intersect? My point in raising these questions is to emphasize that formally and thematically there are variously queered Shakespeares, not a single gay Shakespeare. The 1980s and 1990s Shakespeare films I listed above evince a marked heterogeneity: avant-garde and realist; art house films and mall films; films with straight and gay actors playing gay or straight characters; films made by straight and gay directors. Shakespeare may be aligned with a variety of theatrical modes of reproducing his plays to signify gayness: with the popular, contemporary, and innovative, and with avant-garde and realist, costume drama; with theater and with film.[12]

This heterogeneity of representations generates a host of even broader questions about the project of gaying Shakespeare. What is required to gay Shakespeare? Would only explicitly gay adaptations in films by openly gay directors cast with gay actors do? Or do gay moments of straight productions, either consciously done or as symptoms of the film's queer unconscious (whether the director is queer, straight, or bisexual), count as well?[14] Can an exhaustive survey of gay Shakespeare films, a chronicle of the Shakespeare celluoid closet, be undertaken? Would that undertaking be worthwhile given that some gay directors such as George Cukor, Gus Van Sant, Aki Kaurismaki, and Derek Jarman have made Shakespeare films that either blur sexual identities or leave out gay content altogether?[14] In *Hamlet Goes Business,* for example, Kaurismaki makes Hamlet much stronger than he is in Shakespeare's play (all of the soliloquies are cut) and focuses on a heterosexual romance between the chauffeur and the maid, who kill Hamlet and happily walk off with a bunch of cash at the film's close. But does this plot twist exclude the film from being gay Shakespeare? Or would one want to attend then to a homosexual gaze, a cinematic technique, gay or lesbian auteurship (of the director and/or star), and privilege them over gay content? If so, would there be evaluative criteria for determining good or bad use of them?[15] If so, what would they be?

A related, equally broad series of questions arise over how gay sex is represented in films of Shakespeare, over what counts as gay. Is a gay reading of a Shakespeare play as obvious as it is to the director in *The Goodbye Girl* ("I mean, read your text"), or is it something that has been forced on the play? Would it be better to violate transgressively a straight text or to honor and respect a canonical gay text? Is Lindsay Kemp to be lauded, to take one example, for making the Athenian couples at least temporarily gay in the Coronado film of his theatrical production of *A Midsummer Night's Dream,* thus moving beyond Woody Allen's decision in *A Midsummer Night's Sex Comedy* to keep the play's compulsory heterosexuality consistently in place? Or is a gay Shakespeare redundant within American popular culture, merely a confirmation of a populist image of Shakespeare as something for prissy art fags?

What, if anything, is being disrupted or subverted through gay Shakespeare films? What kinds of deeds can gay sexuality figure? (Similar to Branagh's *Henry V,* the BBC *Richard II* used gay sexuality to figure political corruption by having a gay Bushy and Greene sit in a hot tub with Richard II discussing how they will carve up England.) Does the sexual identity of audiences or critics matter significantly in terms of what they will consider to be a queer Shakespeare film or in terms of the pleasures or politics they are likely to find in a Shakespeare film they agree to call gay? Consider *Kiss Me Kate* (dir. George Sidney II, 1953), a musical in which a group of actors put on a production of *The Taming of the Shrew.* The film inscribes a closeted, gay critique (a critique to which I will return at length in chapter 4) of the stage actors. Precisely because this critique was written from the closet, it is more likely to be recognizable as gay to gays and lesbians, who might have knowledge about the genre of the film musical and/or the director's and actors' sexual orientations, than it is to straight audiences. But this gay critique may nevertheless be readable to straight audiences. Would their knowing or not knowing that it is gay make a difference? Is the film's reception more or less queer if the straight audience receives the critique without knowing that it's gay? Would not knowing constitute a kind of homophobic disavowal and discrediting of gay readings? Or is the gay reading saved precisely by being connoted, thereby escaping the kind of homophobic policing that may be called up by more explicit declarations of gay sexuality?

Shakespeare's canon, derived from a time of all-male transvestite theater, raises one last set of questions. Are we speaking of a strictly gay male Shakespeare? Are there any female homoerotic relations as opposed to female homosocial relations in Shakespeare, or did the fact that Shakespeare's theater was a transvestite theater close off those relations? (See Traub 1992a; Traub 1992b; Callaghan 1996.) If not, is a gay Shakespeare just a reconfirmation of a masculine Shakespeare, a gay male version of the Schwarzenegger-as-Hamlet sequence in *Last Action (Boy) Hero?*[16]

These broad questions, and others equally theoretical and political, arise out of what I have called the nonidentity of gay sexuality within Shakespeare films, a nonidentity I, like many others, take to make gayness irreducibly queer. By distinguishing between "gay" and "queer," I distinguish between a legible, secure identity and position, on the one hand, and a disorienting of such an identity and position, on the other. I am not interested in answering the questions raised above, but in examining how gay nonidentity generates queer effects. Of course, identities and positions are assigned to people practicing particular sexual acts and assumed by them. Moreover, specific values accrue to those identities and positions. For a knowing audience, a straight man playing a gay character may be significantly different from a gay man playing a straight character.

I insist on the term "queer" in distinction to "gay" not because of its greater inclusiveness but because of its greater representational fluidity. As Michel Foucault (1989/1996) and Judith Butler (1993) have argued, it is precisely the performativity of any identity or position that allows its meaning to be contested and resignified.[17] Leo Bersani (1994, 42-55) has objected that this notion of gayness as a queer performance despecifies homosexuality, degays gayness, by taking the sex out of being gay, and thus ironically that it does what homophobes hope to accomplish: eliminates gays. Yet gay sexuality is not something that simply can be outed, nor is being gay identical with having gay sex. As Michael Warner (1993, vii) writes, "Sexual desires themselves can imply other wants, ideals, and conditions." To be explicitly recognizable, gayness has to be represented, coded. Moreover, at stake in gay identity for theorists such as Foucault is a critique of normalization: If the point of being queer is to *become* rather than to *be* gay, why take on an identity? Why assume a fixed position that is subject to pathologization by a normalizing culture rather than resist it? I would argue that representations of gay sexuality, no matter how explicit or literal-minded, will always be more or less queer.

Figure 1.4: Richard III, "Queen" of England, in Herbert Ross's *The Goodbye Girl.*

Crucial for an analysis of Shakespeare as gay signifier in film, then, is attention not only to the means of production and distribution but above all to the coding and recoding of gayness. This has a particular bearing on the popularization of gayness. Consider the difference between *The Goodbye Girl* and *Prospero's Books.* The audience of the former knows that Richard is gay because he is "flaming": Elliot holds his wrist limp, has a slight lisp, adopts "feminine" postures, pinches a fellow actor on the butt, and wears platform shoes and a pink chiffon shirt (see figure 1. 4). An audience of Greenaway's film, however, would not necessarily know that the actor playing Caliban, Michael Clark, is gay[18] (see figure 1. 5). Perhaps his odd latex harness, which constricts and contorts his testicles, marks him for some as a sadomasochistic, taste of latex boy.[19] It is precisely the way he is not legible as gay, however, that makes this leather boy love slave of Prospero seem so queer.

The 1983 comedy *Strange Brew* (dir. Dave Thomas and Rick Moranis), more a spoof of the metadramatic spin-off *Rosencrantz and*

Figure 1.5: Caliban as Prospero's leather boy love slave in Peter Greenaway's *Prospero's Books.*

Guildenstern Are Dead than of *Hamlet,* offers a perhaps even more bizarre example of Shakesqueer cinema. In what might be called a "metacinematic," queer primal scene, the leading characters, two brothers played by SCTV's Moranis and Thomas, stumble upon their parents, who are also played by Moranis and Thomas, having sex.[20] Illegibility and queerness do not go together in any straightforward way, however. Consider Franco Zeffirelli's version of Cassio's dream (as narrated by Iago) in his film of Verdi's *Otello* (1986). Zeffirelli shows Cassio backlit, naked in bed, masturbating (just off-screen) and mouthing the lines sung in a voice-over by Iago, which narrate Cassio's sexual fantasies about Desdemona (see figure 1. 6). Is this a gay moment? Is this an instance of a male cinematic ga(y)ze? Is the camera getting off, that is, on the spectacle of a naked man masturbating? Or is the gaze heterosexual male? Is this a heterosexual moment about a naked man fantasizing about intercourse with a woman? Or is this scene necessarily both gay male and heterosexual? If so, would that make it a queer moment?[21] A film such as Sally Potter's *Orlando* further

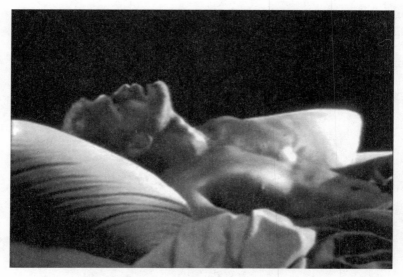

Figure 1.6: The camera getting off on Iago getting off on Cassio getting off on Desdemona in Franco Zeffirelli's *Otello*.

complicates any reduction of queerness to gay identity. On the one hand, it does not contain a nude scene between Orlando and Sasha (for which it was faulted by some lesbian-identified critics. See Straayer 1996: 77; Halberstam 1991: 10); on the other hand, it does show a gay man playing a Queen (Elizabeth I), as it were, in bed with a woman playing a man.

In making a distinction between gay as legible and queer as illegible, a distinction that in some significant respects is always already compromised, I do not want to suggest that popular films can be aligned with a normalization of gayness and avant-garde films with an antinormalizing queerness.[22] I want rather to attend to a variety of popular films in which the very clarity of Shakespeare as a signifier of gayness produces queer effects. At the risk of seeming perverse, I will focus primarily not on Shakespeare films that are self-identified as gay nor on ones made by self-identified gay directors, but on films made by straight male directors that are about heterosexual men or adolescents: *Porky's 2* (dir. Bob Clark, 1986), *The Goodbye Girl* (dir. Herbert

Ross, 1977), *Dead Poets Society* (dir. Peter Weir, 1986), *So Fine* (dir. Andrew Bergman, 1981), and what might appear to be an exception, *In and Out* (dir. Frank Oz, 1997). All are realist films made for popular, mainstream audiences.[23]

My point in examining these films is to show that the least visibly gay Shakespeare films can paradoxically be the queerest films.[24] One could of course legitimately look for gay representations in more obvious places and codes: avant-garde and art house films (Jarman's *Tempest*); camp (Coronado's *A Midsummer Night's Dream*); the melancholy and the pathos of AIDS, hustling, and the closet (*My Own Private Idaho; The Dresser*). Yet this kind of project has the liability of keeping gayness in its predictable, proper place (and in the more paranoid account of D. A. Miller [1992, 18], of enabling the policing of gays). By contrast, the very legibility of gayness in the straight films I will discuss makes them unexpected sites of a proliferating queerness. The degaying of Shakespeare may paradoxically function as a solicitation to queer Shakespeare. As films about the "homosexual panic" (Sedgwick 1989) of straight men, the first three of the above-named films are a useful site for a critique of what Michael Warner (1993) calls "heteronormativity." Except for *In and Out,* all of these films involve acting Shakespeare onstage and thus highlight what Butler (1990/ 1993) calls the performative status of gender. Finally, as popular films, they reach a presumptively heterosexual audience. In this regard, a queer "eruption" in a straight film targeted to a straight audience may prove more dis*orient*ing than a film explicitly marked as gay.[25]

In saying that these films are disorienting, I am not saying that they are subversive or transgressive. Indeed, the reverse is true. The films take up older readings of Shakespeare's comedies as heteronormative: one goes through homosexuality on the way to heterosexuality. To be sure, in *Porky's 2* and *Dead Poet's Society* Shakespeare is partly a metaphor for a rebellious, passionate nonconformity, and productions of his plays are supported by teachers and students opposed to political and religious corruption or to bureaucratic, patriarchal discipline. Though the films are not homophobic, they are nevertheless about heterosexuals becoming better heterosexuals; in short, they enforce hetero- (and pedaro-) normativity. These films may not be subversive or transgressive, then, but they may at the same time be quite interesting and provocative. Indeed, the film I take to be the most repressively heteronormative, namely, *Dead Poets Society*, is, in my view, by far the most disorienting. This is not to say that all the films I am examining are equally interesting, however. They may be placed on a spectrum of the more or less interesting, and how interesting they are has nothing necessarily to do with how anti-heteronormative they are. *So Fine*, I will argue, unsettles any attempt to place these films along a more or less queer axis. These films do not display, then, some essential gay "eruption," but different ways of responding to the heteronormalization of gayness.

In and Out is an exception to the rule these other films construct in that it actually does present us with gay characters in a gay-positive way. Yet far from confining gayness to a few characters, the film universalizes it. Near the end of the film, in a scene echoing the scene after the Romans' defeat of the slave revolt in *Spartacus* (dir. Stanley Kubrick, 1961), everyone at the high school graduation ceremony gets up in support of the gay teacher who has just been canned and declares in turn "I'm gay."[26] *In and Out* attempts a daring normalization of gayness, one that depends, however, both on excluding the representation of gay marriage and gay sex (which can be discussed as long as it is closeted) and on making Shakespeare a bisexual signifier of gayness and of heterosexuality.

At the close of this chapter, I consider the work that the concept of the popular does within academic criticism and turn to a popular video, the *Playboy* production of *Twelfth Night* (dir. Ron Wertheim, 1972). The video rewrites Shakespeare to put lesbian sexuality on display, presumably for straight male viewers.

In focusing on the signification of gayness, I adopt a critique of gay identity politics formulated by Michel Foucault (1989/1996, 332-35 and 382-90), Lee Edelman (1993), and Judith Butler (1990). According to Butler, gender is performed, cited and hence capable of being resignified in a subversive way. Thinking about gayness in terms of Shakespeare draws our attention to other problems, namely, how the films I am discussing may be allied to a political agenda and how to determine which kinds of representations will be politically effective. Moreover, making such determinations can be, in themselves, paradoxical, problematic. As Marjorie Garber (1991) has pointed out, gay coding is complex because the codes must be legible to gays and lesbians but opaque to straights.

For some queer theorists and activists, there is an even more significant problem about coding for gays as well as for straights: normalization. Queer critiques of normalization may themselves become normalized and normalizing. To avoid this problem if only momentarily, a breakdown in codes, or what might be called the "queer sublime," can be politically and aesthetically efficacious (Burt, 1993). According to Butler (1994, 38), the subversive act is to be distinguished from other kinds of routinized political acts. Subversion turns out to be an aesthetic category insofar as it is aligned with a breakdown in reading:

> You can't plan or calculate subversion. In fact, I would say that subversion is precisely an incalculable effect. That's what makes it subversive. . . . I think that subversive practices have to overwhelm the capacity to read, challenge conventions of reading, and demand new possibilities of reading. (1994, 38)

Butler gives examples of Act-Up die-ins. One couldn't read them, she says—know if people had AIDS or not, were dead or not, sick or not. And to them Butler contrasts what she considers to be the less effective because more legible acts of Queer Nation:

> What I worry about are those acts that are more immediately legible. They are the ones that are most readily recuperable. But the ones that challenge our practices of reading, that make us uncertain how to read, or make us think that the way in which we read public signs, these seem really important to me.
>
> The Kiss-Ins Queer Nation did at malls were quite outrageous. . . . They worked for awhile, but they always run the risk of becoming tropes. Once they've been read, once they're done too often, they become deadened tropes, as it were. They become predictable. And it's precisely when they get predictable, or you know how to read them in advance, or you know what's coming, that they just don't work anymore. (1994, 38)

Valued here is not clear recognition of codes but their breakdown. (It is significant that Butler's "you" appears to include straight as well as gay and lesbian audiences.) In the discussion of films that follows, I want to examine the paradoxical queerness of heteronormativity: the process of gaying Shakespeare may be part and parcel of degaying Shakespeare and vice versa.

Smells Like Queen Spirit

I would like to begin my examination of the ways in which Shakespeare may queer heteronormativity with the simplest of the films under consideration, *Porky's 2*. The film is set in the closeted 1950s at a white trash high school on a beachfront town in Florida. Students mount a production of scenes from Shakespeare plays, including *A Midsummer Night's Dream*, that foreground a particular American signifier of gay sexuality: "fairy" (Chauncey, 1994).[27] Some of the boys initially resist performing Shakespeare because he appears to signify being gay. One boy is teased by the others about playing Oberon:

> TIM: Hey Billy. What kind a role you playing? . . .
> BILLY: Oberon. . . .
> MEAT: What's he?
> BILLY: He's sort of like a forest ranger.
> MICKEY: A forest ranger? In Shakespeare?
> BILLY: Yeah. He looks after the woods. . . .
> TIM: Sounds like a fairy to me.
> BILLY: He's not just a fairy. He's the king of the fairies.
> TIM: Oh, you mean like a really big fairy.

The same teasing returns in a subsequent scene. One boy leafs through a copy of *A Midsummer Night's Dream* and asks:

> MICKEY: What the fuck's a Puck?
> BILLY: He's a character. He's a friend of Oberon's. He's like a little forest ranger.
> MEAT: Uh hum. Puck, a little forest ranger? Who plays that part?

Figure 1.7: "Meat" as Thisbe in Bob Clark's *Porky's 2*.

BILLY: Pee Wee.

TIM: Oh, so Pee Wee plays a little fairy and you play a big fairy. That's a lot of fairies. You guys get to run around in the woods together?

In a later scene, the Reverend Bubba Flava, who attempts to stop the production on grounds that it is obscene, cites the line from *A Midsummer Night's Dream*, "Lovers to bed. 'Tis almost fairy time" and comments "God, it's enough to make a real man sick!" On a similar note, he cites the exchange between Petruchio and Katherine in *The Taming of the Shrew* ending with Petruchio's rejoinder "What, with my tongue in your tail?" and explodes: "What kind of a man would do a thing like that?" (In response, many male students happily raise their hands.)

Despite the teasing of the students and the homophobia of the Reverend and his flock, all the boys end up playing parts in the review, and, strikingly, the most phallic character, Anthony, nicknamed "Meat," cross-dresses as Thisbe (see figure 1.7). But *Porky's 2* plays it safe by contrasting Shakespeare as art to Shakespeare as obscenity. Amid the teasing of Billy, one student pauses to say "Hey, come on guys. Let's get serious. This is art here." Similarly, when the Christian fundamentalist preacher Reverend Bubba Flava and his flock try to stop the production, the teacher directing it insists, "This is Shakespeare. It is not filth."

To be sure, this opposition is compromised in a confrontation between Reverend Flava and the principal, Mr. Clark, who shout out dirty parts of Shakespeare and dirty parts of the Bible, respectively. Clark wins, but by making a bawdy pun on "flock." Flava concludes: "Shakespeare must go. So saith the shepherd. So saith the flock. What saith you Mr. Clark?" Clark answers: "Get the flock [fuck] out of here." And, of course, the film itself is marketed for male adolescents whose main pursuit, like the characters', is to get laid.

Yet in using Shakespeare to make a critique of censorship, political corruption, racism, and religious bigotry (and perhaps implying a tolerance of homosexuality), the film is actually far less carnivalesque, far less "politically incorrect," and far less queer than it might be. It is by far the tamest of the four *Porkys* films, with hardly any T and A. Some might lament that it is not properly carnivalesque. But the problem is not that it is insufficiently political; it is rather the way its desire to be liberal (some might say "politically correct") disciplines its carnivalesque energies. As Don Hedrick points out, the film's sentimentality may make it unappealing to its intended teen audience.[28] Moreover, the film's liberal-mindedness is premised on the absence of gays from the student body and general population. One student teases Billy, "So you're playing a big fairy? Yeah? Well, that's good casting." But the joke is harmless because Billy and everyone else is straight. "Hey Turner suck my wand!" Billy quips, in a witty version of that weird heterosexual way of asserting one's heterosexuality by inviting another man to engage in gay oral sex. Shakespeare may be a signifier of gayness precisely because his plays are art, not filth. What is particularly queer about the film is its attention to gay desire in the absence of gay characters. In this high school, homophobia is not only unnecessary, it is impossible, since there is no one toward whom anyone could be homophobic. By the same token, homophobia seems to be inescapable: precisely because gayness can't be localized, it can be anywhere.

TOTALLY F***ED UP SHAKESPEARE: LOOKING FOR BITCHARD

A more complex example of the way a gay Shakespeare may disorient heteronormativity is *The Goodbye Girl,* a film about a straight actor, Elliot Garfield (Richard Dreyfuss), who gets fucked, as it were, but who nevertheless comes out on top through a Shakespearean prosthesis. The film begins with Garfield's discovery that the friend who sublet him his New York apartment failed to tell his just-dumped girlfriend, Paula McFadden (Marsha Mason), and her daughter, Lucy (Quinn Cummings) to vacate it. This difficulty is resolved by an agreement between Elliot and Paula to share the apartment, but it is quickly followed by another unexpected problem: though Elliot has come from Chicago to make it big in New York, he learns to his great discomfort that he must play Richard III as gay[29] (his reactions to the director's gay interpretation of Richard rather than the interpretation itself are what really generate the scene's comedy).

In opening with a story that appears to be about Elliot getting fucked over, the film stages a solution to the breakdown of the nuclear family, namely, the heterosexual "sensitive guy." But the film also discloses a problem with its solution: insofar as the sensitive guy is defined against the "macho, macho man," he is vulnerable to being read or to reading himself as symbolically castrated (in this film, read feminized, read gay). If he has to play Richard III as gay, Elliot protests, he might as well be a transvestite and play a woman: "You want this kind of performance? Let me play Lady Anne." Similarly, after the performance, Garfield conflates gay and transgendered roles: "I was an Elizabethan fruit fly. I was the Betty Boop of Stratford on Avon." Moreover, Elliot voices his fear about how the public will respond by using slang that links him to gayness. He's afraid he is an asshole:

> ELLIOT: The critics are gonna crucify me and gay liberation is gonna hang me from Shakespeare's statue by my genitalia. . . .

MARK: Do you feel foolish?

ELLIOT: I feel like an asshole. I passed foolish on Tuesday.

The reviewers in turn code Elliot's performance as gay and as transgendered:

> ELLIOT: *Times* review said: "Elliot Garfield researched *Richard III* and discovered him to be England's first badly dressed interior decorator." *Daily News* said that. Here, read it: "It never occurred to us that William Shakespeare wrote *The Wizard of Oz*. However, Elliot Garfield made a splendid Wicked Witch of the North."

After the failed performance, then, Elliot appears to be totally fucked, both as an actor and as a lover (Lucy tells him that he is not sexy like Tony, the guy who dumped her mother).[30]

Paradoxically, however, Elliot's transgendered, gay Shakespeare is the means of his romantic and theatrical success. Like "Springtime for Hitler" in Mel Brooks's *The Producers* (1966), what appears to be an absolute disaster turns out to be the opposite. Elliot wins the hearts of Lucy (who asks to go see the performance) and her skeptical, hard-to-get mother; moreover, his performance makes his acting career. After the failed *Richard III* (it closes after the first night) he is asked to join an improv group, and a Hollywood director in the audience is struck by Garfield's daring and invites him to act in his film.

How does *The Goodbye Girl* get to this happy ending? Richard III is crucial since the character provides Elliot with what he needs: a prosthesis to defend against his symbolic castration anxiety. The prosthesis emerges through an implicit pun on "hump," meaning hunchback and sex:

> MARK: How do you see Richard? Mr. Macho? Is that it?
>
> ELLIOT: I don't see him as a linebacker for the Chicago Bears, but let's not throw away one of his prime motivations.
>
> MARK: Oh? What's that?
>
> ELLIOT: He wants to hump Lady Anne!

The hunchback returns not as the macho linebacker but as a hump. Although Elliot follows the director and plays Richard as gay, he fights to keep the hump and the twisted fingers, and eventually he and the director reach a compromise:

> MARK: Do you see where I'm headed?
> ELLIOT: I'm trying Mark.
> MARK: Richard was gay. There's no doubt about it. But let's use it as subtext. We'll keep it but now we can put back the hunchback and the twisted fingers.

Elliot is ecstatic. Once he has his props, he can allay what he otherwise experiences as symbolic castration. The hump functions as the phallus. With Richard stripped bare to his metaphorical hump, Elliot can still hump women, even if he acts the part of a gay transvestite too. Elliot learns how to perform onstage and how to perform in bed. Though the film is not overtly homophobic, it does suggest that Elliot frees himself up by unconsciously equating the stigma of being gay with the stigma of being a cripple.

Elliot has the phallus, and thus the film apparently concludes with a reconstructed, "normal" nuclear family. Yet the process of normalization itself is anything but normal. Like Richard's fingers, the narrative is a bit twisted. What might seem like two separable plots—one about an actor's career, the other about a romance—instead prove to be linked through Shakespeare, who is kept as subtext, as it were, to the heterosexual romance. Though the film never doubts that Garfield is anything but heterosexual, at the heart of his heterosexual romance is a gay character and anality. Anality crops up in a number of places: not only in Elliot's comment that he is an asshole, but when he walks out on a rehearsal (in a wonderful combination of gay lisp and Elizabethanese, he says "Thisith maketh me a horseth ass"), and in his remarks to Paula. When she rebuffs him the day after they sleep together, Elliot exclaims to her: "You are one large pain in the arse. If you weren't such a horse's rectum. . . ." Anality is marked most noticeably in the moment Elliot and Paula hook up, the night of his performance. Elliot comes home so drunk he falls on the floor. Paula

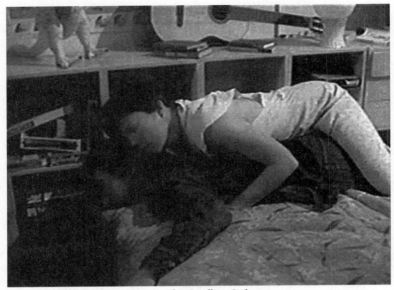

Figure 1.8: Elliot bottoms out in *The Goodbye Girl.*

picks him up and with her arms around his stomach she pushes him forward to his room, and then onto his bed. After he asks her if she thinks he is upset about fourteen negative reviews and answers his own question "You bet your ass I am!" he falls on the bed face down, and she falls on top of him (see figure 1. 8). Feeling as if she is humping him, Garfield comments: "Sorry, this apartment is rated PG." This sexualized moment suggests that their romance is really a story about two assholes falling in love: whereas initially she fucks him up, now she fucks him—up the ass.

The film's anality does not suggest that Elliot is gay, then, but it does raise a problem with the way his Shakespearean prosthesis can serve as a compromise-formation, namely, its mobility and transferability. The prothesis is metaphorical rather than literal: it is a phallus, yet it functions like a dildo. The phallus/penis equation that would link Elliot's gender to symbolic mastery is disturbed by the phallus/hump equation. The scene with Paula on top of Elliot on the bed confirms their interest in each other but raises the question, "Who has the phallus?" The film's answer appears to be a promiscuous "pretty much everyone": Paula's ex-lovers, Paula, the daughter, the director, the theater audiences. At one point or another, all have the symbolic mastery Elliot lacks.

Elliot's solution to the promiscuity of the phallus is theater. Theater, and to a significant degree, specifically gay theater, offers a compensatory mechanism for adjusting an inequality between Elliot and Paula. By making it as an actor, Elliot hopes he can be desirable to Paula in the way she is desirable to him. Through much of the film, Elliot is presented as a romantic loser. He has to assert that he is the wooer, the one who kisses first. He's at least third in line for Paula (he says he hates the "other guys" who have left her, inviting one to ask "how many?"). When he works temporarily as a barker for a strip show on 42nd Street, he is decked by a drunk he isn't able to bounce.

The film's conclusion, while quite sappily making Elliot as desirable to Paula as she is to him, nevertheless cannot quite realize the dream of a reconstructed, "normal" nuclear family. Acting keeps the two lovers separate instead of uniting them: Elliot goes off to make his film alone; rather than go with him, Paula decides to stay home to "spend his money" to decorate their apartment. Their union remains deferred, promised. Love may be better the second time around, but we don't know for sure.[31] To emphasize the pathos of Elliot's potentially broken promise to return, the film closes with the melancholic pop song of the film's title. This lack of closure signals, I suggest, a residual anxiety about Elliot's ownership of the phallus, a fear that his gay cripple theatrical protheses, Shakespearean and otherwise, can't quite fill a fundamental lack of heterosexual symbolic authority.

The Story Must Be Told:
Shakespeare's Fairy Queens

While *Porky's 2* and *The Goodbye Girl* more or less succeed in normalizing Shakespeare, *Dead Poets Society* displays a much more complex process in which degaying Shakespeare opens up the contrary possibility. Set in an elite New England boys prep school during the 1950s, this film stages a pedagogical scene at once far more repressive and far more daring than does *Porky's 2*. In one class, the teacher, John Keating (Robin Williams), codes Shakespeare as gay and contrasts a British theatrical production he brands as effeminate with two straight American cinematic productions:

> Today we're going to be talking about William Shakespeare. Oh God. I know a lot of you look forward to this about as much as you look forward to getting a root canal. We're going to talk about Shakespeare as someone who writes something very interesting. Now many of you have seen Shakespeare being done like this: "O Titus, bring your friend hither." [Williams lisps the line and holds his right wrist limp.] But if any of you have seen Mr. Marlon Brando, [you] know that Shakespeare can be different: "Friends, Romans, countrymen." [Williams imitates Brando's slurred speech.] You can also imagine maybe John Wayne as Macbeth going "Well, is this a dagger I see before me?" [Williams imitates Wayne here, this time provoking laughter in the students.]

Keating degays Shakespeare by moving him from the gay English theater to the (hyper)straight American cinema.

But Keating's degaying ironically works as a solicitation to students to gay Shakespeare and even to become gay while appearing to disavow doing so. The theatricality of Shakespeare is here disorienting: Keating's mimicry of John Wayne, for example, undoes his contrast between straight and gay ways of doing Shakespeare. Wayne becomes an hysterically funny, over-the-top parody of heterosexual masculinity. Keating makes it possible in a number of ways for his students to like Shakespeare, and to like him. And precisely because nothing is going to happen, the homosocial relation between teacher and student can be eroticized: students and teacher permit themselves to have unacknowledged, mutual crushes on one another. The film focuses on one student, Neal (Robert Sean Leonard), who appears to be solicited by Keating. Neal organizes the reconstitution of the Dead Poets Society and decides to disobey his overbearing father, taking to heart Keating's admonition to "seize the day." Neal auditions for *A Midsummer Night's Dream* and, perhaps predictably, gets the part of Puck. His father forbids him to act in the play, but Neal goes ahead with it anyway. Unexpectedly, his father shows up looking ominous at

Figure 1.9: No "fairy" tale ending for this Puck in Peter Weir's *Dead Poets Society*.

the performance. In a series of cross-cut reaction shots, Neal appears to deliver the play's epilogue to his father, as if asking his pardon (see figure 1. 9). Neal gets a standing ovation and Keating tells him that he must stick with acting. But nothing is mended. The father is intransigent, furious at Keating, and takes Neal home directly, informing him that he is to be withdrawn from school and enrolled in a military academy. Neal is crushed and commits suicide. The film concludes with Keating being unfairly blamed by the parents and administration for the suicide and subsequently dismissed. The boys go along with the administration. Yet, in a last stand, as it were, they proclaim their loyalty by standing on their desks and addressing him as "Captain, my captain" before he leaves their classroom for the last time.

Implying an equivalence between theater and homosexuality, the film allows one reasonably to conclude that Neal committed suicide because he was gay and couldn't come out to his father. (Few adolescents commit suicide because their fathers refuse to let them major in acting, but many do because they are gay.) More directly, Neal plays Puck in a production at a girl's school (his performance is quite traditional, not an imitation of Brando or Wayne). As in *Porky's 2,* playing a fairy appears to be code for being gay. After Neal gets the part, he is filmed walking down the hall of his dorm happily reciting the line, "broom faerie, here comes Oberon." This shot is followed by one of his father waiting in Neal's room to forbid Neal from acting. The repressed returns. We also see Neal getting nude before committing suicide; and the crown he wore as Puck, when he places it on his head just before he shoots himself, can be read as a crown of thorns for a young gay martyr to paternal homophobia. Moreover, Neal is a fan of Keating. He digs up a yearbook with Keating's photo in it; he leads the Dead Poets Society; he has Keating's copy of his book, *Five Centuries of Verse,* from which the members of the original Dead Poets Society read aloud; he is the first to address Keating as "Captain, my captain," a title Keating invited his students to call him on the first day of class. The Whitman/Lincoln analogy for the student/teacher relation is reinforced by a photograph of Whitman at the front of the class above the blackboard and by a crucial pedagogical moment for Neal's roommate, Todd (Ethan Hawke): Todd learns how to recite poetry aloud to the class when Keating first coerces and then encourages him to talk about the Whitman photograph.

One might nevertheless argue that a reading of Neal as gay is forced. To be sure, there is no direct evidence for it and the film is, after all, clear about Keating's and the students' heterosexuality, even heterosexism. Keating affirms that "the Dead Poets Society . . . wasn't just a bunch of guys. We weren't a Greek [read gay?] organization. Women swooned." The class on Shakespeare is preceded by a conversation about language and love: "Language was developed for but one endeavor," Keating remarks, "to woo women." Similarly, the first poem he teaches is Herrick's love lyric "Gather ye rosebuds while ye may." The film piles on more evidence: one boy brings two girls to a meeting of the Dead Poets Society; Keating has a girlfriend; and a male and female student hook up while watching the performance of *A Midsummer Night's Dream.*

The absence of direct evidence of gayness and the presence of what looks like counter-evidence can, however, easily be read as disavowal. Keating's girlfriend, he says without explanation, is in

London: "Makes it difficult." And he jokes about the school's "monastic oath. [They] don't want worldly things distracting us from teaching." In addition to his interest in acting (implicitly equated, as we have seen, with gayness), Neal shows no romantic interest in any of the women in the film. The Herrick love lyric, which Keating ventriloquizes and locates in the previous, now dead students (Keating himself is a former student of the school), makes the teacher/student relation a homosocial one and levels the distinction between teacher and student: everyone is a student teacher (rather incredibly, the boys' favorite pastime appears to be meeting in study groups). Moreover, heterosexuality is represented in distinctly unflattering terms. The one male student who does hook up with a female student is very much a stalker/harasser.[32]

But if closeted gayness makes sense as an explanation of Neal's suicide, it isn't a secret the film seems particularly interested in disclosing. Rather, *Dead Poets Society* insists on the queerness of death in general and of Neal's death in particular. In the first class, Keating gets his students to reflect on their own mortality. They will become "food for worms," as did the other boys who went to this school, boys whose photos Keating has invited them to look over. "Did they wait until it was too late?" Keating asks them, and then adds: "You can hear them whisper their legacy to you. *Carpe diem*." This is a conventional enough lay existentialism: live fully because your time is limited. But a weird conclusion to this scene unsettles the conventionality of Keating's lesson. A sequence of reverse shots in close-up establish mirroring images of two students in the photographs and the roommates Neal and Todd. "That was weird. Spooky, if you ask me," two students comment after class. This weirdness and spookiness is emphasized later by a shot of the boys disappearing into fog at night when they first go out to meet as the Dead Poets Society. And eerie music (composed by Maurice Jarré) plays just before Neal commits suicide.

Rather than simply outing Neal, the film seems interested in a much more ambiguous kind of queer pedagogy. While opening up a critique of normalization, the film does not make an overt critique because to do so would itself be normalizing: let's all be nonconformist the same way. This is actually what threatens to happen in a scene in which Keating has the boys walk in a circle (one boy doesn't join in because he wants to be independent), and more pointedly in the final scene of the film. In order to save a queer critique, the film risks lapsing into a touchy-feely *Mr. Chips*–like bathos. The film ends by replacing one triangle with another: Todd stands on his desk and replaces Neal, while Nolan, the repressive headmaster now filling in as English teacher, replaces Neal's controlling father. This new triangle installs a new binary opposition between the good, fired teacher and students loyal to him, on the one hand, and bad, new teacher and students he manages to cow, on the other.

This opposition might appear to affirm the heterosexual masculinity of the students loyal to Keating. Though they earlier betrayed Keating, giving him up to their parents and headmaster, now they appear to seize the day and demonstrate that they have learned the meaning of Keating's teaching. But this apparent affirmation is disturbed in a number of ways. The scene isn't really about the boys' demonstration of their loyalty and respect for Keating. The scene is more about their loss of someone they love. An inverse disturbance is that Keating contradicts his own teaching. He does not fight his dismissal. Perhaps he has attained a Christlike wisdom that places him above petty school politics. But such wisdom, insofar as it is achieved, contradicts his *carpe diem* lesson. Keating is now sizing up the other side, that is, figuring the odds against winning, and thinking ahead: he is most pointedly not seizing the day. (Another possibility is that Keating wimps out because he sees himself as a student being expelled, the fate of the one student who does defend him by decking the student who first betrays Keating and then urges the others to do likewise.)

Perhaps more interestingly, the melodramatic opposition between good and bad teachers, strong and weak students, is disturbed formally by a triangulation between the viewer, Keating, and Todd. The last shot of the film, held for fifteen seconds, is of Todd, framed through the crotch of another boy who is also standing on his desk (see figure 1. 10). It is close to being a reaction shot of Keating, who stands across the room from Todd, but the angle of the shot is so far away from Keating's line of sight that it positions the spectator, not Keating, as the observer. This triangulation is literalized by the shot itself. The boy's legs form a triangle. The shot calls attention to a

Figure 1.10: Boys stand up for teacher in *Dead Poets Society.*

structure of triangulated desire that has been present throughout the film: Neal and Keating's relationship is mediated not only by Neal's father but by his roommate Todd (who at one point sides with Neal's father and at another with Keating). Todd's relationship to the Dead Poets Society and to the class is mediated by Whitman.

Though the film ends by clearly enforcing heteronormativity, the triangulation foregrounded in the closing shot also calls attention to a disorientation that cannot be put right, much less straight. The film's triangles register a desire to reanimate the dead, a process begun when Keating teaches his first class and invites the boys to look at students who have previously attended the school. (Todd's older brother, a distinguished former student, serves as a ghost the memory of whom makes him an oppressive burden for Todd.) Dead poets are reanimated in Keating's original society. Keating appears to reanimate himself as a student by teaching other students about dead poets. Neal reanimates a Dead Poets Society. In the film's narrative logic, he has to die for there to be a story about Keating. The desire to reanimate produces an imperative to narrate: Keating will tell the stories of dead poets, of dead students; Todd will tell Neal and Keating's story. But the triangulation highlighted in the film's closing shot also suggests that narrative here is propelled by a process of continual displacement and deferral: the story that must be told is never the story that can be told. In reanimating the dead poets, Keating doesn't tell the story of his desire to reanimate them for himself, for his students. (Why did he quit his London teaching job and return to this school? Why did he leave his girlfriend in London?) The story of his teaching is displaced and deferred in turn, told by a student whose own story will have to be told by yet another student.

And what doesn't get told is what doesn't get mourned. The film is an instance of what Judith Butler calls "heterosexual melancholy":

> the heterosexual refusal to acknowledge the primary homosexual attachment is culturally enforced by a prohibition on homosexuality. . . . Heterosexual melancholy is culturally maintained as the price of stable gender identities related through oppositional desires. (1990, 70)

In *Dead Poets Society,* however, melancholy arises because of a narrative problem rather than because of a repressed primary homosexual identification. The triangular structure that propels the reproduction of heteronormativity means that there will always be a remainder that cannot be narrated, or, to put it another way, that can be narrated only after the person the story is about is dead or otherwise lost.

Ciao, Shakespeare Professore

In maintaining that *Dead Poets Society* is a more queer and more interesting film than *The Goodbye Girl* and *Porky's 2*, I have argued that there is a continuum along which films may be distinguished as more or less interesting and more or less queer. I want to turn now to *So Fine* to show how any such distinction may sometimes be called into question by the lack of any clear, consistent definition of queerness. Whether *So Fine* is more queer than *Dead Poets Society* is hard to say, and though *So Fine* is not as well made, whether or not it is more interesting is a matter of opinion. *So Fine* registers how varied the paradoxical relation between queerness and gayness is. The film is a fantasy of total ethnic assimilation, but the real wish behind it is that the father can be both left and kept around at the same time. An unconscious bargain is struck between son and father such that the son, an assimilated Jewish English professor at a New England college, can be assimilated back into his father's New York garment district world and then released; the son can save the father and then the father can return the favor. An ethnically marked and adapted Shakespeare allows for a romantic, adulterous coupling between the son and a woman that doesn't unsettle the father and son bond.

Yet the father's inclusion within the heterosexual couple produces uncanny effects. The father is almost always where he's not supposed to be. In keeping the Oedipal bond secure, the film has to degay homosocial bonds and at the same time empower women. The site of this contradiction is the professor's naked ass. The film negotiates a queer resolution to the primal scene (which is here reversed—the father sees the son having sex), displacing what cannot be seen and eroticized by straight men, in this case, the son's ass rather than the parents having sex, with what can be seen, namely, the woman's ass, what all men can safely desire, in the logic of this film.

So Fine adapts *The Merchant of Venice* and *Othello* (with some allusions to *Henry V*) to produce a comedy that ends with two prospective marriages. Bobby Fine is a professor who teaches American literature at a New England college and who cites Shakespeare. He is competing for tenure against another assistant professor who has just published an article (which the Chair praises). By contrast, Fine is viewed as a slacker. After explaining that there is only one tenured position, the Chair, rather oddly, cites Shylock's invitation to Antonio to accept a loan and tests Fine: "What shall [sic] I gain by the exacture of this forfeiture? A pound of flesh taken from a man is not so estimable, profitable neither, as, as what Mr. Fine?" Fine, who had to be nudged awake by a colleague moments before, manages to finish the quotation, to everyone's surprise: "as the flesh of muttons, beef, or goats. I say to buy this favor, I extend this friendship" (1.3. 160-164). After the meeting, when asked by the other assistant professor how he knew the lines, Fine replies, "My father's in the dress business. I always liked *The Merchant of Venice.*"

The film's rewriting of Shakespeare's comedy reverses Jewish and Italian ethnicities and ends with inter-ethnic marriages between Jewish men and Italian women: in this case, a Jewish family is in debt to an Italian one. Bobby Fine is the equivalent of Bassanio, Jack Fine (Jack Warden), Antonio. Jack borrows $150,000 from Mr. Eddie (Richard Kiel), a character who is the equivalent of Shylock. Mr. Eddie takes over Fine's business when Fine can't repay him and demands that Bobby come into the business. There is no equivalent for Portia. Bobby/Bassanio ends up saving the business as a result of having an affair with Mr. Eddie's wife, an Italian immigrant named Lira (Mari-angela Melato). When Mr. Eddie comes home unexpectedly, Bobby has to dress in Lira's sweater and jeans, which are much too small for him, in order to escape undetected. Bobby bends over, rips them across the pockets, and then stuffs the pockets with clear plastic, apparently in a futile attempt to cover his ass. When he returns to the office, buyers getting off the elevator see Bobby from behind and immediately want to order the jeans. The new design (for women only) becomes a huge success and the Fines make enough money to buy back the business from Mr. Eddie.

Quotations from *Henry V* mark how far Bobby Fine has been assimilated into his father's world. When Bobby first speaks to the people at his father's company, he cites (in compressed form) the chorus's description of Henry V going among his men:

> I'm going to go amongst you today and absorb and learn, much in the tradition of Shakespeare's Henry V, "The royal captain of this ruined band, / Walking from watch to watch, from tent to tent . . . / That every wretch pining and pale before, / Beholding him, plucks comfort from his looks."

The employees are not impressed. One says to another, "Do you believe this putz?" A bit later, another character says, "I bet Jack wishes I were his son," suggesting that Bobby isn't so much Henry V as he is the truant Hal at the opening of *Henry IV, Part One.* After his success with the see-through jeans, however, Bobby cites *Henry V* again to his employees before he returns to college. "It's an honor to call you, as Shakespeare's Henry V so aptly put it, 'we few, we happy few, we band of brothers.'" This time, the employees respect him.

Though Bobby can now operate "almost like a pro" in the business world (his wardrobe now consists of very expensive Italian suits), he does not take on the status of a martial hero capable of wooing a princess and marrying her, nor does his analogy to Bassanio admit of a Portia-like wife. Instead, Bobby retreats from romance, breaking things off with Lira so as to avoid Mr. Eddie and returning to his college campus. *So Fine* nevertheless manages to end comically, and it does so not by leaving Shakespeare behind but by radically rewriting the Shakespearean marriage plot in post-Shakespearean terms: adultery is licensed through an adaptation of an adaptation of Shakespeare's *Othello,* namely, Guiseppe Verdi's *Otello.* After the failure of *Henry V* as a full analogue to Bobby's situation, the film then begins to rewrite Verdi's *Otello* in comic terms. Bobby Fine now becomes the equivalent of an adulterous Cassio, while Lira becomes analogous to a now unfaithful Desdemona (in this rewrite, adulterous with just cause). Bobby, Lira, Jack, and Mr. Eddie all meet up at a performance of *Otello* on the college campus. (After Bobby returned to his college Lira followed him there. Mr. Eddie found out about the affair and followed her, and Jack in turn found out that Mr. Eddie had found out and followed him.) In an earlier scene in the film, Lira sang the closing "Liebestod" aria from Richard Wagner's *Tristan und Isolde* as she and Bobby made love, the tragedy suggesting that the lovers are doomed. Performing in the Italianized Shakespeare tragedy *Otello,* however, Lira does make possible a rewriting of tragedy as comedy, taking over the part of Desdemona when Mr. Eddie shows up (the original singer, Ms. Caneloni, is sick with a cough and can't continue). Mr. Eddie then knocks out Enrico Di Rienzi, the tenor, and goes onstage in partial black face, surprisingly able to sing the part of Otello. He then proceeds to rewrite the opera as the story of himself and his faithless wife, but she counters, "You have a limp noodle." As Otello/Mr. Eddie starts to smother Desdemona/Lira on their bed, Bobby tries and fails to stop him. But Jack swings across the stage like a 1940s swashbuckler and knocks out Mr. Eddie. Jack, Bobby, and Lira receive a standing ovation, and the chair awards Bobby tenure (the other professor is caught having sex with a student in Fine's office). This comic revision of Shakespearean tragedy then enables a return to Shakespearean comedy. The film ends by echoing *The Merchant of Venice* a final time, with the two couples, Bobby and Lira and Jack and Lira's servant (who are analogous to Gratiano and Nerissa) riding in separate gondolas in Venice.

Shakespeare is at the center of a series of crossovers in jobs, gender, genre, geography, and language—man to woman, woman to man, father to son, tragedy to comedy, academic world to business world, (New) England to (little) Italy, New York to Venice, theater to opera, Wagner to Verdi—that allow for a comic resolution, that is to say heterosexual union, to take place. Initially, it seems that neither Bobby nor Lira can succeed outside his or her own narrow world. Bobby knows nothing about the dress business and has to be counseled by Jack when first meeting Mr. Eddie: "Don't be a putz. Don't quote *The Canterbury Tales* to him. He's ignorant." Bobby complies, but his status as "putz" is confirmed, as we have seen, when Jack introduces him at work. As it turns out, however, he can cross over. It's significant that Fine teaches at a Department of English and Comparative Literature and that he is an Americanist rather than a Shakespearean. He and his department are multilingual and multicultural. Lira is a fitting match for Bobby because she too can cross-over. At first she seems to be unable to do so, and Fine returns to college because he feels she is a woman whom one can take to Rome, to Florence, or to Paris (a line she later echoes), but not to New England. As her name suggests, however, Lira is a kind of currency, something that can be exchanged. And it is precisely through *Otello* that she is able to cross over from being married to the mob to being married to the academy. Her Desdemona gets her a standing ovation and, apparently, Fine tenure.

Though the film ends recalling *The Merchant of Venice,* it departs from Shakespeare's heteronormative comic plot in making the romantic couples' ability to cross over ethnic boundaries a means of keeping the Oedipal bond intact. The *Otello* performance allows Jack to repay the debt to his son by saving him in turn. Far from straightening out the romance, however, Shakespeare marks a certain queerness in both Fines, registered most clearly in the way Shylock's pound of flesh is displaced onto Bobby's exposed buttocks. Though both men are straight, the father and son have a distinctly homoerotic relationship. Jack's wife is inexplicably absent, never even mentioned. (Another character, we learn, has been married three times. His first two wives died and the present one isn't doing well.) And as a transvestite version of Portia, the son adopts the role of wife. When they first meet and Bobby learns that Mr. Eddie will literally kill Jack if he doesn't pay back the money, Bobby massages his father's neck in a "wifely" way. Moreover, Bobby is attracted to a woman who is already coupled and ends up in bed with her and her husband. Though Mr. Eddie is asleep, he turns over and hugs Fine from behind; Fine blurts out to Lira, "I thought you said he was impotent!"

So Fine's reversals also call into question who is a man. "You gotta be one of them. You gotta be a mensch," Jack tells Bobby in his first performance review. "You are a man," Lira says to Bobby, and he responds diffidently, "I like to think so." His masculinity is not that of the stereotypical, macho Italian sort, however. Lira is the eager, passionate seductress, Bobby the timid, Adonis-like object of her attention. Consistently the aggressor, she decides to take him to Venice at the film's close (though they will return to his college). Moreover, both Fines are feminized. Lira dresses Bobby in her clothes and Jack prostitutes himself to get a women buyer to purchase his clothes. And, on the bus to work, a gay man hits on Bobby, asking if he's seen Bobby at the baths. Similarly, Jack's status as a single parent is implicitly feminized by the plot. Bobby drives the "world's most famous poet" to campus, an old man with long gray hair who looks like an old woman and who tells about exposing himself, and Bobby literally carries him to the reception to escape Mr. Eddie's gangsters, who've come to collect him. Jack is positioned, too, as an older, feminized man whom his son must bail out. Whereas Jack's employees have sex with buyers at the business, Jack ineptly retrieves a dress from a women in her dressing room and almost gets busted by the security guards. The film implies that the Fines are so fine that they are perhaps too fine, a *familia* fabric that can easily be torn.

To be sure, no one in the film is clearly marked as stereotypically masculine. Even the giant Mr. Eddie is cut down to size. Though Jack remarks "Jesus, Eddie, you're really built" when he sees Eddie's penis

Figure 1.11: Bobby Fine trying to cover his ass in Andrew Bergman's *So Fine*.

in a sauna, when Lira seduces Bobby, she says she is a very unhappy woman—that Mr. Eddie is "not a man." Fine asks, "Is he homosexual?" "No," Lira replies, "he's not homosexual. He's not *al dente*." Lira's disclaimer is contradicted, however, by the fact that Mr. Eddie does get an erection when he hugs Bobby from behind in bed (after earlier rebuffing Lira's request to make love).

The absence of any clearly marked "masculine" man in the film is a consequence of the way the film inverts gender positions in order to maintain exclusively heterosexual couplings. The spectacle of the woman's butt displaces the spectacle of the man's butt as the film genders the see-through jeans. Though the buyers ask Bobby whether there are jeans for both men and women, he answers oddly that he is wearing women's jeans and that that is all they market. Moreover, we see Bobby's ass only briefly and even then only obscured after he rips his jeans. He doesn't wear, that is, see-through plastic (see figure 1.11). As if in compensation for showing Bobby's rear briefly and in veiled fashion, however, the film shows us lots of women's rears in see-

Figure 1.12: The spectacle of women's rear ends in *So Fine*.

through jeans and with much larger areas cut out (Bobby's jeans only have small slits). *So Fine* repeatedly delivers shots of women wearing the see-through jeans, first in a Busby Berkeley–like commercial with twelve dancers (see figure 1.12), then at a disco, on the streets, on the college campus, and, in the film's last shot, in Venice, where a plump, middle-aged woman selling gelatti turns around and walks off wearing the see-through jeans. The displacement of focus from Bobby's rear to women's rears serves to keep Bobby's sexuality straight. Oddly, Bobby's transvestism doesn't signify to anyone in the film, except a taxi driver who refuses to pick him up and the gay man who hits on him. For everyone else, the only significant thing about Bobby's dress is his "bare ass." And it's Bobby's ass that the film wants to cover, as it were.[33]

By keeping men straight, this displacement from male to female rears allows, paradoxically, for a homosocial and even homoerotic relationship between father and son. Although Bobby momentarily ends up in bed with both husband and wife, he does manage to escape the husband, Mr. Eddie. But Bobby's father sticks around even at the very end of the film. Moreover, both father and son get off on each other's sex lives. Both father and son see the other hook up with a woman and take pleasure in doing so. Bobby and Jack smile at each other when Bobby sees Jack meet up with the woman to whom he prostitutes himself; and Jack is even more appreciative when he sees Bobby and Lira having sex while Lira sings the "Liebestod," saying to himself with a big smile, "I used to fuck like that." Similarly, at the film's end, Jack and the servant discuss Bobby and Lira, how happy he's made her. "Yeah, he's really made her sing," Jack says wistfully. The servant pleads, "Jack, make me sing too" and brings his face to hers as she kisses him.

So Fine essentially attempts to suture a tear in the men's business of dressing women opened up by generational differences in degrees of ethnic assimilation. In becoming more assimilated, that is, Bobby threatens to leave behind not only his father, but his father's world. The credits open with denim being torn, and when the credits roll at the end, the opening is reversed so that the denim is once again whole. Yet this suturing of a generational tear isn't really successful; rather, it marks the end of the film as a wish that cannot be comfortably fulfilled. The son has been reassimilated back into his father's world and has paid off his debt, and the father in turn has repaid the debt he owes his son by saving him from Mr. Eddy. Yet the father remains in his world. As if expressing a degree of resentment toward Jack, the film registers his inclusion with mockery. Jack's presence in a gondola at the end is not only a surprise , but is subtly criticized as well. "How long have the streets around here been fucked up?" he asks the servant, underlining his ignorance of a world outside New York. The father remains unassimilated and provincial, then, in a way the son does not. Moreover, the father's uncanny presence in Venice is compounded by the return of the maternal in the film's closing shot. The woman we last see, a gelatti vendor, is the only unattractive woman we see wearing the see-through jeans. She is a maternal figure, surrounded by children. She does not provide milk, however, but ice milk, sweet but cold. This final moment seems to be the revenge of the mother: a ghost that forces her way into the picture, even if she is framed by the father's gaze at her comically grotesque ass.

In the end, as it were, the spectacle of a man's butt and the possibility of a homosexual gaze at it are displaced by the spectacle of a woman's rear that is not exactly erotic, at least not in conventional terms. Insofar as the displacement is successfully eroticized up to the film's last shot, however, it also involves a gender reversal in which women are in control of their relationships, able to demand sexual and emotional satisfaction from their partners. The film hints at a troubling excessiveness about female desire for the male characters, a hint registered not only in Lira's adultery ("I fuck around," she tells Fine when they meet at Mr. Eddie's disco), but in a large poster of the opera *Messaline* that hangs near the door of Lira and Mr. Eddie's apartment. In *So Fine's* adaptation of Verdi's adaptation of Shakespeare's *Othello,* Desdemona gets to be unfaithful and escape her husband, while Nerissa/Emilia gets to be turned on by the spectacle of her mistress having sex. (When Lira and Bobby first have sex, Lira has to tell her to leave, and, at a later moment, the servant listens to them in the next room while they have sex).[34] *So Fine* degays the homosocial relations between men in the film, but it effectively queers heterosexual relationships by inverting gender positions such that the male characters are feminized and the female characters are masculinized ("gay" is understood here in popular, heterosexual terms as feminine, passive, penetrated). Though the women's asses are eroticized, they are also the dominant partners. Women are the toppers, and men are the bottoms.[35]

This is not to say, of course, that Lira and Bobby are really somehow gay. My point, rather, is that the film queers heterosexuality (and marriage) by reversing the usual terms in which the relation between heterosexuality and homosexuality is regarded in the dominant culture: instead of homosexuality being construed as a failed imitation of heterosexuality, homosexuality becomes the model for heterosexuality envisioned as anything but normative. *So Fine* not only reworks Shakespeare by displacing Portia with Desdemona, but radically departs from Shakespearean conventions altogether by making adultery the path to (re)marriage.

In and Out of Shakespeare

In and Out constitutes a radical departure from the films I have discussed thus far, and by actually outing, in gay-positive terms, a man who initially thinks he is straight, it marks a post-AIDS mainstream film engagement with gay males. It might legitimately be considered to be the apotheosis of other mid-1990s films such as *Four Weddings and a Funeral* (dir. Mike Newell, 1995), *First Wives Club* (dir. Hugh Wilson, 1996), and *My Best Friend's Wedding* (dir. P. J. Hogan, 1997), all of which regard gayness as a desirable utopian possibility for heterosexuals outside of marriage and heterosexuality.[36] In *In and Out*, a small-town high school English teacher, Howard Brackett (Kevin Kline), who is about to marry his fiancée of three years, Emily Montgomery (Joan Cusack), is outed on national television by a former student turned movie star, Cameron Daze (Matt Dillon), during his Oscar acceptance speech. Initially asserting that he is not gay, Howard discovers that he really is, and he announces it to his bride at the altar and then to the assembled guests. He is fired from his job (though perhaps rehired at the end of the film) and becomes the boyfriend of a supportive tabloid newscaster, Peter Malloy (Tom Selleck), who has encouraged him (partly by kissing him) to come out. Emily hooks up with Cameron after he dumps his anorexic super-model girlfriend, Sonya (Shalom Harlow).

Shakespeare swings both ways in this film. On the one hand, he is aligned with Howard's gayness. Students repeatedly take as evidence of Howard's gayness the fact that he teaches Shakespeare (the sonnets). Hamlet's "what a piece of work is man" speech is written out in large bold type on the back wall of the class (perhaps with camp irony), visible as Howard discusses with his students whether or not they think he seems gay. And Brackett, given to malapropisms, misquotes sonnet 18, making a noticeable Freudian slip: "Shall I compare thee to a summer's gay? / Thou art more lovely. . . ."[37] Yet Shakespeare is also a signifier of heterosexuality. Brackett's fiancée mentions before the Academy Awards show begins that she taught Cameron as a student teacher and that the two of them regularly exchanged quotations from *Romeo and Juliet* in after-class tutorials. When Cameron returns to his hometown, Greenleaf, Indiana (perhaps in a very inside joke, called "Greenblatt" by his supermodel girlfriend) to help Howard, he stumbles upon his former teacher after she's left a bar and declares his love for her and his acceptance of her formerly full figure (she's lost a lot of weight by working out to

Richard Simmons tapes). The two characters discover their love for each other by again quoting (and misquoting) lines from the balcony scene. Cameron misquotes the last word of Romeo's lines "With love's light wings did I o'erperch these walls, / For stony limits cannot hold love out" as "in" (2.2.66-67), and she corrects him, saying, with some distress, "out." Cameron then repeats the word correctly.

In its gay-positive representation of a teacher and its bi-signifying Shakespeare, *In and Out* might seem to be a counter-example to what I have argued thus far. Gayness, that is, proves not to be disorienting to straights at all, and one could buttress this conclusion by arguing that the film is little more than a gay-friendly piece of romantic fluff with some incidental references to Shakespeare popularly understood as both gay and heterosexual. If the play wants to make gayness/secure sexual identities safe for straights through Shakespeare, it also wants to make Shakespeare safe in the same terms: Shakespeare would serve, that is, as a prophylatic against (hetero) confusion about sexual identity, that which enables that confusion to sort itself out as either "really" gay or "really" heterosexual.

Yet the film radically qualifies just how clearly Shakespeare can signify any sexual identity. Given Emily's penchant for gay men, for example, one of whom, Howard, thinks he is straight and who quotes Shakespeare, the other, Peter, who is gay and whom she hits on just before the Romeo and Juliet scene with Cameron, the film invites us to wonder just how straight Cameron really is. (A parallel between Cameron and Howard is set up near the beginning of the film: in clips from Cameron's Vietnam film at the Academy Awards, we see his character getting kicked out of the Army for being gay, thereby anticipating Howard's being fired as a teacher after he outs himself. Moreover, one might argue that his interest in Shakespeare marks him as a version of Howard rather than an alternative to him.) Rather than help a contemporary male decide to be in or out of the closet by virtue of being aligned with sexual identity *per se,* Shakespeare further contributes to the deconstruction of sexual identities insofar as he is neither exclusively gay or straight, in or out of the closet.

Moreover, far from simply representing the acceptance of gay men by heterosexuals, the film, in a very witty and sophisticated way, inverts the normalizing strategies of the other films discussed thus far.

Instead of trying to keep gayness in or out of the closet, distinct from heterosexuality (through an always already gay or straight Shakespeare), and thereby assuage the anxieties and insecurities gayness presents to heterosexuals once it is out of the closet, *In and Out* universalizes gayness. Even straight people, in this film, get to be gay. After Howard comes out at his wedding, four women comfort his mother by suggesting that they all "come out." One woman says that her wedding treat recipe really belongs to a dead woman; another says her husband has three testicles, and so on. In one hilarious moment, after Peter Malloy turns down Emily's offer to sleep with him (she's rebounding after being jilted at the altar) because he's gay, Emily runs out to the street and shouts "Is everyone gay?" And, as I mentioned earlier, the entire community protests the firing of Howard by getting up and declaring in turn "I'm gay," taking the homophobic notion of gay teachers as gay proselytizers whose gayness will "rub off" on their students to a comic extreme rather than denying it.

Despite its charm and gay-friendly intentions, one could regard this universalizing of gayness as accomplishing its actual erasure. Heterosexual women revealing secrets is hardly the same thing as apparently straight women outing their lesbianism (something none of them does in this scene). And while the first student who announces that he's gay at the graduation actually does seem to be gay, the force of his declaration is actually diminished as the rest of the audience, who seem quite clearly to be heterosexual, begins to do the same thing. Moreover, the film momentarily appears to end with a marriage between Howard and Peter but gives us instead a renewal of wedding vows by Howard's bewildered but supportive parents. Except for a single, comically presented kiss, there is no active gay sexuality in this film, no gay marriage. And, significantly, there are no lesbians. (The film's most obvious comparison is between gay men like Howard and full-figured heterosexual women like Emily: women can be overweight and still be loved just as men can be gay, come out, and still be loved.) The universality of gayness isn't really a gay fantasy here, nor is the film an unwitting example of queer theory. The film's fantasy about the universality of gayness is a distinctly heterosexual one (both gay characters are played by heterosexual actors, a point emphasized in the press kit). This is the new rather than the old in and out.

Yet the film does not simply degay gayness by universalizing it. What makes the film often funny and interesting is that it questions what it means to be gay. "What are the signifiers of gayness?" the film asks, as Howard and his family, fiancée, and students struggle to figure out why Brackett was outed and if he is indeed gay. And here Shakespeare plays a significant role as a bifold signifier of hetero and homosexualities.[38] As a signifier that keeps love in and out, Shakespeare crystallizes the film's heterosexual fantasy of gayness as something that deconstructs the opposition between being in the closet and out in public and that allows of the kinds of exchanges and equivalences that allow heterosexuals, particularly women in this film, to come out of their closets. Only the straight man (the high school principal) and the bulimic woman (Cameron's girlfriend) remain trapped in a stultifying realm of sobriety and vomit purges. These exchanges are hard to pin down in terms of political effects. If they erase gayness, they also mainstream it (one reporter asks Howard if he knows Ellen Degeneres, for example). The lack of gay marriage may seem like a sop to conservatives who supported the 1996 Defense of Marriage Act. On the other hand, raising the possibility and then foreclosing it keeps gayness open as a utopian space for heterosexuals precisely insofar as it remains the negation of heterosexual practices, something that can not be entirely reoriented. While not an example of queer theory, then, the film is not reducible to a conservative mimicry of queer theory's notion of mimicry as radical resignification either. Instead of showing that an overtly gay film is less queer than one in which gayness is closeted, then, the film deconstructs, albeit in a very different fashion from the other films I have discussed, the opposition between gayness and queerness by moving the queer beyond the limits of a particular sexual orientation.

Bringing Out Bill

In analyzing these mall films, produced and directed for a presumptively heterosexual audience, I have intended to show ways in which Shakespeare as a signifier of gayness in heteronormative films may be more queer, more disorienting than gayness in self-identified gay

Shakespeare films. In marking themselves as gay, these latter films are in some ways paradoxically quite straight. My queer reading of Shakespeare as a disorienting gay signifier in straight films may, however, produce some skepticism. Can a gay or a queer Shakespeare be popularized in these films without being pathologized? None of the films suggests an affirmative answer to this question. As I conceded at the outset, the films are mostly heteronormative. Moreover, with the exception of *In and Out,* each links a gay Shakespeare to disaster, even though none of them is homophobic. In *The Goodbye Girl,* the director's assertion of the accuracy of his interpretation—"I mean read your text"—is funny because he thinks gayness is obviously in the text whereas most readers of the play will find his reading totally unconvincing. His production of a gay *Richard III* bombs. In *Porky's 2,* a student reads a copy of *A Midsummer Night's Dream* and, bewildered, asks, "What the fuck's a Puck?" The Shakespeare production turns unintentionally into a burlesque, a mannequin's leg at one point replacing Macduff's sword. In *Dead Poets Society,* reading Shakespeare as gay leads to a student's suicide. Learning how to read Shakespeare differently may allow the boys to read Keating differently from his adult peers, but the boys fail even to present their different reading of Keating—"you don't know him like we do"—to their parents, much less to persuade them of its validity. And in *So Fine,* Bobby Fine is marked off from two real loser professors, one, his competitor, who is caught sleeping with a student and denied tenure, and another who tries to curry favor with the chair by finding ways of appreciating the unanticipated changes in *Otello* as an intentional rewriting. The production of *Otello* is a disaster—backdrops from other shows go up and come down—and an academic mode of recuperating that disaster is mocked. When Mr. Eddie appears as Otello, the sycophantic professor comments, "Brilliant. To make Otello a kind of tragic giant?" And when different background sets change as Bobby attempts to escape from Mr. Eddie, he notes, "very surreal."[39]

If these films make a difference, that difference has to do with a certain kind of failure rather than a successful assimilation of gayness to heteronormative culture. But that is not necessarily a bad thing. The failure of these films is not, in my view, reducible to a typical homophobic disavowal or repression; it registers, rather, the queer ways in which what I have called gay eruptions exceed the codes by which gayness is signified in heteronormative culture. The success of these films, such as it is, lies in moments of disorienting breakdown rather than in moments of clear-headed, utopian affirmation.

Shakespeare's Incredibly Queer Will(y)

An American scholar achieved wide popular attention in *People Magazine* and on the front page of the *New York Times* for having appeared to argue (at an academic conference) that he could tell that a certain poem was written by Shakespeare because Shakespeare was bisexual (Anonymous B 1996; Honan 1996).[40] Though it may still produce some controversy or titillation in some quarters, the idea of a bisexual (or gay) Shakespeare is now widely considered normal inside and outside of academia. Some might applaud the release of Shakespeare's queer will in film as a way to normalize gayness. Given the degree to which a country like the United States remains virulently homophobic, it would be hard to disagree. Alan Sinfield (1995, 1-20) regards Shakespeare as something imposed by a dominant culture on subordinated groups and their subcultures (Jews, women, gays, and other minorities). A popular gay Shakespeare might bring relief from the burden of having to enjoy Shakespeare by imagining oneself as other than who one is. The failure of popular films to imagine a gay Shakespeare in terms other than disaster might make some more comfortable with the terrain of the avant-garde, openly gay arty versions of Shakespeare on film. Even if Jarman or Van Sant can do less with the popular because they appropriate it in a clearly marked gay camp context, so the argument might go, they are at least free of the constraints on gay representations put in place by the Hollywood system.

While normalizing films may have social benefits by lessening homophobia, my concern is less with those benefits than it is with the way queer theory and practices may be normalized in academic work. What is the value of a Shakesqueered cinema? What happens to Shakespeare's legacy, to his will, if he is perceived to be gay or queer (Fineman, 1991)? I would like briefly to address these questions by yoking the problem of normalization to Shakespeare's popularization in the cinema. Cultural critics now fantasize that their work can be popularized and so reach a wider, nonacademic audience, but this fantasy is disturbed by the fact that a gay Shakespeare won't signify much of anything progressive. The distinction I am making between gay and queer, much less the concept of the queer sublime, is pretty much meaningless for heterosexual culture outside academia. Moreover, even if the films were subversive in popular terms, saying so would be rather uninteresting in academic terms. (The subversion/containment debate, though played out by the late 1980s, appears to be where much cultural criticism still seems stalled.) Rather than ask how academics can popularize a gay Shakespeare, then (my answer is that they can't), I want to ask how the fantasy of a popular gay (or queer) Shakespeare functions in academic work. At stake in a gay as opposed to a queer Shakespeare is the kind of critical work done in Shakespeare's name. Gaying Shakespeare may allow scholars to do little more than the most everyday kind of textual criticism, deciding what is or is not part of the canon, what is or is not authentic, all on the basis of a presumed gay sexual identity that is most certainly anachronistic. Even an anti-authenticity performance criticism that opens up what counts as Shakespearean to include all reproductions as worthy of study, secures its legitimacy by relating the reproductions to Shakespeare's identity. Laurie Osborne (1996, 124) notes, for example, that nonacademic reproductions of *Twelfth Night* "respond more obviously to the homoeroticism in the play." Osborne says she would include as performance editions of *Twelfth Night* "modern crib sheets like *Cliffs Notes* and *Shakespeare Made Easy* or *Twelfth Night by William Shakespeare: The Cartoon Shakespeare Series*. . . . The dismissal of these versions, either because of their audiences or because of their failure to be faithful to the 'original,' actually registers a perception of the play. *Twelfth Night* has a recognizable identity partially because of the reproductions that challenge that identity" (174). Shakespeare's identity works to secure a textual identity: what appears as a threat to identity turns out to be, in one view, the opposite.

A queer Shakespeare, in my view, is precisely not defined in the terms by which we orient ourselves: gay, straight, or bisexual. It's the very lack of such categories in the plays that allows for queer transformations and adaptations of them and that threatens their textual identities. The force of a Shakesqueer as opposed to a gay Shakespeare may be underlined by considering the reception of the *Playboy* production of *Twelfth Night,* a video to which I will return at length in the next chapter. This video occupies a strategic position in Osborne's argument, for example. She says that we should regard all reproductions as part of the "original": "A particular text's claim to the signifier, to the name *Twelfth Night,* inevitably calls the play into question. Ron Wertheim's softcore film . . . has only the loosest connections to the Folio text, yet, by claiming that title, the film announces itself a reproduction of Shakespeare's comedy" (174). The use of this film as a key example raises at least two questions. Why should a softcore porn version of *Twelfth Night* occupy a central place in an argument confirming Shakespeare's unity rather than multiplicity? Does the porn sex make it straight or lesbian? In closing with these questions, I wish not simply to defend the merits of a Shakesqueer as opposed to a gay Shakespeare but to suggest that queering Shakespeare on film is a way of putting the canonical in question rather than of opening it up. A greater inclusiveness of specifically Shakespearean reproductions may merely reinforce existing textual and sexual identities. More broadly, the heterogeneity of film authorship—director as auteur, star as auteur—and of reception—gossip, scholarship—risks merely confirming an identity politics in which some texts can be read as strictly gay or lesbian rather than opening up a queer space of overlapping kinds of knowledge and reading practices (queer in the sense here of being shared by straights, gays, and lesbians alike, whether fans or not).[41] The "*sub*-lime" breakdowns of a Shakesqueered reproduction question the legibility and identity of what is gay and what is Shakespearean, such that Shakespeare's cultural capital does not necessarily save a given queer reproduction, nor does a queer reading save a given Shakespeare reproduction. One person's reading of a Shakesqueer text may be another's failure to read a Shakespeare text at all; one person's reading of a Shakespeare text may be another's failure to queer it.

CHAPTER TWO

Deep Inside William Shakespeare: Pornographic Film and Video "Classics" and the Castrated Gaze

Talk Shakespeare to Me

Despite the widespread interest in the transgressive sexuality of Shakespeare's plays, even an interest in the pornographic impulse of *Othello,* cultural critics have tended to overlook Shakespeare in contemporary pornography and contemporary pornography in Shakespeare.[1] The earliest instance of porn in Shakespeare (on sound film) I know of is the softcore *The Secret Sex Lives of Romeo and Juliet* (dir. A. P. Stootsberry, 1968), with Foreman Shane and Dierdre Nelson in the leads.[2] Roman Polanski's *Playboy* production of *Macbeth* (1971) soon followed, with a nude, sleepwalking Lady Macbeth and bare-breasted witches. *Playboy* also produced a softcore *Twelfth Night* (dir. Ron Wertheim, 1972) for its television series *Playboy at Night.* Although not billed as pornography, several recent Shakespeare films have included more or less softcore sex scenes.[3] In Zeffirelli's *Hamlet* (1991), Hamlet dry humps Gertrude in the closet scene. Peter Greenaway's *Prospero's Books* (1991) parades naked people of all ages, sexualities, and (trans)genders, including a transsexual actor who took his stage name from a nineteenth-century painter (Felicien Rops) and who plays a character named Pornocrates, a nearly naked Caliban (Michael Clark), a pissing boy (Orfeo) playing Ariel and one pornographic book in Prospero's library, *The Autobiographies of Pasiphae and Semiramis* (Greenaway 1991, 24).[4] Oliver Parker's sexually explicit *Othello* (1995) leaves no doubt as to whether Othello and Desdemona consummated their marriage, showing them undressing and then hopping into bed. It also has Othello fantasizing Cassio and Desdemona having sex in bed, and Iago initiating anal sex with Emilia (both are still fully clothed).[5] And in his recent *Hamlet* (1996), Kenneth Branagh shows Hamlet and Ophelia going at it in bed.

More pointedly, a number of recent, less well-known Shakespeare films have been explicitly marked by or marketed as heterosexual pornography. Troma Entertainment, best known for *The Toxic Avenger* (dir. Michael Herz, 1985) and *Class of Nuke 'Em High* (dir. Richard Haines and Samuel Weil, 1986), released *Tromeo and Juliet* in 1996. This film incorporates porn in a number of scenes: a softcore scene of Juliet and Ness, a character based on the Nurse, having sex is intercut with another of Tromeo, a character based on Romeo, masturbating to an interactive pornographic CD-ROM entitled *As You Lick It* (he passes over other CD-ROMs entitled *Et Tu Blow Job, The Merchant of Penis,* and *Much Ado About Humping*) (see figure 2.1); Juliet dials 1-900 FUL-STAF and has phone sex; she also has a dream-turned-nightmare of having sex with a Fabio-looking guy whose penis turns into a monster; Juliet's father runs a lucrative porn movie business he stole from Tromeo's father; finally, Rosy, a character based on Rosaline, is shown having sex with a guy while on the phone with Tromeo and, later, dressed at the Capulet Ball like a stripper/porn star. A perhaps even less well-known, direct from HBO to video release, *Skyscraper* (dir. Raymond Martino, 1995), stars former *Playboy* Playmate-of-the-year Anna Nicole Smith as the heroine (she exposes her recently enlarged breasts in two sex scenes and one rape scene). The film, which I discuss in the following chapter, is loosely modeled on *Die Hard* (dir. John McTiernan, 1988) and contains a band of high-tech robbers who regularly recite lines from Shakespeare before terminating their victims with extreme prejudice.

There are also a number of equally or perhaps even more obscure hardcore films about Shakespeare productions as well as hardcore adaptations of them. A 1987 spin-off entitled *Romeo and Juliet* directed and written by porn veteran Paul Thomas and starring Jerry Butler (Romeo), Kim Alexis (Juliet), Nina Hartley, and Keisha deconstructs the distinction between porn flick and Shakespeare play. The video tells the story of a group of actors who put on a production of *Romeo and Juliet* to prevent a local theater from being turned into a porn movie palace

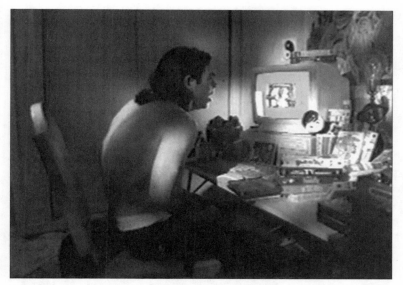

Figure 2.1: Tromeo masturbates to Shakespeare CD-ROM porn in *Tromeo and Juliet.*

(and who are of course filmed having sex with each other in the process). The production turns out to be a hit after Juliet and Romeo end up having sex on stage. Other American hardcore films include a sequel entitled *Romeo and Juliet II* (1988, also directed by Paul Thomas, with Nikki Randall and Jaquline Lorians), and several other spin-offs, adaptations, and citations: *A Mid-Slumber Night's Dream* (dir. Michael Cates, 1988, with Heather Wayne, Christy Canyon, and Erica Boyer), *A Midsummer Night's Bondage* (dir. unknown, 1993, Arlo Productions, with Candy and Lady Simone), *Romeo Syndrome* (dir. Jim Enright, 1995, with April and T. T. Boy), *Othello: Dangerous Desire* (dir. Joe D'Amato, 1997, with Cort Knee and Sean Micheals as Desdemona and Othello), advertised as "a modern re-telling of this interracial classic," and *Taming of the Screw* (dir. Jim Powers, 1997, starring Mila and Tony Martino), which updates Shakespeare's comedy by having Pete (Petruchio) be offered a partnership in a law firm if he'll agree to marry the senior partner's "bitch" older daughter, Kate. Several European Shakespeare

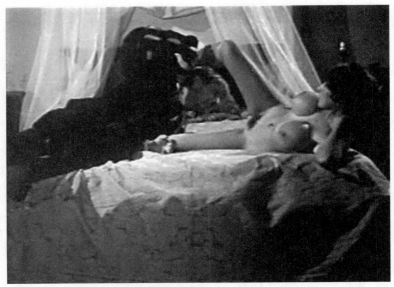

Figure 2.2: Polonius is right about Hamlet in Luca Damiano's X-rated *Hamlet: For the Love of Ophelia.*

porn films that are widely available in the United States include: *Juliet and Romeo* (dir. Joe D'Amato, 1996, with Italian porn star Stefania Sartori as Juliet); and a two-part *Hamlet: For the Love of Ophelia* (dir. Luca Damiano, 1996, with British porn star Sarah Young as Ophelia and German porn veteran Christopher Clark as Hamlet).[6] "Hamlet has forgotten the murder of his father," the ad copy informs us, "and dedicated all of his considerable passion to bagging Lady O." According to this version, Polonius was right about Hamlet after all (see figure 2.2). There are also Japanese animated spin-offs of *Romeo and Juliet* and *A Midsummer Night's Dream* (made in 1995 and 1993 respectively) which are marketed as adult products.[7] While many of these "heterosexual" porn versions of plays contain lesbian scenes, there are no lesbian-identified Shakespeare porn films or videos, to my knowledge.[8] I know of only two gay male porn versions, both spin-offs of *Romeo and Juliet: Le Voyage a Venise* (*Carnival in Venice* in its U.S. release, dir. Jean Daniel

Figure 2.3: Teen sex in the multinationally produced children's series *Shakespeare, the Animated Tales'* adaptation of *Romeo and Juliet.*

Cadinot, 1986 in France; 1987 in the U.S., with Yarrick Bard and Yves Fontenay) and *Romeo and Julian,* advertised as "the first gay romantic musical" (dir. Sam Abdul, 1993, with Grant Larson and Johnny Rey in the leads).[9] Finally, the *Shakespeare, the Animated Tales* (dir. Efim Gambourg, 1992) version of the play, for example, shows a montage of Romeo and Juliet speaking their lines in voice-overs as they have sex naked in bed during the aubade scene. (see figure 2.3). (It is an arty sequence: a little cupid appears shooting an arrow, and the lovers float in miniature form briefly as well).[10]

Given the recent mainstreaming of porn inside academia and out, the inattention to Shakespeare porn (both pornography in straight Shakespeare films and Shakespeare in pornographic films) might seem somewhat surprising, perhaps a function of academic performance anxiety about having one's work attacked for being about more than just mental masturbation. Yet attention to

Shakespeare porn is really quite predictable.[11] Indeed, now that cultural studies has institutionalized itself as a cultural waste management program, it would be quite easy to recycle Shakespeare porn as a legitimate object of academic study. In part, I want to show just how easy it is to recycle Shakespeare porn for academic purposes. I propose to examine Shakespeare porn in light of recent feminist work on porn by Linda Williams (1989), Andrew Ross (1989), Laura Kipnis (1996), Anne McClintock (1993), Constance Penley (1997b), and Judith Butler (1997). Pornography, Andrew Ross points out, is not only what it says it is (1989, 207). Taken together, the work of the above critics argues that however sexist, even disgusting to some viewers porn may be, porn nevertheless seriously explores the question of female desire, examines "male trouble," displays the failure of gender to be anything other than the mimicry of institutionally compelled norms, and offers a critique of class in some cases by exposing the grotesque body. One can concede that porn is a sexist genre, these critics suggest, and still analyze its contradictions and turn them to progressive political account.

The conjunction of Shakespeare and porn, I will argue, in many respects bears out the present pro-sex feminist analysis of porn. All of the films I consider rewrite Shakespeare so as to undo the romantic couple and the institution of marriage. They give reign to a sexual pornotopia, including gay and lesbian sex and even incest, rather than uphold heteronormative sexuality. The hardcore *Romeo and Juliet*s foreground the question of female desire; the *Playboy Twelfth Night* suggests the way gender is always a failed mimicry of unrealizable norms; *Tromeo and Juliet* presents explicit sex in relation to the grotesque body. But the conjunction of Shakespeare and porn, of high and low culture, also complicates this feminist pro-sex account of porn. If porn is to be regarded as a form of popular culture, as Ross (1989) suggests, what happens when a classic is made into a mass-marketed porn film? And what about authorship? Are porn films to be regarded as part of the Shakespeare canon? If so, how do we take stock of the fact that they are shelved not in the Shakespeare or drama section of video stores but in the adult section?[12] And what are we to make of one thing that never happens in Shakespeare porn? Though Shakespeare appears as a character/author in some films, he never gets laid.[13]

To address these and other questions, I situate explicitly porno-graphic Shakespeare films in relation to the remaking of "classics" such as *Cyrano de Bergerac, Alice in Wonderland,* and others as soft- and hardcore pornography. The process of adapting classics as porn began as a way of legitimating and mainstreaming porn in the early 1970s, when Hugh Hefner saw in producing a film of *Macbeth* a chance to prove that *Playboy* had a "philosophy."[14] Now that porn no longer needs the alibi of high culture and is largely immune from prosecution (almost anything is construed as having socially redeeming content), adapting the classics has become a way of increasing the market share of a female star (and the company behind her) who is otherwise overexposed, as it were, and has penetrated the market as far as she can.[15] Shakespeare porn (and other "classic" porn films such as *1001 Erotic Nights, The Ribald Tales of Canterbury, The Hunchback of Nasty Dames,* and *Robin Head*) is now sold primarily because consumers (mostly male, of course) want to see the porn stars in it, not because they want to see an X-rated costume drama or classic (the lowbrow version of Pasolini's *Canterbury Tales, Arabian Nights,* and *Decameron*).[16] *Hamlet: For the Love of Ophelia* trades on the viewer's desire to see its star Sarah Young by postponing a scene in which she has sex until the end of *Part Two.* To be sure, an adaptation of a "classic" still functions as cultural capital, but it does so primarily inside the industry. *Hamlet: For the Love of Ophelia,* for example, won the *Adult Video News* award for best European release in 1996 presumably not just because the sex was thought to be hot but because of the Shakespeare narrative, settings, and high production values.[17]

Porn adaptations attempt to resolve what Slavoj Žižek has termed a structural impossibility in pornography (1991, 111).[18] Pornography, Žižek points out, claims to go all the way, to show everything. But in so doing

> it always *goes too far,* i.e., it *misses* what remains concealed in a "normal," nonpornographic love scene. . . . The unattainable/forbidden object approached but never reached by the "normal" love story—the sexual act—exists only as concealed, indicated, "faked." As soon as we "show it," its charm is dispelled, we have "gone too far." Instead of the sublime Thing, we are stuck with vulgar,

groaning fornication. The consequence is that harmony, congruence between the filmic narrative (the unfolding of the story) and the immediate display of the sexual act, is structurally impossible: if we choose one, we necessarily lose the other. In other words, if we want to have a love story that "takes," that moves us, we must not "go all the way" and "show it all" (the details of the sexual act), because as soon as we "show it all," the story is no longer "taken seriously" and starts to function as only a pretext for introducing acts of copulation. . . . The fantasy ideal of a perfect work of pornography would be precisely to preserve this impossible harmony, the balance between narration and explicit depiction of the sexual act, i.e., to avoid the necessary *vel* that condemns us to lose one of the two poles. (1991, 110; 111)

Porn adaptations of classics are caught within this structural impossibility such that they can either function as porn spectacle intended to arouse the nonacademic viewer and as a textual, sublimated reading of a classic designed to interest the academic viewer (who may also, of course, be aroused). But the adaptation also draws attention to a reflexive element of porn, opening up a paradoxical dynamic: on the one hand, the classic sublimes the porn, creates a critical distance on the sex; on the other, the classic makes porn even sexier by deferring desire, a deferral registered in the puns of so many porn spin-offs.[19] If in adapting classics pornography goes too far, it also often gets somewhere other than the register of a disappointment and lack.[20]

The case of Shakespeare porn suggests that the history in porn of adapting classics is not simply the history of making harder and harder porn more and more socially acceptable. It is instead a paradoxical process. The more Shakespeare's plays are made pornographic, the more Shakespeare as author-function is desexualized and the further one moves away from the text. In softcore and hardcore Shakespeare porn, there are no or next to no actual lines from the plays. And in avant-garde adaptations such as Greenaway's *Prospero's Books,* there is lots of nudity, but no pornographic sex. (One perhaps awaits a porn version of Greenaway's film, *Prospero's Dirty Books.*) This is particularly true of Shakespeare porn, in which not everything is necessarily sexualized. A normative function for Shakespeare as author-function is put in place even as his plays are transgressively adapted as porn. In *Romeo and Juliet II,* Shakespeare comes back from heaven with Romeo to watch Juliet in a three-way and complains that he can't see because Romeo is blocking his view. Similarly, at the very end of *Tromeo and Juliet,* Shakespeare appears laughing in a kind of epilogue. A similar paradox exists in many of these films for the director, who also acts in them: Paul Thomas casts himself as a non-sexually performing Romeo in *Romeo and Juliet II;* Ron Wertheim casts himself as a gay Feste in *Playboy's Twelfth Night;* Luca Damiano casts himself as a lustful but impotent Old Hamlet in his two-part *Hamlet: For the Love of Ophelia;* and Sam Abdul casts himself as a trick Romeo picks up but who is not shown having sex in *Romeo and Julian.*[21]

In what follows, I discuss Shakespeare's paradoxical position as desexualized author of sexualized works in terms of what I call the *castrated gaze.* My account of this gaze is both indebted to and differs from recent feminist work on pornography and cinema. The feminist critique of porn produced by Williams, Kipnis, and others parallels an earlier feminist critique of the male cinematic gaze. The central question about porn debated by Williams and others is whether porn produced by women makes any difference in terms of its sexual politics. As a number of feminist film theorists have argued in a number of different, sometimes conflicting ways (Mulvey 1989; Silverman 1988; Doane 1980), the heterogeneity of the means of film production calls into question any claim for a unified, noncastrated, nonfeminized spectatorial position (of male director, cameraman, or male spectator). Everyone is castrated, according to Kaja Silverman (1993), though men tend to disavow that fact. Feminists have also tended to criticize pornography for its tendency to foreground female desire, as if male desire were too threatening to explore.

The Shakespeare porn I examine is made exclusively by men, and thus, for some critics, might not appear to hold out much hope of producing progressive political effects. I am nevertheless interested in Shakespeare porn because it problematizes this account of the spectator's castration insofar as it makes the phallus paradoxical. Feminist film and porn criticism has tended to assume that one either appears to have the phallus or can be revealed not to have it. Yet the desexualization of authorship in Shakespeare porn throws into relief the way the (pornographic) male gaze both arouses the male viewer while also staging his and the male actor's castration, their position offscreen, outside the pornographic scene.[22] Far from confirming the self-sufficiency of the male spectator by making the woman the spectacle (with the representation of female pleasure its chief aim), pornography necessarily disturbs total identification on the part of the male spectator with the male performer. For the male viewer's gaze cannot be fully sutured to an internally coherent embodied male gaze, actor/character, scene, or narrative. The star, author, and adapting director may be parallel but they can never be identical even when the star also holds the video camera and videos himself having sex (such identity would still have to be shown, thereby separating the camera from the otherwise unified male gaze).[23] The male gaze is thus at once tumescent and castrated. It is impossible to equate, I am suggesting, total identification of the male gaze with the male performer and whatever pleasure porn may provide male viewers. While the lack of complete identification might, for some straight male viewers, disrupt the goal of porn—arousal and ejaculation—it might also further it by opening other kinds of cross-gender identifications. The castrated gaze does not just register the author/*auteur*'s lack, then; it is also productive, taking a variety of more or less imaginative forms, forms that may imply an hysterical equivalence, from the heterosexual viewpoint, of male, female, and gay male gazes.

The castrated gaze marks a queer critical space inside of heterosexual pornography in general and adaptations of classics in particular. If a character does not have sex in heterosexual hardcore porn, he will be read as gay (in the logic of this hardcore porn, only gay men do not have sex). An analysis of the contradictions of authorship in porn, including Shakespeare, the film director, and the film producer, will involve writing a history of pornographic adaptations of the classics in which the more and more sexually explicit, the more and more uncensored, are not always aligned with the more and more significant, the more and more deeply political.

While my account of the castrated gaze is indebted to recent feminist cinema and porn criticism, it does not necessarily yield a critique of Shakespeare porn that confirms the now dominant pro-sex view of porn as liberatory, democratizing popular culture. Some might want to legitimate the study of Shakespeare porn by claiming that it marks an ultratransgressive recoding of Shakespeare. And perhaps others might want to criticize it as tasteless, "politically incorrect," or ultimately heteronormative since it is produced with the straight male viewer foremost in mind. These critiques seem to me to be both predictable and facile. They are also self-defeating, since many of the films are not readily available and are unlikely to be taught in your average undergraduate "Shakespeare in performance" class, even if they may someday be discussed in the pages of *Shakespeare Quarterly*. In characterizing the male gaze as castrated, I mean not just to follow a feminist and queer theory strategy to examine heterosexual male trouble. This move typically involves celebrating queer rewritings of heterosexual narratives and positioning the academic as a fan, if not of the texts themselves, then of their fans. In contrast, I want to examine the academic fantasy of fandom, particularly the fandom of the porn star. Whereas the fantasy of the fan is that the academic can cross over and occupy all positions at once (participant, voyeur, academic, nonacademic, and so on), the case of Shakespeare porn suggests that the academic may not in fact crossover everywhere and adopt all positions: Shakespeare plays can become porn, but can they become academic porn? More broadly, we might ask: Are academic and nonacademic ways of reading Shakespeare porn compatible? In the former case, one would read the film as an interpretation of Shakespeare; in the latter, one would focus on the sex and perhaps be aroused by it. Yet how stable is the relation between these subject-positions? Who is more perverse, the nonacademic porn fan who fast-forwards past the Shakespeare narrative to get to the sex, or the academic Shakespeare fan who fast-forwards through the sex to get to the Shakespeare narrative?

Rather than assuming that Shakespeare porn can serve the purposes of cultural criticism, I am interested in examining the way Shakespeare porn calls into question the academic fantasy of recycling cultural trash for transgressive, democratizing ends. Shakespeare porn, that is, tells us something about academic fantasy because it tells us something new about pornography as well as something new about Shakespeare. If, as Andrew Ross (1989) advocates, intellectuals refuse to endorse a reform of porn that seeks to educate the porn consumer's desire but instead focus on the subversiveness of porn fantasies, then the study of Shakespeare porn can raise broad questions about a now widespread fantasy among cultural critics, namely, that academic desire needs to be educated. In this fantasy, the intellectual is learning from popular genres like porn and its fans, rather than just adopting a patronizing, reformist position.

Juliet Does Verona / Gertrude Does Denmark

Before analyzing the castrated gaze in relation to Shakespeare as author, I want to re-examine what it means for female desire to be regarded as castrated in Shakespeare pornography. In suggesting that to view women as castrated is to misread the anatomical difference between the sexes, to misunderstand further that no one has the phallus, feminists want to level the gender playing field. Yet this leveling risks merely producing an inversion since the mistake is inevitable. One always thinks someone else has the phallus. In terms of pornography, this leveling might produce an apparently stable binary opposition between misogynistic displays of female sexuality for male viewers and displays of women exploring their "authentic" desires; a woman for whom sex is work as opposed to a woman who acts out or acts on her desires.

Shakespeare porn complicates these oppositions insofar as they depend on a narrative as opposed to a scene. The more plot, that is, the more female desire can be represented in these terms. Yet the sex scenes make it harder to differentiate authentic female sex precisely because they denaturalize it, exposing all sex as performance. To be sure, sex and acting are regularly differentiated in pornography. As former porn star turned performance artist Annie Sprinkle says of her career in porn: "The sex was easy. The acting was the hard part."[24] Yet what constitutes "good" acting in porn? Can sex and acting be so easily opposed? I want to pursue these questions by examining a wide range of lesbian scenes and then look closely at lesbianism and gender in one video, *Playboy's Twelfth Night*.

Shakespeare porn, like pornography generally, tends to fore-ground female desire in narrative terms. It's notable that the female characters of Ophelia and Juliet occupy center stage in five hardcore productions and that these productions align female gender and the genre of comedy (all of the porn adaptations of the tragedies rewrite them as comedies). The centrality of women is, of course, not necessarily a gain for feminism. It is due in part to the male viewer's interest in the female porn star (few men achieve porn star status). And in the case of *Hamlet: For the Love of Ophelia,* female sexuality is portrayed in arguably misogynistic terms. Gertrude is insatiable and promiscuous (having sex, she says, with over a hundred people in one day), while Ophelia appears to Hamlet to be a coy virgin who wants him to wait until they marry. After Ophelia gives in to him, however, three guards appear from chests where they've been hiding and Hamlet leaves, calling her a "whore." Moreover, women are sometimes the occasion for male bonding or displays of male virility. Hamlet and Horatio engage in lots of group sex, and *Juliet and Romeo* opens as Benvolio and Mercutio finish a mock swordfight and then come upon Tybalt having sex with two Capulet servants. Tybalt cums too soon to satisfy the two women and rushes off as he is called away by an off-screen male voice (never identified). "I'm still feeling sexy," one woman says. Benvolio and Mercutio then approach the women and have sex with them, leaving them, we are supposed to think, satisfied. Slow motion "money shots" (of the men cumming on the women) in this case further differentiate the two houses.

Even though women may sometimes occasion displays of male virility, the narrative emphasis in many of these films often falls significantly on the woman's desire such that the role of women is expanded and comically celebrated. The focus of the Paul Thomas *Romeo and Juliet*s, for example, is on Juliet's sexuality. In *Romeo and Juliet,* the sexual fantasies of the character playing Juliet place her closest to Shakespeare. She fantasizes having sex with the actor she wants to play Romeo (in her fantasy they have sex as if they were Romeo and Juliet and speak to each other in a *faux* Elizabethan English) and, as Juliet, she initiates sexual intercourse with Romeo onstage during the performance of the play, leading members of the audience to have sex with each other as well. Similarly, the plot of *Romeo and Juliet II* centers on the casting of Juliet's part. The actress who gets the part is taught how to act by the real Juliet (the character, in this version, is also a real person, now residing with Shakespeare and Romeo in heaven). After the play is performed Juliet returns and kneels in front of her, giving her flowers and congratulating her on her wonderful performance. And in *Juliet and Romeo,* Juliet awakens in the tomb in time to prevent Romeo from killing himself. The film closes with a last scene in which the two have intercourse in a sarcophagus. Rosaline becomes a major character in this version of the play, replacing Friar Laurence (who is entirely written out). She "helps" Romeo by having sex with him and later has sex with Benvolio. In addition, two Capulet women are added in this version. In *The Secret Sex Lives of Romeo and Juliet,* Juliet is a "slut" who pretends to be a virgin to Romeo while having an affair with the Prince (during the balcony scene, she receives cunnilingus from her dog, and there are also sex scene with Juliet and the Nurse as well as with Juliet and the Chorus).[25] And in *Tromeo and Juliet,* the sex drives of the protagonists are gendered such that Juliet's is much stronger and more developed than Tromeo's. Rosy, his first girlfriend, cheats on him in a softcore porn scene and tells her new boyfriend that "Tromeo sucks" as a lover. She dumps him at the Capulet ball, where she appears with her new lover. Tromeo masturbates to lame interactive CD-ROM porn, choosing the program "True Love." The porn actress on it says things like: "Would you like to get married? Then I can show you my bosom." Tromeo cums as he repeatedly responds to the woman's "I love you" with "I love you too." Juliet (played by riot grrrl Jane Jensen, whose CDs include "Comic Book Whore"), by contrast, has phone sex, has sex with Ness (a character based on the Nurse), and has a sexually abusive relationship with her father. She dreams of rats coming out of her pregnant belly after it explodes with popcorn and of Tromeo eating the popcorn. Juliet is drenched, so to speak, with sex. To be sure, she is marked in some ways as monstrous: she gets briefly turned into a human transsexual cow, and she dreams of a "penis monster." But Juliet's monstrosity is at once part of what is supposed to make her cool and a function of her father's abusive treatment of her. We are to appreciate her for taking the lead at the end of the film, when she comically licenses Tromeo and herself to marry and have (monster) children, despite the fact that they are brother and sister.

Though female desire is foregrounded in these films, it is difficult to thematize it as consistently authentic or inauthentic because there is no correlation between the narrative, the genre, and how arousing the sex is; that is, the morally good sex and the arousing good sex are not necessarily the same. Shakespeare porn, particularly the *Romeo and Juliet*s, tries to distinguish between acting and having sex, treating the former as artificial, the latter as natural. In *Romeo and Juliet II,* for example, Elena can't (yet) act or find her voice, yet she has no inhibitions about having sex. Sex is presented as easy, natural, unembarrassing. Yet this attempt to differentiate having sex and acting only ignores and displaces how acted/artificial/scripted the sex really is. The film also calls attention to a disjunction between narrative and sex scenes by not casting the star porn actress of the video as Juliet; that is, the central character isn't played by the actress thought to be the most arousing. To be sure, *Tromeo and Juliet* does more clearly thematize a difference between Rosy and Juliet's desires. But that relative clarity is due to the film's distance from hardcore porn: Rosy's softcore, simulated sex scene marks her character as inauthentic, unromantic, sluttish. Nor can authentic sexual desire be aligned with sexual orientation. In *Romeo and Juliet II* and *Juliet and Romeo,* the actresses playing Juliet do not seem to be into the lesbian sex scenes any more than they are into the heterosexual couple and three-way scenes.

Female desire is castrated, I am suggesting, insofar as the tension between narrative and spectacle marks a loss of any unified performance or cinematic gaze. And it is precisely the lack of this coherence that exposes in Shakespeare porn the castrated status of the male gaze. This status can be grasped more fully if we turn to the two-part *Hamlet: For the Love of Ophelia.* In some respects this film follows out Lacan's reading of *Hamlet,* in which Ophelia is the key to Hamlet's desire, reflecting Lacan's account of the play as an allegory of desire back as an account of the pornographic status of desire.[26] Yet again, the tension between sex and narrative compromises any attempt to allegorize fully this film as a literalization of Lacan's reading of Shakespeare's play. The film significantly takes up the question the play poses, according to Lacan, namely, "What does Hamlet want?" The film does not give an answer, however. In this version, Hamlet is less a neurotic than an hysteric, talking to himself throughout a sex scene with Gertrude, two maids, and Claudius. Only after considering several possibilities, engaging in lots of sexual encounters (usually with multiple partners), and receiving several visitations from his ghostly father urging him to have sex does Hamlet settle on Ophelia as an object of desire. The film rewrites Hamlet's relationship with Ophelia in two respects: Hamlet does not turn away from her until the end of the second part; and Claudius kills both Gertrude and Ophelia (it's not clear whether Hamlet and Claudius kill each other or not). Moreover, the film collapses Ophelia into Gertrude as objects of Hamlet's desire. When Hamlet discovers three guards in Ophelia's room he cries out: "I'm *also* a cuckold and we're not even married. My Ophelia is *also* a great whore" (my emphases). Here Hamlet's "also"s mark his identification of himself with Old Hamlet, and Ophelia with Gertrude.

This loss of distinction between Ophelia and Gertrude makes explicit precisely the problem Hamlet faces in Lacan's account of the play as he tries, unsuccessfully, to use Ophelia to separate from his mother in the classic Freudian narrative of Oedipalization. As Julia Lupton and Kenneth Reinhard argue in their Lacanian reading of the play:

> Though Ophelia appears as the means of Hamlet's separation from his mother through the acquisition of a new object . . . Ophelia is nonetheless continually linked in the play to Gertrude, and to Gertrude not as object of incestuous desire but as maternal Other of demand. Thus Hamlet's early conflation of Ophelia and Gertrude in the fantasmatic projection of their voracious sexualities is born out in Ophelia's erotic songs, which use the theater of madness to stage the crossing of the Other of demand and the object of desire in the fundamental fantasy of Hamlet and *Hamlet*." (1993, 81)

Moreover, the pornographic Gertrude literalizes what, according to Bruce Fink (1996), is in Lacan's view Hamlet's construction of Gertrude's sexuality. As Fink comments, Gertrude needs to be "getting it" all the time: "'I am what I am; in my case, there's nothing to be done, I'm a true genital personality—I know nothing of mourning'" (1996, 190).[27]

Yet the pornographic *Hamlet* does not entirely lend itself to a Lacanian reading. Though after Hamlet has sex he meets with his father's loving approval, the sex scenes display a homoerotic supplement to Hamlet's heterosexuality: Hamlet's repeated references to himself "taking it up the ass" and a number of scenes of group sex with Horatio in which the two actors' penises nearly touch all come close to violating the usual taboo on homosexuality in heterosexual porn. And, in narrative terms, far from attaining closure through Hamlet's identification with the lethal phallus, the film marks its own ending as one more instance of the endless deferral of desire. After watching a version of *The Murder of Gonzago,* Claudius stabs Gertrude and Ophelia. When Hamlet stabs him, both actors freeze: in a metacinematic moment, Hamlet tells the audience "this has all been a joke to amuse myself," that the characters "are all only actors," and Old Hamlet then makes an appearance to applause from the crowd. This is *Hamlet* as *Rosencrantz and Guildenstern Are Dead* (dir. Tom Stoppard, 1991). A tension between sex scenes and narrative disrupts any attempt to allegorize the film in Lacanian terms, or more broadly, to thematize male desire in terms that are any more coherent or authentic than female desire is in Shakespeare porn.

Don't Kiss Me, Petruchio

Taming of the Screw might seem to realize Andrea Dworkin's worst nightmare by presenting what is arguably the most obviously sexist pornographic adaptation of Shakespeare made thus far. The male gaze might appear in this case to be anything but castrated. *Taming of the Screw* updates Shakespeare's comedy, making Kate into a ranting Courtney Love look-alike who is considered a "bitch" by all the characters in the video. Kate dresses in a sheer leopard bathrobe over black silk panties and a bra, and her potential lustiness is perhaps heightened by the actress playing her, Mila, who lays claim to the title of "absolutely filthiest girl in porn . . . ever" (Lytle, 1997). Her sister (Jill, in this version) spells out the sexist premise early on: Kate is a bitch because she hasn't been "fucked." Kate in turn calls Jill a "slut" and a "whore," claiming that the reason no one asks her out is that Jill sleeps with all of Kate's prospective suitors first. Kate's father and her future husband, Pete Smith, make Kate's marriage an object of monetary exchange even more crudely than in the play. Pete gets to become a partner in the father's law firm and receives both a home in Bel Air and $100,000 as a dowry. Pete proceeds to tame Kate by acting as a jealous, controlling, "perverted" husband. In contrast to Shakespeare's *The Taming of the Shrew,* no effort is made to make him appear to be acting out of love for Kate. The video constructs a mildly sadomasochistic relationship between Kate and Pete. In a scene recalling Kate and Petruchio's exchange about the sun and the moon, Kate finally agrees she will have sex with Pete after having been carried on his shoulder out the door of her father's house before she can attend her wedding reception and having been forced to have sex with two of her husband's male servants and then, in a later scene, with two women (also at his direction). Kate does consent to the sex with these characters, and is turned on by Pete after they first meet (after he leaves). In the final scene, Kate wins Pete's bet with his brother-in-law and an unnamed character who is Hortensio's equivalent, bringing in Jill and a woman who is the widow's equivalent and forcing them to kneel at Pete's feet and give him a blow job.

Taming of the Screw might be regarded by some critics as a backlash video, using Shakespeare to tame the contemporary feminist, riot grrrl/tank girl reappropriation of the angry, sexy whore who displays her sexiness for herself and other women rather than for men.[28] I would argue, however, that by rewriting the plot to make it even more sexist than Shakespeare's, the video produces a critique of the sexism of porn and allows for a limited but significant degree of female agency by not playing out the play's narrative in its most obviously sexist form. The bedroom scene that Petruchio, at the very end of the play, invites the audience to speculate on is not realized by the video. The most striking thing about the video's rewrite is the absence of any sex between Kate and Pete. Kate asks Pete if he wants to join the two butlers when they begin to have sex with her, but he leaves the room instead, thereby abdicating even the position of voyeur. Nor does Pete watch Kate have sex with the two women. (Kate is the only character to occupy the position of voyeur. In a shot reminiscent of the first shots of Elizabeth Taylor's eyes gazing out of her house on the street in Zeffirelli's film version of *Taming*, we see Kate looking out of her house at Jill and her fiancée having sex by the pool.) Pete never asks Kate for a kiss either. It is Kate who begins to control the sex, even the sex that Pete initiates. Perhaps recalling Petruchio's line about leaving Kate with his "tongue in your tail," she tells one of the butlers to "suck my ass." Similarly, the two women who have sex with Kate because her husband "wants me to be lesbian" say they will teach her to be a better lover. They use dildos, inserting them into Kate's vagina and anus. Yet Kate takes them over and uses them on herself as well as on the two women. (Mila's star status as "filthiest" performer in porn here converges with a character-ization of Kate as "whorish" in that she is the only woman of the three to take dildos both in her vagina and her anus.) And however much better Kate becomes as a lover, her "improved" abilities are not enjoyed by her husband.

The video's ending most clearly gives Kate sexual agency even as it also marks her complete acquiescence to her husband's wishes. Kate ends her final speech about wifely obedience by telling Jill and the widow ("cunts," she calls them) to "suck my husband's cock." Kate then leaves the room with her father (after he reasserts Kate's com-mand to give Pete head against Jill's wish to the contrary) while Jill, the widow, Pete, and Mark (Lucentio) have sex. Her own sexuality remains significantly outside her husband's control; moreover, she redefines married sexuality as being in excess of the monogamous couple. While Kate is not free of her father in the final scene, she is nevertheless able to direct the sex her husband enjoys. By putting him in a three-way at the beginning of the final scene, Kate replicates the opening number of the video in which Pete had sex with two women, a self-identified "whore" and her madam. Although the sex in the final scene is partly normalized as the Hortensio character leaves Mark and Pete to engage in couples sex with the other wives, this normalization is itself undercut by the fact that the couples are not married to each other. Moreover, given the way that Shakespeare's play structures this spin-off, there is a strong implication that Kate and her father are going off to have sex together. *Taming of the Screw* thus (inadvertently or not) subverts the play's comic teleology whereby Kate and Petruchio's relationship defines itself as ideal by virtue of its increasingly public eroticization. And while this subversion, limited as it is, may not disturb at all the male viewer (who might well get off on a woman's sexual agency and willingly entertain the fantasy of being married to a "whorish" porn star), any pleasure the male viewer takes in Kate's agency (or Mila's star status) in the video comes at the expense of the identification the play labors to secure, namely, the male spectator with Petruchio.

I Heard the Mermaids Singing

We can get a fuller sense of what it means to call the male gaze castrated by turning not only to lesbian desire in relation both to soft- and hardcore pornography but also to the heterogeneity of porn film production, particularly the use of sound. Lesbian sex scenes are presented in every soft- and hardcore Shakespeare adaptation under discussion in this chapter. This should hardly be surprising since lesbian scenes are, of course, standard fare in heterosexual pornography. In terms of Shakespeare porn, it is significant that the more interesting and more queer representation of lesbian desire is the softcore *Playboy* production of *Twelfth Night*, "based," the opening credits tell us, "on the play by William Shakespeare." Though *Playboy* went in the direction of a more pornographic Shakespeare by producing this film, that movement was itself paradoxical. On the one hand, Wertheim's *Twelfth Night* has lots of sex in it (whereas Polanski's *Macbeth* is a straightforward adaptation of the play with some nudity). On the other, Wertheim's *Twelfth Night* has no actual Shakespeare lines in it (except for Feste's final song, sung at the film's beginning and ending), though this adaptation sticks pretty closely to the narrative of the play. The "purity" of Shakespeare's play is implicitly left intact by not citing any of its actual lines.

The sex scenes are generally heterosexual, the homosexual ones lesbian rather than gay. Olivia's desire for Caesario is rewritten as a desire for Viola (Nicky Gentile). Olivia (Greta Vayan) is marked as lesbian by a citation of Garbo: imitating Garbo's famous line from *Grand Hotel* (dir. Edmund Goulding, 1932), Olivia tilts her head back as she sits on a couch and exclaims: "I want to be alone." More explicitly, while Caesario sings to her, Olivia fantasizes having sex with

Viola (this sequence is intercut with shots of Olivia's dead brother riding a white horse that moves toward the camera). By contrast, gay male sexuality is pretty much written out of the film's "authentic" coupledom. Orsino (Carlo de Meijo) does ask, amused, if Caesario wants to kiss him, and in one scene Orsino has a fantasy of seeing Viola, half-naked, and Caesario, dressed, in mirrors, then of trying to kiss Viola (who has blonde hair) and Olivia (who has brown hair) as they pass by him; Orsino appears to resolve his gender confusion about Viola/Caesario in the next scene, when he has sex with two women, a blonde and a brunette. The possibility of male homosexuality is displaced here by the actuality of female bisexuality and elsewhere by a racialized and transgendered sexuality. Antonio and Sebastian are made into a racially mixed heterosexual couple: Antonio becomes Antonia, and she is played by a black transsexual (Ajita Wilson).[29] Feste (Ron Wertheim) appears, however, to be gay (in a pointedly double entendre, Olivia tells him he is "much too gay"). (I'm not sure what to make of the fact that Malvolio [Yonathan Lucas], a leather boy submissive in this version, finally ends up with a bare-breasted mermaid.)[30]

Critics have debated the representation of lesbian desire inside of male-consumed, heterosexual pornography. According to Irigaray, "female homosexuality does exist. But it is *prostituted to men's fantasies*. Commodities can only enter into relationships under the watchful eyes of their 'guardians'" (1985, 196). By contrast, Linda Williams (1989, 139-40) argues that representations of lesbian sex in pornography meant to be consumed by straight men can nevertheless have progressive, feminist political effects. Some critics might want to argue that the *Playboy Twelfth Night* is a classic instance of the encelluloiding of the pornographic male gaze. That may well be. Although the *Playboy* 60s adaptation of Shakespeare (here the play is about sex, drugs, and disco) may be a heteronormative representation of (lesbian) sex, even unhip, but its use of sound also marks it as a bizarre, if not queer, instance of porn. Sound is synchronized throughout for realistic effect. This *Twelfth Night* is a softcore film that produces the play, as is generally the case with porn, as a musical (Williams 1989, 122-23).[31] Orsino is a retired rock star. After singing a song (adapted from the play's opening speech), Orsino laments (in verse that I find impossible to scan): "My golden hits have lost their gleam. No more. / It doesn't thrill me anymore, like it did before. / I'd gladly leave behind those days of endless yearnings / That sent me on a zillion psychedelic trips / Of one night stands and group baths for one sincere relationship." (Like this quotation, much of the script is written in badly rhymed couplets with no consistent metric form.)

Sound is, of course, the most bizarre feature of all mainstream hardcore pornography, and it poses a problem of interpretation. Linda Williams notes that the use of postdubbing detracts from the genre's realism:

> In hardcore film and video . . . the relation of sound to image differs from that in dominant cinema, though without having the function of avant-garde deconstruction. In these films, when characters talk their lips often fail to match the sounds spoken, and in the sexual numbers a dubbed-over "disembodied" female voice (saying "oooh" and "aah") may stand for the most prominent signifier of female pleasure in the absence of other, more visual assurances. Sounds of pleasure, in this latter instance, seem almost to flout the realist function of anchoring body to image, halfway becoming aural fetishes of the female pleasures we cannot see. (1989, 122-23)

She asks why "this convention has been so popular in a genre apparently engaged in an interminable quest for realism" (124). It cannot be explained away as a function of low production values, she notes, since even in big-budget hardcore films in which sound is synchronized, it is nevertheless postdubbed in the sexual numbers. She also rejects the notion that the sounds attempt to offer aural equivalents of the visual "money shot," noting that "the 'aural' ejaculation of pleasure, especially in post-synchronized sound, gives none of the same guarantee of truth that the visual ejaculation does" (125).

Williams does not offer an answer to the question of postdubbing. While I do not claim to do so either, I think that *Playboy's Twelfth Night* helps us address it further by broadening the question of sound to include not only female pleasure but the performativity of gender and sexuality as well. The average porn soundtrack calls attention to one of the central disappointments of pornography, namely, that the actors, especially the women, are faking pleasure in general and orgasm in particular. At stake in sound is the performative aspect of porn. Insofar as women's performances are mediated by men, who present male fantasies about female sexuality primarily to other men, sound foregrounds the tendency of porn, even if porn is a normalizing practice, to denaturalize gender, to show that gender is always a copy of a copy. As Judith Butler points out, pornography always involves a failure:

> In fact, although one might well agree [with Catherine MacKinnon] that a good deal of pornography is offensive, it does not follow that its offensiveness consists in its putative power to construct (unilaterally, exhaustively) the social reality of what a woman is. . . . [P]ornography neither represents nor constitutes what women are, but offers an allegory of masculine wilfullness and feminine submission (although these are clearly not its only themes), one which repeatedly and anxiously rehearses its own unrealizability. Indeed, one might argue that pornography depicts impossible and uninhabitable positions, compensatory fantasies that continually reproduce a rift between those positions and the ones that belong to the domain of social reality. Indeed, one might suggest that pornography is the text of gender's unreality, the impossible norms by which it is compelled, and in the face of which it perpetually fails. (1997, 67-68)

The nonsynchronized, postdubbed soundtrack of the sex scenes in porn films may call attention to this failure in a particularly direct way for the porn consumer and may open porn up to parody. It's easy to make fun of the sounds, after all, as in the moment at the restaurant in *When Harry Met Sally* (dir. Rob Reiner, 1989) when Meg Ryan fakes an orgasm. And porn adaptations often self-consciously build in this humor, such as it is, most notably in the titles (*Robin Head, The Tale of Two Titties, Spermacus,* etc).

What is interesting about *Playboy's Twelfth Night* is not its use of sound to register female sexual pleasure, however, but its use of postdubbing to establish gender difference. The question of postdubbing female pleasure does not arise in this *Twelfth Night,* however,

largely because it is softcore porn: the sex scenes are always accompa-
nied by music, both instrumental and songs. (There are no "oohs" and
"ahhs.") Instead of focusing on female orgasm, then, the film focuses
on resolving possible confusion about gender and sexual preference.
As Kaja Silverman notes in a discussion of mainstream cinema, gender
difference is always partly a function of the postdubbing:

> One of Hollywood's most established deviations from synchronized
> sound is, of course, postdubbing, which juxtaposes voices with
> images after the latter have been produced and (usually) edited, so
> bringing momentarily together in the studio the shadow play of
> celluloid and the voices of flesh and blood actors. The latter speak
> the lines assigned to them while closely observing the lip movements
> represented on screen, and their voices are recorded as they do so.
> These actors may be the same or different from those whose images
> they conform to vocally, but in both cases, the aim is usually for
> complete illusion of "perfect unity." (1988, 47)

As we have seen, the film deals with the transvestism and the
possibility of male homosexuality in Shakespeare's *Twelfth Night* in a
number of rather bizarre ways.[32] The soundtrack is perhaps the most
bizarre. It is almost always synchronized (we often even see people
playing the instruments we hear on the soundtrack). The one instance
of postdubbing, however, is Sebastian's voice. Sebastian and Viola/
Caesario are both played by the same actress, Nicky Gentile. As
Caesario, Gentile's Viola is hardly convincing; indeed, the only thing
that marks Caesario as male is his short haircut. When Caesario
speaks, the same voice is used as when the actress plays Viola. So it's
no surprise that Olivia fantasizes about Caesario as a woman. When
Gentile plays Sebastian, however, a male voice-over is used. And when
Sebastian and Olivia have sex, the same song plays as when Caesario
and Olivia had sex, only now we hear Sebastian's voice. (When
Sebastian and Olivia briefly have sex, however, a male body double is
used for a few shots.)

    Even though the film "heterosexualizes" the play, queer sex effects
are nevertheless produced. Though Antonia and Sebastian are portrayed as a heterosexual couple, for example, their heterosexuality is

"performed" through sound: Sebastian's male gender is a function of a dubbed male voice, not a falsetto, female voice. Lesbianism thus remains visually inscribed within the heterosexual couple.

The soundtrack is delightfully contradictory. Gender differences are signaled in the case of Sebastian and Viola but not in the case of Viola and Caesario. Of course, this makes sense as an attempt to distinguish the biological difference between brother and sister versus the biological sameness of sister and her transvestite character. One would also expect, however, that Caesario would at least speak in a lower tone to signal "his" difference from Viola; instead, the two voices are identical. Voice proves, then, to be an inadequate way of signifying gender. This inadequacy is most striking at the end of the film. Everyone shows up at the local disco, and Antonia is the first to see that Sebastian and Viola are both present. Orsino then mistakes Viola for Sebastian, but Antonia draws his attention to both characters. Viola and Sebastian continue to speak in their usual voices and both appear, as at the beginning of the film, onscreen at the same time.

Yet this difference is apparently not obvious enough and has to be pornographically supplemented by a more naked, embodied difference: facing the camera, Viola rips open her shirt and exposes her breasts, exclaiming, "See, I'm a girl!" This gesture doesn't, of course, prove her gender since her pants remain on. Moreover, the realism of the gesture is undermined by a *trompe l'oeil* as Nicky Gentile appears onscreen simultaneously as both Caesario and Viola (see figure 2.4). The film tries (and fails) to show that gender is something other than a performed mimicry. Sound and image do not coalesce to produce a realistic illusion of unified, distinctly gendered subjects.

However queer, the film's mimicry of gender has nothing to do with some subversive resignification of Shakespeare's *Twelfth Night*. Jonathan Crewe (1995) has argued that even a contemporary popular film dealing with transvestism such as *The Crying Game* (dir. Neil Jordan, 1992) doesn't manage to subvert the play's marriage plot and compulsory heterosexuality. I would add that *Playboy's Twelfth Night* doesn't either. (Admittedly, there are no marriage ceremonies nor plans for them, but the play's version of heterosexuality is arguably a distinctly *Playboy* vision of swinging and wife swapping, one that merely recycles sexism rather than transforms it.) The postdubbing of

Figure 2.4: Viola declares her gender difference from her twin brother Sebastian by bearing her breasts in Ron Wertheim's softcore *Playboy* production of *Twelfth Night*.

Sebastian's voice isn't played for laughs, as the scene in *When Harry Met Sally* is. The film suggests, rather, that gender norms are themselves fictions in a different (less radical?) way than Butler allows.

To be sure, porn trades on certain fantasies about size, endurance, of being a sex object attractive to all women, of having sex with women who are into it from the word "action," of the money shot (the fantasy of getting paid to cum instead of having to pay for a fantasy that will make one cum), fantasies that may or may not be at variance with what Butler calls "social reality" (1997, 68). Yet if porn is unrealizable in some ways, that is not primarily because the porn body marks some kind of unreachable ideal; rather, it is because of the low production values of porn film and video and the poor acting in it. Television bodies, by contrast, may be unrealizable because of their telegenic aspects and because a certain celebrity effect attaches to the mere fact that they have appeared on television. In porn, however, it's not bodily perfection that makes it unrealizable for most people but its sleaziness. Size matters, of course. Yet almost anyone can get penile implants or breast enlargements. Plastic surgery makes it relatively easy for most people to reach a porn ideal, if they wish. Porn may depict "impossible and uninhabitable positions," as Butler maintains, but that is not because of some absolute, Hegelian "rift between [them] and the ones that belong to the domain of social reality" (1997, 68), but because most people don't want to have sex that way, make those noises, adopt those poses (since the poses and noises are designed to get the viewer rather than the performers off in the first place). Indeed, porn in some ways is all too easy to realize and inhabit. After all, anyone can have sex; it takes no particular skill as an actor at all. The immense popularity of amateur porn indicates that amateurs do just as well as professionals when it comes to making porn.

The *Playboy Twelfth Night* suggests not only that gender norms are unrealizable in general, but that norms may or may not be realized for a number of different reasons having to do with specific media.[33] In this respect, the fact that this film is softcore is crucial to its queer effects. And by casting himself as a gay Feste, director Wertheim queers the lesbian sex usually displayed for the typical male heterosexual viewer's pleasure. These queer effects do not constitute a queer resignification of *Twelfth Night,* then; rather, they depend precisely on the *auteur*'s sense of his own paradoxical castration.

William Shakespeare, Uncut?

Having rethought the male gaze's castration in terms of the heterogeneity of the filmic apparatus, including a divorce between camera and actor, sound and character, sex and narrative, we are now in a position to consider that gaze more explicitly in relation to Shakespeare as an author. Shakespeare porn effectively inverts the relation between Shakespeare and his plays in his own time. While Shakespeare's contemporaries did not read the plays as pornographic (a practice that didn't begin until the eighteenth century), Shakespeare's own sex life could be the subject of anecdotes such as the one told by John Manningham of the Middle Temple:

"Upon a time when Burbage played Richard III, there was a citizen grew so far in liking with him, that before she went from the play she appointed him to come that night unto her by the name of Richard III. Shakespeare, overhearing their conclusion, went before, was entertained and at his game ere Burbage came. Then, message being brought that Richard III was at the door, Shakespeare caused return to be made that William the Conqueror was before Richard III." (Burgess 1970, 184-85)

Of course Shakespeare punned on the sexual meanings of "will" in sonnets 135 and 136, concluding the latter by identifying his name with desire, "my name is Will" (Booth 1969, 466-69), and, according to Joel Fineman (1991, 191), he performed in *The Rape of Lucrece* a "pornographic staging of the literal letters ["W" and "M," signing the name "William" by chiasmatically yoking its first and last letters] in its lines."[34] In contrast, Shakespeare's plays can now be made into pornography, but Shakespeare himself appears in porn as sexless, either as a benevolent parental figure or as gay (in straight porn, being gay effectively means being castrated since gay male sex is almost never performed).[35] Though the censoring of Shakespeare's works by the Reverend Thomas Bowdler and others was described as Shakespeare's "mutilation" and "castration" (Marder 1963, 112), one of the interesting things about Shakespeare porn is that it does not equate the uncensored Shakespeare with an explicitly pornographic Shakespeare.[36]

In films that rewrite Shakespeare through or as porn, his approval of the rewrite is always desired or asked for when he is mentioned or appears as a character. In *Hamlet: For the Love of Ophelia, Part Two,* Hamlet at one point stumbles and falls on his face and then addresses the camera: "Don't tell Shakespeare about this." More explicitly, if more tangentially, the copy on the jacket inside the CD-ROM version of this video reads, "It would not be impossible to believe, if Shakespeare were present today, that he would laughingly give his approval to the director of this Italian masterpiece." Similarly, though *Tromeo and Juliet* at one point displays a bloodied copy of the *Yale Shakespeare* as a murder weapon, the film directly builds in Shakespeare's enthusiastic approval of its trashy rewriting of *Romeo and Juliet*, not only citing

Figure 2.5: Shakespeare in front of a 42nd Street porn palace. (Publicity still for *Tromeo and Juliet*. Photo courtesy of Troma Entertainment.)

critics who say things such as "Shakespeare would be delighted" and "the Bard would love it" in the press kit, but making him a happy character who appears laughing at the end of the video and in advertisements for it.[37] Though the film introduces pornography into the play, Shakespeare thus remains literally outside the pornographic scene.[38] *Tromeo and Juliet* distinguishes between the two fathers, Monty Q and Cappy, as good and bad porn kings, respectively. Tromeo's father, Monty Q, put together a business called Silky Films that "catered to the art crowd, French babes, soft focus, lots of arty stuff." But after Cappy stole the business, Silky turned out trash: "You should see the stuff Silky turns out now. The worst motherfucking movies in the world." By placing Shakespeare outside the frame of the movie and its pornographic elements, *Tromeo and Juliet* saves itself from being read as merely a bad movie. It asks to be placed in the cult section of video stores, alongside John Waters, Ed Wood, Jr., and Russ Meyers. Similarly, in a publicity still for the film entitled "Shakespeare entering a porn palace" (see figure 2.5) it is notable that Shakespeare is outside on the street; he does not participate in pornography but instead is on the verge of watching it.

Shakespeare's distance from porn (as approving but non-voyeuristic critic rather than as participant sex performer) is even more marked in Paul Thomas's hardcore video *Romeo and Juliet II*. Since few readers will have seen this video, it is worth rehearsing the narrative. The video begins with an audition for the part of Juliet held by Bill (Jamie Gillis), the director, and Charlie (Rick Savage), the new owner of the theater, who wanted originally to make it into a porn movie theater but left it a theater on condition that he be allowed to put his two cents in when it comes to casting the women. This sequel opens with a problem: who to cast as Juliet now that last year's Juliet has gotten pregnant. After rejecting a number of women, the director auditions Wanda (Jaquline Lorians), a friend of his wife's who is "almost a professional." Bill does not immediately accept Wanda for the role, even though this means making his wife extremely angry. The women go off and start having sex. Bill follows them and walks in to join them. (One of the odd things about heterosexuality in porn is that no one ever cheats on anyone, as in ordinary, "real" heterosexuality. Instead, people sleep around and everyone seems to take that for granted.) Meanwhile, Rob (Tom Byron), the actor playing Romeo, has sex with Elena (Aja), whom he wants to play Juliet even though she is so shy she cannot project her voice further than a few feet. So there is a stand-off between the men. Who will get the part of Juliet, they agree, will be decided by holding another audition, and if that fails, by a flip of a coin. As it turns out, Juliet (played by the interestingly named Ariel Knights), the actual character turned historical figure, appears magically on stage, auditions, and gets the part. Elena accepts the role of understudy while Wanda and Lydia storm off (Wanda later seduces Charlie in order to get him to give her a vehicle to make her a star.) Juliet then has a sex scene with Rob. Afterwards, the film cuts back to heaven where Juliet meets up with a jealous Romeo (Paul Thomas) and a distressed Shakespeare (she wasn't supposed to have sex, just help them find a Juliet). The play goes forward with Elena as Juliet and is a success (though in this version Romeo and Juliet do not have sex onstage, a disappointment to Charlie). Juliet returns and has a three-way with

Elena and Rob. Romeo and Shakespeare appear briefly to watch and then disappear. Juliet then disappears too, and the credits roll.

A nonsexualized Shakespeare is used as a means of getting behind the scenes of porn films and videos.[39] This is metaporn. Through the production of a Shakespeare play, the video makes a critique of porn production rather than a critique of the play itself. The video's critique is first visible in the process of casting Juliet. The first woman we see audition disqualifies herself because of a thick Long Island accent. Bill, the director, rejects her, and the pornographer, Charlie, is baffled: "Hey Bill, did you see her? She had great tits." In contrast, Bill responds, "I appreciate your involvement. But this is Shakespeare. We gotta concentrate a little, just a little, on acting." This distinction between pornographer and serious theater director is immediately unsettled, however, as the first sex scene follows. Wanda, a character we might assume will get the part of Juliet partly because she says she has acted and partly because she has sex with the director's wife, Lydia (Nikki Randall), then auditions for the part of Juliet. Yet the funny thing is that the actress playing Wanda can't act either. And the film knows this. (Wanda tells Lydia she's acted in a stage production of *Howard the Duck*.) Wanda is just another bad porn actress who's in this video because she will have sex in front of the camera and because her not-so-great-shape and ultra white skin throw into relief Nikki Randall's more shapely, tanned body. (The distinction between actresses and porn actresses is also humorously compromised when we see a sheet of paper with actresses whose names sound like those of porn stars.) The scene becomes a kind of casting couch number, with the actress agreeing that she "can take direction." Here Bill becomes a porn film director, posing her while she makes love to his wife. They quickly get into a three-way. Bill is thus even more sleazy than Charlie (who is thinking of converting the theater into a topless sushi bar if the play doesn't make enough money).

Romeo and Juliet II's behind-the-scenes critique of porn is also registered in terms of the cast members' ages. An older actress auditioning for Juliet is quickly rejected. ("You bring a real maturity to the role," Bill tells her.) But most of the actors and actresses look like they've come out of retirement (or perhaps should go into retirement). This video desires to do more than porn, an excess that produces a self-reflexive critique of porn's conventionality (though not a Catharine MacKinnon, antiporn sort of critique). Shakespeare opens up a critique of the porn industry from the inside. This critique involves insulting people in the industry who don't know their Shakespeare. After Wanda says she's played Portia, Ophelia, and Lady Macbeth, for example, Charlie says, "Yeah, must be rough playing all those parts nobody's heard of." Yet the video is really about typecasting, about how much artistic freedom one can have as an actor within the genre of porn and about how that freedom is gendered.

This inside critique of porn depends on Shakespeare and the actual Romeo (Paul Thomas, the director) not having sex. Shakespeare is played as sexless or perhaps asexual: though Shakespeare wants to watch Juliet having sex with Rob and Elena, the actor playing him codes him as gay, which is to say, in the context of hardcore heterosexual porn, castrated. Moreover, Shakespeare is not allowed to be even a voyeur. When he appears at the end of the video with Romeo while Juliet is engaged in a three-way, Romeo does not allow him to watch, and Shakespeare then calls them all back to heaven (see figure 2.6). Furthermore, the casting of porn stars for *Romeo and Juliet II* does not correspond to the casting of the characters who audition for parts in the theatrical production of *Romeo and Juliet;* that is, the box cover photo of Nikki Randall implies that she is Juliet, but in fact she has nothing to do with the play (there seems to be no need for the parts of Lady Capulet or the Nurse in this production). Jaquline Lorians gets second billing as Wanda, and Ariel Knights is billed third even though she plays Juliet. Similarly, Jamie Gillis gets top billing as Bill, and Rob (Tom Byron) gets third billing as the character who is cast as Romeo.[40]

The film's insider critique arises out of its contradictory relation to Shakespeare. On the one hand, it is a pornographic film about *Romeo and Juliet* in which Juliet turns into a porn star and in which the actress playing the role also does porn scenes. On the other hand, the theatrical performance of *Romeo and Juliet* and the character of Shakespeare are not sexualized at all: the play's bawdy jokes are surprisingly untapped. And though Juliet and Rob kiss during Juliet's audition, Rob and Elena's performance of the play is completely chaste. Rob and Elena have a sex scene backstage after the play is over. Though the two-part *Hamlet* and *Taming of the Screw* stand in some

Figure 2.6: Romeo keeping Shakespeare out of the pornographic picture in Paul Thomas's *Romeo and Juliet II*.

marginal relation to their Shakespearean "originals," *Romeo and Juliet II* is more typical of Shakespeare porn in being what I call a "post-hermeneutic" replay: there is no dialectic here between Shakespeare text and porn performance.

The sequel attempts to resolve its contradictions by putting back in place the distinction between Shakespeare (genuine theater) and porn cancelled in Thomas's first *Romeo and Juliet* porn video. Yet this distinction is reconstructed not in order to save Shakespeare, nor to degrade his tragedy in a transgressive manner. The video does not offer a critique of *Romeo and Juliet,* nor does it attempt to rewrite it (the scenes actually quote the lines from the play verbatim).

The point of making Juliet a person rather than a literary character appears to be to question the distinction between direction and acting in legitimate theater, on the one hand, and directing and acting in porn, on the other. What porn has over legitimate theater, of course, is the freedom to go all the way when it comes to representing sex. But, as it turns out, even that freedom is constrained from the start: the sex has to be performed in a set number of poses, routines, and scenes; the star performer must have a certain kind of body, and so on. These constraints are of course gendered. It's the women, not the men, who "take direction." In certain respects, however, the women are less constrained. Juliet, for example, does gain some autonomy through her sexuality. She is the one to return to earth to perform (in both theatrical and sexual scenes), not Romeo. And she is in control of her sexuality. She is unfaithful to Romeo; first she has sex with Rob, then with Rob and Elena. (The film does not hold this against her.) Moreover, she is able to teach Elena how to overcome her shyness. Elena initially fails onstage as Bill and Charlie both comment on how bad her acting is. She forgets her lines but remembers Juliet's method-acting advice that she "speak the lines from within" and is thus able to deliver an excellent performance (we have to take the film's word on this point). But Juliet is also constrained in deeper ways than a porn actress is by a director like Bill (or Paul Thomas). She is limited not only by heaven, but by the fact that she is a character. "Don't you ever get out of character?" Rob bemusedly asks her after she auditions. And when told she can have the part, Juliet says, "I am the part." Juliet, that is, can't play anyone other than herself, nor is she even really allowed to play herself in Shakespeare's play.

The constraints on the men are more equivocal. As directors, they have more control over the production than the women do. Bill is able to give Wanda direction and is quite willing to ignore his wife's desires. Yet he too is at all points constrained by Charlie. And the film marks a more radical gender distinction between legitimate acting and porn acting. The casting of Juliet links porn stardom to legitimate acting at all points. The woman who gets the part in the play is also the woman who will be performing in a porn video. But in the case of the characters of Romeo and Shakespeare, there is a divorce between legitimate acting and porn acting. Though one could imagine this distinction as working in a high-minded way to preserve Shakespeare as an ideal that transcends the assumed vulgarity of porn, it doesn't work that way in this film. Their asexual roles suggest rather the impotence of these men, symbolically as much as literally. Shakespeare cuts a reduced figure. To get God to allow Juliet to go down to earth, Shakespeare agrees to do all the skits for the next angels' convention.

He apparently has neither the freedom nor the desire to rewrite his own play. And director Paul Thomas, in casting himself as Romeo at an age (44) even older than Leslie Howard (43) was when he played the role in the George Cukor version (1934), makes his Romeo a somewhat ridiculous, prudish cuckold who ineffectively chastises Juliet for appearing in heaven naked and for being "shameless." In *Romeo and Juliet II*, male artistic autonomy, unlike female autonomy, comes at the expense of the man's ability to have sex.

If artistic freedom is possible in porn, this video suggests, it is not to be found in upscale porn that has remade itself in the image of a classic, such as *Hamlet: For the Love of Ophelia*, but in porn that is badly made—not John Waters kitsch bad, but just plain bad. Artistic freedom paradoxically lies in making one's porn as incompetently and generically as possible. The film isn't really addressed to average porn consumers or Shakespeareans but instead to other porn directors and actors. Whereas a metadramatic play such as Tom Stoppard's *Rosencrantz and Guildenstern Are Dead* suggests that actors are like prostitutes in that they will play in anything that makes money, this video suggests to people in the industry that actors are no more free than porn stars. It succeeds at being a failure as porn. Unsurprisingly, *Romeo and Juliet II* received no stars when it was reviewed by adult video magazines, whereas *Romeo and Juliet* (the first part) received three and a half (out of a possible four).

Shakespeare, in All the Right Places

An account of Shakespeare the author as castrated in porn, paradoxically sexualized and desexualized, enables us to see that the history of pornographic adaptations of classics does not, as I suggested earlier, merely involve a movement in the direction of legitimating harder and harder porn. What we see in the history of Shakespeare porn adaptations is that not everything is sexualized: the play is not simply the excuse for sex scenes, something to be minimized as much as possible, but it may also be the occasion for critique of porn film and video conventions and authorship: Shakespeare porn is also always in some ways antiporn.

The contradictory drives to sexualize and desexualize Shakespeare in Shakespeare porn, as we have also seen, open up a space for critique, not only of Shakespeare's plays but also of the construction of gender and the porn industry. The necessary overlap between Shakespeare as author and the film director as auteur, even sometimes producer, means, however, that the focus of the critique will not always be stable. For adaptation does not mean that one author substitutes for the other (film director for playwright), but that the authorship of a given adaptation is always in question: whose *Macbeth* is it, for example, Polanski's or Shakespeare's? And if it is Polanski's, to what extent can the film be allegorized in biographical rather than strictly formal terms? Neither a strong claim for auteurship nor a deconstruction of authorship stabilizes the director's position as exterior or interior to the pornographic scene. The director or producer is, like Shakespeare, both inside and outside, both sexual and unsexual; moreover, the director's male gaze may be sexualized in contradictory ways. The pornographic male gaze may mark the director (or producer) not only as author of the scene and narrative but as voyeuristic porn consumer, part of the scene rather than apart from it.

To begin to reconceive the history of porn adaptations, I want to examine two more examples of Shakespeare adaptations, Polanski's *Macbeth* and Greenaway's *Prospero's Books,* and situate these examples in the larger context of adaptations such as Pasolini's highbrow, gay adaptation of *The Canterbury Tales* (1972) and the landmark mainstream, straight porn film *Caligula* (dir. Silvano Ippoliti, 1980), produced by Bob Guccione and Franco Rosselini. Consider first the earliest film joining porn to Shakespeare, namely, Roman Polanski's *Macbeth.*[41] *Macbeth* is marked as *Playboy*-influenced porn by more than just nude sleepwalking and bare-breasted witches. There is also the frontal nudity of Macbeth's son being bathed by Lady Macduff, and Macduff's slaughtered children naked and bloodied.

The pornographic aspects of the film are properly viewed in the larger context of the play's concern with masculinity under pressure and Polanski's interest in the grotesque body. In *Macbeth,* Polanski registers how vertiginous the male gaze is. The film's nudity works to unsettle the spectator. Lady Macbeth's nude sleepwalking scene, for example, is less an instance of a pornographic gaze than of the film's blurring of generic boundaries: Polanski recodes Shakespearean tragedy in terms of the American horror film (he had earlier directed *The Fearless Vampire Killers, or: Pardon Me, But Your Teeth Are in My Neck* [1967] and *Rosemary's Baby* [1968]).

Polanski's construction of the male gaze is not so much to eroticize as to disperse it, to make it the hysterical site of Macbeth's and Lady Macbeth's castration. Polanski allows for something like a female gaze in the film, located in Lady Macbeth and Lady Macduff. After Duncan's murder is discovered by Macduff, he, Lennox, Macbeth, and Lady Macbeth go in to see the corpse. The camera follows Lady Macbeth. She turns her head to the right and sees the murdered grooms, and the camera follows her line of vision: she and we see in a briefly held shot that one groom has been cut in half, the other beheaded. She then faints. Here the female gaze is precisely a castrated gaze. There is also a brief shot of Lady Macbeth looking helplessly at Macbeth before he rides off to see the Weird Sisters the second time.[42] In a tracking shot, the camera also follows Lady Macduff before her son is killed when she discovers first a servant being brutally gang-raped and then her slaughtered children. Rather than giving her any power, however, this cinematic technique marks her impotence. More strikingly, Polanski identifies our gaze with Macbeth's after Macduff has beheaded him. In one sequence, Macduff carries Macbeth's head on a stick through a crowd of soldiers, holding it parallel to the ground. Shots of the head are intercut with reverse shots of soldiers looking directly at the camera, implying that we are seeing them from Macbeth's perspective. Our view is then abruptly divorced from Macbeth's when we see a long shot of his head on a spike above the castle battlement. In identifying the male gaze with the audience's, Polanski makes it/us look from the site of decapitation. The question of Macbeth's decapitated consciousness (are we looking from the perspective of death?) is made ambiguous by the shots of the prop of Macbeth's severed head. It is first shot very realistically, when Macduff picks up the crown to give to Malcolm. Indeed, it seems to be alive, especially when the hair moves after the crown is taken off. But in the subsequent shots, the prop seems quite unrealistic, as if it were made for a cheap horror film. Unlike Medusa's head, which, according to

Freud (1922, 212), had an apotropaic effect, turning male to stone (making him erect) in the face of the threat of castration, Macbeth's decapitated head here marks the spectator's own position as castrated.

Because the camera cannot be identified with Polanski the auteur, Polanski's own authority over the film is undermined: he does not distance himself from the scene of castration, gazing at the gaze, as it were, from a noncastrated position. By blurring Macbeth's generic boundaries, Polanski also blurs the relation between the film and his life (the brutal murder of his wife, Sharon Tate, occurred the year before Polanski shot *Macbeth*). She was eight-and-a-half-months pregnant when she was savagely stabbed to death. Polanski vociferously resisted any attempt to link the film to his life, instead equating the making of a graphically violent *Macbeth* with having kept his balls after Tate's murder:

> PLAYBOY: Some critics and moviegoers may feel that you chose *Macbeth* as a kind of catharsis, to purge yourself of the kind of violence you had so recently experienced in your own life. What would you say to them?

> POLANSKI: I would say they are full of shit, because it's not so. . . . Even if *Macbeth* weren't a play about murder, the critics would be asking why I chose to make it after Sharon's death. What if I had made a scene with Macbeth, dagger in hand, going to the king's chambers, and then . . . dot, dot, dot, dot? They would say "After what happened to him, he lost his balls." (Anon. 1971, 98).

Yet it was precisely the perception that the film was an autobiography that also opened up the charge that the film was pornographic. As the *Playboy* interviewer pointed out, "critics might argue that the graphic portrayal of violence is analogous to pornography, not only with no redeeming social value but with harmful effects on those who see it" (1971, 98). Though Polanski of course denied the charge, his subsequent sexual behavior, including having sex with a thirteen-year-old girl and later, an affair with then fifteen-year-old Nastassja Kinski, only reinforced a tendency to link his films to his life, making his *Macbeth* into *Roman Polanski's Baby,* as it were, calling into question a distinction between Polanski as cineaste of voyeurism and Polanski as voyeur of voyeurism.[43]

Ironically, it was precisely this view of the film as Polanski's pathological symptom that *Playboy* ended up taking. Reviewed positively in *Playboy* (January 1972) upon its initial release, *Playboy* later took a different, if unofficial view of the film. *Macbeth* appeared at a fifty-fifth birthday party for Hefner, the Fifty-Fifth Annual Calamity Awards, "an event," James Caan, master of ceremonies announced, "that will live on in the anus of show business" (Miller 1984, 313-14). The nominees for the biggest disaster *Playboy* had funded were all films produced by Hefner, including *The Fiendish Plot of Dr. Fu Manchu* with Peter Sellers and *And Now For Something Completely Different*, "the story of Hef's first attempt at copulation with a woman over twenty-one." *Macbeth* was the winner. (It had been a flop at the box office.) Caan's ten-year-old daughter, "a pretty little blond with bouncing curls," according to Russell Miller, "stepped up to accept the award on behalf of Roman Polanski: 'My husband couldn't make it tonight,' she lisped into the microphone, 'but thank you.' The audience went wild" (1984, 314). One might argue that the real problem with Polanski's *Macbeth* is that it wasn't *Playboy* enough. The nude sleepwalking scene is not really very revealing and the witches are grotesque. Nevertheless, Polanski ends up getting sexualized, not Shakespeare. And in the process Polanski is pathologized, metaphorically castrated, unable to have "adult" sex.[44] He has thus far been unable to make a box office success since he emigrated.[45]

Greenaway's *Prospero's Books* goes the opposite direction of Polanski in marking itself off from pornography and Greenaway off from Shakespeare. Instead of establishing himself as the author of the film, Greenaway deconstructs authorship. There is overlap but no secure identifications among Prospero, Shakespeare, and Greenaway. Instead, the film constantly calls attention to the moment "we split." Mirrors, voice-overs, handwriting, all serve to disembody authorship. This deconstruction of the author involves, among other things, placing the film in a pornographic scene, including, as I mentioned earlier, nude dancers; an almost completely nude Caliban, whose genitals are exposed; a transsexual character, Pornocrates; and a pornographic book. Yet the effect of this nudity is to neuter the pornographic scene.

This paradoxical effect is registered acutely at the moment Prospero reads the one dirty book in his library. Just before the wedding masque, Prospero reads *The Autobiographies of Pasiphae and Semiramis*. This book alone is hidden in a secret compartment, accessible to no one but Prospero. As Greenaway writes in the screenplay:

> Prospero, after putting on a pair of gloves—presses a catch in his especially-constructed bookshelves for the twenty-four books . . . and a panel slides back to reveal a small compartment and a small black book. He takes it out and opens it on top of the other books on his desk. . . . The illustrations leave no ambiguity as to the book's contents. The book is bound in black calfskin with damaged lead covers. . . . The pages are grey green with line-engravings in black, touched out in white—the pages of the book are scattered with a sludge-green powder and curled black hairs and stains of blood and other substances. The slightest taint of steam or smoke rises from the pages. They leave stains on his gloves—like these stains made by acid. (1991, 135)

The force of introducing pornography here, however, is to mark it off as literally ob-scene, as against the film's own scene. Indeed, Prospero is set up as a censor. He not only handles the book with gloves on, a book associated with excrement (and linked both to Caliban, who pissed, vomited, and shat on some of the books earlier in the film; and Ariel, whose piss spills over onto the first book shown in the film) but he reads the book just before the wedding masque, speaking the lines addressed to Ferdinand in which Prospero advises him not to "break [Miranda's] virgin knot." Furthermore, in the screenplay version, his words are illustrated by "lewd mythological figures [that] dance around his desk . . . dusted in the same sludge-green powder as was found in the book . . . with their characteristics provocatively reddened" (1991, 135).[46] The screenplay then indicates cuts to Miranda bathing a naked Ferdinand, "her hands straying to his belly" (1991, 136). But the mythological figures of the masque displace the "lewd figures" associated with the pornographic book, and the film proceeds to celebrate the triumph of married sexuality over pornographic, unbridled sexuality.

The film mutes, one might even say "censors," the pornographic scene imagined in the screenplay, however, leaving out the secret compartment, gloves, and lewd figures. Furthermore, the film de-eroticizes sexuality even as it is present almost everywhere in the film. *Prospero's Books* frames pornography, marking it as grotesque, rather than presents a pornographic version of *The Tempest* meant to arouse the viewer. While waste products such as piss, shit, sludge, and blood are thrown on books during the film, it is notable that semen never is. The force of Greenaway's deconstruction of authorship is not to return us to an early modern moment prior to the modern author-function but instead to anachronistically project onto Renaissance Humanism an opposition between high culture and pornography, an opposition, as Paula Findlen (1993, 48-54) has shown, that was in fact never in place. "The proud lineage of scholarship, stretching from Petrarch to Erasmus," she points out, "ultimately produced Pietro Aretino, the most famous of the pornographers of the Renaissance" (1993, 52). Yet even this de-eroticization of the film's nudity and sexuality did not always convince viewers that the film was not pornographic. Though Greenaway's own sex life never was an issue, the film's nudity was. The Japanese considered it to be pornographic (it violated Japanese codes by displaying pubic hair), and they allowed Greenaway to post-produce his film in Tokyo only because he was only editing the film (and wouldn't show it there) and because the NHK studio facility where he worked is not officially a part of the country (Rodman 1991, 37). The nudity proved controversial for many English and American critics as well (see Lanier 1996, 194).

The history of Shakespeare porn suggests, then, that the more explicit the nudity and sex, the less sexually arousing the film may be. The impossibility of narrating a history of porn adaptations in terms of the progressively explicit exposure of nudity and sex may be appreciated further by situating Shakespeare porn within the broader context of non-Shakespeare porn adaptations. Consider two very different attempts to remake classics or use classical material, Piero Pasolini's *Canterbury Tales* (1972) and Bob Guccione's production of *Caligula*. In his *Canterbury Tales*, Pasolini, as one might expect, constructs Chaucer as an author-function in a more complicated way than Shakespeare is constructed in either *Tromeo and Juliet* or *Romeo and Juliet* II such that Chaucer the author is both sexualized and desexualized.[47] Pasolini constructs Chaucer as an author by inserting scenes of him writing at his desk in between the tale segments. The shots of Chaucer thus frame the narratives that surround them. In showing Chaucer as author rather than as fellow pilgrim and recorder of the tales, Pasolini suggests that the tales are Chaucer's fantasies. This suggestion is reinforced by the way Pasolini makes Chaucer more and more isolated as the film progresses. We see him writing first in a room full of sleeping pilgrims (only one other person is awake), then in his house and library. In one scene, his wife shrieks his name and he awakens and sits up in his chair, as if to get back to work. The effect of this framing is to suggest that the tales are to be read not as public poetry but as Chaucer's own private sexual fantasies, fantasies that function as compensation for his isolation.

The tales can also be read, however, as Pasolini's own compensatory fantasies for his castration as a gay auteur/author. Pasolini casts himself as Chaucer and frames Chaucer as author with his own film; that is, Pasolini establishes Chaucer as author rather than daydreamer through two framing shots. The only times we see what Chaucer is writing down are when he begins and when he ends what he calls *Notes to the Canterbury Tales*. But Chaucer's beginning and ending are in turn framed by Pasolini's film, which begins with the pilgrims meeting at the Host's Inn and ends with a sequence of shots in which we first see a close-up of Chaucer meditating, as if he were recalling the last shot in the previous tale (the Reeve's) of a devil taking a huge fart, then Canterbury Cathedral, then pilgrims receiving Mass, then Chaucer again, then his book, and finally, "The End." As framer of the framer Chaucer, Pasolini as auteur exceeds Chaucer as author.

This excess allows Pasolini both to sexualize the particular tales he tells and to mark his adaptation of the tales as gay. Pasolini's Chaucer does not write a retraction but licenses the telling of the tales for the pleasure of telling them. And in Pasolini's case, that pleasure is distinctly gay. The male gaze here is framed at different points as explicitly voyeuristic, as when the camera looks at people having sex through a keyhole. In the *Summoner's Tale* there is a scene of two men having anal sex (one is later burned at the stake), and throughout the film there are lots of shots of young men from behind and men embracing. Moreover, the scenes of heterosexual sex always show the woman distinctly not enjoying herself. By casting himself as Chaucer, then, Pasolini is able to be both the framer and the framed, both outside the sex occurring in the tales (Chaucer does not have sex and seems to be terrified of his shrewish wife) and yet inside it (since the tales are Chaucer's/Pasolini's fantasies).

A quite different set of tensions emerges in Guccione's production of *Caligula*. Guccione wanted to make the first mainstream film that was also hardcore. In contrast to Hefner, Guccione wanted to be known as a pornographer and had already moved mainstream men's magazines in the direction of hardcore by the time he produced *Caligula*. *Penthouse* was the first mainstream adult magazine to show women's pubic hair (de Grazia 1993, 577-81). Guccione defended the film's sexual explicitness in terms of historical accuracy: since imperial Rome was sexually "pornographic," the film had to be pornographic as well. *Caligula* was a box-office failure, but it may have boosted *Penthouse's* sales, at least partly because it was a strange crossover phenomenon between British stars, budding porn starlets, and a Hollywood screenwriter. It ended up caught between its conflicting desires to be mainstream movie and porn film. On the one hand, it starred Peter O'Toole, Malcolm McDowell, Helen Mirren, and John Gielgud with a screenplay by Gore Vidal in a straight *Fall of the Roman Empire* or Frederico Fellini's *Satyricon* kind of movie, one to be only somewhat more revealing than the Italian-made *Hercules* movies. It thus was a mainstream movie that had the cache of "real" British actors, two of whom had begun to cross over to Hollywood. On the other hand, Bob Guccione credited himself with directing additional scenes, and the film also "introduced" two *Penthouse* models, Anneka di Lorenzo and Lori Wagner. Hollywood stars and porn stars didn't mix well. The former stayed outside of the sex, though McDowell had simulated sex with a woman and simulated anal fisting of her bridegroom.[48] The split within the movie between mainstream star vehicle and porn film was emphasized after it was released. In May and June of 1980, *Penthouse* ran pictorials with the two "introduced" starlets doing lesbian scenes not actually shown in the movie. Gore Vidal sued (unsuccessfully) to have his name removed from the screenplay credits. Instead of merging historical accuracy and porn into an epic film with a star cast, the film's contradictory means of production polarized them. Guccione remained unable to bring porn further into the mainstream.

The force of this effort to historicize porn adaptations of classics is to revise our understanding of the castrated male gaze. Shakespeare pornography stages the castration of the male gaze, one might speculate, as a heterosexual male's defense against penetration. In *Romeo and Juliet II,* Juliet's advice to Elena to speak from within suggests a kind of lesbian penetration that cannot be framed in visual, pornographic terms for the male viewer. Porn, of course, succeeds only partially in going deep inside a porn star in the sense of uniting both male physical penetration and male psychic penetration. Yet how deep inside William Shakespeare can one go? Is it safe for straight viewers or directors to go deep inside him? Just where is one going anyway? Is one being penetrated in turn by Shakespeare's fantasies, if nothing else? Perhaps the way to avoid being fucked, *Romeo and Juliet II* suggests, is by presenting oneself as unable to fuck. One can avoid being gayed (becoming a bottom, in popular heterosexual terms) by being castrated (which is to say, same difference). From a more directly queer perspective such as Wertheim's or Pasolini's, however, castration is precisely a means by which the director becomes sexual, albeit as the orchestrator of other people's sex. Although castration opens up a variety of critical effects, they are not reducible to the overt or ostensible politics of a given film. Guccione's *Caligula,* for example, may be boring as porn and heterosexist to boot, but that doesn't make it a less interesting film than Pasolini's *Canterbury Tales.*

Shakespeares That Matter

At the end of the last chapter, I sought to examine how queerness functions in academic work rather than what effects a queered Shakespeare might have outside academia. What, one might ask, is the force of the foregoing analysis of the castrated gaze in terms of academic fantasy? What is the money shot, as it were, of this chapter? Some critics might now expect that the pay-off of historicizing the pornographic adaptation of literary classics might be a queering of straight porn that would produce liberatory pleasures or a critique of normalization in porn as well as in academia.[49] That expectation will not be met here. I am interested, rather, in posing a question not asked by recent critics of porn. If we take critics such as Andrew Ross at their word, Shakespeare porn should be smarter than academic readings of it. What is it, then, that Shakespeare porn knows that academics don't? Can Shakespeare porn tell us everything we want to know about academia but are afraid to ask cultural critics?

Critics tend to assume that the pornographic and the uncensored are where the real signified is. A pornographic Shakespeare could, some critics might argue, give us access to what the play is really about. Shakespeare porn, in this account, would not be post-hermeneutic but ultra-hermeneutic. Yet what is striking about the Shakespeare porn I have discussed is precisely that there is nothing much to be said about the sex in relation to the Shakespeare play. The uncensored, pornographic sex turns out to be insignificant. One way to confirm this point is to ask whether seeing the porn I have discussed would make any difference to our understanding of porn and of Shakespeare. The premise of most criticism is that a given text or film under consideration has been seen by most readers; by the same token, critics tend to assume that a good piece of criticism will change how a film is viewed. These assumptions turn out to be questionable for Shakespeare porn, however, if there is really nothing to say about the sex scenes. For the pornographic to signify in relation to Shakespeare one would have to be able to construct a love scene, say between Romeo and Juliet, as specifically Shakespearean sex. I can see no way this could be done. While it is possible to "porn" Shakespeare, it would appear that porn cannot be "Shakespeared."

Porn might also be said to know something about the nature of academic fantasy that academics don't, perhaps don't want to know. Academic critics typically allegorize pornography in order to legitimate its study, turn it into another genre such as the musical, interpret it as part of popular culture or the history of print, or conceive it as work so that it can be taken seriously as a political statement. Transgressive sexuality in academia can be transgressive as long as the sex can be said to be about something other than sex; that is, one could teach or publish an article on pornographic Shakespeare films as subversive reinterpretations of Shakespeare's plays or as producing a political critique of gender, masculinity, and so on, but one couldn't teach them or write on them in order to discuss how sexually arousing they were (or use them in order to arouse students and readers) without significantly calling into question whether one was still doing Shakespeare criticism (as opposed to pornography, hence possibly pornographic, criticism), whether one was still a critic or was instead a voyeur/pervert.

It is not at all clear that academics view porn in a way that is compatible with the way nonacademics watch porn. For it is of course sex as sex that sells Shakespeare porn. "Make no mistake," the ad copy for *Juliet and Romeo* says, "great writing, terrific acting and tireless story aside, the sex is the main attraction here." As I mentioned at the outset of this chapter, classic porn is now popular with many of its consumers because it allows porn stars to appear in less generic, predictable settings, not because it offers a new reading of Shakespeare. It creates a new commodity and allows stars to increase their market share.[50]

My point is not that there is something called "sex" that stands outside of academic discourses, however. Sex is, of course, never just about sex (though it may be the case that sometimes a cigar is just a cigar). Even in porn, sex is always, as Luce Irigaray would have it, the sex that is not one. My point is that there are extra-academic discourses that construct pornographic "sex" in radically different terms. There is, for example, an industry-based institution of porn criticism (with its own film reviews and guides, fan clubs, academy awards ceremonies, and even halls of fame).[51] Some cultural critics might believe that it is possible to be both a Shakespeare fan and a porn fan, even celebrate the porn fan's reading of Shakespeare porn films.[52]

To be sure, it is possible to imagine a porn version of academia, a phone-sex line (1-900-STUDENT) with the sex worker saying, "Ooh, yeah. I just love it when you talk academic to me!" And one could imagine academic advisors to porn versions of Shakespeare plays, even academic screenplay writers of Shakespeare porn. It isn't difficult to come up with titles such as *Shrew You!* (with a sequel called *Shrew You Two: Petruchio's Revenge*), *Coriole's Anus, The Merchant of Venus, Mac-boner, The Comedy of Eros,* and so on.)[53] I would argue, however, that

Shakespeare porn can be assimilated to the present Shakespeare database only by excluding the industry-based institution of porn criticism, since it evaluates pornographic films and videos in terms that are incompatible with academic considerations.[54] Academic Shakespeare porn may be possible, but it would probably fail as porn precisely because it would be an academic rewriting of a Shakespeare play as pornographic: it would be about the play rather than about sex.[55] Shakespeare porn of the hardcore variety assumes a nonacademic audience of men and couples. They will watch *Juliet and Romeo,* for example, because they want to get off, not because they want to learn more about *Romeo and Juliet* or to compare this adaptation to other cinematic adaptations. "Honey, wanna see a porn version of *Hamlet* tonight?" is presumably a more enticing question than "Honey, wanna see *Slick Honey* tonight?" If we imagine an academic asking the former question, it seems likely that the answer would not be "Sure, baby, that sounds fun" but "God, don't you ever stop working?!" (Perhaps there is a market for obsessive, industrious academic couples, but one suspects it is a rather tiny one.)[56]

Shakespeare porn perhaps also tells us something about the way the academic viewer's identifications with porn, like all identifications, are ambivalent and contradictory.[57] Academic writing on porn wants to be both outside and inside sex. On the one hand, the critic identifies with the pornographer, who can recycle everything, even Shakespeare. On the other hand, the cultural critic tends to identify with the porn star, the sex object (see Wallen, 1993). "When sex is discussed, the discussion itself is sexy," according to Marjorie Garber (1995, 144). Perhaps attempting to take this point a step further (suggesting, that is, that discussing sex makes the one discussing it sexy), two pro-porn feminists befriended a feminist porn star and appeared on a panel with her (Lord 1997, 40). Cultural critics want to have it both ways: they want both to desexualize their work and to have their work, in some cases even themselves, sexualized, as in "what a sexy critique" (or "critic").

Whether this means that cultural criticism takes the form of AC/DC, open to all comers, as it were, is open to question. For the identifications with pornographer and porn star are not symmetrical. The sexualization of the critic is possible only because there is a surplus of capital produced by the criticism itself, what amounts to academic stardom. Insofar as the critic is like a porn star, some critics might conclude that this surplus, or stardom effect, raises problems for cultural critics. For some, academic stardom might call into question, if it does not entirely subvert, the critic's claim to be politically transgressive in writing about porn; stardom might translate into inequitable academic distributions of symbolic and economic capital. For others, the problem might be that the critic writing on porn might be sensationalized, unfairly attacked by right-wing journalists or academics as a pervert for exploring the perfectly legitimate topic of sexual politics.

I am interested in another problem, however, one that I think is more obvious but one that tends nevertheless not to be recognized or discussed. This more obvious problem, in my view, is that the analogy between academic star and porn star suggests just how far from real stardom the academic is. For if writing about porn does make a critic sexy, we might ask "sexy to whom?" The cultural critic may fantasize about being read and recognized by everyone, but like the porn star, he or she is actually known only by a narrow circle of people, and by almost no one outside it. The academic's identification with the porn star suggests something else about the value of academic criticism. Unlike Hollywood stardom, which thrives primarily on exclusion and offers only the illusion of democratic access (we all know that not everyone can be discovered at Hollywood and Vine), porn stardom has become increasingly democratic. Bill Margold, a porn actor who founded a porn hall of fame in Las Vegas called "Legends of Erotica," chastizes *Adult Video News* precisely because the editors induct everyone into their Hall of Fame, particularly the more recent, still-performing stars.[58] This tendency toward greater and greater inclusion is partly designed to extend the otherwise short shelf life of most porn stars (the average career in porn films is two years). The analogy between academic stardom and porn stardom suggests, then, that academic stardom may be relatively open and democratic, but that its accessibility is precisely a function of its cheapness.

Of course, one could argue that a truly transgressive, queer, postmodern criticism would attempt to "pervert" everything and not be worried about being called perverted or about academic stardom.

This critic would abandon, that is, the modernist distinction between art or criticism, on the one hand, and pornography, on the other. There is no escaping normalization, however, at least not in academia.[59] As Jane Gallop (1997) and other critics who connect teaching and sex explicitly show, when under pressure, the cultural critic will always have recourse to normalizing strategies in order not just to keep his or her job but to defend the integrity of his or her criticism *as* criticism rather than as pornography.[60]

If Shakespeare porn and, more broadly, historicizing pornographic adaptations of classics does not deliver the academic version of the money shot, namely, a critique of normalization, what, then, does it deliver? I suggest that academic attention to Shakespeare porn raises the question of whether the recycling of cultural trash (in this case, Shakespeare porn recycled as academic subject) can properly be regarded as a transgressive, democratizing move. The fantasy that cultural criticism can recycle every kind of cultural trash is part of a larger fantasy about the ways in which the dominant modes of accumulating cultural capital can be subverted through transgressive rewritings.

The cultural critic may imagine that every piece of cultural trash, including cultural criticism, can be recycled, but the instance of Shakespeare porn suggests otherwise. For there is not an equivalence between porn as waste (along with the waste it produces, namely, semen) and cultural criticism of Shakespeare porn as waste (criticism doesn't produce bodily waste products).[61] Though porn can recycle Shakespeare (as well as almost everything else), and though academics can recycle Shakespeare porn as criticism, academic porn readings of Shakespeare cannot be recycled in Shakespeare porn. No porn director is likely to consult an academic for advice on how to do an adaptation of Shakespeare, not because it would not be sexy, but because it would be sexy primarily, perhaps even exclusively, to academic viewers. Academic work on Shakespeare thus meets the reception academic work typically meets outside (and sometimes inside) of academia: it is considered to be useless, even masturbatory, "work." Whether cultural critics find it flattering that their criticism is regarded by the porn industry as unrecyclable remains to be seen.

CHAPTER THREE

Terminating Shakespeare with Extreme Prejudice: Postcolonial Cultural Cannibalism, Serial Quotation, and the Cinematic Spectacle of 1990s American Cultural Imperialism

I Shot William Shakespeare

In the romantic comedy *L. A. Story* (dir. Steve Martin, 1991) Harris K. Telemacher (Steve Martin), a television weather forecaster going through a mid-life crisis, brings his date Sara (Victoria Tennant) to a graveyard where "lots of famous people" are buried: "Rocky Marciano, Benny Goodman, and, of course, William Shakespeare." As Telemacher pulls away overgrown ivy that has obscured the headstone, we first see engraved on it "William Shakespeare / Born 1564 / Died 1616" and then, as the camera pans down, "Lived in Los Angeles / 1614-1616." Telemacher adds, "I think he wrote *Hamlet, Part Eight: the Revenge* here." The humor of this line depends on an opposition between Shakespeare and Hollywood, an opposition the film at once affirms and deconstructs. On the one hand, Shakespeare is the fountainhead of English high culture, in short, of Western civilization; on the other, Hollywood mass culture is conceived as repetitive, derivative, capable only of cannibalizing itself. Telemacher's joke about a Hollywood *Hamlet, Part Eight: the Revenge* opposes *Hamlet,* which is an original masterpiece, and tragedy, to *Friday the Thirteenth,* parts 1 through 8, which are a number of sequels, and the teen horror film. In opposing high and low culture in these terms, *L. A. Story* conforms to a dominant English view of American mass culture as a culture in which the sequel rules. When making a film of his play *The Madness of George III*, Alan Bennett, for example, had to retitle it *The Madness of King George* because American backers feared their audiences would think they had missed the first two parts. Bennett comments ruefully: "apparently . . . there were many moviegoers who came away from Branagh's film of *Henry V* wishing they had seen its four predecessors" (1995, xix). (Also notable in this regard is Kenneth Branagh's satire of English provincial actors, *A Midwinter's Tale* [1996]. Joe, the character who plays Hamlet, goes off at the end of the film to star in a Hollywood science fiction film trilogy.)[1]

Yet *L. A. Story* does not merely appropriate the ex-colonizer's supposedly superior civilization.[2] Although the film embraces Shakespeare, it also Americanizes him, making him a dead resident of Los Angeles; moreover, it ironizes him, producing a comic hodge-podge of quotations and allusions to *Richard II, Hamlet, Macbeth,* and *The Tempest.* Shakespeare marks the leading character's psychological development but also marks him as a cosmopolitan Angeleno, different both from a specifically English, wimpy male character, his main rival for his date's affections, and from a more comic, less romantic character (Rick Moranis), a version of the third gravedigger complete with faux Cockney accent. Telemacher is helped through his mid-life crisis by Shakespeare. (Telemacher loses his job, finds out his girlfriend has been having an affair with his best friend, dates a young woman who lives with her boyfriend, and falls in love with Sara, a woman his age who also knows her Shakespeare.) Yet the film maintains a clear distance between the two men. For Telemacher, Shakespeare is dead and buried in misrecognized form as an emigré who left the London theater to work in Hollywood films. Moreover, if Martin the director knows Shakespeare in a way Telemacher does not, it is nevertheless Sara, an Australian journalist, who actually cites Hamlet's lines about Yorick from the graveyard scene. If Shakespeare has been re-interred in America, his ghost is still called up through a voice with a foreign accent.[3]

In this chapter I want to examine a number of films that take revenge both on Shakespeare as cultural icon and on American mass

Figure 3.1: Arnold Schwarzenegger as an apocalyptic, "not to be" action-hero Hamlet in John McTiernan's *Last Action Hero.*

culture. In varying ways and with varying degrees of self-consciousness, *The Naked Gun: From the Files of Police Squad!* (dir. David Zucker, 1988), *Skyscraper* (dir. Raymond Martino, 1995), *Last Action Hero* (dir. John McTiernan, 1991), *Star Trek VI: The Undiscovered Country* (dir. Nicholas Meyer, 1992), *Independence Day* (dir. Roland Emmerich, 1994), and *The Postman* (dir. Kevin Costner, 1997) push an American, usually ironic, ambivalent identification with Shakespeare to the point of breakdown. Shakespeare is terminated in a variety of ways, including misquotation, the killing of actors in a Shakespeare performance, and the displacing of a traditional Shakespeare film with a cartoonish trailer.

The Naked Gun is a comedy in which we learn that a bumbling cop named Frank Drebbin (Leslie Nielsen), a parody of Clint Eastwood's Dirty Harry, has killed actors performing *Julius Caesar* in the park, but he nevertheless manages inadvertently to save Queen Elizabeth II from being assassinated during her visit to Los Angeles. In *Last Action Hero,* a somewhat parodic send-up of the typical Arnold Schwarzenegger vehicle, Laurence Olivier's diffident, even effeminate Hamlet is replaced by Schwarzenegger's macho, decisive action-hero Hamlet (see figure 3.1). As I noted at the outset of the previous chapter, the less well known, direct from HBO cable to video release *Skyscraper* is about a band of high-tech robbers who regularly recite lines from Shakespeare before killing their victims. And in *Star Trek VI* a group of Shakespeare-quoting Klingon villains plot to assassinate the leader of the Federation and destroy the possibility of peace.[4]

In order to show how Shakespeare's postcolonial status in American popular culture complicates both reactionary and progressive national fantasies articulated by the 1990s action film genre, I compare near the close of this chapter the reactionary *Independence Day* and the liberal-minded *The Postman*. Shakespeare is alluded to but not cited in the former film, which cites repeatedly other films in the science-fiction genre, whereas he is cited repeatedly in the latter, which defines itself against the sequel as a post-Western. A signifier of empire rather than republicanism, Shakespeare's presence, whether by allusion or citation, disturbs the opposed political aims of both films.

Shakespeare appears in these films, I suggest, as an unconscious symptom of an American ambivalent postcolonial identification with British colonial culture, at once foreign and native, a figure both of a revolutionary break with Britain and of a prerevolutionary identification with it. As such, Shakespeare is an icon to be both destroyed and worshipped, both abjected and incorporated. Whether the United States can be considered under the rubric of the postcolonial has recently been the subject of rather heated debate. Laurence Buell (1995) maintains, for example, that American literature of the nineteenth century emerges as a postcolonial phenomenon, while Vera Kutzinski (1995) counters that this literature bears no significant resemblances to the postcolonial literature of an Achebe or Ngugi. In adopting the term "postcolonial," my concern is not to take sides in this debate but to show that the films I am discussing construct America's relation to British culture as a vestigially postcolonial one.[5] As Buell observes (438), there is no decisive moment at which one can say that postcolonialism comes to an end in the United States. The postcolonial thus necessarily intersects with American imperialism rather than is entirely displaced by it. *The Naked Gun* begins somewhere in the Middle East, for example, as Fidel Castro, Idi Amin, Mikhail Gorbachev, Mohammir Khadafi, Yassar Arafat, and the Ayatollah Khomeini sit around a table plotting an assassination that will humiliate America. Frank Drebbin, disguised as a servant, then reveals himself, beats them all up (in cartoon fashion), and exits saying, "Don't ever let me catch you guys in America." But the rest of the film is devoted to problematizing who an assassin is, and it shifts the figure of the assassin away from recognizable Arab and Russian leaders to an anonymous group represented by a Mr. Papschmir, returning to the domestic only to have the domestic retriangulated through an assassination plot on Queen Elizabeth II (rather than the President of the United States).[6]

By understanding these films in terms of their postcolonial relation to Shakespeare, we can address a striking question they raise: what does the citation of Shakespeare enable these films to do on both the foreign and domestic fronts that *Rambo* (dir. Ted Kotcheff, 1984) or *Die Hard* cannot? I will argue that Shakespeare serves contradictory purposes. Shakespeare functions both as the signifier of a foreign, excessively violent villain or villains *and* as a native icon that legitimates their termination by American heroes and heroines.[7] On the one hand, he triangulates America's relation to the foreign. As icon of (Western) civilized values, Shakespeare authorizes an all-out attack both on the Third World and on immigrants (and ethnic and racial minorities) while at the same time distancing the U.S. from British imperialism. On the other hand, Shakespeare gives rise to a national fantasy of supplanting America's postcolonial status altogether. He is Americanized. Shakespeare's citation in films such as *Last Action Hero*, among others, registers a problem (if not a crisis) both in the legitimation of American imperialism (it's unmasked as racist terrorism rather than multicultural liberation) and in its means of cultural production (it's shown to be exhausted, parasitic on an earlier, colonial literary formation). This problem is focused acutely on the sequel, the site of American postcolonial anxiety about America's status as mere mimicry, in Homi Bhabha's (1984) terms, a sequel itself, a British Empire II, as it were.

Shakespeare enters the films I discuss less as a saving alternative to Hollywood mass culture, a reminder of a mythic WASP moment prior to multi-ethnic immigration when originality and innovation were supposedly still possible, than as a colonial icon the destruction (and partial reassimilation) of which saves a national fantasy about native artistic originality. Hollywood was of course largely the creation of Eastern European immigrants eager to forget their past and become "American" (Gabler 1988; Baxter 1976).[8] Whereas the earliest silent Shakespeare films to assimilate immigrants and to legitimate film generally could count on the audiences' familiarity with Shakespeare, these more recent films I discuss here were produced at a moment when Shakespeare as signifier of America's supposed multicultural universality was being eclipsed by a new signifier of what had actually been American cultural imperialism all along, the action hero.[9] By the late 1980s, entertainment had become, after aerospace technology, the second biggest export industry for the United States: the exportation of missiles converged with the exportation of action film spectaculars that displayed hard male American bodies, often under duress (Jeffords 1989).[10] The international distribution of the action hero was shadowed by the international distribution of its explicit parody: the Sylvester Stallone *Rambo* series, for example, was quickly followed by *Hot Shots!* (dir. Jim Abrahams, 1991) and *Hot Shots! Part Deux* (dir. Jim Abrahams, 1993).[11] Moreover, these newer action films (and their parodies and knock-offs) were made with multiple domestic and foreign markets in mind. A film such as *Last Action Hero* might be a box-office disaster in the United States but then recoup its production costs in sales on video and abroad.[12] And a film such as *Skyscraper* is recognized to be so bad during production that it is never even meant to be released in movie theaters, much less to an international market. Instead, several trailers at the beginning of the video try to increase the market for similar cheaply made action videos containing lots of gratuitous sex and violence.[13]

   In the context of a global market for made-in-America entertainment and weapons, Shakespeare the icon enables the articulation of a foreign critique of the racism underlying an American imperialistic multiculturalism. The Klingons call humans "racist" in *Star Trek VI*, and *The Naked Gun* displays its racism as it turns away from foreign leaders such as Castro and Kadafi toward American ethnic and racial minorities. The lone black protagonist, a cop named Nordberg, played bizarrely enough by O. J. Simpson, is subject to assault both from the villains and from Drebbin. Moreover, the villain and assassin-programmer, Vincent Ludwig (played by Ricardo Montalban, who performed, among many other roles, the Prospero-like Mr. Rourke in the 1970s television series *Fantasy Island*), is Hispanic. Similarly, Ludwig programs an African American man (played by the baseball star Reggie Jackson) to kill Queen Elizabeth II. And, *The Postman*, though ostensibly progressive in promoting racial equality, nevertheless kills off one partly African American character (who saves the Postman) and keeps another limited to the role of sidekick.

In the films under discussion, Shakespeare's citation registers a contradiction in a national fantasy about both the exporting of United States politics and culture and the immigration of foreigners (who can also cite Shakespeare). The fantasy is that the United States can resolve its own internal ambivalence about its colonial past as it projects that ambivalence onto countries it colonizes. Shakespeare's citation registers a lingering American postcolonial nostalgia for British colonialism. By yoking Shakespeare to the action picture, these films paradoxically recode American imperialism as a postcolonial cultural and political export: the United States brings a revolution to those it colonizes, and colonials cannot, in the logic of this fantasy, legitimately revolt in turn from the revolution.

These films register a problem in the means of cultural production through which a national fantasy is forged. Shakespeare isn't just terminated but rewritten as well. Though these films are ostensibly interested in serial killing, they are really interested in serial quoting. The villains in *Skyscraper* are serial quoters, and the film models itself on *Die Hard* and its two sequels; a "trailer" for the Schwarzenegger *Hamlet* is squeezed between the end of *Jack Slater III* and a screening of *Jack Slater IV* in *Last Action Hero*; *Star Trek VI* cites Shakespeare in serial fashion, departing from the typical one player-per-one-episode citations or adaptations in the *Star Trek* television series; and, like *Star Trek VI*, *The Naked Gun* is itself part of a sequel series. It's worth adding that the films enumerated at the beginning of this chapter, with the exceptions of *Independence Day* and *The Postman*, are the products of a number of directors and stars who often work in sequels. John McTiernan directed *Die Hard* (1988) and

Die Hard With a Vengeance (1995); the former was knocked off by Raymond Martino in *Skyscraper;* David Zucker directed a *Naked Gun* sequel, coproduced another, and worked with directors of other similarly generic parodies and their sequels such as *Airplane!* (dirs. David Zucker and Jim Abrahams, 1980) and *Hot Shots!;* and Nicholas Meyer directed *Star Trek II: The Wrath of Khan* (1982) and *The Voyage Home: Star Trek IV* (1986).[14]

The films I will examine implicitly or explicitly deconstruct a distinction between Shakespeare original and Hollywood sequel, but not by informing their audiences of what Shakespeareans know, namely, that Shakespeare wrote for a theater in which hack writing was the norm and that he wrote his own sequels (*Henry IV*, of course, has two parts; and *Henry VI*, has three) and prequels (the epilogue to *Henry V*). He also recycled characters such as Falstaff. Instead, these films call attention to a fantasized Shakespeare by underlining the way that the foreign, alternately coded as British and Third World, is itself an American construction, a projection that licenses its own self-cannibalizing mode of cultural production.

Though the Hollywood production of sequels and rip-offs is a product of cynical marketing, it is also of course limited by its redundancy: the typecasting of the same actors, the recycling of the same plots, the same car chase, sex, and gun play scenes, the same formulas for jokes, and so on may all produce a kind of reassuring familiarity but they may also easily produce a boring predictability not only for the audience but for the actors and directors as well. Serialization makes its demands felt crudely, leaving actors and directors little chance for autonomy or innovation.

The severe constraints serialization places on artistic autonomy and innovation are played out in the films under consideration here in terms of an embattled masculinity. As the editors of *Nationalisms and Sexualities* note in their introduction, "nationalism favors a distinctly homosocial form of male bonding. . . . Typically represented as a passionate brotherhood, the nation finds itself compelled to distinguish its 'proper' homosociality from more explicitly sexualized male-male relations, a compulsion that requires the identification, isolation, and containment of male homosexuality" (Parker et al. 1992, 6). The films I discuss in this chapter are no exception to the homosocial imperative of American nationalism, though the threat to masculinity comes less from homosexuality than from women.[15] The (male) hero of these films is typically feminized and infantilized (or otherwise threatened) by powerful women, who include ex-girlfriends, ex-wives, and bosses. In *The Naked Gun*, a woman mayor constantly berates the hero for his gross incompetence. Similarly, in *Last Action Hero,* Jack Slater's wife has left him; when she calls, he plays a tape of himself and props it next to the telephone receiver saying "yes," "uh, huh," and "whatever you say." (As it turns out, Slater gets the local grocery clerk to call him at the station and pretend to be his wife so that his fellow officers will think she still cares for him.) Slater's daughter establishes herself as *his* daughter by kicking an assailant in the balls and getting his gun. And in *Star Trek VI: The Undiscovered Country,* a Starfleet woman turns out to be a traitor. To be sure, *Skyscraper* does put at its center a heroine who flies a helicopter to transport businessmen around town and who eventually frees a number of people held hostage by a group of terrorists. Yet the casting of Anna Nicole Smith marks the heroine as grotesque. As we will see, Smith doesn't fit the romantic part physically. Plastic surgery has made her breasts larger than ever, and her sex scenes are awkwardly out of place, as if they were grafted onto the film from one of her *Playboy* softcore videos. *The Postman*'s ostensibly progressive politics allow women and young teens in the army and postal service, but Shakespeare-citing remains an exclusively adult male practice, and Costner's own antimilitaristic, "sensitive guy" post-man masculinity is, on the face of it, ridiculous (his outfit is a joke, and the only real action sequence is a shot of him on horseback grabbing a letter out of a little boy's hand). Costner's "post-man" is precisely that, wooden.

The films I will discuss are, for the most part, just plain bad. There is little redeeming about them. They bear no resemblance to the witty British film *Theatre of Blood,* (dir. Douglas Hickox, 1973). In that black comedy, there is a sense of poetic justice. An actor named Edward Lionheart (Vincent Price), who has pretended to commit suicide after years of bad notices, kills off his critics one by one and stages the murders as scenes from eight of Shakespeare's plays, citing them extensively and accurately as he does so. Each murder is designed to fit each victim. Furthermore, the audience is expected to be familiar with a wide range of Shakespeare's plays, including *Troilus and Cressida* and *Cymbeline*. The film also makes some in-jokes, casting actors who actually performed Shakespeare on stage and in film such as Diana Rigg, Michael Holdern, and Milo O'Shea in this black comedy about a bad Shakespeare actor.

In contrast, the films I discuss are distinctly American in exceeding any notion of "poetic" justice and in assuming that an audience won't know much Shakespeare, if any, or care about their ignorance. Shakespeare is usually misquoted when he is quoted at all. For the most part, these films were box-office flops, and were considerably worse, in my view, than a British film such as *Theatre of Blood*. I am interested in them not because of their formal complexity but because their very lack of it helps us think through what I call the infantilization of American mass culture. By infantilization, I mean not simply that these films appeal to an audience of young boys or of men who wish to remain "boy eternal." I mean rather that it is precisely in being bad "all the way," in excessively fulfilling the conventions of a genre, that they produce a critique of Shakespeare and American mass culture, a critique quite different, as we will see, from an avant-garde critique of realist, Hollywood cinema. However limited these films may be in aesthetic terms, they nevertheless raise broad questions both about the way Shakespeare is a symptom of the United States' postcolonial national unconscious and about the constraints of a serialized mode of cultural production on lowbrow filmmakers. In so doing, they implicitly invite a reconsideration of recent critiques of the notion of cultural imperialism (Wasko 1994), a point to which I will return at the close of this chapter.

Off Target: Ass-assinating Shakespeare

What is more surprising than the fact that Shakespeare should turn up in American films responding to post–Cold War international terrorist politics is the *way* he turns up. He is regularly misquoted or turned into a pastiche, and generally made up of a very limited number of plays: *Hamlet, Julius Caesar, Romeo and Juliet,* and *The Merchant of Venice*. In *Skyscraper,* for example, the villain, Mr. Fairfax (Charles

Huber), garbles his quotations. Prior to killing his partner Jacques, Fairfax conflates Hamlet with Juliet: "Alas, poor Jacques, I knew you well. Parting is such sweet sorrow." Fairfax cites a relatively obscure line from *Henry VI, Part One* when he first meets Carrie (Anna Nicole Smith) when taking a ride in her helicopter, a line she misidentifies:

FAIRFAX: A prettier pilot than I am accustomed to.

CARRIE: So, do you have a problem with women pilots?

FAIRFAX: When a world of men could not prevail with all their oratory yet have a woman's kindness overruled.

CARRIE: Henry the . . . Fourth!

FAIRFAX: Yeah! I feel in good hands already.

The line is actually spoken by Talbot before he meets the Countess of Auvergne (*Henry VI, Part One* [2.2.48-50]). Given the way the film sets up Anna Nicole Smith's character as a white- trash bimbo, it is perhaps surprising that Carrie nearly gets the quotation right. Perhaps she's dyslexic. (At least she doesn't pronounce the Roman numeral IV as if it were the capital letters "I" "V.") One could try to pursue the analogies between Carrie and the Countess of Auvergne and between Fairfax and Talbot (the film inverts their roles in the play such that Carrie defeats Fairfax rather than vice versa, as in Shakespeare's play). Yet the point seems rather to be that neither he nor most members of the average audience knows or cares that she has gotten the source wrong. This film's apparent assumption about its audience's indifference to Shakespeare is played out quite clearly when Fairfax meets up with another partner, Cranston, whom he plans to rip-off and kill. This time he adapts a line from *The Merchant of Venice*: "I am merely a man, and if you prick me, I do bleed." Cranston's reception underlines the lack of value the film assumes its audience places on Shakespeare: "Oh, Jesus. Are you still doing that Shakespeare crap? Can we get on with this?!" Shakespeare, not to put too fine a point on it, is shit.

Unsurprisingly, the villain who cites Shakespeare tends to get blown away. Fairfax may have an IQ of 175, but he is nevertheless psychotic, justly killed off, according to the film's logic. Citing Shakespeare and the villain's demise are even more closely linked in *Star Trek VI*. The film's climactic battle scene is punctuated by an orgy of quotations from *Henry V, Hamlet, The Merchant of Venice, Julius Caesar,* and *The Tempest,* cited, often incorrectly, by the Klingon General Chang (Christopher Plummer). When Chang realizes he will be destroyed, he says in English, having earlier said it in the Klingon language, "To be or not to be?"

The license granted to Shakespeare terminators is starkly revealed in *The Naked Gun,* which doesn't even bother to cite a line from Shakespeare directly. The mayor (Nancy Marchand) chastizes the rogue cop hero, Frank Drebbin, for having shot some actors performing *Julius Caesar:*

> DREBBIN: When I see five weirdos dressed in togas stabbing a guy in the middle of the park in full view of a hundred people, I shoot the bastards! That's my policy.
>
> MAYOR: That was the Shakespeare in the Park production of *Julius Caesar,* you moron! You killed five actors! Good ones!

The rogue cop who doesn't know Shakespeare, can't tell a theatrical performance from an actual murder, and can't tell the difference between good acting and bad acting is nevertheless licensed to kill. Similarly, in *Last Action Hero,* Hamlet is transformed into a contemporary action hero. Something may be rotten in the state of Denmark, the announcer says, but this "Hamlet's takin' out the trash." Hamlet's sword is quickly replaced by a machine gun and he ends up blowing up the castle after answering the play's most oft-cited question, "To be or not to be?" with a stoic, impassive, "Not to be." By reconceiving Hamlet as an "unfair Prince," *Last Action Hero* can reduce Olivier's film of *Hamlet* to a three-minute trailer.

Yet these films do not simply demonize Shakespeare in jingoistic, sexist fashion. If Shakespeare is shit, we might ask, why do these films bother to cite him at all? A partial answer is that these films are ambivalent: the genre is fractured by an American postcolonial identification with prerevolutionary colonial British culture. On the one hand, their postcolonial status makes Americans superior to the British: Americans have democracy and they don't. On the other, Americans remain culturally inferior: Shakespeare remains the measure of American culture. A long-standing anxiety about the worth of American culture vis-à-vis European culture reappears in these films.

This anxiety is registered partly in the way both the villain and the hero are contradictory figures. The villain, for example, is the revenger as well as the one on whom revenge is taken. As we have seen, Fairfax and Chang cite the same lines by Shylock. And Chang's citations of *Julius Caesar* make him both the assassinated (Caesar) and his avenger (Antony) rather than the assassin. (Similarly, he cites Prospero rather than Caliban.) The hero of *The Naked Gun* is also contradictory: rogue cop Frank Drebbin is the assassin of the assassins. His difference from other assassins is secured only by the fact that his killings (and general brutality) are accidental. When plotting Queen Elizabeth II's assassination, Vincent Ludwig (Ricardo Montalban) discusses the best kind of assassin with his fellow conspirator, Mr. Pahpshmir:

> LUDWIG: In all the world, who is the most effective assassin?
> PAHPSHMIR: Well, I think anyone who manages to conceal his identity as an assassin.
> LUDWIG: Yes, there's an even more ideal assassin, one who doesn't know he's an assassin. It seems to me anyone can be an assassin.

Ludwig trains his assassins to be perfect killing machines through "sensory induced hypnosis." In contrast, Drebbin is the accidental assassin. At the end of the film, he means only to stun Ludwig with bullets from his cufflinks, but Ludwig inadvertently falls over the railing to his death. (He is then run over by a bus, then by a steam roller, and, finally, by the University of Southern California marching band.) Nevertheless, even this distinction is partly compromised in terms of the ethnicities and eating habits of the heroes and the villains. Though the terrorists and assassins are all foreign and all the cops except for Nordberg (O. J. Simpson) are white, Drebbin masquerades at one point as an Italian opera singer, Enrico Palazzo, in order to protect the Queen. After he saves her, his co-partner is just about to identify him to the mayor when a spectator blurts out "It's Enrico Pallazo!" *Last Action Hero* similarly complicates a distinction between licensed and unlicensed terminators. As Hamlet, Schwarzenegger is himself a kind of terrorist. After Polonius says to him, "Stay thy hand, fair prince," Schwarzenegger responds, "Who says I'm fair?" and blasts away. Even the unironic *Postman* can't make Shakespeare a stable signifier of progressive values. General Bethelem, the film's competing messianic figure who leads a fascist group called the Klan, also cites Shakespeare.

In addition to representing heroes and villains as contradictory, these films more generally both mock and affirm English culture and politics. *The Naked Gun*, for example, repeatedly humiliates Queen Elizabeth II (Jeanette Charles), both as person and as icon. At a press conference about the Queen's impending visit to Los Angeles, Drebbin horrifies the mayor by saying: "As silly as the idea of having a Queen may be to us, as Americans we must be graceful." Moreover, Drebbin wears a radio microphone and inadvertently broadcasts the sound of himself urinating while the mayor finishes the press conference. He is eventually dismissed from the force when he tries to save the Queen from what he mistakenly thinks is an assassination attempt. (The Mayor has Ludwig present Queen Elizabeth a revolutionary war musket.) Drebbin jumps on top of her to protect her but, as the two skate across a long table, with him between her legs and with her legs up in the air, it looks as if they are having sexual intercourse. Here the film "fucks" with English culture, as it were. Nevertheless, Ludwig's assassination attempt is foiled (and "God save the Queen" is played when Queen Elizabeth arrives at a ballgame). A postcolonial nostalgia for the monarch(y) is inscribed here: you can kill Shakespeare(ans) and you can insult and humiliate the Queen, but you can't kill her.

An American ambivalence about Shakespeare is also registered in the way he is often partly reclaimed rather than terminated wholesale. *Last Action Hero* rewrites Hamlet as the assassin rather than destroying him (like Wiley Coyote in a *Roadrunner* cartoon that follows this trailer, he survives the apocalyptic destruction of Elsinore), and in *Star Trek VI*, Captain Kirk (William Shatner) reappropriates Shakespeare from the Klingons. Unlike the television series in which Shakespeare is always the province of the Federation, here Shakespeare is cited almost exclusively by the Klingons, who regard Shakespeare as one of their own. At a dinner party aboard the Starship Enterprise, Chancellor Gorkon cites Hamlet's "To be or not to be" soliloquy, toasting to "the undiscovered country, the future." After Mr. Spock (Leonard

Nimoy) identifies the quotation ("*Hamlet*. Act three, scene one") the Chancellor responds "You haven't experienced Shakespeare until you've read him in the original Klingon." At the very end of the film, however, after Kirk and his cohorts defeat another assassination attempt on the new Klingon Chancellor, Azetbur (Roseanne de Soto), daughter of the assassinated Chancellor Gorkon, Kirk cites the same line from Hamlet's "To be or not to be" soliloquy and salvages intergalactic peace:

> CHANCELLOR: What is the meaning of this?
>
> KIRK: It's about the future, madam Chancellor. Some people think the future means the end of history. Well, we haven't run out of history quite yet. Your father called the future "the undiscovered country." People can be very frightened of change.

Yet even this reclamation of Shakespeare betrays a further ambivalence. For Kirk's citation of the assassinated Chancellor's citation of Shakespeare secures peace, restores the daughter's faith in her assassinated father and Kirk's in his murdered son (both were advocates of peace). The film is thus an anti-*Hamlet*. *Star Trek VI* rewrites Shakespeare's tragedy as a comedy in which the cycle of revenge ends and in which relations between genders and generations are harmonized.

Perhaps the most extreme instance of American ambivalence about colonial culture is to be found in *Last Action Hero*. The film opens with what turns out to be *Jack Slater III*. This film-within-a-film reveals itself as such when it literally goes out of focus just as it is about to end. Danny, a young truant, is the only person watching it in the theater except for a sleeping drunk. He goes upstairs to tell Nick (Robert Prosky), the projectionist, to put the film back in focus. By the time Nick does so, however, *Jack Slater III* is over. Nick offers to let him see the next sequel before it officially opens and gives him a special ticket. Later the boy watches *Jack Slater IV,* and the ticket magically transports him into the world of the film.

Shakespeare makes his appearance in the school to which Danny returns late after watching *Jack Slater III*. Joan Plowright, Laurence Olivier's wife and a Shakespearean actress in her own right, is cast as the teacher. She uses Olivier's film to popularize *Hamlet* (1947) for her students (Hamlet was "the first action hero") and insults Olivier's move into advertising and mass-marketed movies, informing her students that they may recognize Olivier from his work in a Polaroid commercial or as Zeus in *Clash of the Titans* (dir. Desmond Davis, 1981). If Danny's Schwarzenegger fantasy Hamlet might be regarded as Hollywood's revenge against Shakespeare, the end of the film might even be read as Shakespeare's revenge. After the villain from *Jack Slater IV* escapes from the film to the "real" world, he accidentally releases Death, played by Sir Ian McKellen, from an unlikely screening of Ingmar Bergman's *The Seventh Seal* in an art house theater on Manhattan's 42nd Street. Death insults the truant Danny: "You are a very brave young man. Unfortunately, you're not very bright." And McKellen's extra-cinematic self-characterization as a gay Shakespearean effectively outs the homoeroticism and pedophilia of the action movie genre. (About a third of the way through the movie, Danny's mother and Slater's daughter drop out of the film for good, not to be replaced by any other women characters.)

Boob Jobs

Addressing this American ambivalence about Shakespeare and British colonial culture requires that we situate the Shakespeare citations in these films in relation to the way they cite other American films and genres. The contradictions displayed in these films in terms of the global, transnational circulation of American film do not produce a saving or coherent critique of American imperialism. Though most are easy enough to criticize for their conservative politics, what is compelling about these films is the way their criticism spills over from a coherent critique of the racism of American imperialism to a critique of the film industry and the films themselves. Shakespeare quotations and in-jokes about Shakespearean actors may be obscure or unrecognizable to many members of an American audience, but other kinds of citation are unmistakable to the average American moviegoer. In *Skyscraper,* for example, a scene in which Carrie hangs from the roof from a fire hose and eventually breaks through a glass window, then narrowly escapes being dragged out of the room by the weight of the hose, pointedly recalls, by its very length, the similar scene from *Die Hard*. Several trailers preceding *Skyscraper* are about similar overtly generic, cheaply made rip-off films. The comedy of *The Naked Gun* and *Last Action Hero* also comes from citing other films. In the former film there's a parody of the scene in James Bond films in which Q tells Bond about various weapons and gadgets he's perfected (in this version, Drebbin gets a pair of cufflinks that shoot stun bullets) as well as a parody of the film noir male voice-over. Similarly, in *Last Action Hero* a Sharon Stone lookalike stands outside the police station dressed as her character in *Basic Instinct*, and then the more advanced terminator of *Judgement Day: Terminator 2* walks out dressed as a cop. Later Sylvester Stallone appears in a cut-out poster for *The Terminator* in a video store when Danny tries to prove to Slater that he's really a character in a film.

Shakespeare citations occur, then, within a larger context of cinematic citation. This citation registers a self-reflexiveness in these films. Except for *Star Trek VI*, each film has a more or less overtly thematized metacinematic dimension: *The Naked Gun*'s[15] resolution is played out on a huge TV screen in the ballpark; video monitors in *Skyscraper* screen shootouts for the villain; and *Last Action Hero* is a movie-within-a-movie. The double citation of Shakespeare and Hollywood film is part of a metacinematic critique of serialization focusing on stardom, typecasting, narrative/generic/metacinematic clichés, and the apparent displacement of theaters by home video. These films register a marked tendency in film production of the late 1980s and early 1990s. As Janet Wasko comments, "The other unmistakable trend [in addition to the productions that travel well internationally] is the proliferation of remakes and sequels of successful films. For instance, the list of sequels released during the summer of 1990 seemed endless. Several others were scheduled for release the same year" (1994, 237). This trend is itself a product of several developments in the late 1980s: a national merger of film with multimedia, licensing of merchandise, and product placement tie-ins; the acquisition of movie theaters by the major studios, ending a prior separation between production and exhibition; and the use of market testing before a film went into production.

These films register a rather deliberate, excessive citation of Shakespeare and of other American films. In *Star Trek VI*, Shakespeare becomes a serial signifier. Whereas Shakespeare was reworked into the plot in episodes of *Star Trek*, *Star Trek: The Next Generation* turned him into a signifier of Captain Picard's cultivation and Lieutenant Data's humanity, in some cases simply using a phrase from a play as an episode title. *Star Trek VI* cites this citation of Shakespeare the signifier. The battle at the end of the film consists of shots of Chang at the helm of his Klingon warship citing lines from Shakespeare's *Henry V, Hamlet, The Merchant of Venice, The Tempest,* and *Julius Caesar* intercut with shots of the Enterprise sustaining more and more damage and of those plotting to assassinate the new Klingon Chancellor:

> I can see you, Kirk. Can you see me? Now be honest, warrior to warrior. You do prefer it this way, as it is meant to be. No peace in our time. Once more unto the breach, dear friends. *Tak Pah, Tak Beh?* ["To be not or not to be?" in the Klingon language] Tickle us, do we not laugh? Prick us, do we not bleed? Wrong us, shall we not revenge?

After the Starship Excalibur arrives on the scene, Chang adds:

> Ah, the game's afoot, huh? Our revels now are ended, Kirk. Cry 'havoc!' and let slip the dogs of war. I am constant as the northern star. To be or not to be?

Is this a parody or not? Hard to say. A generic undecidability arises because the excessive number of citations of a film such as *Star Trek VI* not only deconstructs the distinction between the original and the (parodic) sequel but also undermines the capacity of the original or sequel to open up a controlling critical distance from the film's narrative and genre.

Far from confirming a distinction between original action picture and parody, these films show how parody is already built into the original. *Die Hard,* for example, was itself a parody of the Sylvester Stallone and Schwarzenegger action picture, a send-up of the cowboy myth underwriting the action hero. Shakespeare's termination in the films of these action directors can be understood in terms of a breakdown of a distinction Frederic Jameson (1996) has drawn between pastiche and parody.[16] Jameson sees a decline from modern parody, which has some critical force, to postmodern pastiche, which does not.[17] In the films I am considering, however, the stability of the term "parody" has itself been undermined because the "original" parodies itself. Drebbin's inability to distinguish between an assassination and its simulation is a comic version of a high theory point, as if Jean Baudrillard were the film's academic consultant. This is not to say that these films do not have a critical function at all; it is to say that the critical function is itself unstable, off-target. Indeed, the sheer inanity at the base of so much in these films might be read as the way they can't entirely fail, even at failing. Insofar as they critique the way critique can't function in popular film but always misfires, they go wrong, since they thereby have paradoxically succeeded at critique.

One register of this unstable critical function is the way the metacinematic dimension works: as they reflect on the genre of which they are a part and so distance themselves from it, these films criticize not only the film industry's production of generic films but the films themselves, particularly their stars. The *Die Hard* scene in *Skyscraper* offers a kind of critique of Hollywood by its very length. The film is all about excess, an excess that is critical, though not parodic, of other Hollywood/HBO cable films. Carrie wants to get big, literally. She and her boyfriend fight at the beginning of the film because he doesn't want to get her pregnant. (However, she doesn't seem particularly tall in this film, as opposed to her appearance in *The Naked Gun, Thirty-three-and-a-third: The Final Insult*.) The length of the *Die Hard* scene lends itself to an allegorical reading of Smith's relation to the film industry. Carrie takes forever to get into the building as a man shoots at her from the roof. The very obviousness of the citation invites one to read the scene metacinematically: Smith is trying to break through the "glass ceiling" of the industry when it comes to blonde "babes." She wants to crack out of being typecast as a big-breasted bimbo.

The Naked Gun also offers a metacinematic critique of its own happy ending. As Randy Newman's "I Love LA" plays on the film's soundtrack, strife between the ballplayers and between the fans stops as they collectively pause to watch Drebbin declare his love for Jane projected on the stadium screen. But a kind of strife continues, albeit in parodic fashion, as Nordberg, shot repeatedly and then hospitalized at the beginning of the film, is flung from his wheelchair after Drebbin accidentally pushes him down a flight of steps. This film rewrites the pastoral sport of baseball as "don't take me out at the ballgame."

One effect of this self-reflexiveness is a critique of serialization as homogenization. *Last Action Hero,* the most overtly self-reflexive of the films I discuss here, builds serialization into its narrative and produces the most overt critique of Hollywood. After Slater returns to the film *Jack Slater IV,* he enters his captain's office and makes a critique of the film's conventionality, telling his captain that they are all puppets: "Put a sock in it. I'm not deaf. You know why you're shouting? It's in the script. You're the comic relief. You know what else? I'm the hero. So shut up! You see, Hollywood is writing our lives. And you know something? I don't want to shout anymore and to blow up buildings." In the dilapidated theater in which *Jack Slater III* is screened, the film registers the closing of movie theaters in the 1980s (see Wasko 1994, 174). That decade marked the end of a divorce between film production and exhibition as the major studios bought up chains of theaters and converted many to cineplexes in order to have greater control over distribution than cable or video allowed. This meant closing a fifth of the then-active theaters (Wasko 1994, 177-78). A critique of the constraints of typecasting is also implied when Danny sees the Sylvester Stallone cut-out advertisement as Jack Slater in the video store. "That's impossible!" he remarks. While a mark of Schwarzenegger's star status is that only he can play his roles, a mark of Schwarzenegger's limitations is precisely that he can only play his action-picture role.

Yet far from insulting Hollywood from some high-minded, high culture position, these films insult themselves as well. The criticism focuses on the characters, even the films' stars. In *Skyscraper,* the heroine is ironized by Smith's inability to transcend her own previous typecasting. Her earlier crossover effort in *The Hudsucker Proxy* (dir. Ethan Cohen, 1993) was a bit part as a blonde bimbo, and she played the same kind of action heroine the year before in *To the Limit* (dir. Raymond Martino, 1994). There's a parodic excessiveness about Carrie. We see a lengthy close-up of her hand on the control stick of the helicopter at the beginning of the film, for example, but the phallus is less the stick than it is her incredibly long fingernails (see figure 3.2). And then there is her body. Though she hadn't yet gained the

Figure 3.2: Anna Nicole Smith takes control in Raymond Martino's *Skyscraper.*

amount of weight that entirely subverted the *Playboy* ideal, Smith's lips and initially quite ample breasts were enlarged before this film was shot. Her porn star body and her action heroine character don't cohere. It is tempting to read Smith's white-trash "excexiness" as an instance of what Laura Kipnis (1996) calls the pornographic grotesque body, part of a critique of class. Her large breast size recalls in transgendered fashion the oversized body of Rambo. But as "Rambimbo," Smith plays a very traditionally feminine character whose only "masculine" behavior is working as a pilot.

Smith is thus the opposite of her contemporary ex-*Playboy* star Pamela Lee Anderson, who, through a series of plastic surgery operations on her face, breasts, and thighs, became more and more the *Playboy* ideal and who did manage to crossover successfully on the television series *Baywatch* and, less successfully, in her movies *Naked Souls* (dir. Lyndon Chubbock, 1995) and *Barbwire* (dir. David Hogan, 1996). In the latter film, Anderson manages to integrate softcore displays of her naked body with her "don't call me babe" character. Anderson may do nude scenes, the film implies, but she's no bimbo. By contrast, Smith hasn't been able to cross over, not even from *Playboy* softcore video to direct from cable to video. She still does the softcore porn in the same *Playboy*-style way. There are two sex sequences, neither of which is at all integrated into the plot of the movie; rather, they're prompted by the weak narrative excuse of fantasy flashbacks. Moreover, they look like scenes from softcore videos, not like sex scenes in mainstream movies; that is, the romantic scenes don't work because her breasts get in the way. Smith's acting talents are further insulted by the fact that Carrie has pictures of Marilyn Monroe all over her apartment. Smith is, of course, no Monroe.

In *The Naked Gun,* Drebbin is similarly insulted. He's constantly sexually humiliated by being put in the woman's position. In this comedy, there's no room for a sensitive, feminized man. Instead, the comedy relies on the audience's awareness that he has crossed generic codes for gender. When Drebbin unexpectedly finds Jane cooking at his house, for example, he asks her, "You mind if I slip into something a little more comfortable" (and comes out wearing a suit and tie). When Jane says to him, "I'm a very nice woman," he replies "So am I." After the credits, we learn that Drebbin's girlfriend has left him for another man. "[The new boyfriend]'s an Olympic gymnast and it's the best sex he's ever had" Drebbin's partner Ed Hocken (George Kennedy) tells him. Later Drebbin declares, "Having your nuts bit off, that's the way I want to go," and at one point he accidentally detaches a penis from a statue while escaping a hotel room.

In *Last Action Hero,* both the character Jack Slater and the actor Arnold Schwarzenegger are insulted. Slater's final critique of Hollywood is abruptly cut off, as if the film knew it would fall on deaf ears. Before he can finish his consciousness-raised rant, Slater gets drowned out as the camera cuts back to the movie theater in which Danny and Nick are watching, and then Nick nostalgically tells him about an earlier time of entertainment prior even to cinema when he went to see Buffalo Bill and got backstage to meet Sitting Bull. (Nick had explained earlier that Houdini gave him the ticket that allows Danny to enter the film world of *Jack Slater IV.*)

Last Action Hero is in some ways about the revenge of the generic character on the typecast actor who plays him. After the villain Benedict (Charles Dana) from *Jack Slater IV* brings the villain Ripper (Tom Noonan) from *Jack Slater III* into the real world, he explains to him that by killing the actor playing Slater he can be free: he will no longer have to play the same role over and over again in *Jack Slater III.* And Schwarzenegger the actor is insulted by his wife, Maria Shriver, who plays herself. As they approach reporters at the premiere of *Jack Slater IV,* she tells him not to plug his restaurant chain Planet Hollywood. He agrees not to but goes ahead and does it anyway. She then lambasts him, telling him, "You embarrass me, you low forehead. It's humiliating." Similarly, when character and actor meet up at the premiere, Slater curses Schwarzenegger: "You've caused me nothing but pain."

Even the high-minded *Postman,* largely a testament to Kevin Costner's egomania, insults Costner's acting abilities. In this post-western, Costner plays a former actor turned drifter nicknamed "Shakespeare" (because he used to perform Shakespeare) who puts on the uniform of a dead postman and leads a group of civilians to resist the film's villain, a Hitler-like figure named General Bethelem (Will Patton). Near the beginning of the film, "Shakespeare" stages a one-man Shakespeare show, citing snippets from the end of *Macbeth,* with his "ass" (a mule) as his partner, dressed as Birnam Wood. (The ass then holds a sword in his mouth while Costner engages him in combat.) The audience is largely made up of children, who laugh at the appropriate points. After the performance, a man from the audience who was an actor tells "Shakespeare" that his acting stinks. (Costner and a woman from the audience then disagree with him.)

A parodic self-reflexiveness doesn't save these films, then; there is not much in them that could be considered politically or formally progressive. One might even want to distinguish among them in terms of gender, reading gender difference itself as a symptom of male postcolonial anxiety about the male author's secondariness. A hyper-male body such as Schwarzenegger's could be read as a defense against the male body's possible feminization, a defense that is parodied in Drebbin's characterization. In this reading, the female body would function as inescapable sex, the male body as action hero, such that the female body becomes the balloon of bile, the bouncing bed of ambivalence. A specifically male post-colonial (castration) anxiety would be assuaged by differentiating a male excessiveness from a female one, hard muscle as excess flesh from soft fat as excess flesh.[18] Thus, Smith remains completely trapped in her roles, a bimbo celebrity outcast, while Schwarzenegger appears to have a thing called "him" beyond his roles that enables him to wield them like a hero.

Far from securing such differences, however, the films suggest their breakdown, notably by shared eating disorders. A kind of radical anorexia prevails in these films. Anna Nicole Smith may have gained weight for *Skyscraper,* but she did so offscreen; in *Last Action Hero* no food is even present; the Enterprise crew is grossed out by Klingon eating habits at the dinner party in *Star Trek VI* and don't partake of the Klingon dishes; in *The Postman,* "Shakespeare" gives away his food (containing parts of his mule) to another conscript and doesn't eat; and in *The Naked Gun,* neither Ludwig nor Drebbin manage to ingest. Ludwig bites down on a hotdog and discovers a finger with a ring on it. He spits it out in disgust. Drebbin too has trouble getting anything down. At one point, he cleans out his refrigerator full of rotten leftovers, pouring out spoiled milk in his kitchen sink as two radio announcers excitedly tell of the Queen's visit. And at a reception for the Queen, we see a cake with the Queen's face on it cut up and served for dessert. But Drebbin does not actually eat the piece he is served (nor does anyone else). When his girlfriend Jane (Priscilla Presley) cooks dinner for him, she asks "How was your meat?" and sucks his finger, suggesting that his meat is not only what he's eaten but what she will eat (metaphorically).

The eating disorders (of both genders) in these films, particularly the failed cannibalism of *The Naked Gun,* reveal the extent to which Shakespeare cannot be fully incorporated in American popular culture. Shakespeare does not occupy the position of what Freud (1913) called the primal father, whose murder and subsequent cannibalization would introduce gender difference along national lines, producing a band of brothers. Shakespeare doesn't go down well precisely because he is foreign, a step-primal-father, so to speak, with Americans as his stepchildren (perhaps bastards at best, with Shakespeare as the sperm donor). Shakespeare remains encrypted and incorporated and thus unmourned in American popular culture, a point to which I will return in the conclusion.[19]

A kind of anorexic refusal to cannibalize Shakespeare and English culture may be read as a defense against the prevailing cultural cannibalism implied by the sequel. Caught between the twin fears of being a mimicry of England (the true original) and being bound to a mode of cultural production that can only produce mimicry, these films can't produce in any coherent fashion either a national fantasy of American multiculturalism or a critique of that fantasy. I find it striking that *Skyscraper,* the least self-reflexive film of the bunch, is arguably the most progressive. The actors are almost all clearly American. The accents of the terrorists, with one exception, are all obviously fake (whereas Alan Rickman affects a very convincing German accent in *Die Hard*). Furthermore, the villains are not thieves mistaken for political terrorists as in *Die Hard;* in this case, they *are* political terrorists, members of the People's Democratic Liberation Army (its national origins are unclear). This group is radical, perhaps even American, precisely because it is democratic.

The most self-reflexive film, *Last Action Hero,* is arguably the most conservative. It displays a nostalgia for a kind of native colonialism. Houdini figures a nonthreatening construction for the immigrant as entertainer (perhaps of Arnold himself), and Buffalo Bill and Sitting Bull figure a similar view of American Westward expansion as pacifying entertainment. The film's last shot is of Schwarzenegger driving off into the sunset, waving, establishing the rogue cop action hero as the modern-day heir of the cowboy. The cowboy hero mocked by Bruce Willis's character in *Die Hard* returns here with a vengeance. Moreover, self-reflexiveness fails to get *Last Action Hero* anywhere in terms of narrative or generic complexity. Ironically, *Last Action Hero* sinks back into the film-within-the-film it initially tries to rise out of, merely recycling the plot of *Jack Slater III,* with Slater's son being replaced by Danny, the only difference being that Danny is saved whereas Slater's son had died in *Jack Slater III.*

In this nostalgia for a native myth of the hero as loner cowboy (or post-western postman), a myth that disavows the American imperialism it enables, we can perhaps best understand why Shakespeare should be cited so ambivalently in these films. In the face of the exhaustion of American genres such as the Western, film noir, the gangster picture, and the rogue cop or action picture, the actor and director of *Last Action Hero* wish to return to an even earlier moment, a moment prior to Houdini, prior to the action picture, the moment of (Olivier performing) Shakespeare's *Hamlet*. But Shakespeare doesn't provide any real critical leverage any more than any of the citations of American films do. As we saw earlier, Olivier is insulted by Plowright for making television commercials and bad Hollywood fantasy films. And although Schwarzenegger might appear to trump Olivier by rewriting *Hamlet* in contemporary terms, perhaps the film's biggest insult to Schwarzenegger lies in showing that he can't play Hamlet straight. His parodic update depends precisely on a distance between his character type and Shakespeare's tragic hero. Schwarzenegger couldn't do Shakespeare if he wanted to, not unless he could turn *Hamlet* into an action picture. He can only do Hamlet, that is, as Jack Slater (his line to Claudius, "big mistake," quotes a line he gives to the villain in *Jack Slater III,* later twice quoted by Danny).

The same is true of the other films. The closest Leslie Nielsen has ever gotten to serious Shakespeare acting is in the spin-off of *The Tempest, Forbidden Planet* (dir. Fred McLeod Wilcox, 1956), a film in which he played straight the very character type he parodies in *The Naked Gun* and its sequels. And the closest William Shatner or Leonard Nimoy have ever come to Shakespeare on the screen is in a *Star Trek* episode or movie.[20] (The obvious exception from later *Star Trek* films, Patrick Stewart, is of course British.) Shakespeare can't simply be terminated by Americans, then, because he functions not just as a signifier of foreign evil but as an ideal American actors and directors can never reach. They can't do Shakespeare the way it is supposed to be done.

This failure is most overt in *The Postman.* Though fully identified with Shakespeare as a signifier of high culture and human dignity in a non-ironic way, *The Postman* nevertheless presents us with a leading actor who can't do Shakespeare straight even when he wants to do so. Kevin Costner had the freedom to star in and direct the film, and he had a large budget to boot. Yet his creative freedom only underlines his failure as an actor, particularly as an actor of Shakespeare. The first scene in which "Shakespeare" does part of *Macbeth* is not a burlesque of Shakespeare, though it is light-hearted, and, as we have seen, Costner's character defends his acting abilities when challenged by a man in the audience. Similarly, in a later scene, General Bethelem's troops applaud the general and laugh at "Shakespeare" each time the two trade quotations (from Henry V, Marc Antony, and Hamlet) until Bethelem interrupts his troops and says, "No, no. He's pretty good." Yet when the film signals its conclusion through the Postman's citation of the same lines from *Henry V* Bethelem cited earlier ("Once more unto the breech, dear friends . . ."), as if "Shakespeare" were now claiming all of Shakespeare as his own, Costner betrays his lack of confidence in his own acting, giving the lines in a voice-over and cutting away from himself to his miraculously appearing cavalry. Shakespeare becomes, inevitably it would appear, a symptom of American abjection, part of L. A. ('s) Shakespeare Story.

Slick Willy II, or The Post-Shakespeare Man

We can appreciate more fully the political complexity of Shakespeare's status in the 1990s action-film genre as a symptom of U.S. postcolonial anxiety about the secondary, sequel status of American popular culture by turning to *Independence Day* and looking more closely at *The Postman*. The former film extensively cites earlier films from the genre but does not cite Shakespeare literally, while the latter does the reverse. The two films thus frame the limits of the 1990s conjunction of Shakespeare and the serial: in one case, hyperserialization is thematized in the literal absence of Shakespeare citations; in the other, hypercitation of Shakespeare is thematized in the context of a post-Western, an attempt to move beyond the sequel or serial altogether.[21]

Independence Day knowingly recycles and cites a host of science-fiction films and television programs from the 1950s to the 1990s (with their sexism fully intact), including *E. T., The Day the Earth Stood Still, Close Encounters of the Third Kind, The X-Files,* and *The War of the Worlds.* The President of the United States (Bill Pullman) rallies his young, green troops to do final battle with invading aliens on July 4 and invites them to celebrate all future Independence Days as a universal rather than a strictly American holiday. Though this speech faintly recalls Henry V's St. Crispian's Day speech, the interesting thing is that Shakespeare is not literally cited in this film at all. Why, we might ask, would the film want to allude to Shakespeare and yet not cite him explicitly? In my view, the film's imperialistic ambition, its construction of the (still white male) President as a former combat pilot who leads his (multiracial but still all male) troops into battle, and its epic register inevitably call up Shakespeare's imperial, Anglo-Saxon warrior king, Henry V, and perhaps Malcolm as well. (Like Shakespeare's heroes, the President keeps his distance from women. Though married from the start, the President sees his wife only when she is on her death bed, and other major male characters are separated [physically or by divorce] from their female counterparts, who wait passively to be saved by them for most of the film.) The pressure Shakespeare exerts here may in part be due to a deepening cynicism about the Presidency and the splitting of the President in several popular films that followed *Independence Day* into two types: some cast him as an action hero (*Air Force One*, dir. Wolfgang Petersen, 1997), and others as a corrupt man (*Absolute Power*, dir. Clint Eastwood, 1996; the more moderate *Murder at 1600*, dir. Dwight H. Little, 1996; and *Wag the Dog*, dir. Barry Levinson, 1998, in which the guilty president's face never appears on screen).[22] Henry V, as Americanized in films such as *Renaissance Man* (dir. Penny Marshall, 1994) would thus function to rehabilitate the otherwise tarnished image of the President as villain/conspirator. Yet Shakespeare cannot explicitly appear in *Independence Day* because the film paradoxically legitimates the universalization of a post-apocalyptic America as leader of the (free?) world through an anti-imperialistic rhetoric of republicanism (after all, it's the aliens who are doing the invading and who refuse to agree to a truce, not citizens of the United States). The President clearly cannot overtly align himself with a (Shakespearean) king and remain a legitimate leader of a democratic (now transnational?) republic as opposed to a multicultural fascist state. (The one President in recent memory to create [symbolically] what contemporaries called an "imperial Presidency," Richard Nixon, was ridiculed for his tasteless sense of style and his megalomania.)

Based on the 1985 David Brin novel, Kevin Costner's *The Postman* (set in 2013 after a nuclear winter) is in many respects the inversion of *Independence Day,* fully thematizing Shakespeare citation and defining itself as a post-Western blockbuster rather than as a sequel (except for brief citations from *Universal Soldier* [dir. Roland Emmerich, 1992]; *The Sound of Music* [dir. Robert Wise, 1965]; and *She Wore a Yellow Ribbon* [dir. John Ford, 1949, starring John Wayne], a frame of which morphs into a frame of *The Postman;* there are no quotations from other films). *The Postman's* politics are also the reverse of *Independence Day's.* In the liberal *Postman,* which takes a jab at Emmerich's earlier post-apocalyptic *Universal Soldier,* the civilians are integrated racially, and women have equal rights (the cavalry at the end of the film, for example, is composed "mostly of women"). Bethelem's army, in contrast, admits only "ethnically pure" men, and women do factory work. In a new variation of what Amy Kaplan (1990) calls the American "romancing of empire," *The Postman* wants to be post "man," transcending via Shakespeare the sexism and racism that typically marked the John Wayne cowboy hero of the Western.

Yet the wannabe progressive politics of *The Postman* are compromised by the film's identification with British imperial culture, an identification that enables the legitimation of an American imperialism misrecognized as democracy. This misrecognition takes the form of a translation of Shakespeare into American terms. When asked by a fellow conscript what Macbeth's line about dying "with harness on our back" (5.5. 50) means, "Shakespeare" answers with New Hampshire's motto, "Live free or die." Similarly, the Postman's identification with Henry V is made parallel with his belief in "the United States," a belief that enables him to defeat Bethelem in single combat. The film's progressive political ambitions are premised, however, on an all too familiar U.S. imperialism that is at once geographic and cultural and of which the translation of Shakespeare is only the most glaringly obvious symptom: a postnuclear world is equated with the United States (only once does a character ask about Europe) and with American cinema, and the film assumes that American film is inherently populist. Even *The Sound of Music,* preceded by close-ups of the film projector and preferred by Bethelem's Nazi-like troops, appears to be evidence of what is actually their antifascist sentiments (since the film is anti-Hitler). Hence they violently reject *Universal Soldier,* a film one would assume they would prefer. *The Postman* fails to be post "man" or post-Western, however. Indeed, its attempt to transmute the Western only returns the film more securely to its origins: the invocation of Shakespeare calls up the Postman's forebear, the itinerant, drunken actor who performs part of Hamlet's "To be or not be" soliloquy in John Ford's *My Darling Clementine* (1946).[23] Moreover, the film's imperial unconscious is marked by the adjective "restored" (rather than "reconstructed") in the Restored United States of America, written on the American flag, this despite a reference in the film to a second civil war. There is no mention of the U.S. Constitution or the Declaration of Independence in this film, and the President is actually a fictitious character invented by the Postman. Restoration, indeed. In contrast to the high-tech postnuclear capacities of the U.S. in *Independence Day*, *The Postman* projects an empire of mail routes; it celebrates a low-tech New Age post-apocalyptic future in which "things are getting better" for dispersed microcommunities connected by an archaic mail system (somehow electricity exists for film projectors and ham radios, but not for television sets or telephones).

If Shakespeare's literal absence in *Independence Day* marks the point at which a national fantasy of multicultural fascism cannot (yet?) be celebrated as such, Shakespeare's presence in *The Postman* marks the collapse of a New Age fantasy of a postpatriarchal white-guy, liberal multiculturalism. In *The Postman*, women are predictably limited to traditional roles (Abby, the woman who saves the Postman from execution, falls back into the traditional role of bearer of his child; similarly, the Postman's daughter, who is also the narrator and historian of his life story, is displaced at the end of the film by a statue of the Postman on horseback about to take a letter from a little boy). More surprisingly, "Shakespeare" has to claim membership in the Klan in order to defeat Bethelem, before going on to relegislate the Klan's basic commandments. (A similar blurring of the distinction between Bethelem and "Shakespeare" is signaled when Bethelem's order to burn "Shakespeare's" copy of Shakespeare's plays is alluded to first at the moment Costner's character burns a letter to keep warm and later when he forges a letter from the fictitious President ordering the young postmen [and women] to disband and burn their uniforms.)[24] Like *Independence Day*, *The Postman* founders on a contradictory national fantasy of an American imperial republic.

It's a Bomb!

Recent debates over U.S. cultural imperialism have divided those who think that imperialism works as a one-way, "shove it down their throats" exportation of a Disneyfied cultural politics and those who think of it as a two-way process, with active, sometimes transgressive receptions on the colonized side (Tracey 1985; Sepstrup 1989; Roach 1990; Kaplan 1990; Kaplan and Pease 1993; Wasko 1994). In having analyzed a series of mainstream films with an American ambivalence about both Shakespeare and their own status as Hollywood films, I want to consider the possibility of another way of thinking about self-reflexive critique of U.S. cultural imperialism, what might be called the box-office bomb. I am maintaining that the films' critical interest lies in the way they bomb rather than in the way they might encrypt a secretly coded critique to be discovered by Shakespeareans who happen to be interested in popular culture.

If these films are not *Theatre of Blood,* they're also not avant-garde, anti-American critiques such as Gus Van Sant's *My Own Private Idaho* (1991) or Jean Luc-Godard's *King Lear* (1989). While these films may have a more clearly thought out critique of American myths of the cowboy and the gangster, they nevertheless face the same problems as do films such as *Last Action Hero.* In its own way, *My Own Private Idaho* terminates Shakespeare as well. Van Sant harnesses Shakespeare to a critique of class in contemporary urban life (Burt 1993; Wiseman 1997), rewriting *Henry V* and both parts of *Henry IV* as stories of gay hustling. Yet he also separates Shakespeare from the main character, Mike Waters (River Phoenix), such that the film's critique does not in fact rely on Shakespeare at all. Moreover, the film's use of Shakespeare is so unmarked that most viewers who see the film don't even realize that Shakespeare is being rewritten at all.

A similar problem exists in Godard's *King Lear.* The film attacks Hollywood, particularly the Cannon Group formed by the Israeli Menahem Golan and Yoram Globus who funded the film, by demonstrating the impossibility of a sequel to Shakespeare (as well as to itself). Godard's *Lear* begins and ends twice. For Godard, there are only approaches, attempts at doing Shakespeare's play on film. Shakespeare can't be redone. In Godard's *Lear,* Hollywood's destruction of European culture is figured by American gangsters' invasion of Las Vegas. Yet this critique was also made in an inverted form by an American director of a sequel series. Francis Ford Coppola used *King Lear* as a source for *The Godfather III* (1990), casting his daughter Sofia in a Cordelia-like part (Cowie 1994, 235-36 and 240; Breskin 1992, 32).[25]

If criticism of American cultural imperialism can't be salvaged in avant-garde films, it can't be salvaged in films such as *Last Action Hero*, as I suggested earlier, in terms of their relative self-consciousness. The less self-reflexive films are not necessarily more interesting or more progressive than their opposites. To be sure, one can place these films along an axis of the more or less conservative. But this would be somewhat misleading. For what is particularly interesting about these films is the way their criticism is always off-target. In *Skyscraper,* Carrie breaks through the glass side of the building rather than through the "glass ceiling." In *The Naked Gun,* Drebbin's killings and brutality are always accidental. *The Postman* simply fails to deliver, as it were. Perhaps the most interesting example of the off-target critique is the line "It's a bomb," in *Last Action Hero*. Schwarzenegger delivers it as he runs out of a house that then blows up. Is this line an intentionally self-reflexive criticism of the film? Or was its appropria-tion by reviewers as a description of the film their own witticism? Rather than try to decide these questions, I want to suggest that they are the wrong questions to ask, since they can't rightly be answered in terms of a straightforward opposition between intelligence and stupid-ity. In my view, films such as *Last Action Hero* might be considered in terms of a different opposition, namely, smart bombs and dum(b)-dum(b) bombs. In terms of critical intelligence, these films lag behind the weaponry that they are exported alongside. Their explosiveness is paradoxically a function of their knowledge that, unlike the truly smart bomb, they'll never hit their target.

CHAPTER FOUR

When Our Lips Synch Together:
The Transvestite Voice,
the Virtuoso, Speed,
and Pumped-Up Volume in
Some <u>Over</u>-heard Shakespeares

Bi Any Other Word: Strictly Balls Room?

In the spectacular, Las Vegas–style Capulet ball sequence in Baz Luhrmann's *William Shakespeare's Romeo and Juliet* (1996), a bearded Mercutio, played by black actor Harold Perrineau, is the "very pink of courtesy," performing in full drag on a staircase in front of a huge painting of the Virgin Mary and baby Jesus, surrounded by six male dancers (who flash their star-crossed buns to the camera) and flanked by two male go-go dancers. Shot as if he's in an MTV music video sequence in quickly paced zooms, zips, and pans, Mercutio wears a matching sequined cape, necklace, bodice, and miniskirt with exposed garters, stockings, and panties; white, long-sleeved, satin gloves; pumps; false eyelashes; heavy mascara and eyeshadow; bright red lipstick; and a large white fright wig. While dancing a showgirl number complete with above-the-head alternating leg kicks, Mercutio lip-synchs a pumping, Latin disco song entitled "Young Hearts Run Free" (sung by Kym Mazelle) and, extending his tongue at certain moments, makes a striptease-like address to the camera as well as to Romeo. We also see Juliet's father give his own drag performance at the party, dressed apparently as a garishly made-up Bacchus, singing

"Amore" in a red sequined toga that looks like a dress and miming Mercutio as he hikes his toga above his panties and gives his own leg kicks. Old Capulet's performance is all the more queer given its dated sense of romantic music and that he covers a male voice, Tony Bennet's, rather than a female voice. Some viewers may recall that the actor playing Tybalt, John Leguizamo, played a drag queen two years before in *To Wong Foo, Thanks for Everything Julie Newmar* (dir. Beeban Kidron, 1994).[1]

Luhrmann's film can be allegorized in relation to feminist and queer readings of the play and to earlier film versions, but what is of interest here is less the way the film produces a gay or bisexual reading of Mercutio in particular and of the play in general than the way it produces a certain paradox, one, as we shall see shortly, in which the nonsynchronization of sound and narrative is central. Even as the transvestism of the Capulet ball exceeds the text as an unwarranted interpolation, it is a consequence of Romeo's diminished capacity, his drug-induced hallucination. Before the ball, Romeo meets Mercutio at a sex theme park (neon signs flash "Mistress Quickly" and "girls") and Mercutio gives Romeo the House drug of choice, Ecstasy. Mercutio's "I see Queen Mab hath been with you" is code for drug taking: Queen Mab is the hallucinogenic drug personified.[2]

The paradoxical way the scene exceeds the original even as it is also a diminishment of its poetry registers the film's reversal of the usual account of stardom and transvestism. Whereas stardom is usually conceived as freedom from the pressures of social conformism (bisexuality is acceptable in celebrities, but not in noncelebrities, for example), here stardom is conceived of as conformist: to become a star, one must subordinate one's character to one's pre-assigned role, to the rules and norms already governing performance.[3] The film is less an account of the play than it is of Romeo and Juliet's mediatization, their legacy as star lovers of Western culture. Mercutio may opt for divadom but he really has nowhere to go, just as Romeo and Juliet are already bound to their roles and their families from the start, a point underlined by the frequent intercutting of Romeo and Juliet in the tomb at earlier moments in the film.

Luhrmann's account of stardom as conformist in *William Shake-speare's Romeo and Juliet* can be more fully appreciated if we compare it to Luhrmann's earlier film *Strictly Ballroom*. In *Strictly Ballroom*, Luhrmann stages a comic solution to the problem of conformism as the path to stardom, opposing the failed, apparently weak father who, we're mistakenly led to think by his wife and one of the judges, didn't win the contest he danced in as a young man because he danced as he wanted to, and the strong son who is apparently a loser because he wants to follow in his father's dance steps, as it were, and do the dance moves he wants to do instead of limiting himself to moves recognized and authorized by the judges. (As it turns out, the father failed because he didn't dance the way he wanted to. He caved into his assigned role.) An inter-ethnic romance enables a macho father and a grandmother to be brought in as the teachers of their ugly duckling, untrained daughter and of the professionally trained young man. The result is that the apparent losers dance an innovative set of moves, overturn the corrupt judges, defy the son's excessively cautious, domineering mother, and get both fathers' approval.

In *Strictly Ballroom*, incorporating unrecognized moves from the Flamenco dance form enables the loser couple to transform the rules such that the contestants and the audience judge the judges. This transformation has a distinctively heteronormative effect, but one that depends on the boy's father's sacrifice. Though the younger couple affirm heterosexuality as they fall in love, their coupling depends on the boy's father having been castrated by his "bitch" wife. The couple may have lost the dance contest in order to win a more significant, enduring romantic victory, but that victory depends on a misrecognition of the son as different from rather than a mimic of his father.

In contrast, a number of queer effects in *William Shakespeare's Romeo and Juliet*, including an extremely flat-chested Juliet, an Old Capulet in drag, and a Romeo who hallucinates Mercutio as a drag diva, among others, may be read as Romeo and Juliet's inability to break out of the hold their families and American youth culture has on them. Of particular note among queer effects is the use of sound in both films. In *Strictly Ballroom*, sound is generally miked realistically. At certain moments, however, such as the final dance contest, we hear the audience clapping in a way that exaggerates the sound and slows down the speed of the film. Yet these unrealistic effects nevertheless serve a realistic dramatic function, heightening suspense.

In *William Shakespeare's Romeo and Juliet,* sound effects are no longer subordinated to dramatic function. This is Shakespeare on drugs. Actors' accents, for example, call attention to the vocalizable at the expense of the significant. Romeo and Juliet as well as most of the other characters speak in American accents. Some adopt accents that exceed whatever justification might be given by the mis-en-scene of this film. The actor Paul Sorvino (who plays Old Capulet) affects a terrible Italian accent. (Brian Denehy, who plays Montague, does not.) The Nurse does a Cuban accent and Lady Capulet does a bizarre Jessica Lange imitation. The insubordination of the soundtrack to dramatic function is registered pointedly in Mercutio's lip-synching at the Capulet drag ball. It is not clear at all points who is singing or lip-synching "Young Hearts Run Free." At the theme park we hear Mercutio in falsetto singing the words and the disco tune in the background. Then we see the boys in the car and hear the actual disco tune as Mercutio lip-synchs (intercut with shots of the Capulet party) in slow motion with fireworks overhead as the music switches from Mercutio's song to the theme song of *Romeo and Juliet.* Then we get a long shot of Mercutio on the staircase with the song playing at full volume. At this point we hear only Mazelle singing, but her deep voice makes an uninformed audience wonder, at least initially, whether Mercutio is now singing or whether he is lip-synching.[4] Moreover, sound effects take an unrealistic form as the film is regularly sped up and as "zip" sounds are attached to zip pan shots.

Mercutio's lip-synching and other examples of a nonsynchronization between sound and spectacle, I suggest, register a new, more radical solution to the problem of stardom and conformism, a problem felt most acutely in the relation between Luhrmann and Shakespeare. Even as the film claims to be William Shakespeare's "classic" play, it does not conform to the original but instead achieves a degree of freedom by flattening and drowning it out through the nonsynchronization of high and low cultural registers, or what might be called noise. Noise is the film's compensatory strategy for the diminishment Romeo and Juliet undergo as they become "little stars." The adaptation of Shakespeare paradoxically involves drowning Shakespeare out in order to produce the authentic Romeo and Juliet by William Shakespeare. *William Shakespeare's Romeo and Juliet* is Shakespeare in stereo: Luhrmann blasts on both the popular and the Shakespearean speakers.

In foregrounding the transvestite voice and its relation to stardom in Luhrmann's film, I want to ask what it means to drag Shakespeare into American popular culture, so to speak.[5] Addressing this question, as will be clear momentarily, demands that we must first theorize the transvestite voice in relation both to feminist criticism of the female voice in psychoanalysis and cinema and to queer theorizing about the operatic voice. This means rethinking the controversy among feminist and queer theorists over whether the phallus is gendered male. Transvestism is now typically theorized in relation to Lacan's notion of the phallus, a notion that has generated a sustained controversy over the politics of the male transvestite. Insofar as the phallus is, pace Lacan, gendered male since it is thought to be inseparable from the penis, some feminist critics argue that the male to female transvestite merely confirms a tendency in Lacan's work to reproduce homosocial phallocentrism, erasing women (who famously don't exist for Lacan anyway) by what Luce Irigaray (1989) calls "homm/o/sexualité." As in Freud's account of castration anxiety, sexual difference is converted by the Lacanian phallus into symbolic deficiency: women lack, while men are whole. Other feminist and queer theorists have tried to use Lacan's notion of the phallus to open up the possibility of resignifying gender norms in parodic, subversive ways.[6]

Film theory has of course turned to psychoanalysis, and feminist work on cinema has drawn attention to the way voice is gendered and sexual difference is secured by assigning genders to different positions on and off the screen. The voice-over is almost always male, the female voice generally hyper-embodied so that it is consistently synchronized; the male voice occupies an exterior diegetic position, the female voice an interior diegetic position. Feminists have argued further that the female voice is represented as faulty in a variety of ways, ultimately incapable of enunciating and authoring meaning. While my account of the transvestite voice is indebted to this account of the voice and gender, it also calls into question some of its basic assumptions about meaning, authorship, and gender. The transvestite voice demands a rethinking of the phallus/penis equation and the gendering of voice in the cinema by marking a non-synchronization of voice and body, of original and copy.

Typically at issue and coded in a comic register is the volume and speed of the voice. It should not be surprising that in films in which a man lip-synchs to or mimics a woman's voice, jokes about penis size come up. These jokes register the way a male falsetto voice is assumed to be a function of (partial) castration. To compensate for a potential loss of virility, physical penis size gets displaced onto vocal size as male performers pump up the volume, as it were, and pick up the tempo to maintain their vocal and penile potency. The transvestite voice involves what I would call an ambi*dick*sterity.[7] Yet lip-synching to this voice places a limit on any performer's ability to cross over: it registers an inevitable lack of fit between performer and part, a lack that centers on a particular body part, namely, the man's penis. If the transvestite voice allows one to supplement one's lack by enabling one to be a virtuoso, it also foregrounds the very lack that this supplement is meant to mask.

The presence of penis jokes in relation to the male transvestite voice demonstrates that the male transvestism excludes women after all by equating the phallus with the penis, and it marks a further loss for women's speech in obviating a pun on female lips: a man's lips refer only to his mouth while Irigaray's "lips that speak together" may refer, as Jane Gallop (1988) points out, to the labia as well. My point is not that the phallus can be separated from the penis.[8] It can't. My point is rather that no penis can ever bear the weight of the phallus, not simply because the penis changes shape but because size will always remain an issue (for both genders) even when the penis is erect.[9]

The use of a diva or star's voice when lip-synching may be understood as a response to this pressure. As Mary Ann Doane (1980) notes, voice in classic cinema is meant to produce the illusion of embodied presence.[10] This illusion is enabled significantly through the star's voice:

> The voice [that] is not detachable from a body . . . is quite specific—
> that of the star. In the cinema, cult value and the "aura" resurface in
> the star system. In 1930 a writer feels the need to assure audiences
> that post- synchronization as a technique does not necessarily entail
> substituting an alien voice for a "real" voice, that the industry does
> not condone a mismatching of voices and bodies. Thus, the voice

> serves as a support for the spectator's recognition and his/her
> identification of, as well as with, the star. (36)

The star's voice is the voice that can always pass as itself: the original and the copy cannot be differentiated. As Doane notes, not even the ardent fan can tell if it's live or if it's Memorex (1980, 35). This ability to pass secures gender difference such that, in Lacan's terms, the female star is the phallus and the male listener and spectator has the phallus. Moreover, the star's voice has an author-function. Like the voice-over, the star voice presents itself as enunciator, or, as Kaja Silverman puts it, "a metafictional voice, the point of discursive origin" (1988, 51).

The male transvestite lip-syncher, in contrast, is a virtuoso, a mimic of the star. He never passes as himself but mimes other voices, accents, and vocal registers. And since the transvestite voice is lip-synched, it exposes a technology that the star's voice is meant to mask in classic cinema. The lip-synching of the male transvestite is a symptom not of the way all men are castrated but of the way all men are more or less castrated.[11] The male transvestite lip-syncher has or is the phallus insofar as he is a kind of castrato, a virtuoso performer whose ability to pass as the opposite gender perhaps depends on a loss of literal virility.[12] Unlike the star, who can cover an older tune and still appear to be an author because of his or her singing signature, the transvestite voice is at best a DJ, a *poseur* whose claim to authorship is limited to remixing and sampling codes already enunciated by others (though in a brazenly open manner, to be sure).

In distinguishing the virtuoso from the star I don't mean to imply that the transvestite voice is inherently critical in that it demystifies the illusion of the star's unity and self-presence, as if the disembodied, nonsynchronized female voice could be aligned with a feminist avant-garde cinema, and the embodied, synchronized female voice with heterosexist classic cinema.[13] This account of the female voice and cinema has to naturalize and essentialize the voice in order to gender it. Yet queer opera criticism has questioned whether voice is in fact gendered.[14] As musicologist Joke Dame writes in a discussion of the castrato, "does voice have a gender? One is inclined to say that it does. After all, in most cases we do hear correctly whether a voice comes from a female or a male body. Nonetheless, pop music provides crafty examples of gender-disguised singing. Equally in Western music and non-Western music there are examples that might give rise to doubts as to the 'genderedness' of the voice" (1994, 140). The gender of the recorded voice is a consequence primarily of speed, as Wayne Koestenbaum makes clear in his study of the opera queen:

> Record speed was not standardized until 1927. . . . Turn Caruso into a woman by speeding him up; turn Galli-Curci into a man by slowing her down. Who hasn't tried this trick? A recorded voice is genderless sound waves. Thus a disc's revolutions teach something truly revolutionary; that the pitch of a voice, which we take to be an indicator of gender, can be changed once sound passes into the home listener's magic cabinet. (1993, 61)

Insofar as the voice in cinema is always a recorded voice, its gender is always a function of the recording apparatus.[15]

I am contrasting star and virtuoso voices in order to suggest that the technologies attached to the transvestite voice deconstruct attempts in classic cinema to gender the voice by calling into question the opposition between a disembodied, extradiegetic male voice-over and an embodied, diegetic, synchronized female voice. This deconstruction enables a critical, excessive *over*-hearing and transcoding that yields an unspeakable adapted ShaXXXspeare text, an overhearing and transcoding that becomes more overt as the virtuoso transvestite capacities of the voice are openly acknowledged to be a function of the speed of the recording apparatus and other technologies of cinematic reproduction. Yet this critique may appear to be uncritical insofar as its speed marks it as either too fast, hence thin, or too slow, hence retarded, dated, belated. Vocal volume is registered in terms of the speed at which the voice is recorded or played back: the slower the speed, the greater the density; conversely, the faster the speed, the thinner the sound. In enabling a critique, the transvestite voice proceeds through a certain thick-headedness, as it were, or, to put it slightly differently, a kind of semantic denseness. If semantic thickness allows for ambiguous meanings, hence multiple interpretations, the very obviousness, often literal-mindedness, of the terms by which a given critique is produced may appear to flip density over into its opposite, semantic thinness, or the trans-sensical: noise, as in *William Shakespeare's Romeo and Juliet,* or the inane, dumb (in both senses), the stupid, and the retarded, as the case may be. What might strike some critics as semantic denseness in a positive sense, as unspeakable and hence transgressive, might strike other critics as semantic denseness in a negative sense, as simply too stupid or trans-sensical to be worth a listen.

The concept of *over*-hearing might strike some critics as just another symptom of male castration anxiety, the flip side of the voice-over insofar as both may involve disembodiment. As such, it would, all too predictably, be yet one more way of disavowing (heterosexual) male lack, of course at the expense of women. This objection depends for its force, however, on the very assumption the transvestite voice calls into question, namely, that voice has a gender. I am posing the problem of the transvestite voice somewhat differently in terms of the relative denseness of a given critique of heteronormative adaptations of Shakespeare's (perhaps always already heteronormative) plays.

Cultural critics tend to think about what Judith Butler calls "subversive resignifications" of gender norms in terms of some alternative sense, usually regarded as parodic, or in terms of the breakdown of heteronormative intelligibility. In her reading of drag as documented in the film *Paris Is Burning* (dir. Jenny Livingstone, 1991), for example, Judith Butler discusses the practice of "reading" in which one drag queen insults another in terms of who can or cannot be "read." The judge of drag balls (who is also a "legend") is the one who can "read," who can tell the transvestite who is "real" (who can pass as a woman, even to other drag queens) from one who isn't. As Butler comments:

> Significantly, [drag] is a performance that works, that effects real-ness, to the extent that it cannot be read. For "reading" means taking someone down, exposing what fails to work at the level of appear-ance, insulting or deriding someone. For a performance to work, then, means that a reading is no longer possible, or that a reading, an interpretation, appears to be a kind of transparent seeing, where what appears and what it means coincide. (1993, 129)

In contrast, I am suggesting that anyone who performs can always be read (even the critic will be "read" by other critics). The apparent coincidence of performance and signification in the drag balls noted by Butler is a hermeneutic fantasy, for the judge (and queer theorist) is the one who is able to read unreadability, which is not unreadability in general but a specific unreadability to outsiders that only an insider can appreciate.[16]

In shifting questions of adaptation, authorship, and resignification from the unreadable to the unspeakable, as I have, one could, of course, try to assign noise (and its variations) itself a critical function, as so much interference in heteronormative cultural transmissions.[17] While noise may work this way in local cases, my interest in the unspeakable lies in the way it poses a generally unacknowledged problem for cultural critics, namely, the potential triviality of transvestite resignifications of gender in popular film. Butler dismisses popular films dealing with drag such as *Victor/Victoria* and *Some Like It Hot* as heteronormative fluff:

> This is drag as high entertainment, and though these films are surely important to read as cultural texts in which homophobia and homosexual panic are negotiated, I would be reticent to call them subversive. Indeed, one might argue that such films are functional in providing a ritualistic release for a heterosexual economy that must constantly police its own boundaries against the invasion of queerness. (1993, 126)

By turning to the transvestite voice as the focus of unspeakable resignifications, I want to draw attention to the way that subversion for cultural critics always implies a kind of volume and density that threatens to come up short. A given text may be dismissed on the grounds that it is too easy to read, that it's not hard enough, as it were. Lip-synched resignifications of Shakespeare may make sense, as we will see, but not necessarily of the kind some queer theorists would consider subversive, since they may not be properly parodic but instead appear to be trivial. The question for cultural criticism is not only whether there's a subversive critique in a given adaptation but whether a given critique can be fully separated from the trans-sensical in all its varied forms. Shakespeare may prove to be unsinkable in any adaptation, but that may be because the adaptation produces a Shakespeare lite.

Theorizing transvestism and castration in relation to penis/vocal size and speed enables us to understand Shakespeare's entry into American popular culture as a transvestite act in several ways. First, it broadens what counts as transvestism. In addition to the more literal, recognizable visual forms, vocal transvestite effects include the following: men mouthing words to songs sung by women; the falsetto, boy soprano, countertenor; post-dubbing a male voice over a female actress; men singing in their own voices songs written for women singers. Moreover, the transvestite's lip-synching figures a general lack of synchronization in any mediatization of Shakespeare as cultural registers and various archaic or modern technologies of sound and music clash. The lack of synchronization between cultural registers may yield a rewriting and recontextualization of someone else's words, not merely a secondary miming of them. A given Shakespeare reproduction's dominant plot may be rewritten through double entendres and puns, but any rewriting may also push a given adaptation to the point of noise. To mediatize Shakespeare is potentially to overcode him, to *over*-hear him, in the Nietzschean sense, to drown him out in the act of updating him.

Perhaps most significantly, the transvestite voice enables us to ask what status Shakespeare has as an enabling cultural signifier in the United States when his plays are mediatized. Delicately put, just how big is Shakespeare's will when it comes to American popular culture? In present critical accounts of drag, Shakespeare's centrality in relation to transvestism has gone unquestioned. He is often assumed to be foundational, though critics may disagree as to whether Shakespeare is a help or a hindrance in the contemporary political scene. Some critics think Shakespeare has the phallus because he is already a part of popular culture, while other critics think that only a post-Shakespearean comedy has it.[18] However, if we take lip-synching to be a metaphor for mediatizing Shakespeare, a less foundational model of his circulation and resignification is opened up. As a cultural signifier of transvestism, Shakespeare occupies neither gender, hence he both is and is not the phallus, both has and does not have the phallus.

To show how Shakespeare's mediatization in terms of lip-synching enables a critical adaptation that may be retarded by its own semantic thinness, I will consider a number of adaptations and reproductions that link the transvestite voice to recording technologies and to the star and the virtuoso. I begin by contrasting a musical adaptation of Shakespeare, *Kiss Me Kate* (dir. George Sidney II, 1953), and two films that pit the "natural" voice against technological alterations of it, *Porky's 2* and Trevor Nunn's *Twelfth Night*. *Kiss Me Kate,* an adaptation of *The Taming of the Shrew,* originally shot in 3-D, is about the symbolic castration of the male leads and the transsexualization of the female singers. The 3-D visual technology puts pressure on the male body's claim for phallic potency (both literal and symbolic). *Porky's 2* and Nunn's *Twelfth Night* attempt to naturalize the voice, opposing it to technology in order to secure gender difference (men can't pass vocally as women). In *Porky's 2,* a character named Meat dresses up as Thisbe but fails to speak in a falsetto. Nunn's realist *Twelfth Night,* which tries to be as faithful to Shakespeare as possible, was nevertheless forced by the film's American producers to interpolate a prequel that dislocates the voices of the twins Sebastian and Viola, both of whom perform as a vaudeville act on board a ship. Nunn's is the one example of female transvestism I consider. Yet far from offering a feminist and/or lesbian reading of the comedy, Nunn offers instead an apology for the male gaze. His film is the least flexible and the most heteronormative of any of the reproductions considered in this chapter. Ambiguities about gender and voice and the homoerotic possibilities they raise are resolved by making the body a visual spectacle and by displacing the female voice with a male voice-over or male musical accompaniment.

To show how voice, gender, and speed enable a critique of a 1960s noncollaborative Hollywood mode of film and television production that effectively voids itself by being too slow, I will next consider an episode of the 1960s TV sitcom *Gilligan's Island* entitled "The Producer," in which *Hamlet* is adapted as a musical. The analysis of this example is longer than any other because it thematizes most fully the concerns I take up here. Vocal and visual transvestism is at the center of a contest between an individualistic model of literary authorship as appropriation (the Producer) and a collaborative model of literary production as the joint recycling of available cultural resources (the castaways). The episode's comedy turns on speed: both the producer and the castaways want to use the musical for their own purposes, and the central difference between them is less a moral one than a technical one: who can work fastest to capitalize on the castaways' greatly sped-up rewriting of *Hamlet*. Shakespeare's tragedy is condensed to roughly five minutes, and radically rewritten parts of the play are set to the two most famous arias from George Bizet's opera *Carmen* and to the "Barcarolle" from Jacques Offenbach's opéra fantastique, *Tales of Hoffmann*. Gilligan appears as a vocal transvestite Hamlet and sings a version of the "To be or not to be" soliloquy to the tune of Carmen's famous "Hanabera" aria. Though the castaways hope the show will help Ginger return as a movie star and get all the castaways off the island, they are left behind by the faster producer, who stages his version of the musical in New York with great success.

Though my focus in this chapter is primarily on U.S. examples, I also develop the contrast between American and English versions of transvestite, lip-synched Shakespeare by focusing on two English films, Greenaway's *Prospero's Books* and Peter Yates's *The Dresser* (1983). Both films thematize the male voice in terms of the male actor's aging body and consequent loss of mastery and control. I first take up John Gielgud's transvestite voice in relation to *Prospero's Books's* many exposed, wagging penises and the singer Sarah Leonard, who performs Ariel's songs, and then turn to Albert Finney's "straight" voice in *The Dresser*. My analysis of these two English examples is meant to highlight, through contrast, significant ways in which nationalism and sexuality are linked in the United States through Shakespeare. In England, virtuosity is located in the male actor's trained voice. American versions of the transvestite voice are untrained. The transvestite voice in the American Shakespeare examples I consider here is yet another symptom of America's postcolonial relation to Britain, to be regarded as an attempt to compensate through a variety of forms, including the musical, situation comedy, and music video, for the inadequacy of the actor's voice, an inadequacy always registered, even in actors with trained voices trying to do Shakespeare straight, by American accents. To gesture toward ways in which the theoretical issues broached here in relation to a lip-synched Shakespeare might be pursued elsewhere in American and English film, I conclude with an excursus on Derek Jarman's *Edward II* (1991) and Chris Columbus's *Mrs. Doubtfire* (1993), both of which take up the transvestite voice in relation to children.

Shrew You, or Shakespeare in Tights

In *Kiss Me Kate,* a musical in which a group of actors put on a production of *The Taming of the Shrew,* the leading characters, Fred Graham (Howard Keel) and Lilli Vanessi (Katherine Graveson), are divorced when the film begins and appear to reconcile at the end as a result of performing the play. As is often the case in Hollywood musicals, romantic conflicts between the principal characters get worked out as they act, dance, and sing in the show-within-the-show. *Kiss Me Kate's* narrative doubling allows for a queer reading, one that focuses on the deflection of the musical's heterosexual romances, their lack of fulfillment along the straight patriarchal lines of Shakespeare's play.[19] Cole Porter, the lyricist and composer, was gay, and Hollywood musicals in general are gay or lesbian produced or inflected (Doty 1993, 11-13).

This film contains a series of double entendres focusing on Vanessi/Kate's ass and Graham/Petruchio's inadequate penis size: off-stage Graham tells Vanessi he knows that she left him because he wasn't "big enough for the role"; Petruchio and Kate struggle over sausages and a banana (Carmen Miranda had already established the banana as dildo equivalent in a lesbian number, "The Lady in the Tutti-Frutti Hat," in *The Gang's All Here*); the ex-husband acknowledges that Vanessi prefers a Texan, who drives a Cadillac with a set of Texas longhorns on its hood, because of his cattle meat; Graham's difficulties in the theatrical production with his ex-wife (who walks out during a performance) activate a pun on Petruchio's line "I know she will not come" (though delivered while Petruchio is waiting for Kate to come after wagering on her obedience, a pun on "come" seems to express Graham's fear that he is unable to get Vanessi off); and in a number called "Brush Up Your Shakespeare" two gangsters advise Graham to kick his future girlfriends "in the Coriolanus" if they criticize his behavior (which seems like bad advice given that Vanessi left the play during its performance because he spanked her onstage). These puns inscribe a closeted, gay critique both of the theatrical adaptation of *The Taming of the Shrew* in the film and of the male characters who play the Shakespeare parts (despite what might be thought to be a misogynistic characterization of the women—Lois Lane [Bianca] promiscuously loves her boyfriend "in [her] own way" and Vanessi, who sings a song entitled "I Hate Men," is frigid—the failure of the domestic relationships is laid squarely at the feet of the men).

The play's subtle critique of patriarchal masculinity is centered on a disruption of the penis/phallus equation. The more hyperembodied the male body in this film, the less synchronized sound secures sexual difference. Unlike Elliot in *The Goodbye Girl,* who partly secures his heterosexuality through a prosthetic hump, Graham/Petruchio more openly displays his castration through the exposure of his limp penis in tights. As Kaja Silverman observes, when it is embodied the male voice is weakened, the speaker in one case even terminated:

> There is a general theoretical consensus that the theological status of the disembodied voice-over is the effect of maintaining its source in a place apart from the camera, inaccessible to the gaze of either the cinematic apparatus or the viewing subject—of violating the rule of synchronization so absolutely that the voice is left without an identifiable locus. In other words, the voice-over is privileged to the degree that *it transcends the body.* Conversely, it loses power and authority with every corporeal encroachment, from a regional accent or idiosyncratic "grain" to definitive localization in the image. Synchronization marks the final moment in any such localization, the point of full and complete "embodiment." (1988, 49)

Silverman cites Yves Bonizter's commentary on *Kiss Me Deadly* (dir. Robert Aldrich, 1955), a film in which the villain who has spoken offscreen is shot and killed after he appears onscreen.

Kiss me Kate conventionally positions Graham as orchestrator and director of the two women stars and gives him the position of a chorus who delivers a non-Shakespearean prologue when the musical begins. The film foregrounds Petruchio's phallic mastery in 3-D at certain points. When the recently married couple arrives at

Petruchio's house, Petruchio takes a sausage out of Kate's blouse (where she's hidden food so she can later eat it). Then, addressing the camera when speaking the "Thus have I politicly begun my reign" aside, he picks up a banana and throws it at the camera. The more hyperbolically embodied Graham is, however, the less voice synchronization secures sexual difference. The film's 3-D visual technology heightens Graham/Petruchio's castration and enables a transsexualization of the female singers as the phallus becomes a kind of aural dildo. Who has the phallus and how big it is are matters determined by the women. One critic has commented that only the men are shot in 3-D, but both women in fact also get 3-D moments.[20] At the beginning of the film, Graham tries to trick Vanessi into playing Kate by pretending he'll cast Lois Lane (Ann Miller) in the part. Lane has performed a song and dance number called "Too Darn Hot" in which she addresses the camera and flings her glove and scarf at the camera in a 3-D shot. Ann Miller's leggy Lane is thus positioned as being the phallus, as spectacle, as a woman who can't really act but who can entertain men who have the phallus. As her competitiveness and jealousy get the better of her, Vanessi agrees to play Kate and so too becomes subject to the same male gaze.

From the very start, however, the equation between having the phallus and having a penis gets disrupted. Cole Porter, playing himself, questions Graham's judgment in having his ex-wife come to his apartment to discuss acting in the play. Graham demures and we see that he has made himself into a spectacle, hanging a large painting of himself dressed as (Edwin Booth's) Hamlet above the fireplace. Yet Graham is master of neither women. He has failed to tell Lane that "Too Darn Hot" has been cut from the musical because it "just didn't fit. There was no place for it." Furthermore, Lane arrives early. Similarly, before Lane's arrival, Graham attempts to lure Vanessi to take the role by having her sing a duet with him in which both people declare their love for each other. In getting her to sing the words, Graham forces her to say what he wants her to say, that she loves him. Yet this momentary synchronization of song and actress is quickly disturbed as he tells her she'd be perfect for the part of the shrew (she frowns), and when Cole Porter, accompanying the two on piano, says she'll the love the number "I Hate Men."

Failing to secure women in the place of spectacle and synchronized song, the film falls back on a secondary difference between the
two women. Thematically, the women are differentiated in terms of
moral principle, backbone, depth of feeling, sexual fidelity, pliability,
and submissiveness to men. Formally, the women are differentiated by
song and diegesis. Lane is positioned in relation to the number more
clearly as spectacle, hence as exterior in terms of the diegesis, while
Vanessi, who never displays her legs and doesn't dance, is positioned
as interior in the diegesis. While, as in the original play, this distinction
serves to distinguish Vanessi as the more desirable of the two, it also
subverts any claim the film might make for male mastery over the
women. It is precisely through her dance numbers that Lane is able to
assert her mastery over her body, a body that her song aurally
transsexualizes. In a dance number in which Bianca is being pursued
by suitors, she becomes a chick with a Tom, Harry, or Dick, so to
speak. The song inverts the usual order of the names (Tom, Dick, or
Harry), and Bianca at one point repeats the final name "Dick". Her
later number, in which she declares to her boyfriend that she is true to
him "in [her] own way" also reveals her willingness not just to be
turned into the phallus but actively to turn herself into it (the
difference being that she, not her boyfriend, controls her sexuality).

Vanessi's difference from Lane is undercut by her 3-D moment: in
her "I Hate Men" number, Kate throws a beer mug at the camera. And
though she dumps her fiancée and returns to the play, kneeling to
Petruchio and smiling at Graham, the two plots don't run parallel (as
if they told the same story of female submission). As Graham has told
her earlier, it's the theater that Vanessi loves; that's why she can't leave
it. Her return thus does not initially entail any commitment to Graham
or any desire to remarry him. Moreover, the frequent if subtle puns
suggest an alternative recoding by Vanessi of Kate's willingness to put
her hand under her husband's foot. A frigid woman in their marriage,
Vanessi's apparent willingness to give Graham a "hand job" is a kind of
compromise. Perhaps the clearest sign of a dysfunction, however, is
the way Vanessi indicates her love for Graham. After finishing Kate's
speech, Vanessi silently mouths the word "really" to him. The film can
neither synchronize Vanessi's voice with a song from the show nor
with her character. The film departs from Shakespeare's narrative in

continuing past this scene to a dance number with Bianca and Lucentio and two other couples in which the question of sound becomes all the more striking as there is no song, only instrumental music, and hence no synchronization.

Life Is a Cabaret, or the Unsinkable William Shakespeare

If the technological apparatus of *Kiss Me Kate* opens up a critique of patriarchal mastery by enabling the aural transsexualization of the female singer, other adaptations attempt to do the opposite, largely by presenting the voice as natural, hence naturally gendered. *Porky's 2*, for example, presents a scene in which Meat appears cross-dressed as Thisbe. His appearance contradicts his defiant insistence in the previous scene that he won't participate in this "faerie" activity, and the camera begins with a close-up of his feet and moves up his body, thereby shooting him the way only women are shot in classic cinema. The teacher asks him to speak his lines, which he does. Since his bass voice makes him sound so obviously like a man, she asks him to try to raise its pitch. After several embarrassing, failed attempts, he pleads with her to let him stop: He can't do it, he explains, not because he's unwilling but because he's unable as a "real" man. By securing gender through an account of the voice as natural, *Porky's 2* keeps in place a semantic difference between two puns, one on heterosexual "meat" and the other on homosexual "faeries," between, that is to say, men who have penises and men who don't.[21]

Trevor Nunn's *Twelfth Night* offers a more sophisticated and perhaps more conservative account of the voice as essentially gendered.[22] The film opens with a vaudeville performance on board a luxury ship in which Viola (Imogen Stubbs) and a cross-dressed Sebastian (Stephen MacKintosh) appear as veiled and heavily made-up harem girls performing a version of "O mistress mine." Their performance measures the (in)adequacy of Sebastian's male transvestite against what we are to consider a real woman's voice, namely Viola's. This scene, interpolated and intercut with a male voice-over, pseudo-Elizabethan verse prologue that begins "I'll tell thee a tale," presents the twins, Viola and Sebastian, performing for some of their shipmates prior to a storm that will soon separate them. In addition to their appearance as veiled harem girls, their genders are questioned further by their singing voices. Sebastian and Viola perform a duet in a soprano and mezzo-soprano range, but one voice keeps falling into a baritone register, making it clear that one of the "girls" is actually a "boy" who is trying, and at moments failing, to sing falsetto. (This effect is actually achieved by alternately overdubbing two female voices and one male voice.) Because the "women" are wearing veils, however, it is impossible to say who is which gender. As if to criticize the male for giving away his gender through his failure to sing a falsetto consistently and convincingly, the female twin turns to him and pulls off "her" veil to reveal a "masculine" face, here established by a moustache. It appears then, that a male voice has been synchronized with a male face. Rather than simply establish the moment as a virtuoso one a la Julie Andrews in Blake Edwards's *Victor Victoria* (1992), however, the film raises the possibility of an infinite regress of false revelations in which any gender marker always has to be put in quotation marks as a performative signifier. The "clarification" is in turn revealed to be an illusion as the "woman" who has remained veiled pulls off the "man's" spirit-gummed moustache: "he" is actually a "she." The twin exposed as a woman after all then pulls off her twin's veil and reveals another "male" signified face, complete with moustache. Rather than stop here in a moment of final clarity, however, the game continues as "she" reaches to pull off "his" moustache, only to be interrupted as the boat runs into a rock on which it will flounder.[23]

The film thus initially works against the usual manner in which voice and gender are synchronized and localized, a manner that Michel Chiron has compared to a striptease:

> In much the same way that the feminine sex is the ultimate point in *deshabille* (the point after which it is no longer possible to deny the absence of the penis), there is an ultimate point in the embodiment of the voice, and that is the mouth from which the voice issues. . . . As long as the face and mouth have not been revealed, and the eye of the spectator has not "verified" the coincidence of the voice with the mouth . . . the vocal embodiment

is incomplete, and the voice conserves an aura of invulnerability
and of magic power. (1982, 32-33)

Nunn's *Twelfth Night* opens with an interrupted, softcore tease with
regard to voice and gender.

Yet instead of using the interruption generated by the shipwreck
to defer the question of the performers' genders, Nunn's film does the
reverse, giving the viewer private visual access to the gender of both
singers and providing further clarity through an unquestionably male
voice-over narrating an interpolated prologue. As the ship founders,
both twins tear off their costumes and run for the stateroom to pack
their dearest belongings. Viola is revealed to be very much a female,
with long, flowing blond hair and a long, flowing dress. Sebastian,
while also possessing somewhat feminine features, is quickly proven
to be capable of quite "masculine" behavior: as Viola is swept
overboard, Sebastian breaks away from sailors who attempt to restrain
him and dives into the water to save his sister. Underwater, Sebastian
finds Viola, and their genders are once again clarified visually as they
reach out and touch one another, grasp hands, and hang briefly
suspended in the water in a Gemini-like configuration. The ocean's
force then divides them: Viola swims to the surface while Sebastian,
nowhere in sight, appears to have drowned. Viola's next reversal of
gender is made clear as the credits roll; we, along with the captain, are
this time made privy to the spectacle of her cross-dressing as we see
Viola transform herself into Caesario: she cuts her hair, takes off her
corset, pulls on pants, inserts a piece of cloth into the crotch, straps
down her breasts with a piece of cloth, and then, in a separate location,
shouts in a low voice. Picking up a discarded photo of herself,
Sebastian, and their father, she places her false moustache over her
face in the photo.[24]

In intercutting the opening vaudeville act of ambiguously embodied male and female voices with an unambiguously male voice-over
and a pseudo-Elizabethan verse prologue and then letting us see Viola
disguise herself as a boy, Nunn rather conventionally and uncritically
returns us to the scene of castration, as Kaja Silverman puts it, the male
disavowal of which secures sexual difference at the expense of women:

"By isolating the female subject from the production of meaning, [the corporealization of the female voice] permits the male subject to pose as the voice that constrains and orchestrates the feminine 'performance' or 'striptease' as enunciator rather than as himself an element of the enonce" (1988, 62). Yet to represent the voice as naturally gendered, Nunn's *Twelfth Night* has to invoke and disavow a very conventional cinematic technology.

Nunn's attempt to naturalize the voice as always already gendered has consequences for the film's take on the relation between voice and sexuality in Shakespeare's comedy. If Olivia's lesbianism is the central issue in the *Playboy Twelfth Night,* in Nunn's version Viola/Caesario's homoerotic relation with Orsino is central.[25] Olivia (Helena Bonham Carter) is "straightened out" so that her desire for Caesario is essentially heterosexual. Consider the following exchange between Olivia and Viola/Caesario:

> OLIVIA: I prithee tell me what thou think'st of me.
> CAESARIO: That you do think you are not what you are.
> OLIVIA: If I think so, I think the same of you.
> CAESARIO: Then think you right; I am not what I am.
> OLIVIA: I would you were as I would have you be. (3.1.138-42)

The scene is played strictly for laughs: the visuals effectively rewrite the paradoxical lines about identity—"You are not what you are" and "I am not what I am"—to mean "You are not a woman" and "I am not a man." Similarly, at the end of the film, when Olivia realizes she has fallen in love with a woman, she experiences consternation as Sebastian tells her she is "betroth'd both to a maid and a man." Her consternation quickly gives way to comfort, however, as Nunn interpolates a line in which Olivia calls Viola "sister" and hugs her, and so is further distanced from any possible lesbian desire.[26]

To be sure, two scenes with Caesario and Orsino (Toby Stephens) do admit of homoerotic possibilities. Nunn shifts two pivotal scenes from the public setting of Orsino's court to private, even intimate settings to foreground these possibilities. In the first scene, in which Orsino instructs Caesario about how he is to approach Olivia, Orsino is in a bath and asks Caesario to scrub his back. Viola is clearly moved by the physical contact, but the scene stages it as a heterosexual moment, not only because Orsino, after all, is talking about Olivia, but because we see past Viola's disguise to her heterosexual attraction to Orsino, who in turn seems to see past Caesario to Viola.

A second pivotal scene closes down even more firmly on the homoerotic possibilities it initially broaches by adding another interpolation, this one involving Feste (Ben Kingsley), whose role is greatly enlarged in this version of the play. Perhaps aware that Caesario is in fact a woman (he's seen Caesario emerge from the cave) and apparently willing to help her win Orsino, Feste plays a love song for Orsino and Caesario when the three are in a horse stable. The female voices of the opening have been displaced by the voice of a male who occupies the position of the voyeuristic male gaze. Orsino and Caesario almost kiss as they can get carried away by the song, but the song ends before they can do so. Like the storm, which interrupted the transvestite vaudeville number, this interruption of music halts the homoerotic potential of the kiss. The fundamentally heterosexual nature of their relationship is underscored when Viola's near open declaration of her love for Orsino follows immediately: "Say some lady, as perhaps there is, / Hath for you love as great a pang of heart / As you have for Olivia . . ." (2.4.90-92). The lady in question is clearly Viola, and Nunn makes sure we understand that she is a woman after all by focusing the camera tightly on Viola's face as she gazes adoringly at Orsino. Caesario tries to convince Olivia not to pursue Orsino because Viola wants him for herself. Viola speaks here, but she does so as a woman, not as a eunuch who lacks a "little thing." Her singing voice from the beginning of the film is displaced by Feste's. The film might be read as an apology for the male gaze: insofar as it is equated with Feste, who in yet another interpolation returns Viola her pearls at the end of the film, the male gaze works benignly. Yet of course what Nunn (and his version of Shakespeare) take to be benign others might regard as an unwanted heterosexist imposition, a diminishment of Viola's agency, and a disavowal of the play's homoeroticism through a corresponding disavowal of the film's own technological apparatus.

What's Hecuba to Him, Or He to Hecuba?: Car-men Meets Hamlet on the Cast(ing)away Couch

If my contrasting *Kiss Me Kate* on the one hand with *Porky's 2* and *Twelfth Night* on the other, shows how openly acknowledging the voice's gender as a function of a technological recording apparatus opens up a critical overhearing of an unspeakable Shakespeare, we may see how that criticism may also subvert itself if we turn to adaptations in which the voice is contextualized in relation to stardom and the virtuoso producer. As a prime example, I would like to consider an episode of *Gilligan's Island* entitled "The Producer" (airing first in 1964) that triangulates a female movie star, a male-run castaway collective, and a male producer as it restages the play-within-the-play of *Hamlet* as a musical within a sitcom. An overbearing Hollywood producer named Harold Hecuba (played by guest star Phil Silvers), or HH for short, crashes his plane but nevertheless arrives on the island in style and treats the castaways as if they were his servants. Everybody submits to him, even though they see him as a "self-centered, abusive, overbearing human being," in order to get off the island through his help. Ginger in particular sees an opportunity to advance her career as a movie star. She attempts to impress and perhaps seduce him by serving him food while dressed successively as two movie stars, Sophia Loren and Marilyn Monroe (she imitates Loren and Monroe in dress, voice intonation, accent, and dialect).

Ginger wants to show Hecuba "what a versatile actress" she is, but he is not impressed and laughs in her face. Humiliated, Ginger tells Gilligan she won't leave the island if they're rescued because she can't face returning as an "unknown, a has-been." She threatens to become a version of the famous movie star who retires: "I'm going to spend the rest of my life alone on this island." It occurs to Gilligan that if they "put on a musical with Ginger as a star, HH would see how great an actress she is," and, after considering a number of inappropriate books owned by the castaways, Gilligan suggests that they can adapt and produce *Hamlet*. The musical stars Gilligan as Hamlet; the Skipper as Polonius; Mr. Howell as Claudius; Mrs. Howell as Gertrude; Mary Ann as Laertes; and Ginger as Ophelia. A quite inane, highly compressed version of *Hamlet* follows in which the tragedy gets rewritten as a comedy (no one dies in this version).

The castaways' version begins with an instance of vocal transvestism as Gilligan/Hamlet sings the following version of the "To be or not to be" soliloquy to a very crudely rearranged version of Carmen's "Hanabera" aria: "I ask to be or not to be, a rogue or peasant slave is what you see. A boy who loved his mother's knee, and so I ask to be or not to be. So here's my plea, I beg of you, and say you see a little hope for me. To fight or flee, to fight or flee, I ask myself to be or not to be." (The music for the other set pieces of the musical is rearranged in an equally crude fashion: Ginger/Ophelia sings a speech set to the "Barcarolle" from Jacques Offenbach's opéra fantastique *The Tales of Hoffmann,* and Polonius's speech of advice to Laertes is set to the bullfighter Escamillo's "Toreador" aria from *Carmen.* The "Barcarolle," we may note in passing, itself involves vocal transvestism, as it usually employs a female mezzo-soprano to sing the male part of the duet.[27]) Eventually, Hecuba takes over the production and performs it entirely himself, cross-dressing as Ophelia but unable to do a falsetto to effectively mimic her voice. He falls from exhaustion before he can finish, saying "goodnight, sweet prince" just before he faints. Later that night, Hecuba gets off the island alone, and the disappointed castaways later hear on the radio that their musical has become a big success on Broadway. One of Gilligan's many crackpot ideas ends up being perfectly viable in the public sphere off the island.

The episode opposes two models of authorship, the self-aggrandizing, virtuoso individualism of the Hollywood producer, and the collective collaboration of the castaways.[28] The former involves appropriation of others' goods and the latter the joint recycling of commonly held resources. The castaways arrive at the idea for a musical together. The Skipper thinks Gilligan's idea is stupid but goes along with it when the Professor says he likes it, and the Professor first has the idea to adapt one of the books and records they have before Gilligan suggests they use *Hamlet.*

This episode of *Gilligan's Island* owes its exemplary status in this chapter to its production on television at a moment when the hold male directors and producers had over the medium was just beginning to loosen. One might read "The Producer" as a critique of the material and gendered constraints under which the writers and producers of shows such as *Gilligan's Island* worked. The episode itself was the result of an unusual cross-gendered collaboration: it was co-produced and co-directed by Ida Lupino and George M. Cahan, and the screenplay was similarly collaborative, written by Gerald Gardner and Dee Caruso. In the 1950s Lupino left the cinema, in which she had moved from acting to directing, for television, and "The Producer" invites its own allegorization as an insider's appreciation of Lupino's difficulties as a television director and producer. (Lupino had already directed several episodes of *Gilligan's Island,* along with episodes of shows such as *Bewitched* and *The Twilight Zone*). In alluding to the Parisian composers Bizet and Offenbach, who were contemporaries, the episode projects an allegory of the limits placed on collaboration, cross-gendered or otherwise, by its own material conditions. The mix of Shakespeare and opera is less a clash between high and low culture than a utopian recoding, through the American musical, of two earlier popular forms, one, theater from Shakespeare, the other, comic opera from Bizet's and Offenbach's bohemian counterculture (Gould 1996, 19-60), which was opposed to the pretensions of Italian and German grand opera and the reactionary (sexual) politics of the Second Empire. "The Producer" echoes constraints that undermined the bohemian critique of an earlier form and historical moment. For the means of opera production divided Bizet and Offenbach. Whereas Bizet wrote for the state-licensed Opéra-Comique (one of two subsi-dized opera houses in Paris) and for the Théâtre-Lyrique, Offenbach composed for the less prestigious but also less rigid and less conserva-tive operetta theaters. Indeed, a star singer, Zulmar Bouffar, whom Offenbach had discovered was Bizet's first choice for the role of Carmen (she turned it down), and Bizet and Offenbach competed for collaborating librettists: two long-time collaborators of Offenbach's, Henri Meilhac and Ludovic Halévy, wrote the libretto of *Carmen.*

The possibility of a cross-gendered collaboration to have been involved in "The Producer" was undercut by the material conditions of Hollywood television production—as in cinema, women were largely restricted to acting; directing and producing being the province of men.[29] As an actress, scriptwriter, director, co-producer, and "self-proclaimed team player" (Kuhn 1995, 9), Lupino was a notable exception to the rule of gender in television and film production and direction. Even so, her creative freedom as an auteur was limited in film and even moreso in television.[30] As Mary Celeste Kearney and James M. Moran point out, the role of the director was always secondary to that of the producer in television, and Lupino's television work can't be considered in auteurist terms precisely because her influence, especially "on formulaic series such as *Gilligan's Island*" (1995, 139) was minimal:

> The figure of Lupino as a "female Hitch" [Alfred Hitchcock], whose nomenclature suggests the freedom to call her own shots and the status of an auteur, is rather misleading within the context of a television industry whose creative efforts are shaped and controlled almost exclusively by producers rather than directors. . . . For this reason, in contrast to her body of cinematic directorial work . . . Lupino's scattered work in television must, by the very nature of the industry, resist any auteurist approach. More of a freelance substitute than a series regular, Lupino established her career with an accumulation of random "guest" spots rather than pursuing long-term contracts with any particular programme or network. Such job security was reserved for her male colleagues. (138-39)

The transvestism of "The Producer" also echoes Lupino's media representation in androgynous terms, as both masculine and feminine. It also distances her from the movie star gendered female here. One could also read the episode as a comment on Tina Louise's (and Ginger's) typecasting as a B-movie star. As the producer of the series, Sherwood Schwartz, notes, Louise became so identified by her audiences with the part of Ginger that the series effectively destroyed her career outside it (1988, 145).

While enabling a critique of gender inequities in Hollywood television and cinema production, "The Producer" nevertheless calls that critique into question. To be sure, we are clearly meant to prefer the wacky, free-wheeling democracy of the castaways to the controlling, selfish tyranny of the producer. Hecuba is regarded as a kind of thief. When he tells the cast, "Get ready to rehearse Harold Hecuba's

Hamlet," Gilligan corrects him: "Don't you mean Shakespeare's *Hamlet?*" Hecuba's response is telling: "If he was alive today, I'd have him working on a full rewrite." Moreover, Hecuba can't do the whole thing alone. As I noted above, he faints before completing the rehearsal in which he plays all the parts. And Hecuba's transvestism is meant to erase everyone other than himself, one might say. The more archaic play-within-the-play of *Hamlet* performed by the First Player turns Hecuba from being a mourning figure of narrative report and spectatorial comment to the active, now male producer of the musical. In contrast, transvestism among the castaways might be regarded as an incidental matter having to do with their limited cultural resources, nothing of any real significance, or perhaps a register of the castaways' relatively democratic social arrangements (the Professor takes on the menial task of producing sound so that Mary Ann can act). Transvestism in the case of the producer might register his inability to distinguish between original and adaptation, author and producer (his nickname "HH" suggests a redundant lack of difference, as does the radio announcer's description of his new film: "a musical extravaganza, called *Musical Extravganza*").

The episode's use of transvestism suggests, however, that the differences between the characters and, by extension, the models of authorship they represent, are not all that secure. Transvestism, for example, is employed by both collaborative and individualistic virtuoso models of authorship. One might want to argue that the aural transvestism of Gilligan's Carmen-inflected Hamlet, Mary Ann's Laertes, and Ginger's aural transvestism in her Nicklause-and-Giulietta-inflected Ophelia constitute a kind of liberating democratic practice in which the castaways are free to cross genders, in contrast to the overbearing, "I can do it all the best," autocratic practice of HH, but this distinction is compromised of course by the fact that Hecuba, too, cross-dresses (as Ophelia). The gender distinction between Ginger as movie star and Hecuba as virtuoso similarly breaks down when examined critically. Hecuba's name alludes to a Queen in *Hamlet,* and, like Gilligan, Ginger performs an aural transvestism as I noted above.

The aural transvestism of the castaways' *Hamlet* adaptation collapses the distinction between transvestite and virtuoso in that the transvestite is not simply the one who crosses gender boundaries (moving from one identity to another) but the one who occupies a number of possible roles that, to be sure, cut across gender, but also range from composer to storyteller to singer: just as Gilligan is not only Carmen but also Bizet, a fellow adapter of "trash" for the masses, so, too, Ginger's performance calls up other female Shakespeare characters besides Ophelia (Juliet and Gertrude), a man and a woman in *Tales of Hoffmann* in which the man's part is itself sung by a woman, and even Offenbach and the storyteller Hoffmann. Like Offenbach and his double, the melancholic Hoffmann, Ginger is a would-be virtuoso who wishes to demonstrate her versatility but who misses what she aims for (Offenbach, a child prodigy and cello virtuoso, always wanted to write grand opera and never succeeded, even though he often parodied the dictatorship of grand opera. [Kracauer 1938, 153 and 347].) Like Carmen, Ginger is a mimic; unlike Carmen, however, Ginger is a failed mimic: she can't act, as we've seen. Furthermore, Ginger's dyed red hair permanently marks her throughout the series as a B-movie star (she's an imitation, a second-rate Marilyn Monroe).

And in adapting *Hamlet,* the castaways are clearly borrowers. The castaways' collective recycling of their cultural leftovers from the shipwreck has its own hierarchies, particularly when it comes to gender. In the episode, collaboration is gendered male. Though the musical is ostensibly for her benefit, Ginger is excluded from adapting *Hamlet.* Her exclusion and marginalization are registered in several ways. In contrast to Mary Ann, who plays a male role, Ginger plays a starring woman's part. Secondly, Ginger's speech is not derived from the play, as are Gilligan's and the Skipper's (except for a reference to "the conscience of the King," none of her lines bear on the play). Finally, the speech she sings is set not to music from *Carmen* but from Offenbach's *Tales of Hoffmann,* and it is not reprised with other members of the cast as is the case with Hamlet's and Polonius's arias.[31] Ginger's acting, the allusions to the femme fatale of "Barcarolle," and Ginger's part as Ophelia all confirm HH's low estimation of her abilities as an actress. At various moments Ginger tries to upstage Gilligan, even knocking him off balance at one point. And though Ginger is linked through Offenbach's opera to a femme fatale character, the courtesan Giulietta who dies by accidentally drinking poison meant for the poet Hoffmann (perhaps also linking her to Gertrude), Ginger is no femme fatale as far as HH is concerned. Indeed, as Ophelia, Ginger is also opposed to the temptress Carmen, who dies, though at the hands of an ex-lover rather than by suicide or by accident. Gilligan/Hamlet makes a joking reference to Ophelia's death when he tells Ginger/Ophelia "don't go near the water." As if confirming Hecuba's assessment of her the episode subtly suggests that Ginger's career is indeed at a dead-end.

The episode's conclusion further calls into question suggested moral differences between Hecuba and the castaways. Gilligan and the Skipper discover that Hecuba has left the island and the two of them discuss with the Professor what's happened. The radio announcer later asks, "Who but Harold Hecuba would think of an idea as brilliant as that [the musical]?" "Us, that's who," Gilligan responds. Like Carmen's voice in Gilligan's version of the "To be or not to be" soliloquy, Ginger is absent from his "us," and her response to Hecuba's departure is simply left unseen. The castaway men may be upset at Hecuba for first ripping them off and then deserting them, but they used Ginger to try to get off the island the same way that Hecuba used them to make his new musical.

The moral clarity of the differences between the two literary models of collaborative recycling and virtuoso individualism is muddied by the means of cultural production available both to Hecuba and the castaways. The castaway collective appropriates and mimics, after all, not only opera but opera as a musical. Making *Carmen* into a musical was hardly an original recycling in 1964. *Carmen* had in fact already been adapted and Americanized as the musical *Carmen Jones* (dir. Otto Preminger, 1954), set in the South and played out as love affairs among African Americans.[32] Moreover, both Offenbach's *Tales of Hoffmann* and Bizet's *Carmen* were themselves adaptations. Offenbach's opera was an adaptation of an adaptation, based on the dramatic adaptation by Jules Barbier and Michel Carré of three of E. T. A. Hoffmann's stories; *Carmen* was taken from Prosper Merimée's novella. Offenbach, a notorious self-plagiarist and self-recycler, took the music for the "Barcarolle" from his earlier romantic opera *Les Ondines du Rhin* (1864). Similarly, Bizet borrowed from three of his earlier works in composing *Carmen* (McClary 1992, 17), and Charles Gounod thought

Bizet had stolen Micaela's aria in the third act from him (McClary 1992, 28). Bizet's opera involved different kinds of mimicry as well. Carmen, for example, is herself a mimic of others. The opera's gypsy music isn't really Spanish, and Bizet took Carmen's "Hanabera" aria not from music played in Havana but from local Parisian nightclubs (where imitations of Spanish gypsy music were fashionable).

The episode's moral distinction between recycling and theft as forms of mimicry and appropriation falls apart, then, as Ginger and Gilligan are shown to be no more original and to have no more virtuosity than Hecuba. Moreover, the castaways invoke property rights only when their own adaptation is "stolen." They can take whatever they wish from Shakespeare, Bizet, and Offenbach, but what they've recycled is effectively their property in their view. Though Gilligan attempts to correct Hecuba by preserving Shakespeare as the author of *Hamlet,* the force of his correction is radically called into question by the fact that Hecuba's *Hamlet* is only a redoing of the castaway's musical rewrite, hardly the equivalent of Shakespeare's tragedy.

A critique of the self-aggrandizing, male-centered individualism of Hollywood television and film production is compromised not only by the way that collective recycling and virtuoso appropriation both involve mimicry, but, more crucially, by speed. As Kearny and Moran note, Lupino had mixed feelings about the speed of television production. She initially praised television "as exciting because it moves so fast. . . . You film a television picture in three days and you can see the finished product a week later. It's not like making motion pictures which take months to film and then more months to complete. . . . By the time a motion picture is finished you've forgotten it" (1995, 139). Years later, however, she complained that it is "harder to direct TV than movies. TV people want quality and they prefer it to be done in a short time. Sometimes that's impossible. I want to go back to movies because it would be like a vacation" (1995, 139-40). Whether due to Lupino's ambivalence or not, speed is the most radical deconstructer of the episode's moral opposition between the producer's and the castaway collective's models of authorship. Other than a more pronounced transvestism as Hecuba dresses as Ophelia, the only real difference between the castaways' version of *Hamlet* and the producer's is the speed of their productions ("I'll show you how to do it with pace! Tempo!" Hecuba says to the assembled cast, and he later says to the Professor, who is turning the record player by hand, "give me a better tempo! Faster!").

Hecuba's desire for a faster tempo rather than a substantive rewrite of the musical seems inexplicable until we consider that speed has been crucial from the outset. After the Skipper and Gilligan see Hecuba's plane crash, Gilligan is shown in time-lapse photography driving his cart to Ginger to obtain the radio so they can send messages to the rescue party. Yet Ginger is listening to the radio and won't give it up until her Hollywood News show is over. The announcement that Hecuba has been out searching for people to cast in his new musical turns out to be the (apparent) means of rescue. Ginger is already several steps ahead of the Skipper. Speed also already marks the musical adaptation before Hecuba intervenes. A four-and-a-half-hour play is reduced to a five-minute musical, and Ginger/Ophelia's version of the "Barcarolle" is particularly accelerated.

Yet the castaways are behind the producer, reconfirming their consistent belatedness on the show in general. The series itself is all about cultural adaptation, surviving on an island under duress. The fiction is that the castaways have next to nothing. In fact, though, they have quite an extensive reserve, so that anything they happen to need, such as opera records or costumes for *Hamlet,* is always on hand. The inadequacy of their reserves is nevertheless consistently registered in terms of their datedness. The record player has to be turned by hand, for example. In "The Producer," only Harold Hecuba is quick enough on his feet to bring *Hamlet* up to date. The show follows suit: its comedy depends on making literary history into an accelerated process of what I would call "speedy-adaptation."

A Tempest in a Pee Pot

In characterizing Nunn's *Twelfth Night* as conservative in the above discussion, I implicitly drew attention to a national difference between the examples on which I focused. I would like to clarify that difference now by considering a signal difference in American and English versions: the difference between the trained and untrained voice, between those who speak Shakespeare with an English accent and those who do not. The cultural conservatism of Nunn's *Twelfth Night* was emphasized in its promotion as embodying some kind of essential difference between the English kind of Shakespeare and the kind implicitly associated with American models. As the Telluride announcement for Nunn's *Twelfth Night* asserts, with a barely concealed sneer: "the film succeeds in part due to Nunn's decision to ignore the box office lure of Hollywood stars, and to cast all the parts with outstanding British actors who can actually speak Shakespeare's lines with proper cadence and clarity."[33]

We can further examine the way that the transvestite voice both allows for a critical re-enunciation of Shakespeare texts adapted by Americans and calls that critique into question by considering English counter-examples of the virtuoso voice that link it to a slowed-down, aging male body, hence the loss of authorial mastery, a loss registered most fully in death. *Prospero's Books* and *The Dresser* both dramatize a loss of patriarchal control in an older virtuoso male actor's voice. *Prospero's Books,* in which Gielgud speaks the parts of all of the characters for almost the entire film, explicitly raises questions about authorship, and when critics have debated the extent to which Greenaway enlarges Prospero's powers, a consideration of Gielgud's voice has been crucial. Douglas Lanier writes, for example, that Greenaway adds "a third variable" to the longstanding conflation of Prospero and Shakespeare:

> our awareness of John Gielgud's stature as the last of the great triumverate of "heroic" Shakespearean actors, one of the few capable of bringing off a performance of all the play's parts. The merging of author, character, and actor is deepened by the sense that Gielgud, like Prospero and Shakespeare, is here giving a valedictory performance. . . . By casting Gielgud as Shakespeare/Prospero and deepening the resonances of this triple identification, Greenaway manages to conflate virtuoso performing with the act of writing: at least within the fiction of *Prospero's Books,* Gielgud's performing becomes the source of *The Tempest*'s text, rather than the text the source of his performance. (1996, 196-97)[34]

Recent feminist film theory might be used to support this reading. In her book *The Acoustic Mirror* (1988), Kaja Silverman argues that the female voice is generally coded as the lost maternal voice and that in classic cinema male castration is disavowed through the abjection of this view; consequently, castration returns in a number of threatening, paranoid forms. Following this logic, the use of Gielgud's voice for all the characters might be thought to be an attempt to usurp the female body's generative capacities. The problem with this reading, however, is that Gielgud's voice isn't exclusively male. It's a transvestite voice. Gielgud manages to play all the parts precisely through the digital remastering of his voice, effectively disguising its pitch, tone, timber, age, and gender as necessary.

The loss of mastery implied by the aged sound of Gielgud's voice might be read in relation to the operatic voice. In *The Angel's Cry* (1992), Michel Poizat argues that the pleasure a listener takes in the operatic cry is about a fantasy of a quest for a lost vocal object, and he maintains that the castrato's, and later the *travesti*'s, popularity lay in the way he/she could represent a radically purified, angelic voice, that is to say, a voice in the higher registers. The remastering of Gielgud's voice might be understood as an attempt to purify it in a similar manner.

Yet in obvious contrast to the castrato, who could reach the high pitch of the boy soprano and whose voice, like the operatic voice generally, was not miked in performance, Gielgud's transvestite voice is old, fully adult, and prosthetically amplified through the newest recording technology. Any claim for its purity depends not on Gielgud's technical self-mastery of his voice, but on its re-mastery through a sophisticated recording apparatus. Though Gielgud speaks all the parts only until Prospero releases his prisoners in Act 5, it's not easy to tell the difference between the real voices and Gielgud's ventriloquization of them because his voice has been altered beyond recognition when he speaks a part other than Prospero's. Moreover, the film subverts a claim for Prospero's mastery in several ways: Gielgud's voice is not synchronized with the other characters (Miranda is asleep while Gielgud speaks most of her lines from 1.2., for example, and even when awake, she never speaks, as is the case with everyone else in the film, until its end); Gielgud's voice is inconsistently synchronized with

Prospero, who is often doubled in the film (there is also a stand-in for Gielgud, Jasper van der Linden), and Prospero regularly goes in and out of his own voice when reciting lines of other characters.

Any claim for Prospero's authorial, patriarchal mastery is of course centered on his books, and critics have discussed the way that the film deconstructs authorship into the author-function and the book into discourse. Gielgud's words are not synchronized with the text. The beginning of the film is typical: we see the word "Boat-swain" being written on the screen and Gielgud repeating it several times in voice-over, the word echoing each time. This lack of synchronization both extends and undercuts Prospero's mastery not only by extending his sway over the diegesis but by putting Gielgud in an extradiegetic space as well. Many of Prospero's lines are spoken in voice-over, and Gielgud speaks as well the lines describing each of Prospero's twenty-four books.

The film also questions Prospero's mastery by counterpointing his voice with a supplemental vocal transvestism. All of Ariel's songs are lip-synched, overdubbed by a woman, Sarah Leonard. The songs on the soundtrack, always sung by women, bring into relief the limited range of Gielgud's voice in particular and the male voice in general. When Gielgud speaks Miranda's lines, we hear two voices in two registers, one high and one low, almost simultaneously. Yet he clearly cannot sing Ariel's songs. Even the boy actor performing Ariel (Paul Russell) can't do a falsetto to reach the quite high treble notes. Sarah Leonard's ability to hit these notes as well as much lower ones marks her as an alternative off-screen virtuoso separate from Gielgud/ Prospero. Ariel/Leonard, serving as a vocal prosthesis for Prospero, is divided not only in terms of gender but by the actors playing Ariel. Ariel's voice is never singular. Even when he speaks for the first time in his own voice, we see three Ariels onscreen writing down the lines (none of them mouth the lines). Ariel's own voice remains multi-disembodied.[35]

Gielgud is thus inside and outside of Prospero, inside and outside of Shakespeare. Through this deconstruction of authorial identity, the film defines itself as avant-garde cinema, displaying a contradiction built into classic cinema involving the embodied male voice. As Silverman writes:

Even as it issues and reissues this sexually differentiating edict [aligning diegetic interiority with the embodied female, exteriority with the disembodied male voice-over], dominant cinema works against it, holding its male as well as female characters to the imperative of visibility, and securing both within the limits of the story. Hollywood thus erects male subjectivity over a fault line, at the site of a major contradiction. In order both to conceal this contradiction and to sustain the male viewer/listener in an impossible identification with the phallus, classic cinema has elaborated a number of strategies for displacing the privileged attributes of the disembodied voice-over on to the synchronized male voice—mechanisms for reinscribing the opposition between diegetic and extradiegetic within the fiction itself. As a result of these mechanisms, interiority and exteriority are redefined as areas within the narrative rather than as indicators of the great divide separating the diegesis from the enunciation. "Inside" comes to designate a recessed space within the story, while "outside" refers to those elements of the story which seem in one way or another to frame that recessed space. Woman is confined to the former, man to the latter. (1988, 54)

Gielgud's voice secures and calls into question this engendering of the voice, particularly in terms of the way it literally frames Prospero with mirrors throughout the film.

In the screenplay, Greenaway writes:

The mirror is apparently held by dark, almost unseen, black figures—dark fleshed, ambiguously-sexed, naked—and they strain and grunt to hold up their large heavy mirror . . . as though this first conjured image of Prospero's imagining is torturously arrived at. Later this device of mirror and mirror carriers will be developed and many changes rung from its possibilities. When the image in the mirror is optimistic, the mirror-carriers will be light-skinned, handsome, young . . . and the mirror easy and light to lift. When the image is pessimistic, its carriers will be haggard, ugly, misshapen and dark, and the mirror heavy and burdensome. These figures will be more and more revealed until the idea is made concrete that Prospero's imaginings—good and bad, fair and foul—are always

> "reflected" in mirrors held by minions . . . as though a mirror was
> always necessary for Prospero to make his imaginings manifest.
> (1991, 47-49)

Any attempt to see the mirrors as exterior indices of Prospero's inner state are compromised, however, by the lack of synchronized sound such that diegetic and extradiegetic cannot be aligned with female and male respectively.

In addition to the mirror as a metaphor for the split in authorship, Gielgud's nonsynchronized and technically altered voice returns us to the question of the film's relation to pornography. As we saw in chapter 2, the filmed version swerves away from the more explicit representation of pornography called for in the screenplay. I would add now that though the film shows plenty of penises, none of them is ever erect. There is a multiplication of the penis (and breasts), a symptom, according to Freud, of fetishism. Caliban's penis is displayed quite openly, though, as we saw in chapter 1, it dangles in a completely bizarre way from Michael Clark's body. In addition to questioning male authority by showing us only limp penises, the film questions Prospero's mastery in particular by keeping Gielgud's penis out of view, though we do see him naked when he bathes. Prospero's "oh so potent art" has its limits. We do see lots of urination, as when Ariel pisses a long, continuous stream during the storm, but no ejaculation.

One might imagine that the use of a technological prothesis to extend the range and power of an aging voice might imply that when younger, the voice was fully intact. I want to turn now to *The Dresser* to show that the opposite is the case. Here the male voice is distinctly not a transvestite voice. Its coherence is conferred retrospectively, however; it is a function of a eulogy delivered by his servant, the Dresser (Tom Courtenay), at the end of the film. Albert Finney plays an aging Shakespearean actor, Sir, who is losing his sanity while doing a production of *King Lear* in Britain during the blitz. Sir's ability to act depends on his voice, the size of the actress playing Cordelia, and a gay servant who does his make-up, the Dresser of the film's title. The character's aging and madness, parallel to Lear's, is countered by his voice. The film is conventionally realistic in its use of synchronized sound. The actor's command is demonstrated when he and the cast arrive at the station late for their train and the actor booms out (in close-up) "Stop the train!" The train in fact stops and waits for them to board. Yet Sir also turns out to have limited strength of another kind: he can only carry a light Cordelia. In a strange and comic scene, Sir appears to take up with a young actress named Irenee intent on seducing him. Sir initially appears to respond to her advances, but the scene takes a funny turn as Sir appears to be inspecting her body more than he is turned on by it:

> Do you have good legs? [She looks puzzled. He motions with his hand to have her raise her skirt. She looks frightened and a bit daunted but complies. He motions her to do it higher, so that her stocking top shows.]
>
> Higher. [She complies again. He wheels his chair closer to her and touches her leg and gropes her.]

What looks initially like an erotic behind-the-scenes act of hot adultery is cut short as Sir picks Irenee up, stumbles, drops her, and dismisses her. She thinks he is attracted to her youth but, as the Dresser explains, he is in fact interested in her size:

> Never mind about a young Cordelia, ducky. He wants a light Cordelia. Light, ducky, light. Look yourself at the ladyship. You don't understand he needs youth. You're lighter than she is. You're not the first one to be placed on the scales. How do you think her ladyship got the job? Her ladyship went from map carrier to Cordelia in a single night. . . . It's not youth or talent or star quality he's after ducky, but a moderate eater.

This exposure of Sir's secret and his inability to carry even a Cordelia lighter than his wife is quickly followed by his death in his dressing room.

It is precisely Sir's death that most fully secures a hierarchy of voice, character, and genre. Once he is dead, the Dresser can out himself and declare his love for him. The Dresser gets the last word, but there's no one to bitch, whine, and mourn him as he does Sir. Moreover, the dresser's mourning is represented in distinctly melodramatic rather than tragic terms. Though Sir may have been a self-centered, mean-spirited person, the film endorses the hierarchical relation between actor and dresser by representing the former's short-comings as the consequences of unendurable suffering and the latter's as the manifestations of a bitchy queen.

Prospero's Books might seem like a queer film in contrast to *The Dresser* in the former's eschewing of nostalgia for either an unamped human voice or an England whose citizens were mobilized by Shakespeare to participate in a national fantasy of English stoicism in the face of adversity (in *The Dresser,* watching or performing *King Lear* above ground at night during Nazi air raids). While there are important differences between these two films, the point of contrasting them to the American examples I have earlier considered is to show how they both celebrate a virtuoso, English male voice that is adequate to Shakespeare, even if that virtuosity is revealed to be lost, due either to the actor's advanced age or the character's death. In this sense, *Prospero's Books* and Nunn's *Twelfth Night* present themselves as antitransvestite voice films either by calling up a memory or fantasy of the male actor's voice when it was fully intact, or by locating Shakespeare in the nineteenth-century English music hall, thus metaleptically trumping the American move to translate Shakespeare into the musical.

Walk (Like a) Man

Though it has focused on Shakespearean examples, the foregoing analysis of the ways in which the transvestite voice subverts a critique of American-adapted Shakespeares by marking them as retarded, as noise, or as nonsense raises theoretical issues that clearly extend beyond the scope of Shakespeare. One thinks of Sandra Bernhard doing lesbian covers of Billy Paul's "Me and Mrs. Jones" and Prince's "Little Red Corvette" in *Without You, I'm Nothing* (dir. John Boskovich, 1991); or an art film such as *Farinelli* (dir. Gerard Corbiau, 1994), about the famous castrato, in which there is a dialectic between penile and vocal potency; or more mainstream films such as *The Adventures of Priscilla, Queen of the Desert* (dir. Stephen Eliot, 1994). I would like to compare two 1990s non-Shakespearean examples, one avant-garde gay and one mainstream heterosexual, to show that the same kind of problem with regard to volume and critical weight exists outside Shakespeare. In *Edward II* (1991), Derek Jarman embraces adaptation as a distinct secondariness through the female star and the male silent transvestite. In *Mrs. Doubtfire* (1993), Chris Columbus tells the story of a divorced father and unemployed voice-over mimic who ends up as a transvestite television mimic positioned as a child.

Jarman's film explores an explicitly thematized notion of authorship as secondary revision. Jarman's *Edward II* sets up a struggle between Mortimer (Nigel Terry), who has the phallus and speaks through the microphone, and Edward (Stephen Waddington), who is castrated and overhears while in prison. Prince Edward (Jody Graber), who both has the phallus (he overhears and rewrites through puns) and yet is castrated (a boy), displaces Mortimer and Edward II as recoders. Mortimer is in the conventionally masculine coded position of exterior diegesis and Edward II is in the conventionally coded feminine position of interior diegesis. Jarman rewrites Marlowe's play in terms of new media technologies, the main apparatus of state power. State power has a history, coded in terms of theatrical props from throne to the string quartet. History of state coincides with technical innovations: press conferences, microphones, family portrait photograph, the spotlight used by Isabella, and so on. Placing the ear over the eye as a means of rewriting allows for new, queer-positive forms of cultural reproduction. Edward's line "Something still buzzes in my ears," for example, is metonymically linked to taking it up the ass (as in the pun on "arse" in Joe Orton's play *Prick Up Your Ears*).

In placing the ear above the eye, the film moves from women such as rock diva Annie Lennox and Isabella (Tilda Swinton), whose clothing recalls Evita and Jackie O, to the transvestite boy Prince Edward. An all-woman string quartet performs Mozart and then breaks into a tango as Edward and Gaveston (Andrew Tiernan) campily dance and exchange a cigarette. A spotlight previously used on Isabella is now focused on Annie Lennox, who doubles her, during the dance between Edward and Gaveston. Well-known for her male drag wear, Lennox appears wearing a man's suit and covers Cole Porter's "Every Time You Say Goodbye" after Edward II has banished

Gaveston. The song plays first as background music, then there is a cut to Lennox, then back to Edward and Gaveston dancing in pajamas, then to Edward and Gaveston in spotlight, then to Lennox moving into the spotlight (which recalls Isabella in spotlight, with the microphone in front of her), back to a close-up of Edward and Gaveston kissing, back to Annie Lennox; and finally, the camera pulls back to reveal all of them, and then Lennox walks off the set. Lennox's cover recodes the gender orientation of the song so that it is not only about the two male lovers saying goodbye but about a woman letting go of the men as well: Lennox is the one we actually see exit. She is saying goodbye to Edward, leaving him in a way Isabella won't. The recoding of Marlowe's play arises out of a marked secondariness, then. Annie Lennox doubles Isabella and is associated with the song cover, with the secondary, rather than with the famous politician's glamorous wife or with a movie star.

Jarman also rewrites the play by enlarging Prince Edward's part and making him into a silent transvestite virtuoso. Unlike the play, in which he has a very small part, Jarman's version has him appear throughout the film. Prince Edward is a virtuoso and a transvestite. He first plays with his mother's hat and she prays and others comment that she is a saint. Prince Edward later appears cross-dressed, wearing long earrings and slick- backed hair parted in the middle that mirrors his mother, as well as lipstick and heels. He also imitates his mother's behavior. After she kills Kent by biting his jugular vein in vampire fashion, he licks blood from Kent too. But Edward's transvestism is insubordinate rather than subservient mimicry. He is not a "momma's boy." When Isabella signs the order for Gaveston's recall from France, for example, Edward traces her name in dust on the table, as if he's rewriting her. Prince Edward plays aggressively, perhaps exceeding his mother (who we see shooting a dead deer with a bow and arrow at one point): After the butcher scene in which Edward and Spenser kill the soldier, Prince Edward is seen dressed as a terrorist (he wears a black ski mask) and playing with a toy machine gun. In an earlier scene, Gaveston and Prince Edward play with Edward II's sword as if it were a machine gun.

Though Prince Edward only literally speaks at the very end of the film, his silence is made to speak just before the end as he stands cross-dressed on a cage in which Mortimer and Isabella sit dejectedly and listens to a walkman while mock-conducting Tchaichovsky's "Dance of the Sugar Plum Faeries" from the *Nutcracker* ballet. The soundtrack activates puns on "faeries," "nut," and "man" so that we can read the imprisonment of Mortimer and Isabella as the revenge of a ball-breaking gay boy who has learned to walk like a man.

In celebrating a boy transvestite as future ruler of England, Jarman might appear to be doing something transgressive. Yet his critique is limited by the way his rewrite of Marlowe depends on a macho "rough trade" representation of gayness, one that feminizes Marlowe as a "queen." As Jarman writes in the screenplay: "Neither Edward nor Gaveston were the limp-wristed lisping fags so beloved of the tabloids. . . . Marlowe drops classical references like confetti through the text to prove he's up-to-the-minute. Such an intellectual queen" (1991, 30 and 14). Yet Jarman, too, is an up-to-the-minute intellectual queen. In perhaps a rather predictable way, Jarman can regard his own film as "heavy" by marking it off from a notion of rewriting as feminized fluff.

The transgressiveness of Jarman's rewrite is also potentially moderated by consideration of the way the transvestite voice has been taken up in the mainstream comedy *Mrs. Doubtfire*. Robin Williams plays a vocal mimic, Daniel Hillard, who does voice-overs for children's cartoons and is fired at the beginning of the film because he won't read dialogue that, in his view, portrays smoking cigarettes positively. His wife, Miranda (Sally Fields), leaves him soon after (he can never hold down a job), and she gets custody of the kids (he gets extremely infrequent visitations). To see them more often, he replies to her advertisement for a housekeeper and adopts, with the help of a gay brother (Harvey Firestein), the persona of Mrs. Doubtfire. He is hired, harasses and spies on his ex-wife's new boyfriend, fixes up an apartment, and in a tour de force scene, tries to land a job at a local television show dressed as himself and prevent the new boyfriend from proposing to his ex-wife while dressed as Mrs. Doubtfire (both at the same restaurant). His wife finds him out, however, and, though she will not take him back, he does get to see his children more often and he gets the television job. In the afternoons, they watch him as Mrs. Doubtfire on TV.

The comedy is clearly directed at divorced fathers and is skewed in favor of the husband and against his "bitch" wife Miranda. If its "backlash" politics are not exactly those of Jarman's film, *Mrs. Doubt-fire* nevertheless offers an interesting take on the same material. Here the divorced, heterosexual white male father is recuperated not by becoming suitable marriage material (he never even dates in the film) but through his virtuoso talents as a vocal mimic and, finally, as a children's television entertainer. Williams's own gifts as a mimic are given full rein, particularly in a scene in which he is first made up by his gay brother. Williams goes through a whole range of types and stars, including Barbara Streisand, before settling on Mrs. Doubtfire. By the film's end, Hillard is able to see his children more frequently, but he remains a castrated figure not only as an ex-husband without a new partner (or even a date) but also as a father. He is able to get more visitations because he wins a job as a host of an afternoon's children's show in which he continues to use his Mrs. Doubtfire persona, a show his own children watch. His paternal authority shrinks to the size of a television image, an image that is distinctly asexual. Whereas Hillard begins with a virtuoso male, disembodied voice-over mimicry, he ends with an embodied, transvestite, feminized vocal mimicry, his voice now confined to a single character impersonation.

Jarman's transgressive child transvestite Prince Edward remains transgressive, we might say, only as long as he remains a child. As an adult, Prince Edward can look forward to being a childlike, castrated Peter Pan father whose transgressions are intensely regulated, and, when regarded by the eye of the divorce court as the signs of an unfit father, meet with severe punishment: supervised visitations, one visit a week.

Unheard of Shakespeares?

In analyzing some Shakespearean and non-Shakespearean examples of the transvestite voice, I have sought to show not how Shakespeare has been resignified in some subversive "queer" way by being lip-synched, but that whatever subversive, transgressive force the American examples have is compromised by their own means of cultural transmission. (The English examples of Shakespeare I have considered I do not consider to be transgressive.) Even *William Shakespeare's Romeo and*

Juliet, which dumbs down Romeo and Juliet in order to show how their suicides issue from their participation in Verona Beach's gang banging, drug taking, party-all-night-long family feud rather than from their rejection of it, has literally to retard itself, as I will show in chapter 5, in order to make its pedagogical point clear to its targeted teen audience. These American films and television episode are not simply inane, I hope it is clear. But neither are they redeemable through some kind of political analysis that would seek to convert ostensibly trivial texts into serious (i.e., political) texts. For many, if not all, of the readings I have engaged in here might strike some readers as themselves not worth the trouble (the texts don't bear this kind of scrutiny) or as thin examples of an excessive overhearing, a hallucination of meanings by an eccentric critic. Put more broadly, I have tried to show that any attempt to redeem trivial, "lite" popular culture by reading it in terms of serious, "heavy" politics will fail. As I suggested in the Introduction, politics has no necessary purchase on the serious but may itself be regarded as a trivial pursuit, especially by avowedly more serious political critics who subsume a narrow definition of politics (as a Rights discourse) by cultural politics.

My So-Called Shakespeare: Mourning the Canon in the Age of Postpatriarchal Multiculturalism, or the Shakespeare Pedagogue as Loser

Yo! Shakespeare Raps

Political critics have tended to assume that the popularization of Shakespeare will contribute to a critique of capitalism, American imperialism, and, eventually, a progressive social transformation.[1] The present displacement of a literary Shakespeare, the author of canonical plays and poems, by "Shakespeares," the representations, performances, and author-functions, and the broader displacement of literary by cultural studies has been regarded by cultural critics as a means of renewing interest in the plays and of multiplying audiences for recodings of them. The Shakespearean or cultural critic also tends to assume that he or she can include all reproductions in the database of Shakespeare studies and that he or she can adopt both low and high positions inside and outside of academia, can both get all the elite in-jokes and appreciate the general view, can work through the contradictions between these positions to make possible new subjectivities and open up new kinds of oppositional, dissident readings. The hip and the politically radical go together in this account. A corollary assumption is that Shakespeare reproductions, Shakespeare cultural criticism, and youth culture are all mutually interpenetrating subcultures: everyone can see, or with some instruction can be brought to see, Shakespeare in the same subversive way (Sinfield 1995).

A crucial site of critique, given these assumptions, has been pedagogy. Cultural critics have tended to look to subcultures as the sources of dissident readings, and the notion of a subculture has been virtually coextensive with youth culture.[2] The fantasy here is that intellectuals have access to the "minds of the children of the ruling class" (Mathews 1991, 58). Rewriting Shakespeare differently in the classroom will mean, it is assumed, that power outside the classroom will be reproduced differently (Ferguson 1987; Sinfield 1984). This has meant decentering Shakespeare in the classroom, moving away from a "coverage" model and toward historicizing the plays through noncanonical documents (Howard and O'Connor 1987, 5-11). It has also involved the introduction of new technologies of cultural reproduction. Students in an average college-level Shakespeare class are now less often shown a single production of a given play in its entirety (such as a BBC production from the 1970s and early 1980s) than they are select scenes from two or more versions. (CD-ROM editions of the plays have furthered this fragmentation.)[3]

The new popularization of Shakespeare on film might seem fruitful ground for cultural critics in part because it draws on a youth market (the same could be said for other multimedia and electronic Shakespeares). Yet a review of recent films in which Shakespeare is a signifier in a pedagogical context disturbs rather than confirms these assumptions in that they align the pedagogue and his students with the figure of the loser. In films such as *Renaissance Man* (dir. Penny Marshall, 1994), *Quiz Show* (dir. Robert Redford, 1994), and *Last Action Hero,* as well as in a 1997 episode of the television sitcom *3rd Rock from the Sun* (dir. Terry Hughes), Shakespeare is a means of saving the loser white male father or is an unconsoling symptom of his absence. It is not an accident that *Hamlet* and *Henry V* predominate in these recent cinematic representations of the teacher as loser.

Shakespeare Rerun

The films and the TV episode mentioned above mark a shift away from the earlier *Brady Bunch* and *Ozzie and Harriet* episodes as well as from the 1952 film *She's Working Her Way Through College* (dir. H. Bruce

Humberstone), discussed in the Introduction, and toward a more direct view of the Shakespeare teacher as loser. In *The Brady Bunch* episode (originally aired in 1971), patriarchy is implicitly under threat from the reconstructed or "blended" family, but the stepfather's authority (and Shakespeare's) is never really questioned (nor is the teacher's). The *Ozzie and Harriet* episode, "An Evening with *Hamlet*," also puts the father at the center of the drama. It is a complex episode because it ambivalently positions the father as both for Shakespeare and against him, moving him between a literally unspeakable Shakespeare and a hyper-spoken Shakespeare.

The episode begins at breakfast with Ricky announcing that the television set is on the blink. After Dave mentions that he is reading Hamlet in high school, Ozzie recites from memory the first five lines of the "To be or not to be" soliloquy and then suggests that the family read the play aloud that night. Ricky objects, complaining that the play is "corny," but Dave and Ozzie overrule him. Ozzie supplements the high school teacher by displacing the broken television, teaching his sons to appreciate Shakespeare. Ozzie's self-appointed pedagogical role is enlarged to include the neighborhood as well. Ozzie invites a neighbor (Don de Fores) over to join them, but the neighbor, who disliked Shakespeare in high school, has already planned a poker game he wants Ozzie to join that night. Ozzie resists the offer but then inexplicably changes his mind and attempts, unsuccessfully, to get out of the family reading (Harriet thinks the reading is a great idea and suggests, to Ozzie's dismay, that they do a reading once a week).

Ozzie's ambivalence about Shakespeare is signaled that night by his (non)performance. When the family meets to begin reading, Ozzie takes the lead, but he cannot speak a line from the play he holds in his lap. He stalls, asking for water, complaining about "the fine print" as he holds the book away from himself, and he manages to read only the title of the play (three times in a row) before he is interrupted by the doorbell. A mysterious actor named Cameron Whitfield (John Carradine) enters and suggests, anticipating pedagogical practices of the 1990s, that the family act out the play rather than simply read it aloud.[4] (Whitfield, who appears asking for directions to 1623 Avon, appears initially to be Shakespeare's ghost doubling as Old Hamlet, 1623 being the year of the First Folio's publication and Avon of course being an allusion to Stratford-upon-Avon.)

Ozzie's and his family's ambivalence is never fully resolved in terms of the diegesis, and everyone, including the television repairman and the neighbors who want Ozzie to play poker, performs parts of *Hamlet*. What is remarkable here, however, is that the performances are pretty good. Instead of reading from the text, as Ozzie initially tries (and fails) to do, everyone recites it from memory as if they were either possessed by Shakespeare or were trained actors.[5] In a quasi-Brechtian moment of estrangement, the actors playing the characters appear to step out of character and inadvertently reveal themselves to be professional actors. The episode's deepest ambivalence is reserved for Whitfield's characterization. Whitfield appears at first to be the "spirit of Shakespeare" who read a mysterious sign that drew him to the Nelson house, but the epilogue suggests he is perhaps a con-man who just happens to know some Shakespeare: seeing a sign Ricky put in front of the house advertising *Hamlet* for a quarter, the actor gains admission to the Nelsons' home not in order to elevate the family through Shakespeare but to gain entree into the poker game that succeeds the reading of *Hamlet*. The final shots of the episode are of Ozzie and his friends' jaws dropping as they see Whitfield shuffle the deck and deal with incredible dexterity. The episode's resolution, such as it is, depends in any case on a stranger who acts as a supplement to the father but whose excessiveness in relation to the Nelson family and their neighborhood compromises the episode's naturalism.

She's Working Her Way Through College is concerned less with saving the father than with saving the husband. This film positions the theater professor as loser insofar as he is identified with Shakespeare. Professor John Palmer (Ronald Reagan), who teaches at Mid-West State, is engaged in a long-standing rivalry with a former all-American football quarterback, Shep Slade (Don de Fores), for the affections of Palmer's wife, Helen (Phyllis Thaxter). In a parallel subplot, an ex-showgirl turned student named Angela (Virginia Mayo) is desired by a student, Don (Gene Nelson), the current football quarterback, who already has a girlfriend named "Poison" Ivy (Patrice Wymore). (Angela worked in burlesque in order to save money for college and is eventually exposed by her rival.) The "cool" students at Mid-West

State do not like Shakespeare. The loser girlfriend Ivy identifies with Shakespeare's Juliet, and Don even addresses her mockingly by that name. Striking a similar note, on his return to campus for the big game with Michigan, Shep says unashamedly that he never read *Macbeth* and asks Palmer, "How did that brawl turn out?" And Palmer goes from loser to popular winner as he agrees to let his students stage a new musical written by Angela rather than *Romeo and Juliet*. He subsequently wins his wife's loyalty for good, and rival Shep is exposed as dumb, lecherous, and relatively spineless.

As *She's Working Her Way Through College* rehabilitates Palmer, positioning him as a "swell" instead of an "egghead," it also increasingly distances him from Shakespeare, who is on the side of a "morally proper" cultural monopoly of Anglo-identified, academic tradition, while Palmer is on the side of a (potentially) "morally improper" free market of American show business. Defending his decision to stage a musical rather than a Shakespeare play, Palmer points out to the college president that attendance at last year's "Shakespeare thing" was sixty people. In contrast, the musical is selling advance tickets, Palmer notes, and "might even run for a week." To make sure that the musical isn't "improper," the president, who thought *Oedipus Rex* was "dirty," appoints Shep as censor, to Palmer's dismay. And once Angela's past as a showgirl is exposed in the school newspaper, the president insists that Palmer expel her from the play. Instead, in a scene anticipating Reagan's role as spokesman for General Electric, Palmer praises Angela in front of the assembled student body, even though it means he will be fired, and he defends at length the cultural importance of American "show business."[6]

Yet *She's Working Her Way Through College* redeems Professor Palmer from loserdom not just by opposing his freewheeling, free-market philosophy to the cultural elitism of Shakespeare but by displacing the opposition between traditional (foreign) Shakespeare and innovative (American) musicals onto an opposition between male professor and ex-showgirl student, the latter of which is oddly on the side of both the musical and Shakespeare. Angela does manage to save herself from expulsion and get Palmer a promotion to full professor (she confronts the president, who had propositioned her when she was in burlesque), and she does star in the musical. Yet as Palmer is progressively distanced from Shakespeare, Angela is brought into closer proximity to him. Rather than reject Shakespeare, some of Angela's musical numbers incorporate him. In one number that mocks Freudian psychoanalysis of dreams, for example, the refrain is Prospero's line "This is the stuff that dreams are made of" [sic], and near the close of this number we hear a brief quotation of the wedding march from Felix Mendelssohn's *A Midsummer Night's Dream*.

The consequence of Angela's increasing closeness to Shakespeare is that her moral and intellectual standing begin to be compromised. Shakespeare's compromising presence is felt most acutely in the actual musical, *Give Them What They Want*, the title of which alludes to the subtitle of *Twelfth Night*, namely, *Or What They Will*. Angela's musical is about a number of famous women through the ages who were dumb in school but who were nevertheless "successes." The first of these women (all of whom are played by Angela) is Cleopatra, whose only "easy mark," we are told by a chorus girl, was Antony. Angela's Cleopatra misquotes Shakespeare's Cleopatra's "give me to drink mandragora" (1.5.3) as "give leave to drink of this nectar" to Antony, played by boyfriend Don, who has come onstage smoking a cigar. She then says to the audience, "I know that one day Shakespeare will write" followed by the refrain "This is the stuff that dreams are made of," sung by Egyptian guards. The proximity between Angela and Shakespeare helps legitimate the free market by displacing the moral, aesthetic, and intellectual problems it presents onto famous, street-smart, and unschooled women who manage to get their men: Angela's Cleopatra, in an obviously misogynistic anti-intellectual musical number, makes Angela into precisely the gold-digging vamp that the college president had accused her of being and that Palmer had vigorously denied she was. (This Cleopatra poisons Antony to get his gold and then survives him rather than commits suicide.) Palmer palms off the ills of the free market, as it were, by holding up Cleopatra, and by extension, Angela, as a model of cut-throat market success based on street-smart feminine wiles rather than on an academic education. (Ivy was supposed to play the second lead in the musical but, except for one musical number, simply drops out of the end of the film).

While American television shows such as the *Ozzie and Harriet* episode about *Hamlet* have sometimes required a supplement to the father's authority over Shakespeare and while a film such as *She's Working Her Way Through College* saves the male professor from loserdom by displacing his identification with Shakespeare onto a morally suspect woman, the character who teaches Shakespeare, whether male or female, is unambiguously portrayed in more recent films and television sitcoms as a loser, obsolete, already behind his or her more innovative students, who are in some cases both more crass and more canny than their teachers.[7] In the *3rd Rock* episode, for example, the father, Dick (Jon Lithgow), an extraterrestrial who works as a college physics professor whose students cheer when they manage to do well enough to get D's, fails miserably at directing a "spaced out" production of *Romeo and Juliet* and is replaced by the sports coach (played by Mike Ditka). Dick alone sees Shakespeare as something to study and mime, whereas other characters, including his son Tommy who wants to play Romeo so he can make out with the girl playing Juliet, either mock Shakespeare or appropriate his work as their own. Moreover, an Anglo Shakespeare is identified with the alien. Dick watches Olivier's *Hamlet* and bases his acting technique on it. In contrast, an earthly suitor to his daughter recites lines from the balcony scene of *Romeo and Juliet* and claims he wrote it.

A preachy episode of *The Cosby Show* works similarly. Aired first in 1987, this episode is about son Theo Huxtable's difficulty reading and appreciating Shakespeare in his high school English class. Theo's father, Heathcliff Huxtable, gets Theo to appreciate Shakespeare only by inviting over the celebrity actor James Earl Jones, who recites passages from *Julius Caesar.* The displacement of the teacher (and the father) by the famous actor implicitly marks Theo's teacher as a loser. Shakespeare doesn't need to be taught presumably because there is nothing to say about his plays; one need only recite his lines and marvel at their beauty.[8]

One could, of course, criticize recent popularizations of Shakespeare pedagogy for expressing and endorsing a conservative, "backlash" national fantasy whereby Shakespeare the cultural icon upholds the authority of white male patriarchy under pressure from feminism (divorce), immigration, and corporate down-sizing.[9] *Renaissance Man,* for example, fantasizes a kind of multicultural fascism whereby all antagonisms arising from ethnic and racial differences are resolved through the militarization of the teaching profession and the idealization of Shakespeare as student and soldier.[10] The redemption of "dumb as dog shit" soldiers into fighting machines and an uncaring adman into a caring teacher and father through a "'ten hut!" salute to Shakespeare is perhaps what the writers of *The Shakespeare File* have in mind as a sort of *Dangerous Minds* (dir. John Smith, 1994) solution to what they take to be the present academic dumbing down on college campuses. Similarly, the ostensibly progressive comedy *High School High* (dir. Hart Bochner, 1996) displaces anxieties about white males as losers onto urban, disenfranchised African Americans, equating urban renewal with a gentrified stripclub in which an "over the hill" black stripper performs incompetently as Lady Macbeth with two strippers in the background, receiving a tip in her bra from a man in the audience (see figure 5.1).[11]

Yet to imagine that a more progressive popularization would turn away from the loser would be to miss the complexity of the loser figure in American popular culture. Critics assume that students don't want to regard themselves as losers. In her afterword to the anthology *Shakespeare Reproduced,* Margaret Ferguson, for example, rehearses Pierre Bourdieu and Claude Passerson's account of education in which students who are members of subordinate social formations are regarded by their teachers and perhaps themselves as "academic failures" (1987, 278). The move political critics make here is to recode that failure as dissidence: what the dominant regards as a lack of intelligence and sensibility, the cultural critic regards as political resistance on the part of the disenfranchised. Alan Sinfield begins his book *Cultural Politics: Queer Readings* by telling an anecdote about his brief encounter with a young Jewish security guard at Heathrow airport on his way from London to the United States. The guard turns out to dislike Shakespeare intensely. Sinfield celebrates the inspector's lack of appreciation of Shakespeare as a sign of his subcultural dissidence: as a Jewish reader, he cannot be expected to love and celebrate *The Merchant of Venice.* Conversely, critics tend to regard any minority identification with Shakespeare as politically conservative. For example, in their history of the Vitagraph silent Shakespeare films produced at the beginning of this century, Uricchio and Pearson write: "The reception of these films might be interpreted in terms of appeals

Figure 5.1: "Live Nude *Macbeth*" as urban renewal in Hart Bochner's *High School High*.

to the assimilationist and upwardly mobile tendencies of the workers and immigrants alleged to have constituted the bulk of the nickelodeon audience" (1993, 6). Furthermore, cultural critics assume that students will embrace progressive popularizations of Shakespeare (or progressive readings of conservative popularizations) because they are hipper, more contemporary than the more traditional popularizations (and pedagogical approaches) that sacralize Shakespeare.

What happens to this account of dissident reading when the dominant no longer views itself as the winner, but instead embraces the position of the loser, when there are many different kinds of losers, and when "loser" can be a term of praise as well as a term of abuse? How might cross-racial identifications on the part of white male teenagers complicate these accounts? A film such as *Renaissance Man* still presumes a primarily white audience: the rap version of *Hamlet* performed by mostly African American student soldiers appeals precisely to a white suburban teenage male audience, who make up the bulk of rap's consumers. What are we to make of cultural criticism's identification with youth culture, its interest in aligning itself with the student rather than the teacher? What might it mean for cultural critics of Shakespeare to embrace a youth culture that presently transvalues stupidity as cool and in which Shakespeare doesn't necessarily have the phallus?

To address these questions, we may observe first that far from being clearly aligned with hipness, cultural criticism, like Shakespeare, may be considered uncool by its intended student consumers. As we've seen in the *MTV Romeo and Juliet Special, Dead Poets Society,* and *Looking for Richard,* students can be expected to respond to Shakespeare with boredom, or, as in *Clueless,* to be more interested in a secondary, film version of a Shakespeare play than in the original play itself. In order to make Shakespeare teachable, films such as *Renaissance Man* try to negotiate an acute contradiction between Shakespeare as authentic ("old") and Shakespeare as *au courant.* Whereas in an earlier pedagogical scene such as that represented in *My Bodyguard* (dir. Tony Bill, 1980) Shakespeare might be introduced as "classic" (here *Romeo and Juliet*) and opposed to a "contemporary" American musical adaptation (here *West Side Story*), more recently, the Shakespeare film tries to occupy both positions at the same time.[12] In almost all of these recent films, Shakespeare is presented in conventional theatrical terms; one of the two exceptions, *Last Action Hero,* presents Shakespeare in a dated 16mm black-and-white version; the other, *Clueless,* displaces Shakespeare's Hamlet with the film-star hunk Mel Gibson. Learning Shakespeare is understood in equally contradictory terms: On the one hand, teaching is represented archaically as rote memorization and recitation, learning by heart, in Mr. Chips-ish terms. On the other, learning involves updating and adapting Shakespeare to new technologies and American linguistic, cultural, and musical forms such as rap.

Though many Shakespeareans might want to see the Shakespeare pedagogue represented as using the internet, multimedia film and video comparisons, and CD-ROMs, it's hard to see how that would make much of a difference. Given the speed at which new technologies are produced, today's hip technology is tomorrow's archaic left-over.[13] As Andreas Huyssen remarks, the contemporary is always already the soon-to-be-dated: "our fascination with the new is always already muted, for we know that the new tends to include its own vanishing, the foreknowledge of its obsolescence in its very moment of appearance. The time span of presence granted the new shrinks and moves toward the vanishing point" (1995, 26). The problem for Shakespeare teachers is not just that students might get a "quick fix" from a reduced, fragmented, mediatized Shakespeare that could be considered a regressive form of instant entertainment instead of a moment of liberatory bliss. For the transvaluation of failure as cool in kiddie culture, as I argued in the Introduction, makes it difficult to differentiate consistently stupidity from intelligence. Shakespeareans (and critics in general) might divide each other into "young turks" and "old farts," trading insults like "out of it" and "old-fashioned" versus "fashionable" or "trendsuckers." Yet this division as to who has the real authentic Shakespeare or the real cool "Shakespeares" may be collapsed into the same side of another opposition altogether in which both Shakespeare and "Shakespeares" may be thought to be uncool by nonacademic consumers. Cultural criticism's commitment to newer forms of cultural reproduction, more some right-wing smear campaign, makes it inevitable that the cultural critic (or any other critic) will at some moments be positioned as a loser.

Before pursuing this point further, it is worth exploring the figure of the loser a bit more fully. The loser is the pivotal figure of American culture, the one through whom national fantasies are always projected.[14] The loser is the one who gets to have a secondary version of what he can't have, and this secondary version is both more and less than what the winner has. The loser is thus a paradoxical figure, one who settles for less, knowing that getting more, being the real thing, only means one becoming a more massive loser. Rather than try to become the star, for example, who is unhappy being a star anyway, the loser backs off and settles for something less, such as performing as a stripper. Into that work a woman might bring idealized fantasies of free women such as the 1920s flapper, idealized because decontextualized from all constraints placed on them by family, boyfriends, or husbands. Yet the loser always remains fixated on the thing she or he didn't go for and so never really manages to accommodate to having settled for less.

If the loser is the dominant figure of American culture, he is not a self-consistent one. Indeed, the loser has undergone a number of changes as he or she emerged as a figure in the 1990s. *Beavis and Butt-Head,* for example, depart from the romantic loser in that they will never get anything, particularly women and romance. Similarly, in *Clueless* Cher departs from the loser figure insofar as she doesn't know the original play. The true loser would know, and wouldn't give an answer to a question to which she didn't know the answer. Moreover, there's nothing really marked about her personality. She's pretty much vapid and does all the right "good" things, whereas the real loser gets the compensation of collecting and using all kinds of colorful, quirky fantasy material for which no one else has any use. This recent historical shift to faux losers who have even less or will never have anything might be accounted for in political and economic terms as the loss of access to secure middle-management jobs, loss of upward mobility, loss of the nuclear family, loss of whiteness as unmarked ethnicity. In literary terms, it might be read as the loss of high (literary) culture as a fixed referential point, of a particular icon such as Shakespeare as the phallus. In its place is an expanded and flattened out notion of "culture" in which everything can be referred to as a cultural artifact or text.[15] This displacement of the literary by the cultural might also be read as a displacement of book culture by movie culture.

In positioning the Shakespeare teacher as loser, popular films implicitly question whether the Shakespeare teacher has anything left to teach. And in adapting teaching to newer forms of media, they question as well what function the teacher serves, what cultural functions might now be lost, and perhaps most crucial of all, they question the contemporary response to that loss: Has what has been lost also been mourned? Is it even possible to mourn it? Is it possible to evade mourning it? The emergence of the loser in the 1990s may be read at least partly in relation to a central aspect of kiddie culture: it imagines it can skip over the work of cultural mourning in a postpatriarchal moment through new electronic technologies and archival modes that enable the past to be recycled in the present, the present always retrofitted to the past. From one point of view, dumbing down can't really occur because information and knowledge can always be permanently stored and instantly retrieved, as in the case of the television brain on MTV's *Idiot Savants*. This is the transmission of knowledge as imagined in terms of video: one can rewind and fast-forward without loss, unlike print culture, in which type fades, paper crumbles, pages get torn or ripped out, books get lost or stolen, go out of print, and so on.[16] The acceleration of new technologies also produces, however, a sense of being obsolete, of aging, of death, the sense that a particular text is yours (and that you can keep it out of circulation, if you wish). As Laurence Rickels argues in *The Case of California,* the cost of this ghost-busting through headsets, videos, and other gadgets is that the adolescent overcomes melancholia only through an identification with a group whose formation moves to sado-masochistic rhythms. "The disruption of mourning," Rickels comments, "is always the origin and onset of technologization" (1991, 25). The loser might be read, then, as kiddie culture's melancholic reply, perhaps against itself, to its own attempt to fast-forward through mourning in order to escape the American categorical cultural imperative to "have a nice day."

In considering the Shakespeare teacher as loser, I want to raise two related questions: first, what kind of cultural functions might be lost as the mediatization of Shakespeare threatens to make the Shakespeare teacher obsolete? And, second, what possibilities might be opened up for a Shakespeare pedagogy that embraces its own obsolescence instead of trying to be a la mode? In portraying Shakespeare as the means by which the loser pedagogue or the student redeems him or herself, the films *Renaissance Man, Quiz Show,* and *Last Action Hero* idealize and mythologize an American past or present. Shakespeare's citation shows him to be a symptom of a melancholic fixation on an earlier moment of white patriarchy. In portraying Shakespeare as the redemption of the academic loser, however, we don't see the loss of Shakespeare as the therapeutic enabler of a successfully terminated mourning; rather, we see that this notion of mourning is itself a fantasy. In the films I examine, mourning bleeds into melancholic nostalgia: mourning just isn't what it used to be in the United States.

I want to expand on this point about mourning by contrasting the figure of the Shakespeare pedagogue as loser as he is constructed in *So Fine* and *Dead Poets Society,* and the even earlier *Harry and Tonto,* on the one hand, and *Renaissance Man, Quiz Show,* and *Last Action Hero,* on the other. All of these films are concerned with saving the father, but whereas the father is positioned as the real loser in the earlier films from the 1970s, the more recent 1990s films redeem fathers as well as sons who fail their fathers. And all of these films have fairly simple accounts of the loser such that the loser figure is redeemed either as winner or as tragic figure. With the exception of *Last Action Hero,* these films set Shakespeare in opposition to newer media such as television. Shakespeare is what one has internalized through rote memorization.

Harry and Tonto is about the loser as loner, a retired teacher (Art Carney) who lives in New York and who cites *King Lear* when he meets with adversity (he is mugged and later forcibly evicted from his apartment building) or when he talks to his children. Unhappy after he moves in with his eldest son and his family, Harry leaves New York with his cat Tonto to stay with his daughter in Chicago, and when that doesn't work, he goes to Los Angeles to say with his youngest son. Shakespeare registers a generation gap. The children are indifferent to Shakespeare. When Harry asks his eldest who Lear is, he says, "I dunno," and when he cites Lear on speaking of Cordelia to his daughter, who owns a bookstore, she responds, "No more Shake-speare, Harry." This is Shakespearean tragedy rewritten as comedy, a Crosby and Hope road picture with a man and his cat as the buddies, recalling John Steinbeck's *Travels with Charley.* Harry himself chooses to leave each of his children without any provocation from them; indeed, it is clear at all points that Harry's children deeply love him.[17] Nevertheless, the film takes itself seriously as an adaptation of *King Lear,* and the analogy between Harry and Lear suggests that the patriarchal authority of the Shakespeare teacher is still in place.

In *So Fine* and *Dead Poets Society,* the teacher-as-loser theme emerges more directly, though the teacher's situation as loser is temporary and unsought rather than a self-identified position. Bobby Fine is more of a dark horse than a real loser. Similarly, in *Dead Poets Society,* Neal's father is the true loser, as is the school headmaster, while the teacher, John Keating, loses the battle but wins the war, retaining his students' loyalty even after he is dismissed. However, a certain ghost effect occurs in both films, registering a blocked mourning for the mother in one case and the father in the other. A maternal figure appears in the final shot of *So Fine,* and, as we saw earlier, the son can't disentangle himself from his father. *Dead Poets Society* has explicitly thematized affinities with the ghost story. Keating can't really succeed as an alternative father to the students by displacing real fathers with literary fathers such as Whitman or Shakespeare but is instead idealized as a fellow student. And he too is stunned to learn both that the headmaster had first taught in the same classroom he teaches in, and that he taught the same subject, English literature.

The 1990s films *Renaissance Man* and *Quiz Show* take a more positive view of the pedagogue as loser but are equally stuck in the past: both fixate on *Hamlet,* and both evince a marked absence of women. *Renaissance Man* is a sentimental, idealizing story of a loser temporarily down on his luck who makes good. One could call this film *The Color of Shakespeare.* The central character, Bill Rago (Danny Devito), is a divorced ad writer who has a troubled relationship with his daughter (she wants to become an astronomer and he's unsupportive). After he's fired because he misses a meeting and loses a client, he takes a job teaching English to "dumb as dogshit" white trash and African American soldiers at a local Army base who are on the verge of being honorably discharged due to their gross incompetence. In order to teach them English, Rago decides to teach them Shakespeare. In the very unrealistic narrative that follows, they all love *Hamlet* and even produce their own rap version of the play. He later takes them to see a theatrical production of *Henry V.* Of course Rago makes a mistake and gets the brightest student hauled off to jail after Rago attempts to help him, but the narrative is, on the whole, upbeat: he falls in love with a woman sergeant on the base, whips the students into shape, and buys his daughter a telescope. The soldiers prove him to be a swell teacher. At one point, Sergeant Cass (Gregory Hines), who takes a very dim view of Rago's efforts, tries to humiliate the soldiers by asking them to recite Shakespeare. After several fail to do so, one of them recites Henry V's St. Crispian's Day speech, and Sergeant Cass is duly impressed.

The film's fantasy is that there are no losers. It celebrates the formation of a multiethnic Army through a transnational Shakespeare such that a black sergeant, a white Jewish teacher, black and white trash students, men and women soldiers can all view themselves as winners. (Not one of the students fails an exam on *Hamlet*.) Even the student soldier who ends up in jail, ironically because of Rago's efforts to help him, nevertheless writes to Rago about *Othello* and ends his letter by citing *Hamlet*.

Yet *Renaissance Man's* sappy idealization of the loser is so over the top that it compromises the film's overt claims to have healed race and gender divisions through Shakespeare and to have mourned the Vietnam War. (One initially wimpy soldier's MIA father turns out actually to have been the war hero the soldier has fantasized him as being.) Fast-forwarding through the mourning of fathers means erasing the presence of women in the war and the armed forces or moving them into positions of abjection. Though Rago's daughter sits beside him during the film's graduation ceremony scene, the one female student, who sings about Ophelia in the rap version, disappears by the end of the film. The film closes with a final citation of *Hamlet* in a sound-off led by Sergeant Cass. Here Gertrude gets a bad rap: "Hamlet's Momma, she's the Queen / Buys it in the final scene. / Drinks a glass of funky wine, / Now she's Satan's valentine." For mourning to take place between sons and fathers, someone is still required to take the place of the abject, and that person here is gendered female.[18]

Renaissance Man broaches the possibility of a mediatized Shakespeare in a scene in which the students perform a rap version of Hamlet. The film subordinates this rewrite, however, to the more authentic moment of the student's recitation of Henry V's St. Crispian's Day speech, which in turn enables Sergeant Cass's rewriting of the play in his sound-off. *Quiz Show* privileges an orally recited Shakespeare even more sharply above electronic media, in this case, television, and marks a more serious portrait of the loser as tragic figure, a more deeply ambivalent view of American multiculturalism. The film is based on the true story of the Van Doren family and the national scandal in the 1950s over the rigging of the television game show *21*. Whereas academia in *So Fine* and a military academia in *Renaissance Man* are spaces in which everyone can be assimilated, and Shakespeare can be transcoded and adapted with an apparently infinite elasticity, academia in *Quiz Show* is the distinct province of an aristocratic, WASP culture. The film contrasts two overlapping triangles: one involves a youngish WASP professor named Charles Van Doren (Ralph Feines), a poor Jew from the Bronx named Herbert Stempel (John Turturro), and an upwardly mobile Washington, D.C.–based, assimilated Jewish investigator named Dick Goodwin (Rob Morrow); the other triangle involves Goodwin, Charles Van Doren, and his professor father, Mark Van Doren (Paul Scofield). Goodwin is an ambivalent outsider, admiring of the corrupt Charles Van Doren and his WASP family yet also the one who brings it down.

Quiz Show narrates the story of the tragic fall of academia into television, of education into entertainment, of learning and wisdom into trivial pursuits. The transformation of the television audience into "America's largest classroom" is shown to be a con, a way NBC can get higher ratings and the show's sponsor, Geritol, can make more money. Yet the film inadvertently deconstructs the opposition between quiz show and academia on which its nostalgic attachment to a pre-television American culture depends. Academia itself turns out to be a game in the Van Doren household. Charles and Mark Van Doren regularly play a game in the company of family and friends in which they recite lines from Shakespeare and win by identifying their source. The contest takes place at Mark's birthday party after Charles has become famous—"like Elvis Presley," a young woman remarks—due to his success on the game show "21," and after he has outstripped his father financially. After Charles says he has won $122,000, Mark is stunned, but recovers by citing Shakespeare:

MARK: "Some rise by sin, and some by virtue fall."
CHARLIE: *Measure for Measure.* "To do a great right, do a little wrong."
BUNNY: [interjects to Dick Goodwin] This is a game our family plays.
MARK: *Merchant of Venice.* "O what men dare do, what men may do, what men daily do, not knowing what they do."
CHARLES: *Much Ado About Nothing.* "Things without remedy should be without regard. What's done is done."
MARK: "Without *all* remedy." *Macbeth.*
MRS. VAN DOREN: "How ill white hairs become a fool and jester."
Now, professor, open your presents.

The father uses Shakespeare's comedies as exempla of moral corruption or folly in the heroes (Angelo's rationalization of his intended seduction of Isabella and execution of her brother; Claudio before he shames Hero in the Church scene) to teach his son the error of his ways, leaving open in particular the possibility of some comic remedy. Yet his authority as teacher is undercut both by his wife, who casts him as a disavowed father figure, and by his son, who misses his father's point entirely, answering him with citations from equally or even more deeply corrupt characters (Bassanio at Antonio's trial pleading with the Duke not to honor Shylock's contract; Lady Macbeth telling her husband not to think about having murdered his King); moreover, Charles gives his father a television as a birthday present. The film also ironizes Charles's attempts to keep his distance from the show as an academic. At one point he confronts the show's producers, who attempt to console him by telling him "It's entertainment." "I'm a college professor," Charles shouts back, but his transformation into media celebrity is immediately registered as the door opens and someone says, "The professor is needed in make-up."

The compromising of the distinction between academia and entertainment is also registered in the way the film adapts Shakespeare. When Goodwin won't call Charles as a witness because he has become overly attached to him, his wife chastizes him, calling him "the Uncle Tom of the Jews." "Quiz show hearings without Van Doren," she concludes, "is like performing *Hamlet* without Hamlet." But in this version, young Hamlet, not Old Hamlet, is corrupt. Moreover, Mark's Old Hamlet turns out to be really old, always too slow to understand his son. When Charles appears at the end of Mark's class to discuss his testimony at the oversight committee, Mark's inability to understand either his son or the present cultural moment is registered by the fact that he is teaching *Don Quixote*. Whereas Mrs. Van Doren had earlier played Henry V to her husband's Falstaff, the reference to Cervantes now signals the way even Mark's self-identification with a chivalric ideal amounts to so much tilting at windmills. In contrast to the Lear-identified Shakespeare professor of *Harry and Tonto* of the 1970s, this restrospective, tattered post-Lear patriarch is all that's left in 1950s (and, by implication, 1990s) American culture.

There isn't much of a son left either. When Charles confesses to his father that he is a fraud, that he gave answers given to him by the show's producers, Charles tries to play their Shakespeare citation game again by turning to another comedy, *As You Like It:*

> MARK: It was a god-damned quiz show, Charles.
> CHARLES: "An ill favored thing, sir."
> MARK: This is not the time to play games.
> CHARLES: "But mine own." It was mine.
> MARK: Your name is mine.

In identifying with Touchstone, Charles registers his own castration: at thirty-three, he is neither married nor involved with a woman; there is no equivalent in the film, that is, to Touchstone's "ill-favored thing" (5.4.55-56), Audrey. Moreover, Charles can't control his relation to Shakespeare. He's less a witty fool who can avoid a quarrel through an elastic, literary "lie" than he is Hamlet, a "Crown Prince of education," as Herbert Stempel mockingly puts it, trying to get away from his father's ghost and destroying himself in his attempt to do so.

By suggesting some gender-bending in the Van Doren family, the film's citations of Shakespeare further undermine rather than reinforce its idealization of WASP culture. In the game played at Mark's birthday, Charles takes up Lady Macbeth's position, and his mother takes up Henry V's. Whereas a cross-gender citation might signal the strain Charles feels here, it doesn't for parents, who can cite any character they wish precisely because they are just playing a game without much riding on the outcome.

Yet whatever tragic grandeur Charles achieves as loser depends less on his knowledge of Shakespeare than on the fact that he is telegenic. Charles can be read as tragic rather than merely corrupt precisely because he is a television star, not because he has lost some moral purity he had prior to his appearance on *21*. Herbert Stempel, the contestant Charles beats in his initial triumph, remains the real loser, an embarrassment to Goodwin and the real agent of Van Doren's downfall. Thus the film reinvokes the spectre of the unassimilated, resentful, and above all, untelegenic Jew who'll take the money and take the dive so that it can idealize the WASP male as more than a corrupt, money-grubbing loser.[19]

In contrast to films that try to save Shakespeare from electronic media in order to save the academic (father), *Last Action Hero* openly joins Shakespeare to the medium of film, using Shakespeare to pair a son whose father is dead with a father whose son died in front of his eyes at the hands of one his enemies. Significantly, Shakespeare's initial mediatization is gendered female, linked to a maternal figure. This is the one film in which the Shakespeare teacher is a woman. Moreover, mediatization is doubled, split between the obsolete and the new, between the old and the young. You will recall that Danny plays hooky in order to see *Jack Slater III* for the third time, but he manages to make it to school in time to hear his teacher, played by Laurence Olivier's wife, Joan Plowright, telling her students about the pleasures of *Hamlet*: "Murder, madness, incest, sex, and violence. Shakespeare's *Hamlet* couldn't be more exciting." She shows the students a clip from Olivier's film in which Hamlet delays killing Claudius (who is deep in prayer), informing them that they may recognize Olivier from his work in a Polaroid television commercial or as Zeus in *Clash of the Titans*. Danny is bored by Hamlet's delay, however, and, as we saw in chapter 3, he displaces Olivier's film with his own fantasy version. In an imagined trailer complete with voice over, Arnold Schwarzenegger plays Hamlet as action hero, killing everyone in sight and surviving the apocalyptic destruction of Elsinore. Combining Shakespeare's Hamlet and Old Hamlet, Jack Slater enables Danny's repositioning as Jack Slater's son, one Slater is capable of saving. Yet the film works precisely by being an unrealistic wish: a young boy can be rescued by an action hero and rescue him in turn because the father figure is the cinematic idealization of a boy who is blind to the film's own "adult" mockery of Slater. Moreover, Shakespeare has to be doubled, both rejected and introjected, for this fantasy to take place: Hamlet is split between a feminized Olivier and a masculinized Schwarzenegger.

These recent and not so recent films are about Shakespeare as melancholic symptom of a fixation on an earlier American moment that is more or less acknowledged to be lost. In *Harry and Tonto*, mourning is explicitly thematized. Harry cries when he identifies an old friend's corpse at a morgue so it can be buried; he appears to lose his cat, Tonto, in a graveyard; he is saddened to meet an old flame who now resides in an old-age home and who doesn't remember him; and, finally, Tonto dies. The whole film is about Harry's letting go of his past, and his readiness to face his death is signaled by the disappearance of Shakespeare: Harry stops citing *Lear*. In contrast, the more recent films tend to skip over mourning or marginalize it in a subplot. *Renaissance Man* is the least affecting among them precisely because of its refusal to accept that the past is no longer present, its insistence on using Shakespeare to enable a national fantasy in which the son who failed his father during the Vietnam War becomes the father whose own son he is able to save. Yet even the St. Crispian's Day speech cited by the soldier is about the dead as well as the living, about those who won't survive the battle of Agincourt as much as those who will. And the soldier's MIA father can be idealized precisely because of the war's remoteness from a younger generation.

The more melancholic *Quiz Show* mourns not just the son's corruption but the fall of high-brow academic WASP culture and education into low-brow television entertainment, the fall of the professor into media star. What is particularly interesting is the way that WASP culture is mourned by an assimilated, Harvard-educated Jewish lawyer (the film is based on Goodwin's memoir).

In *Last Action Hero,* Death literally appears as a character and is held at bay. Nevertheless, Death marks the mourning of the passing of the European art film, and the film's framing of Slater's cowboy riding off into the sunset registers a nostalgic twilight of the nonparodic cinematic version of the cowboy myth.[20] Shakespeare's doubling into two Hamlets, one English and one American, is a symptom of the film's blocked mourning of an earlier patriarchal moment. The more explicitly Shakespeare is mediatized, the more explicitly the maternal comes to the fore. *Last Action Hero* complicates the mourning of the Shakespeare teacher insofar as its use of Shakespeare positions viewers as insiders or outsiders: more likely than not, viewers who recognize Plowright and appreciate the humor of casting her as the teacher will be middle-aged or older, hardly the film's target audience. Only a certain kind of viewer can appreciate the passing of her Hamlet. Yet even as the film marks this passing, it doesn't really mourn it so much as mock it, suggesting that the time for mourning is long past, since Olivier had already left Shakespeare in his own lifetime to do television commercials and bad movies.

Don't Cry for Me, America

If recent films tend to portray the Shakespeare teacher as the representative, if not the enabler, of a partriarchal American social harmony, what might the cultural critic's alternative fantasy of teaching Shakespeare be? How would it differ from the fantasy expressed in these popular films? It would, I think, necessarily involve a mediatized Shakespeare. Out of the mourning of the present postpatriarchal moment, some might hope to see the emergence of new subjectivities based on heterogeneity, hybridity, fragmentation. Those who resist would be called on to "get over it, get used to it." By embracing a mediatized Shakespeare, cultural critics might imagine they would further their own mediatization as intellectuals, taking as their province not a narrowly defined corpus of literary, canonical texts but the global, transnational cultural field.

Cultural studies has taken a "postmodern" turn in valuing the media as a resource rather than devaluing it as an obstacle, a source of co-optation. Cultural critics have turned to popular culture, especially its visual forms, and to the popularization of criticism as a means of legitimating the value of their work. They have sought to use journalistic media literally and figuratively to make criticism more accessible, accountable to audiences beyond academic ones. Dana Polan (1993) argues that the intellectual is always "mediatized" and "spectaclized". Gerald Graff (1993, 111) says that the profession is show business, part of the culture industry, and advises cultural critics to do better at public relations if they are to make ours a more democratic society. And Stanley Fish likens the "commodities" available to critics on the academic conference circuit such as "attention, applause, fame, and ultimately, adulation" to those "usually reserved for the icons of popular culture" (1993, 103). Similarly, Jennifer Wicke (1994) wants to use what she calls the "celebrity zone" to advance materialist feminist purposes as defined by academic feminists.[21] According to Michael Bérubé (1994), criticism will never be popular until it is televised. Perhaps it is unsurprising that in 1992 the Modern Language Association (MLA) hired a public relations firm.

This fantasy of the intellectual's mediatization carries with it fantasies about pedagogy as well, fantasies about students that might well be characterized as patriarchal. In typical accounts of cultural criticism as a pedagogical practice, the student is presumed to mirror the academic, to reproduce outside the classroom the oppositional readings he or she has learned to do in the classroom. The investment in mediatization and technology is about staying young. All hostile critics of cultural criticism are typically regarded as obsolete, out-of-it losers, while the political, the significant are equated with the new, the latest technology. What the representation of the loser in film makes clear, however, is precisely that this presumed mirroring of the teacher by the student is a delusion. The mediatization of the intellectual and of pedagogy throws into relief the academic unconscious rather than bypasses it. Cultural criticism has taken increasingly hybridized forms: book reviews are presented as articles or as chapters in books of criticism; critics include interviews with themselves in their books. One could add that another symptom of the academic unconscious is the way texts conventionally considered marginal, such as book blurbs, footnotes to other critics, prefaces, acknowledgments, even critics' clothes and the colors on dustjackets, are increasingly the focus of critical scrutiny.[22]

To illustrate how the pedagogical fantasies of cultural criticism recycle patriarchal elements, I want to compare the scene of Shakespeare pedagogy as staged in *Last Action Hero* with two anecdotes about teaching Shakespeare told by Houston Baker, Jr. and Alan Sinfield. The dated feel of Olivier's *Hamlet* in *Last Action Hero* may be accounted for in part by the way the scene marks a new relation between the plays and their audience, one in which there is no longer a sense of embodied intimacy between the audience and Shakespeare himself, one that is much more cool. The displacement of Olivier by Schwarzenegger marks the disappearance of an older sense of the actor as someone who really knew Shakespeare, who talked to him, who even thought he himself actually was Shakespeare.[23]

To clarify this point, consider an account of teaching by an Americanist, Houston Baker, Jr. At the end of his book *Black Studies, Rap, and the Academy*, Baker tells a story about a trip he made to London's North Westminister Community School, where he taught *Henry V* by using new media:

> To make a pedagogical story brief, we took off—as a group. I showed
> them how Henry V was a rapper—a cold dissing, def con man,

tougher-than-leather and smoother-than-ice, an artisan of words. . . .
It was time for *Public Enemy*'s "Don't Believe the Hype." Because all
that Agincourt admonition and "breach" rhetoric (the whole, hybrid,
international class of London GSCE [General Certificate of Secondary
Education] students knew) was a function of the English Church
being required to pay the king "in full." . . . Patriotism, a show of
hands by the class revealed, is a "hype" if it means dying for England.
. . . *Hybridity:* a variety of sounds coming together to arouse interest in
a classic work of Shakespearean creation. (1993, 98)

Baker explains his own (uncritically assumed) success, unanticipated
by the school head, in terms of his technological literacy:

What the head had not factored in the apologetics was the technology I came bearing. I carried along my very own Panasonic cassette
blaster as the postmodern analogue of both "the message" and the
"rapper's delight" that Shakespeare himself would include in his
plays were he writing today. At a site of postmodern, sonic (twenty-
two languages) hybridity produced by an internationally accessible
technology, I gained pedagogical entrée by playing in the new and
very, very sound game of rap. (1993, 99)

Yet Baker's oppositional, postcolonial account of Shakespeare's monarch
as a rapper simply substitutes a Harlem Renaissance Man for the adman-
turned-teacher of *Renaissance Man,* reinscribing the humanist dream of
Shakespeare's universality with the new dream that the cultural critic
(and his or her students) can occupy all possible positions, high and low,
classic and contemporary, so that the intellectual *cum* rapper is now the
one who can sample all codes and recodings.

Moreover, to be politically oppositional, Baker finds it necessary
to exclude hipness from politics even as he presents his own criticism
as new, youthful, worthy of journalistic coverage, the latest techno-
thing. Earlier in the same book, Baker mounts a critique of what he
calls "start in the middle of the game" expert witnessing, a practice he
sees in someone such as Henry Louis Gates, Jr., who testified in court
on behalf of *2 Live Crew,* whose CD *Nasty as They Wanna Be* was
prosecuted for being obscene:

the demand felt by forty-something experts seems to be get "hip" and provide instant-replay analysis in the fashion of commentators for Monday night football. However, the instant-replay mode vis-à-vis historically situated and resonantly important forms of transnational cultural expressiveness constitutes only a self-aggrandizing act of scholarly hipsterism. It is, one might say, a totally self-interested form of popular hucksterism. (1993, 81)

To this irresponsible hucksterism Baker contrasts his own in-depth knowledge of rap as an expert black studies scholar. But the trumping of instant expertise by in-depth knowledge doesn't really serve to uphold the morally serious distinction between hipness and expertise (or authenticate him as an American postcolonial critic of Britain) because his hipness only serves, in an all too self-aggrandizing fashion (he trumpets press coverage of his class on Shakespeare), to establish Baker as "The Man" who is really hip, really in the know.[24] As if.

This kind of problem is hardly specific to American academics. Alan Sinfield's anecdote about the Heathrow security guard is similarly self-congratulatory. Nevertheless, his anecdote is about a trip to the United States and thus indicates the hold American academic fantasies have come to have on their British counterparts. Sinfield anticipates the guard's negative response and manages to make his flight despite the guard's negative view of English literature by adopting the position of student examinee and by dissing Shakespeare:

Well, he was quite cute, and of course I was charming, so we joked around a bit; eventually we got to be buddies. So he said: "OK, I'll test you. Who was the guy who wanted his pound of flesh?" "Got it!" I exclaimed: "Shylock in *The Merchant of Venice.*" And, exhilarated that I was on the point of winning through, added: "Isn't that a horrible play?" "YES!" he shouted, astonished at the convergence of our judgments, "Isn't that a horrible play!" The young man was Jewish, I deduced. And my journey had been threatened by the insults he had experienced as a student, and by his belief that I must be committed to the universal wisdom and truth of *The Merchant of Venice.* "We don't do it like that anymore," I told him. . . . He enthused "That's just great!" So I gained an endorsement for at least some of my humanities work, and caught my plane. (1994, 1)

In this anecdote, there is a precise convergence between an uneducated worker and an educated cultural worker who both have the same "*diss*-ident" take on Shakespeare. Shakespeare may now be done differently, but the teacher's investment in the (maladjusted) student's endorsement seems quite familiar.

If cultural critics are *in loco parentis* as educators whether they like it or not, they might want to imagine themselves as street parents along the lines of the Falstaff character Fat Bob in *My Own Private Idaho*. "He taught me more than school did," Scott says to Mike. This alternative pedagogue, however, isn't really much of one; Falstaff is a disavowed, rejected father figure in Van Sant's film.[25]

In addition to unconsciously recycling patriarchal relations in their fantasies about alternative pedagogical practices, cultural critics often miss the way that conventions continue to circulate outside the academic sphere of cultural reproduction. The fantasy is that if we change the way Shakespeare is reproduced in academia, we will have changed the way he is reproduced everywhere else. But of course such is not the case.[26] If the drive for authenticity in Shakespeare studies has been exposed as an illusion (Orgel 1984; Greenblatt 1997), a different drive for it in popular multiculturalism remains powerfully in force. In rap, street credibility is essential, and the lasting dominance of gangsta rap is largely about the rapper's need to prove again and again that he is in fact what he sings about. Similarly, a 1990s way of representing urban gang warfare authenticates the feud in Luhrmann's *William Shakespeare's Romeo and Juliet*. Yet the cultural critic's credibility is itself dateable since it relies on contemporary narrative conventions to establish a given critic's authenticity. *West Side Story* seemed daring on its release for transcoding *Romeo and Juliet* to American New York street gangs, but now it seems incredibly tame. The glitzy Baz Luhrmann update will no doubt soon feel dated as well.

A film such as *Last Action Hero* calls into question the way cultural critics always regard academia as an emergent, advanced (sub-)culture, and everything outside academia as residual, anachronistic, and archaic. The cultural critic may be producing a critique that is not receivable by its intended younger market precisely because these consumers will regard it as beside the point, belated, out-of-date, irrelevant, perhaps worst of all, old. What drives the student's recoding of *Hamlet* in *Last Action Hero* is his sense that Olivier's *Hamlet* is boring, too slow, well past its sell-by date. And what may be dismaying for cultural critics is that the teacher, who is herself a kind of cultural critic, fails miserably on her own terms to make *Hamlet* "relevant" by recoding it not only as a film but in relation to Olivier's acting career in contemporary advertising and popular film.[27] Whether this means a total pedagogical failure is what the film implicitly questions. Critics such as Baker (and, perhaps, the teacher) want to set the terms of the student's reproduction. But the student succeeds in doing exactly what he is asked to do, namely, recode the teacher's recoding for his own contemporary purposes. He just doesn't do it the way many cultural critics would like him to do it. He hasn't been "feminized." Indeed, he rejects Olivier as a kind of femme Hamlet.[28]

The problem of the intellectual's identification with a youth culture that is constantly outstripping him or her may be grasped more fully through a final comparison of Baz Luhrmann's *William Shakespeare's Romeo and Juliet* and Lloyd Kaufman's *Tromeo and Juliet* in terms of their position *vis-à-vis* pedagogy. In comparing these films we might consider whether there is anything to be gained by adopting an antipedagogical relation to Shakespeare as an intellectual. Both films are intended for youth markets, and both recode Shakespeare's tragedy in relation to the Generation X-ualization of American teen film (as in Greg Araki's *The Doom Generation*, 1995).[29] Whereas Luhrmann's film is an instructional guide to better Shakespeare for teenagers, marketed, as we saw, through an MTV special full of students, Kaufman's porn version is anti-instructional. And while the Luhrmann film is formally better, it also more retarded, as it were, in its pedagogical commitment to its intended teen audience.

Luhrmann's film recodes the play in terms of a doomed youth culture and offers a sociological reading of contemporary (gang) youth: Romeo and Juliet are not innocent flower children destroyed by a stale, older, violent generation; they no longer have any distance from violent, drugged-out gang thuggery but participate in it fully (both wield guns, for example) and in a debased (because, in this film's logic, it has been commodified) version of romantic love as well, even its Shakespearean version. Luhrmann registers the commercialization of love and of Shakespeare (a large Coca-Cola-like billboard derived from a Coke ad in the set of *Strictly Ballroom* reads "l'Amour," as if love were a product like Coke, and ads citing Shakespeare's plays appear frequently throughout the film).

William Shakespeare's Romeo and Juliet makes itself teachable to its teen audience by putting spectacle above verse and by slowing down the speed of the actors' line delivery so teenagers can easily follow the plot. Moreover, the Chorus's opening speech is delivered twice, first by a news anchorwoman on television, then again in fragments in a male voice-over as what might be called a movie trailer for the film flashes past. Similarly, when Father Laurence explains his plan to Juliet, the film flashes forward so the audience can watch the plan unfold visually. Insofar as the film has a message, it's not at all clear what use Shakespeare is in getting it across.

The same account of contemporary youth culture's dead end can be found in openly cynical films such as *The Doom Generation* and *Natural Born Killers* (dir. Oliver Stone, 1994) in which teen crime is viewed as the consequence of (usually sexually) abusive parents (these films might be regarded in part as a backlash against whiny, twenty-something comedies of the early 1990s such as *Singles* [dir. Cameron Crowe] and *Reality Bites* [dir. Ben Stiller]). Showing Capulet who turns out to be a wife-and-daughter beater succeeds only in turning Shakespeare into a belated mimic of more contemporary, realist cinema.

In contrast, Kaufman's film has no message and nothing to teach.[30] It takes the sociological material of contemporary youth culture and cashes in on its shock value. As he tries to seduce his sister, Crystalmeth, Sammy Capulet encapsulates the film's philosophy: "Oh come on, you know the way the world is. Now we've got gang bangers, we've got perverts, we've got anorexia, everything is in style. If we just throw incest into the mix, the world will be like one big hug." Far from regarding incest as a source of shock, however, the film endorses it. Though Sammy's sister violently refuses him, the play celebrates an incestuous union between Tromeo and Juliet. The film tries to shock by presenting its rewrite of *Romeo and Juliet* as an assault on civilized values. The film rarely cites Shakespeare, and then only in moments of dramatic sincerity (which it usually subsequently mocks). Yet this antipedagogical position doesn't get the film's account of a doomed youth culture any further than Luhrmann's. It too draws on the same signifiers to establish a cool youth culture: pierced nipples, tatoos, drug use, and current fashions in clothing and music. Is anyone really going to gasp in horror at the destruction of Shakespeare as high art? Haven't we seen that before? And the film's sense of fashion is often quite dated as well. While Luhrmann uses the latest MTV bands, Kaufman uses Lemmy, a relic of days gone by, as the Chorus, and betrays a nostalgia for the music of long-forgotten bands like The Meatmen. Similarly, the film's juvenile sense of humor is boringly dated as well and probably doesn't fair well with contemporary teenagers' sophisticated, ironic sensibilities.[31] Harder to take than scenes with severed fingers and heads, dead squirrels, and nipple piercings are the painfully obvious jokes about policemen eating doughnuts and priests as pedophiles.

Both Luhrmann and Kaufman reveal less about youth culture than they do about the way middle-aged directors perceive it. As such, any attempt to reach a teen market by teaching teens or, in a supposedly cool move, by refusing to teach them anything at all, will inevitably, it would appear, wind up seeming dated and sometimes embarrassingly off the mark.

Free Willy?: Infantile Censorships, Kiddie Shakespeare, and the New Bowdlerism

At the end of the Introduction, I raised as a question the possibility that children's television programming in the United States cites Shakespeare in a more conservative fashion than more adult popular media such as film and video do. In various children's shows, Shakespeare arguably isn't a loser, isn't unspeakable. I would like to engage that question now. We can begin to understand how children's programming is the master example rather than the exception to loser kiddie culture by contextualizing Shakespeare's citation in this programming in terms of a historical shift in the censorship of Shakespeare.

Initially, American film and schools followed Victorian England's lead in producing expurgated editions of Shakespeare suitable for the whole family, as well as adaptations of the plays for children in the tradition of Charles and Mary Lamb's *Tales of Shakespeare*. As Uricchio and Pearson note in their study of Shakespeare silent film:

> Shakespeare was a good tonic for everyone, although some required a diluted form. Theodore Weld . . . praised those Shakespearean editors who produced a G-rated version of the Bard. . . . On the principle of discretionary selection and omission, Bowdler's *Family Shakespeare* was long since compiled. Near twenty years ago, Prof. Hows of Columbia College, New York City, published his Shakespeare reader as a school text book. . . . More recently, Rev. Henry N. Hudson of Boston has published his *School Shakespeare,* an admirable text for advanced classes. And Mr. W. J. Rolfe, AM, and the Clarendon press have printed their judiciously expurgated editions. (1993, 93-94)

What differentiates children's programming now is that it appears to evade the need for censorship by addressing two audiences, children and adults, separately.

The innovation of a show such as *Sesame Street* was that it could be watched by both adults and children. The adults could appreciate the parodies and allusions children couldn't get. Beginning in the 1980s, many children's shows, such as *Pee Wee's Playhouse* and animated shows, followed suit, notably *Ren and Stimpy, The Simpsons,* and *Animaniacs*. Thus in episodes using Shakespeare, adults can get the tag lines and parodies while children can enjoy the silliness and pop culture references.[32]

The *Animaniacs* Shakespeare episodes, written by Deanna Oliver and directed by Rusty Mills, proceed by citing excerpts from Shakespeare's plays (*A Midsummer Night's Dream,* Puck's epilogue; *Hamlet,* 5.1, Hamlet and Horatio discussing Yorick; and *Macbeth,* 4.1, the witches over their cauldron). The excerpts are introduced in each episode with the same line (only the title of the play and the characters' names vary). The "Hamlet" episode begins, for example, as follows: "And now, the Warner Brothers in a scene from Shakespeare's *Hamlet,* translated for those viewers who, like Yakko, have no idea what he [Shakespeare] is saying." The excerpts are then translated into abbreviated modern, sometimes grotesque equivalents.[33] In the "Macbeth" episode, Dot, Sloppy, and Nurse say "Double, double toil and trouble. Fire burn and cauldron bubble!" and Yakko translates: "loosely translated, that means 'abracadabera.'" Usually, the character translating the lines also makes some jokes or pop references, as, for example, when Dot translates Hamlet's "my gorge rises at it" as "I'm going to blow chunks," or when Yako and Wakko make up their own witches' recipe:

SLAPPY: Scale of dragon.
Tooth of wolf.
Witch's mummy.
Maw and gulf.
YAKKO: Those are the ingredients of a hot dog!

After Puck's line "And Robin shall restore amends," Dot quips, "And the Boy Wonder will save us." The Batmobile drives up and Robin stands up to let the Warners in. They drive off and leave some annoying pixies behind. Similarly, the "Hamlet" episode weaves in a subplot in which the singer Cher appears getting out of the grave and Yorick's skull chases after her. In the "Macbeth" episode, Jerry Lewis appears and sings, only to be knocked on the head by Dot and fall screaming into the witches' cauldron. Adults disaffected with Shakespeare can here join in appreciating Shakespeare's reduction to base matter, indeed.

To be sure, expurgations of Shakespeare's plays do remain in some of these episodes, though after a politically correct rather than a puritanical fashion. In the *Animaniacs Macbeth,* for example, the line "liver of blaspheming Jew" is cut. And these episodes would seem to contradict the idea that Shakespeare is a loser since they do rave about him. In *Sesame Street's Monsterpiece Theater* (a parody of *Masterpiece Theater*), for example, episodes of *"The Monsters of Venice," "The Taming of the Shoe," "Much Ado About Nothing,"* and *"Hamlet"* are introduced by Alistair Cookie (played by Cookie Monster). In the "Hamlet" episode, for example, Alistair Cookie introduces the play as follows: "One of the best loved classics in the whole world, a play that explores feelings that bubble deep inside all of us. Hamlet, Prince of Denmark. It doesn't get any classier than this." This episode affirms Shakespeare's high value through parody. It stars Mel Gibson reprising his Hamlet from Zeffirelli's film of the play and Elmo as himself (in place of Polonius), and they act out a version of the scene in which Polonius questions Hamlet, presumably because it is a scene in which Hamlet is reading. Elmo enters, saying, "Elmo spieth Hamlet, Prince of Denmark! Reading a book!" and has the following exchange with Hamlet:

> ELMO: Hamlet, what doth thou read?
>
> HAMLET: Words, words, words.
>
> ELMO: Oh, Hamlet. Pray tell Elmo what maketh thee so sad?
>
> HAMLET: (sadly) Words, words, words.
>
> ELMO: Again with the words, words, words! Prince Hamlet doth not give to Elmo a straight answer! Uh, oh! Uh, oh! A dark cloud doth sweep across Hamlet's brow! He seemeth . . . angry! What doth thou readeth that maketh thee so angry, oh great prince?
>
> HAMLET: (angrily) Words, words, words.
>
> ELMO: Okay! That does it! Elmo's fedeth up!

In frustration, Hamlet finally tells Elmo, "Get thee to a library!" In this episode, *Hamlet* is made safe as a classic and as an illustration of the importance of reading for children. Parents can believe that television will not displace reading entirely in their children's lives (while feeling let off the hook for not reading to their children), and as adults presumably enjoy the clever rewriting of the scene.

Episodes of *The Muppet Show* and *Muppets Tonight* that cite Shakespeare work similarly. In one *Muppet Show* episode, Dr. Bob pays a tribute to Shakespeare that stands in contrast to a parody of *Swan Lake,* called *Swine Lake,* that was performed by the host Rudolf Nureyev and Miss Piggy. An episode of *Muppets Tonight* stages a parody of the balcony scene from *Romeo and Juliet,* this time at Miss Piggy's, not Shakespeare's, expense. The parody begins after country singer Garth Brooks, the episode's host, announces he wants to do something different and sings "If I Were a Rich Man" from *Fiddler on the Roof* and Tom Jones's "It's Not Unusual." The balcony scene that follows is a disaster. Miss Piggy reads her lines off cue cards and gets them wrong. Piggy's nephews burst onstage and introduce themselves as "the two gentlemen from Bologna." The scene ends when the balcony collapses under Miss Piggy's weight. Only the ending pokes gentle fun at Shakespeare. The two old men, Statler and Waldorf, comment on the spectacle of Miss Piggy lying on top of the now prostrate Brooks. Statler remarks, "Shakespeare would have hated that," and Waldorf responds, "You should know. You dated his sister!"

Though these examples seem pretty straightforward and are, to be sure, hardly unspeakable, they are nevertheless supreme examples of loser Shakespeare in that they appeal to an adult audience who really dumbs down as far as they can go. Far from disappearing from children's programming, censorship has taken new "infantile" forms (quite apart from FCC regulations) as the adult audience (as constructed by these shows) become the de facto censors, not by prohibiting meaning but by limiting the potentially nonsensical play of adaptation and translation to predictable parodies and cultural trademarks.[34] In his book *Walter Benjamin for Children,* Jeffrey Mehlman discusses Benjamin's essay "Aussicht ins Kinderbuch" [Prospects in Children's Books] and notes Benjamin's

> preoccupation with the very materiality of textual transformation. Words appear in costume; children are caught up in a "masquerade" of script in which meaning itself, insofar as it inhibits the scriptural whirl, functions as a form of "censorship": "Children, when thinking up stories, are stage managers, who do not allow themselves to be censored by meaning [die sich vom 'Sinn' nicht zenserien lassen]." (1993, 6)

In addressing adults and children, one might want to argue that shows such as *Sesame Street* and *Animaniacs* seek to preserve the very kind of childhood Benjamin so dearly treasures by keeping children's reception separate from the adults'. The adults, that is, are the ones who appreciate the parodic meanings, the ways in which a classic text such as *Hamlet* is travestied, while the children enjoy the sheer nonsense. The child's uncensored freedom would be defined, in this account, against the educational agenda parents seek to impose on them. The commercial network shows would actually be more progressive than the public television shows in allowing for a wider range of nonsense. What might look to a high-minded adult like a regrettable dumbing down of Shakespeare, for children would, from the point of view of the cultural critic, look like a liberation from an adult sacralization of high culture.

This account, while plausible, ignores the collapse of child into adult audience; that is, there really isn't nonsense here to which children might have access. The collapse of audiences into a single adult one in children's television mirrors the same collapse in film. The problem with G-rated films in the 1990s is that adults don't want to see them precisely because they are not addressed to adults. Films made in the G and even PG category have by and large disappeared. PG-13 films run pretty much all across the mall marquee. In movie terms, childhood now ends at 7 (the age children are now marketed to as consumers of PG-13 movies). The end of childhood is marked in movie-making, moreover, by the way that even the few G and PG movies that do get made seem geared to adult fantasies about their own childhoods, as in the case of Steven Spielberg's *Peter Pan* spin-off, *Hook* (1993). In Spielberg's retelling, Peter is a grown-up, Yuppie neglectful father who redeems himself (and saves his kidnapped kids) by becoming Peter Pan once again.

Far from reversing the recent collapse of children and audience audiences, the fantasy rehearsed above that children watching shows such as *Sesame Street* would somehow be free of censorship is precisely an adult fantasy about remaining a child forever, a fantasy in which the adult paradoxically acts as censor by constructing childhood as a time free of adult censorship. In this new Bowdlerism, in which adults are the real audience for children's shows, we see a more extreme instance of the adult loser's identification with youth culture: parental guidance is superfluous in the fantasy world of an uncensored childhood. The adult loser's fear that he will be regarded as obsolete and over-the-hill by his hipper, younger audience is thereby minimized, since young children have far less capacity, if they have any, to resignify the culture that is produced for them by adults.

A show such as *Wishbone* that adapts the classics for preteens might nevertheless be thought to be an exception to the rule of loser Shakespeare in 1990s American visual popular culture since it is not

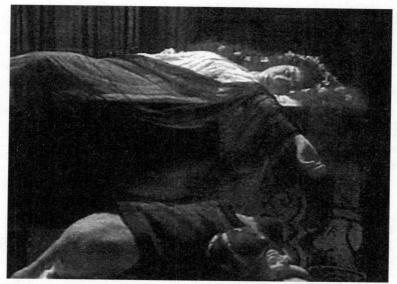

Figure 5.2: Wishbone's Doggystyle Romeo in the *Wishbone* adaptation, "Rosie, O Rosie, Oh."

geared to adults. Using a male terrier named Wishbone who talks as either the leading character or a sidekick in the subplot presentation of the classic, the shows teach (with small bits of joking around) the classics to preteens (who are represented in suburban, middle-class, multicultural terms, of course). A given classic is made instructive by being presented as somehow analogous to the conflicts and problems the preteens face in the main plot. While the series is straightforward in its intentions, the use of the dog as an alternately human or humanized character to popularize the classics adds a rather odd, if not "queer" dimension to the classics that get retold.

Consider, for example, the *Wishbone* retelling of *Romeo and Juliet*, "Rosie O, Rosie, Oh!" (dir. Richard Jernigan, 1995).[35] As is customary in the series, this episode consists of two parallel plots, though in this episode the main plot is comic while the classic is a tragedy. The main plot involves Wishbone falling in love with a dog named Rosie whom he meets in an animal shelter after he is caught without his dog collar. The children Wishbone lives and plays with rescue him and ask their parents to let them adopt Rosie (primarily to save her from being exterminated, but also, by implication, to enable the two dogs to hook up). To the children's dismay, however, the parents refuse. At the end of the episode, the children learn that a nice family came by at the last minute and took Rosie home.

In Wishbone's retelling of *Romeo and Juliet* (which is occasioned by his desire to communicate how deeply he loves Rosie), Wishbone plays Romeo and a young woman plays Juliet. The analogy between human and dog love has some presumably unintended consequences. It's hard not to see the feud in this version as species-driven, the forbidden love being between a dog and a human rather than between two humans from feuding families. This perception is strengthened by the fact that the feud has so often been retold in American films as an interracial one (*West Side Story; China Girl; William Shakespeare's Romeo and Juliet*); moreover, African American rappers such as Snoop Doggy Dog (whose biggest fan base is white suburban teens) have translated "undercover," transgressive sex into dog metaphors, as in his CD *Doggystyle* (see figure 5.2 for *Wishbone's* version). To be sure, nothing untoward happens in this *Romeo and Juliet*. Wishbone's Romeo is a gentleman. He never licks Juliet on the mouth (or anywhere else for that matter) and the aubade is cut, predictably enough.[36] Nevertheless, the tragic ending of the play (versus the happy, same-species ending of the main plot) appears to be a consequence of Romeo and Juliet's violation of the taboo on interspecies sex.[37] Wishbone's Doggystyle Romeo pays the price of acting on his love by going to the "Dogg" pound, as it were.

Spectres of ShaXXXspeare: Loser Criticism, Part Duh

This book has been concerned with reading American Shakespeares in the 1980s and 1990s as symptoms, some of them rather queer, of an American national and academic unconscious. In examining the figures of the fan, the porn star, the transvestite, and the loser in terms of the castrated subject position produced by what I have called kiddie culture, I have also sought to rethink the extent to which cultural politics can underwrite a new model of the academic intellectual as fan, one founded on the liberatory and transgressive advancement of a heterogeneous, progressive political agenda. This intellectual "gets down" with popular culture, unlike the older intellectual, who was a hectoring, authoritarian reformer of popular culture from above. In analyzing queer, postherme-neutic replays of Shakespeare in the context of American kiddie culture, my larger aim has been to rethink the intellectual not as the one who is into technoculture but as the loser. What are we to make, then, of the loser academic intellectual? Is the loser the one who can't lose, or is the loser a figure of the loss of loss, of a nostalgia for mourning?

Some critics might want to ask a slightly different question: what does one gain from seeing the cultural critic as loser? What exactly has the loser lost? Following Pierre Bourdieu's (1996) work on what he calls the "literary field," some might want to regard opting for the loser as only another way a critic might accumulate symbolic capital in the present cultural scene. The loser, in this account, would not really lose anything at all. In response, I would argue that the loser has nothing to do with class position nor with having been disenfranchised politically or economically; that is, even if material and symbolic goods are distributed unevenly and unjustly so that we might in many cases distinguish winners (the dominant) from losers (the subordinate), the loser can as easily be found among the wealthy as he or she can among the poor. Moreover, Bourdieu's model assumes a subject who always and only wishes to be upwardly mobile, who would disavow, if possible, all engagement with market forces. In short, the loser, either as a literary writer or a cultural critic, is not possible in Bourdieu's model (he would be regarded only as a winner trying to win by masquerading as his opposite). In Bourdieu's account, the "'loser takes all' (1996, 21)".

In calling into question Bourdieu's notion of the literary field by dialogically internalizing forces that deny there is any value in the loser's symbolic goods, however, the loser calls Bourdieu's model of cultural criticism into question as well. Consider the example of the Shakespearean academic who invokes a Shakespeare with supreme cultural capital. Typically, Shakespeare is identified with bourgeois interests such as his shares in his theater company, real estate, coat-of-arms, and so on. In a Bourdieuian version of this account, one might argue that Shakespeare identified his plays as aristocratic entertainments (not only the obvious cases of A Midsummer Night's Dream and The Tempest, but all the plays). Shakespeare walked backwards (facing the court, in other words) to the market where the Globe (and even Blackfriars) audiences are seen as gate-crashers.[1] Anticipating writers like Gustave Flaubert, Shakespeare helped create a realm of autonomous art against the supposedly corrupting forces of the market. In the typical academic account, then, Shakespeare is always already upwardly mobile, a Hal who knew us all from the start. The higher Shakespeare's stock, the more central his place in the literary canon and in the culture, the greater force a critique of Shakespeare and his works will presumably have.

Nonacademic writers, in contrast, typically depict a Shakespeare who is not (yet) a winner, and spend a great deal of time fantasizing about his personal life (and relatively little trying to interpret his plays and poems).[2] Leon Rooke's Shakespeare's Dog, for example, develops Shakespeare's story from the point of view of his dog.[3] In Shylock's Daughter (1995), Erica Jong's heroine, a contemporary movie star, goes back in time as Jessica (an actual person, in this novel, who inspired The Merchant of Venice) and meets Shakespeare in Venice before he became

"Shakespeare, the great writer." There they have a passionate affair (resulting in three boys) that ends only at Jessica's insistence so that Shakespeare can return to London and write the plays that made him famous. Neil Gaiman goes further in representing Shakespeare as a loser, devoting three issues of the *Sandman* series to his depressing life composing his plays.[4] In Gaiman's account, from the beginning to the pinnacle of his career, Shakespeare is abject. In the "Midsummer Night's Dream" (1991a) episode, his son, Hamnet, complains to a boy actor that his father spends all his time away from home, and in "The Tempest" episode, Shakespeare's daughter, Judith, is illiterate, unmarried, and courted by a dullard. In scenes recalling Pasolini's portrait of a hen-pecked Chaucer, his wife, Anne, has no regard for his plays and doesn't listen to him when he recites lines from his plays we recognize as famous. Moreover, "The Tempest" (1996) episode ends by recording Shakespeare's failure to compose another play by himself, and the deaths of Shakespeare, Judith, and Anne.[5] Whatever cultural capital accrues to Gaiman through the citation of Shakespeare proves to be rather illusory, the episodes in particular and the series as a whole imply, since no one and everyone owns Shakespeare's stories in this postmodern moment of their transmission and reception.

Of course, one may argue that these nonacademic writers only construct Shakespeare as a loser in order to enhance their own prestige as authors.[6] To take the most obvious example, Jong elevates her heroine (with whom Jong all too transparently identifies) by imagining her to be the sexy, passionate woman who made Shakespeare a success. By the same token, however, Jong's fantasy of "success" is what makes her such a total, insufferable loser as a writer, her novel basically unreadable. In a more complicated move, Gaiman imagines a counter-narrative to the dominant narrative of Shakespeare as the pinnacle of literary history; in the "Men of Good Fortune" (1991) episode, Christopher Marlowe is regarded as the superior playwright. Shakespeare worships and emulates him, and, until Dream gives him stories, he is a literary failure.[7] As a character named Robin (Hob) Gelden tells Dream, Shakespeare's writing "is crap." Moreover, Shakespeare is not central to the *Sandman* series. Other authors such as Geoffrey Chaucer appear, and Gaiman strews quotations from John Webster, W. B. Yeats, John Milton, the Bible, among others, throughout his text. Whether or not nonacademic writers like Gaiman gain prestige and legitimacy for their chosen medium through the citation of Shakespeare, their decentering of Shakespeare as loser throws into relief the way the Shakespearean who identifies (with?) Shakespeare as upwardly mobile might too be considered a loser insofar as Shakespeare remains a loser in American popular culture.

One might also regard the academic loser as having contacted a bad case of what Walter Benjamin (1974a) called "left-wing melancholy," someone who sees injustices from a left perspective but who has long ago given up on the possibility of seeing any social changes that would correct them. But the question remains: from what non-loser, non-melancholic position could a Left critique be articulated? What kind of authority does such criticism have, given the radical decline in value that criticism has outside (and perhaps even inside) the university?

If the academic intellectual is now, like it or not, in the position of loser, we may ask whether that is a losing proposition for the academic intellectual. One rather optimistic answer is that the loser embraces his or her own obsolescence, refusing a tech-no-future through melancholia. The endless "whatever" refrain of the 1990s might be read not as a return to adolescent indifference and a culture of narcissism, but as an uncalculated commitment to knowledge without a program, without an economy either of total loss or of less is more. For an example of this kind of loser, we might turn again to Walter Benjamin for an early version of it. In his essay "Unpacking My Library," Benjamin notes the passing of his paradoxical mode of collecting books he never reads:

> The book borrower of real stature whom we envisage here proves himself to be an inveterate collector of books not so much by the fervor with which he guards his borrowed treasures and by the deaf ear which he turns to all reminders from the everyday world of legality as by his failure to read these books. . . . You should know that in saying this I fully realize that my discussion of the mental climate of collecting will confirm many of you in your conviction that this passion is behind the times, in your distrust of the collector type. Nothing is further from my mind than to shake either your

conviction or your distrust. But one thing should be noted: the phenomenon of collecting loses its meaning as it loses its personal owner. Even though public collections may be less objectionable socially and more useful academically than private collections, the objects get their due only in the latter. I do know that time is running out for the type that I am discussing here and have been representing to you a bit *ex officio*. . . . Only in extinction is the collector comprehended. (1974, 62 and 66-67)

For Benjamin, the obsolete is identified with childhood, with what is not usable from an adult perspective.[8]

Yet a Benjaminian notion of the intellectual as outmoded is itself outmoded in the 1990s. As Thomas Bernhard makes clear in his novel *The Loser* (1993), the loser is always too late, always misses what Bernhard's narrator repeatedly calls "the ideal moment." Precisely because of the self-defeating way the loser embraces the dumbing down of kiddie culture, a culture that registers, as I noted earlier, the loss of the kind of childhood Benjamin prized, it is now difficult to decide whether the loser is really about defeating loss or about staging a nostalgic desire for melancholia in a moment when mourning is no longer possible. Thus, the current version of the intellectual as loser, that is to say, the poseur, the data dandy or dilettante, may always be regarded as a loser (in the insulting sense of the term) paradoxically because he merely poses as the loser (in the laudable, cool sense of the term).

If the undecidable status of the Shakespeare teacher as loser enables neither a clearly defined alternative mode of pedagogy nor a new model of the intellectual, it does nevertheless raise the question of what it means to teach Shakespeare in forms so reduced they may be characterized as unspoken and perhaps forever "unspeakable." Assuming that mourning and interpretation are roughly equivalent, we might wonder whether post-hermeneutic ShaXXXspeares that cannot be mourned can still be interpreted and taught. Are the replays and citations I have analyzed for the most part as "unteachable" as they are "unspeakable?" If not, how exactly might post-hermeneutic unspeakable ShaXXXspeares, those in which there are no genuinely dialectical relations between the "original" texts and their mediatized citations, be integrated into canonical Shakespeare courses? If the texts cannot be located as part of a play's performance history or in a traditional Shakespeare filmography, what referent would legitimate their study in the classroom?

I confess I have no answers to these questions, no pedagogical program. Call me a loser, if you wish. I would argue, however, that the very demand for answers, made either by avowedly progressive or conservative teaching approaches to Shakespeare, much less any answers put forward, would seem to reinscribe rather than transcend loserdom, premised as the demand and the answers are on some notion of Shakespeare as fully spoken, on the assumption that Shakespeare's mediatization simply enlarges his cultural capital. As we have seen, self-identified progressive cultural critics think a rearticulated Shakespeare can have liberalizing political effects. And while conservatives may deplore the dropping of Shakespeare as a required course for English majors, they remain blind to the fact that the object of their devotion no longer serves as a national cultural icon the way he perhaps once did. To invoke Shakespeare in this anachronistic way, as did a sportscaster who ran the St. Crispian's Day speech from Branagh's *Henry V* before the 1997 Superbowl game and billed it as the "greatest pep talk ever," is now to open oneself to ridicule (see Pinkerton 1997). Similarly, conservative journalists and critics seem pathetic as they parade Shakespeare as a member of yet one more embattled group (DWMs, or Dead White Males), positioning themselves as a less attractive and more widely received version of the loser, namely, the victim (see Gates 1993). The new, self-appointed arbiters of cultural literacy are in any case a pale simulacrum of middle-brow 1950s New York intellectuals like Mark Van Doren, to whom many middle-class Americans did pay attention when it came to matters concerning cultural literacy and taste. Intellectuals may still try to tell the nation what every one of its citizens needs to know, but what counts as knowledge has already been significantly dumbed down. According to E. D. Hirsch (1987), for example, you don't have to have actually read *Hamlet* to be culturally literate. You just have to know the story and its author's name.

Moreover, Shakespeare can't serve what amounts to a PG cultural function given that there is no longer a patriarchal authority to provide students with the kind of parental guidance conservatives want.[9] Even a film such as *Looking for Richard* that adores Shakespeare reveals the inevitable failure of his popularization in America. Pacino's search for an authentic *Richard III* leads him back to Shakespeare's birthplace at Stratford-Upon-Avon and then to the reconstructed Globe theater in London. Pacino self-mockingly parades his abject inadequacy by holding up the *Cliffs Notes* version to the camera. The film very much resembles an updated CD-ROM version of a Signet edition of the play: performances of scenes surrounded by footnotes and annotations; sources; excerpts from critical essays; and a bibliography assembled at the end of the edition (the CD-ROM update of the Signet would include video clips and an annotated bibliography). Yet Pacino's film is less a hypertext version of the play than a radically reduced one: commentary and criticism on *Richard III* are quite limited since only about a tenth of the play is actually discussed and performed. If Shakespeare has taken on newly reduced forms in the 1990s, however, he hasn't been entirely lost—the flip side, as we have seen, of the American fantasy that he can be entirely preserved. However old and tattered, the prominence of Shakespeare's *Hamlet* registers a continuing postpatriarchal investment in a very old model of paternity.

This book depends for its existence on the very technologies that have eclipsed a literary Shakespeare, namely, the internet and video. Without them, I would not have discovered, much less had access to, many of the films I have discussed. Putting Shakespeare online has generally been regarded as a good thing in that it creates a larger database, one that makes various research activities much easier or even possible. At the same time, however, this process has produced Shakespeares in excess of any canonical archive (even if the entries mentioned here were to be archived, others will still have been missed). In writing about what I have called unspeakable (and perhaps unteachable) ShaXXXspeares, my wish has been not merely to add to an archive conceptualized as a place from which everything can at some point be retrieved and hence spoken, but the opposite. The unspeakable is about a wish for an unarchivable remainder, for an "ex" that remains inaccessible rather than for an X that can be violated. It is about a hope that certain things are in fact lost, dead, can't be reanimated, retransmitted, spoken to—even if they always call us back as ghosts.[10] Unspeakable ShaXXXspeares exist somewhere between the library and the shopping mall, between arcana and ephemera, between the obsolete and the new. The unspeakable is about a felt but an unknown, undetectable loss. As such, whether unarchived, post-hermeneutic ShaXXXspeares are worth mourning or are in fact no big loss will remain, at least in the foreseeable future, open to question.

Notes

Preface

1. Recent work by Jonathan Bate (1999) and Michael Dobson (1992) has shown that, even in England, Shakespeare was adaptable because, among other things, his texts were always a prop to British nationalism and colonialism.
2. According to Lacan 1966, the name of the father is the means by which the subject is castrated, that is to say, the means by which the subject enters the symbolic. Kiddie culture marks the loss of a paternal name, and hence the loss of the symbolic, tradition and the master or teacher as the one who is supposed to know, as the site of transferential knowledge.
3. On the importance of Hollywood as a site of Shakespeare production in the 1990s, see Boose and Burt 1997.
4. Just what constitutes the boundaries of United States popular culture is difficult to determine. Is a transnational or multinational popular Shakespeare opposed to an American popular Shakespeare, or does the dominance of the United States both as an exporter of its own products and as a market for foreign imports so deeply penetrate even the production of popular Shakespeares made elsewhere (forcing them to define themselves in relation to American popular culture) that national boundaries are effectively dissolved, with the consequence that American popular culture is universalized? Shakespeare in Japanese *anime* (animated cartoons) is an interesting example. These cartoons and comics are extremely popular with Generation X-ers. And the Japanese refer to Ozamu Tesuka, the "father of *anime*," as the "Disney of Japan" (all the while thinking that *anime* is so indigenous that it will not translate outside of Japan). See Levi 1996, 1-21.
5. This book's subtitle itself marks the extent to which academics are regarded as unmarketable losers outside of academia. It originally was "*Academic Fantasy, Queer Theory, and Kiddie Culture*." If St. Martin's had published this book as a scholarly and reference book, there would have been no problem. But since it was published as a trade book (with my full agreement), the title had to be approved by the trade division. Unfortunately for me, the Trade division did not want the word "academic" in the title since, they argued, it would put off buyers working in nonacademic bookstores. I later tried to substitute "loser criticism" for "academic fantasy." Ditto for "criticism." So much for the fantasy of the academic critic who announces himself as such

crossing over into the larger public sphere of Barnes and Nobles (etc.) bookstore/cafes.

6. The Shakespeare filmography at http://us.imdb.com/m/person.exact?+Shakespeare%20William, for example, does not list any of the Shakespeare porn films and very few spin-offs. Ken Rothwell's excellent history of Shakespeare on film will devote a chapter, however, to "transgressive Shakespeare." See Rothwell forthcoming.

7. An analysis of Shakespeare in other national cultures, particularly British and German, is beyond the scope of this study. There are several episodes of *Monty Python* (Chapman, 1989) and *Black Adder* (dir. Fletcher, 1986; dir. Shardlow, 1990) dealing with Shakespeare. What is necessary now is to place an "American" or Hollywoodized Shakespeare in a transnational context. A 1995-1997 Berlin musical entitled *Shakespeare and Rock 'n Roll* interestingly Americanizes Shakespeare, adapting *The Tempest* along the lines of the 1950 science fiction film *Forbidden Planet* and using American 1950s rock hits as the music.

Introduction

1. For another example, consider Anne Rice's *Pandora* (1998), her first novel in a series of vampire tales. Lestat advises the vampire Armand to read or see all the plays of Shakespeare in order to "understand the human race" (27). But this typically high-culture moment takes a pop turn as we learn that "Armand sat through the plays [and] watched the brilliant new films with Laurence Fishburne and Kenneth Branagh and Leonardo DiCaprio" (27-28).

2. In the American production of *Romeo and Juliet* (directed by Australian Baz Luhrmann), Leonardo DiCaprio plays Romeo, and Claire Danes (star of TV's "My So-Called Life") plays Juliet. In all American-made film versions of *Romeo and Juliet,* the culture has inscribed itself into forms of racial tension replayed within an ethnically marked youth culture, as in *China Girl* (dir. Abel Ferrara, 1987), *West Side Story,* (dir. Jerome Robbins and Robert Wise, 1961) and the Luhrmann production, which is set in a Cuban-American community in Florida. Such casting and the co-construction of youth culture as popular culture was the box-office stroke mastered some time ago by Zeffirelli in both *Romeo and Juliet* (1968) and *The Taming of the Shrew* (1966). Indeed, as Robert Hapgood aptly suggests (1997), if Zeffirelli's *Hamlet* was less of a success than were his earlier Shakespeare films, it was because his *Hamlet* was oriented to an older audience. Similarly, Molly Ringwald played Miranda in Mazursky's *Tempest* (1982) and Cordelia in Godard's *Lear* (1987).

3. Like many other popular television shows for children, *Wishbone* has a spin-off book series. See Aronson 1996 for the *Romeo and Juliet* book version.

4. The first announced use of Shakespeare in *The Sandman* was the September 1990 issue, "*A Midsummer Night's Dream.*" It has been reprinted in the

February 1998 issue. The story begun in this issue was then completed in the March 1996 issue "The Tempest," also the last issue of the series. See also "Men of Good Fortune" in *The Doll's House* (Gaiman 1990) and "Sound and Fury" in *Preludes and Nocturnes* (Gaiman 1991). The characters Robin Goodfellow and Titania appear in a number of issues. There are also three issues of *Ranma 1/2* that involve a high school production of Romeo and Juliet (Part Four, no. 6-8, reproduced in volume five as a graphic novel). And there is a single issue of *O My Goddess!* entitled *A Midsummer Night's Dream*. There are videos of both as well (dir. Atsuko Nakajima 1995 and Honda Takeshi, 1996, respectively). On the popularity of these and other comics and animated film series with Generation-Xers, see Levi 1996. In 1998, *Classics Illustrated* released a never-before-published Shakespeare comic, *Henry IV, Part One*. Shakespeare in children's cartoons is not itself new. In a 1970s *Scooby-doo* episode, for example, the ghost of Old Hamlet appears; Scooby-doo also rewrites Hamlet's "To be or not be" line as "To be Scooby or not to be Scooby? That is the question."

5. In between these segments ran the usual MTV ads for Ralph Lauren and various candies, and, not so usually, several for the film itself. MTV News did a segment on the film the same week. The marketing campaign proved successful: *William Shakespeare's Romeo and Juliet* came in first at the box office the week of its release in the United States according to E! Television, November 4, 1996. Perhaps the ultimate statement of just how thoroughly the film constructed itself as a part of youth culture lay in the way it was market tested. At the screen tests done at U. C. Berkeley the summer before the movie's nationwide opening in November 1996, studio moguls handed out market surveys that specifically asked that they be filled out only by viewers who were 39 or younger. According to one teacher, the question-naire included a query that asked "whether the Shakespeare language in the film bothered you or not." For adolescent responses, see Smith 1996. Of course, age may take its revenge on youth through the use of Shakespeare. Consider the rehabilitation and recovery of George III and with him the institution of the monarchy through the use of *King Lear* and *Henry IV, Part 2* in the 1994 film *The Madness of King George* (dir. Nicholas Hytner).

6. It is ironic that the nerdy status of a character named Brian on the television show in which Claire Danes starred, "My So-Called Life," is signaled by the way his occasional citations of Shakespeare are met with a cold reception by his fellow students.

7. For a similar view of Shakespeare and education, see the website for *Looking for Richard,* particularly Activity One of the "Viewer's Guide and Lesson Plan" (http://www.r3.org/pacino/activ1.html), entitled "Run for the Hills—It's Shakespeare." In Part A, students are asked to respond to statements such as "I would not enjoy watching a Shakespeare play" and "That's old stuff; Shakespeare has no relevance to life today." Perhaps responding to the *Shakespeare File,* Part C invites students to argue that Shakespeare should or should not be dropped from the curriculum.

NBC's adaptation of Aldous Huxley's 1932 novel *Brave New World* (original air date April 19, 1998) offered another interesting example of

Shakespeare's loser status in an educational context. John, or "the savage," a frequent citer of Shakespeare in the television version, performs by memory *Romeo and Juliet* (apparently the entire play) for young schoolchildren, all of whom find the play incomprehensible and senseless. Though their indifference is supposed to measure their cultural loss, their disparaging comments echo quite closely those made by students in the MTV *Romeo and Juliet* special.

8. For a transcript of the parody, see http://www.geocities.com/Hollywood/Lot/8897/rjmtv.html.

9. There is a possibility of a rearguard British response, but it is not a very strong one. Here is Ian McKellen's remark about the difficulty he had in finding producers in Hollywood to fund the kind of *Richard III* film he wanted to make: "Of course, if Ken or Mel, or best of all Arnie or Sly were cast as Richard, it would have been easier" (McKellen 1996, 25-26). Kenneth Branagh made a canny compromise in his 1996 *Hamlet,* casting American stars not as leads but in cameo parts. The film that was most risky of all was Adrian Noble's 1996 production of *A Midsummer Night's Dream:* the cast was made up not of Hollywood stars but of a core of the same actors who played in the 1995 Royal Shakespeare Production. The film may not have been released in the United States for this reason. It would seem that the postcolonials are triumphing. Baz Luhrmann (an Australian) put "William Shakespeare" in the title of his *William Shakespeare's Romeo and Juliet,* almost as if to insist on its authenticity, but cast American stars.

10. Consider the following from a 1907 issue of *Harper's Weekly:* "Nearly everyone of the educated class who was questioned had read one or two [Shakespeare] plays, usually at school, but nearly all held mistaken ideas about what they had read, and had a most superficial knowledge of the construction of the plays, the significance of the characters, and the points of preeminent excellence" (cited by Uricchio and Pearson 1993, 76-77).

11. Lawrence Levine has shown that there was a deep knowledge of Shakespeare across classes in the nineteenth century that has been gradually reduced to recognition of a few stock scenes in a few plays. He sees this as a move toward more elite, less democratic "sacralization" of Shakespeare and high culture by the end of the nineteenth century. By contrast, William Uricchio and Roberta Pearson argue that Shakespeare has maintained a more complex function for the masses even in reduced form (1995, 17). Alan Sinfield (1995) also disputes Levine's schema, arguing that there have been conflicts all along.

12. Kenneth Rothwell notes in private correspondence that the silent Shakespeare films varied in length from one minute to two hours by 1916.

13. The episode is titled "An Evening with Hamlet" and was written by Ben Gershman, Don Nelson, Bill Davenport, and Ozzie Nelson. The episode was directed by Ozzie Nelson.

14. Despite the title, this episode has nothing to do with Shakespeare. In the 1936 episode "Pay as You Exit" (dir. Gordon Douglas), however, the gang performs "Romyo and Jullet." When Darla refuses to play Juliet because of Alfalfa's bad (onion) breath, Spanky replaces her with Buckwheat. See also

the Bugs Bunny cartoon "A Witch's Tangled Hare" (dir. Levitow, 1959), which has a character who appears to be Shakespeare going around writing down quotations from *Macbeth* and *Romeo and Juliet*, delivered by a witch and by Bugs. *As You Like It* and *Hamlet* are also cited.

15. See also Barbara Hodgdon's discussion of what she calls "Shakespeare-speaking" (1991, 237).

16. On Al Pacino as uncool, see Powers 1996. There is even a website called "Shakespeare Sucks" at http:www.schoolsucks.com/papers/english/shakes/index.html for students who don't like the language. For an uninteresting attempt, at least to my mind, to make Shakespeare seem cool by virtue of his bawdiness and general "political incorrectness," see Marcone 1997. Also of note is *Shakespeare For Beginners* (Torpov 1997) which lists "Some Cool Things About" each of the plays discussed.

17. In a bizarre case of backward adaptation, the video jacket for the Gwyneth Paltrow version of *Emma* (dir. Douglas MacGrath, 1996) refers to the story as the basis of *Clueless* and nowhere makes any mention of Jane Austen. I have heard, but cannot confirm with a printed source, that Paltrow was cast because of her resemblance to Alicia Silverstone.

18. It is worth noting that Cher, like Marcia, is the product of a broken home. Her mother is inexplicably absent, and Cher plays a maternal role for her father, making sure he sees his parents, whom he calls "lowlifes," and eats well. Nevertheless, her "postfeminism" allows her greater freedom than Marcia has, even if that postfem freedom is only of a yuppie sort. Cher plans to go to law school.

19. An earlier instance of this was the term "baby boomer." Baby boomers did not self-identify, however, as babies.

20. For rather adult, pedestrian analyses of Beavis and Butt-Head and of "kinder-culture," see Kellner 1997 and Steinberg 1997.

21. An episode of *Star Trek: The Next Generation* entitled "The Defector" interestingly shows the citing and surpassing of Shakespeare by a (human-ized) machine. The episode begins with the android Lieutenant Data playing Henry V in disguise discussing the impending battle of Agincourt, coached by Captain Picard. After Data/Henry V says "The King is not bound to answer the particular endings of his soldiers," Picard interrupts: "Listen to what Shakespeare is telling you about the man. A king who has true feeling for his soldiers would wish to share with them on the eve of the battle." Shakespeare enters the episode as a signifier of military-intelligence gathering: in disguise, Henry V seeks to learn how his troops are doing. The episode clearly sets limits on the Shakespearean model of military intelli-gence, however. Picard later has to decide whether to do battle with the Romulans after a Romulan defector comes aboard and disguises himself, like Henry V, as a low-ranking officer. Sitting alone in his ready room, Picard cites Williams from Henry V: "Now if these men do not die well, it will be a black matter for the king who led them to it." On the one hand, Shakespeare signals the difference between human and machine, the difference between good and bad warrior. Yet Picard's ability to be the humane, intelligent warrior depends more on new technology than on Shakespeare. Shakes-

peare exists here not on the page or the human stage but on the holodeck, and Patrick Stewart plays one of Henry's soldiers as well as Captain Picard (and is thus human and manufactured image); moreover, the analogy breaks down such that Picard needs Data's "smartness." When Data enters the ready room, Picard asks for his "clarity of thought" and goes on to say that "it's very possible that we are about to go to war. The repercussions of what we do in the next twenty-four hours may be felt for years to come. I want you to keep a record of these events so that history will have the benefit of a dispassionate view." Picard then takes on a role analogous to Henry V's, asking Data, "How's the crew's spirit?" "They are concerned, Captain, of course, but confident," Data responds. "Do you not see that, sir?" Picard smiles at Data and replies, "unlike King Henry, it is not easy for me to disguise myself and walk among my troops." The analogy between Picard and Henry V breaks down because Shakespeare can't be brought up to speed. Visual technology has made Picard's face familiar to his crew. The captain thus depends more on a machine than he does on Shakespeare to fight effectively.

22. A number of other "genius" icons, such as Socrates, appeared with each successive question. And even "Give 'Em What They Want," the musical in *She's Working Her Way Through College,* could be considered an update of Shakespeare, playing off of *Kiss Me Kate* and Shakespeare's *Twelfth Night, or What You Will.*

23. For another example, see Grace Catalano's (1997) biography of Leonardo DiCaprio, subtitled *Modern Day-Romeo.*

24. The work I focus on in particular is the essay "The Signification of the Phallus" in *Écrits* (Lacan 1966).

25. In an article on computer hackers, Andrew Ross defends youth culture as "proto-political" and takes other cultural critics to task for not appreciating its progressive political potential (1991, 122). See also his co-edited collection on youth music (Rose and Ross 1994).

26. What Jameson sees as a problem with this model may thus also be a virtue for some cultural critics: the distance that has to be overcome between the "real" fan and the academic ethnographer underscores a particularly Derridean turn in the transformation of the "people" into "fans": "where the first of these was a primary substance, calmly persisting in its essence, and exercising a powerful gravitational effect on the insubstantial intellectuals who fluttered near it, the new version opens up a hall of mirrors in which the 'people' itself longs to be a 'people' and be 'popular', feels its own ontological lack, longs for its own impossible stability, and narcissistically attempts, in a variety of rituals, to recuperate a being that never existed in the first place" (1994, 43).

27. Penley writes "The fans . . . could not speak from a feminist position" (491).

28. For another example of this move, see Joyrich 1993. "When asked whether I am interested in analyzing Elvis because I am a fan," Joyrich notes, "I like to respond that what I am actually a fan of is the fans themselves" (85).

29. Responding to John Fiske, who sees her as a fan, Penley says, for example: "I think you only see one side of my project when you characterize me as

having aligned myself with the fans, experiencing and learning from their reading practices. . . . I am learning from the fans, but much of what I learn comes from recognizing and acknowledging the distance between us" (1992, 496).

30. As Terry Castle puts it more strongly in her celebration of lesbian opera diva worship, some fans are deranged, "maddened—sometimes horrifyingly—by their adoration" (1993, 237).

31. A brilliant (non-American) portrait of the loser, see Thomas Bernhard in his novel *The Loser* (1983). See also Lieberman 1993.

32. This may or may not be self-delusion. In Martin Scorsese's *King of Comedy*, for example, failed stand-up comic Rupert Pupkin gets the applause any comic on national television would usually get, and the film ends ambiguously, allowing one to think either that Pupkin actually does succeed in becoming famous or that the last sequence about his fame is only another one of his fantasies.

33. Koestenbaum writes: "A record can't limit the voice's meanings; a voice, once recorded, doesn't speak the same meanings as originally intended" (1993, 51).

34. Andrew Hulktrans takes the show to be about "watching watching TV" (1994, 8).

35. This shift from the literary to the cinematic may be traced back to Vladimir Nabokov's *Lolita*. See Power 1996.

36. Fandom presents political criticism with another problem. It is itself regulatory; it performs critical functions that are anything but liberatory (rewrites as based on what the fan thinks a given show is really about, what its creators intended it to be before corporate control ruined it). Fandom is like criticism in that it codes in advance how one is supposed to respond. A bunch of jocks who show up at a punk rock concert to slam dance, for example, will be despised by punks for totally missing what the music is about, for not getting it. Similarly, one watches a show such as *The Brady Bunch* to make fun of it and insult it, not to say how good it is. Fans, like critics, distinguish between those who can properly appreciate something and those who can't.

37. For a recent replay of this debate, see Butler, 1997a and Fraser 1997.

38. See Musil 1937 for a fascinating and quite humorous discussion of stupidity. For an attempt, unconvincing in my view, to make stupidity in popular music a site of political resistance, see Savage 1996. See also Dechter 1994.

39. The journal *American Literary History* even puts quotations in the margins of the articles, following the practice of newspapers and magazines.

40. As we will see in Chapter Two, however, the *Shakespeare, the Animated Tales* version of *Romeo and Juliet,* marketed through HBO, might count as an exception. On television as a conservative medium, see Weber 1996, 126.

Chapter 1

1. Clause 28 made it illegal for gays and lesbians to express affection for each other in public and to promote homosexuality in school as a valid lifestyle. Some reviewers did see McKellen's Richard as gay-inflected, but he disputed this account: "And though some observers have seen homoerotic overtones in his portrayal of Richard III, he thinks the ambitious soldier-turned-king is unquestionably heterosexual. If Richard were gay, 'that would be another story altogether,' McKellen said" (Ring 1996, 1).

2. The Kemp/Coronado production of *Hamlet* (1976) in which two Hamlets run around clothed only in jock straps much of the time, is not even out on video. On this film, see Murray, 1996, 417.

3. In a more complicated move, Kenneth Branagh writes homosexuality into his film of *Henry V* in order to write it out. He plays up the homoeroticism of Henry's relation to Scroop ("the King's bedfellow," Branagh allows Exeter to say) only to cut Exeter's later speech (4.6.7-32) in which York is reported to "kiss the gashes" on Suffolk's corpse and to have "kissed his lips," thereby "seal[ing] / A testament of noble-ending love."

4. Whether Branagh could be considered a "queer" director/actor is something of an open question. Branagh's films suggest a certain gay preoccupation. He directed and starred in *Peter's Friends* (1991), for example, a comedy about a male character whose sexuality is indeterminate until he reveals at the end that he has been celibate because he has AIDS (from gay sex).

5. In the 1990 science fiction thriller sequel *Highlander 2: the Quickening* (dir. Russell Mulcahy, 1990), comically resignifies Hamlet as Yorick's gay lover. One of the immortal Scottish Highlanders now living on the planet Zeist, Ramirez (Sean Connery), magically appears in the middle of a 2024 Earth production of *Hamlet*:

   > ACTOR PLAYING HAMLET: Alas, poor Yorick! I knew him, Horatio.
   > RAMIREZ: Actually, the name is Ramirez.
   > ACTOR PLAYING HAMLET: (whispers to Ramirez) Will you get out of here?!
   > RAMIREZ: Excuse me.
   > ACTOR PLAYING HAMLET: A fellow of infinite jest, of most excellent fancy.
   > RAMIREZ: Forgive me for interrupting, but . . .
   > ACTOR PLAYING HAMLET: He hath borne me upon his back a thousand times; and now, how abhorred my in [sic] imagination it [sic] is! My gorge rises at it. Here hung those lips I have kissed I know not how oft.
   > RAMIREZ: SIR, whatever you gentlemen felt for each other when your friend was still alive is certainly none of my affair.

6. Orlando turns to the camera after the performance and quips "great play!" The film also includes a scene in which Orlando reads a Shakespeare sonnet.

7. One reviewer quipped that the Capulet ball was done as *Priscilla, Queen of Verona* (Maslin 1996: C12). It is also worth noting that the success of *Clueless* and other Jane Austen adaptations led to a transgendered recoding of Shakespeare. *Time* ran two stories, one entitled "Shakespeare: The Old Jane Austen" (Anonymous A 1996), and the other "Shakespeare is the New Jane Austen," (Corliss 1996: 3). For another account, see Lane 1996. On Mercutio as gay, see Porter 1988 and Smith 1991. On Romeo and Juliet as sodomitical, see Goldberg, 1994.

8. Michael Hoffman's *A Midsummer Night's Dream* (Fox Searchlight Pictures, scheduled for release in 1999) appears promising as a gay version as well. It stars Rupert Everett as Oberon and Kevin Kline as Bottom.

9. The film was made in the U.K. and was released there in 1997. It opened in the U.S. on March 13, 1998.

10. Nicholas Hytner's 1998 romantic comedy *The Object of My Affection* introduces multiple references to Shakespeare in its adaptation of Stephen McCauley's novel of the same name: Paul James, the gay lover of the principle character, George Hanson (Paul Rudd, who played Paris in Luhrmann's *William Shakespeare's Romeo and Juliet*), appears as Romeo with an African American woman as Juliet in the palmer's kiss sequence of a modern dress production. George's female roommate, Nina Borowski (Jennifer Aniston) refers bitterly to Paul as "Romeo"; Rodney Fraser (Nigel Hawthorne, who starred as a Shakespeare-citing monarch in Hytner's earlier *The Madness of King George*), a theater critic who loves musicals and Shakespeare, mentions plans to go see *King Lear*, wishes a hunky friend of George's had been cast as Mercutio, and slams the modern dress production of *Romeo and Juliet*; and in a critic's conference, George's ex-lover, Dr. Robert Joley (Timothy Daly) disparages *West Side Story* as a distortion of *Romeo and Juliet*. *The Object of My Affection*, a film that gives new meaning to the genre of "screwball comedy," goes even further than *In and Out* in using Shakespeare to chart a gay utopia, though initially of an even more heteronormative kind. Though no one in the film is at all homophobic and though all gay people appear to be "out" with comfort, the first Act of the film indulges a heterosexual woman's romantic fantasy about turning a gay man straight. After deciding that they are in love the protagonists George and Nina decide to continue living together and raise her baby without the biological father's involvement (George wants to have a child himself; apparently, the thought of raising a child with another man has never occured to him). In a sex scene with the couple, the film seems to go all the way in erasing gayness. But just as George and Nina are about to have sex, the phone rings with George's ex-lover Dr. Robert Joley on the line. George then declines Nina's offer to continue where they left off and decides to go with Joley to a "critic's convention" at George's old college in order to reunite romantically.

Shakespeare enters the film as it takes a turn to affirm gayness in what I call "homonormative" terms. (These references are the film's addition—they are not in the novel. There is a reference in the novel to a performance in the middle ring of a Ringling Brothers Circus show, however [McCauley 1987, 266]. I develop my account of homonormativity else-where [see ch.2, note 9].) Gayness and Shakespeare are equated. At the critic's convention, Joley, a professor who has just published a book on

George Bernard Shaw, sides with with Shaw, Shakespeare (*Romeo and Juliet*), and Berlin avant-garde caberet against American musicals, while his English antagonist, Rodney Fraser, loves both musicals and Shakespeare and has no patience with contemporary theater. At this conference, George meets Paul. The two have sex and quickly fall in love. As the two form a couple, a modern dress production of *Romeo and Juliet*, complete with sitar music, dark lighting, and an interracial, tatoo ornamented and semi-naked cast, becomes the means by which they disentangle themselves from Nina and Rodney.

The *Object of My Affection* also signals its rewriting of Shakespeare extradiegetically. Paul Rudd makes an in-joke about his role as Paris in the Luhrmann film when he says that he and a possible date are leaving for Paris that night. Paris has been recoded as the site of romance rather than of exclusion from it. Nigel Hawthorne's mention of *King Lear* also may recall to some viewers his performance of King George III doing a scene from *King Lear* in *The Madness of King George*. (His role as Malvolio in Nunn's *Twelfth Night* is also mildly hinted at insofar as he is the jilted lover.)

Gay characters have a monopoly on Shakespeare in the film, and a younger generation's appropriation of *Romeo and Juliet* yields a comedy in which the truly happy couple is gay and has sex. There are several post-coital scenes with George and Paul, and, with the exception of George's Lothario-like brother Frank (Steve Zahn), no one in the film, especially the heterosexuals, is having sex. In one particularly funny moment, Nina, after having discussed not having sex with George, asks George as she lies on top of him in bed whether married couples are as happy as they are. And even at the heteronormative occasion of George's brother's wedding, George and Nina, not the married couple, are the stars, dancing by themselves while everyone else stops to admire their skill, and constituting the model couple for everyone there.

In calling the citation of *Romeo and Juliet* "homonormative," I mean to call attention to the way *The Object of My Affection* constructs homosexual romance in heterosexual terms. Like the heterosexual characters, all of the gay characters are looking for a romantic lover. Except for Dr. Goldstein, an "ear, nose, and throat" specialist, himself a hunky caricature whose advances George spurns repeatedly, no one cruises in this film. (One wonders, however, whether a different scenario in which George were psyhcologically intimate with a woman and capable only of casual, non-romantic sex with men would be any better.) The film does not produce a "queer romance" that radically breaks with the conventions of heterosexual romantic comedy and allows gay male sex into the film only under the rule of the couple. Yet it is precisely the film's conservatism that ends up extensively queering the heterosexual family as reconstructed in this film. Rather than letting go of the female fantasy of marrying a gay man after the "living together without sex" experiment fails, the film does not return to traditional heterosexual couplings. When Nina's baby, Molly, is born, for example, Vince shows up at the hospital as if to claim his "rightful" place, but as the camera pans right we see that George is already there, holding Molly in his arms. And the film closes with a flash forward scene of a new first grade production by George (starring Molly). As the camera tracks right down a row of seats, our expectation that the characters are all arranged in couples is repeatedly unsettled: We first see Vince and Nina, but then we se Nina holding hands with her new boyfriend Lewis, an African American cop she met earlier in the film; we then see Nina's step-sister and husband with their now punk-rock daughter; and finally Paul with Rodney. After the show, Rodney arranges to babysit Molly, and Nina, Uncle George, and Molly go off to have coffee. Through the citation of Shakespeare, *The Object of My Affection* opens up a utopian fantasy designed more for heterosexuals rather than for gays, in which the family is no longer constructed in terms of who's in and who's out of it: instead of the married couple at the head of the family, we have an extended family run by a number of "uncles" (of whom the biological father is considered to be one) and a single mother.

11. In the earlier, 1968 film *The Secret Sex Lives of Romeo and Juliet,* the Nurse is also lesbian.

12. When not adapting the plays directly, films such as *The Goodbye Girl* stage theatrical productions rather than film productions of Shakespeare. This is true of straight productions such as Al Pacino's *Looking for Richard* and Kenneth Branagh's *A Midwinter's Tale.*

13. On Laurence Olivier, for example, see Garber 1995.

14. Aki Kaurismaki (1991) is opposed to representing any explicit sex in his films, regarding it as a Hollywood tendency.

15. The probability of a failure in this regard may be glimpsed in a controversy over Franco Zeffirelli. One critic reads him as insufficiently political (van Watson 1992); another reads in him a critique of patriarchy (Donaldson 1990). For attempts to theorize gay authorship, see Dyer 1991 and Mayne 1991.

16. I explore lesbian sex in a number of heterosexual pornographic adaptations in the next chapter. The Paul Czinner *As You Like It* (1939) starring Laurence Olivier and Elizabeth Bergner also holds some promise for a homoerotic reading of Rosalind and Celia. The two are almost always shot together and are almost always touching, embracing, holding hands, even kissing in one scene. More pointedly, the film interpolates a scene inside Rosalind and Celia's house with the two on a bed (fully clothed, to be sure). Rosalind sings happily to an equally happy Celia, in marked contrast to an earlier scene, just before the messenger arrives with an excuse for Orlando's delay, in which Celia had serenaded a distressed Rosalind. The interpolation delays Orlando's imminent arrival and disrupts Orlando's encounter with the messenger and his news of Rosalind's reception of his excuse. It provides a kind of pastoral suspension of the play's movement toward marriage and heterosexuality. It's also worth noting that when dressed as Orlando, Bergner looks very much like Greta Garbo as Queen Christina.

Also worth checking out is *Outrageous Fortune* (dir. Arthur Hiller, 1987). This comedy parodies the buddy road-picture and tells the story of two women who were initially rivals for the same man but who bond as they discover he's a Russian spy who wants to murder both of them. An aspiring actress, Lauren's (Shelley Long) ambition is to play Hamlet. Porn actress Sandy (Bette Midler), by contrast, has never heard of the play. The film gives the homoeroticism of the genre a lesbian spin, most markedly through Shakespeare. The film ends with a curtain call for a performance of *Hamlet* in which Lauren stars as Hamlet and Sandy as Gertrude, thereby recoding the incestuous relation between mother and son as a lesbian relation between a cross-dressed butch and a femme. *Eve's Bayou* (dir. Kasi Lemmons, 1997) offers a kind of *Die Bitteren Tränen der Juliet von Verona* take on lesbian identification among the sisters, mother, and sister-in-law, in which their only love is born of their only hate for each other. The sisters, who consistently form the film's closest couple, identify with male characters from *Romeo and Juliet*. Cicely, the oldest, addresses Eve and Po, her younger sister and brother, as Mercutio and Tybalt, respectively, and, to make them stop fighting, cites Romeo's lines to them: "the Prince hath expressly / Forbid this bandying in Verona's streets" (3.1. 82-82). In a later scene, Cicely plays Romeo to Eve's Juliet doing the balcony scene. And when her mother cuts herself while preparing dinner and anxiously awaiting her cheating husband's return home, Eve cites Mercutio's lines about his wound from Tybalt "'Tis not so deep as a well, nor so wide as a church, but 'tis enough. 'Twill serve" (3.1. 92-93). While *Romeo and Juliet* marks the deepness of the same-sex bond between the sisters, it also marks heterosexual couples as failed—adulterous, incestuous, or cursed (the sister-in-law Moselle, despite the fact that she knows she is a "black widow" whose husbands all die, ends up marrying an effeminate, long haired man named Julian [who, of course, dies right after they marry]).

17. For example, gay sex in *The Goodbye Girl* is a source of comedy, whereas in theatrical productions of Shakespeare in the 1990s gay sex is played straight, as the moment of greatest emotional pathos.

18. Probably, one would have to have read gay journalistic coverage to know about Clark's sexual orientation. See Chunovic 1991, for an example.

19. Michael Clark explains, "I wanted to kind of change it [his penis] into something less familiar, so I did what I could do with it. I basically tied my penis in a knot by putting it around my balls and stuffing it back into a pair of flesh colored rubber pants that I got from a sex shop in Amsterdam" (Chunovic 1991: 96).

20. I would like to thank Josh Ruddy for drawing my attention to this film.

21. Some critics might answer in the affirmative. "Queer" in this sense includes readings by straights as well as gays and lesbians, and includes gays and lesbians of all political affiliations (see Doty 1993, 15). But the very inclusiveness of the meaning of "queer" would appear to empty it of specificity, and hence empty it of meaning.

22. This opposition can itself be deconstructed. In his *Tempest* (1979), Derek Jarman, for example, brings popular culture into his avant-garde adaptation, closing the wedding festivities near the end of the film by bringing in Elizabeth Welch, a black singer famous in the 1930s, to sing "Stormy Weather" after the sailors from the shipwrecked boat have done a musical number.

23. In addition to these examples, *Withnail and I* (dir. Bruce Robinson, 1985) deserves a mention. The English comedy *Withnail and I* is about two straight male Hamlet-identified out-of-work actors (Richard E. Grant and Paul McGann) who leave London for a weekend visit to Withnail's ponce uncle's (Richard Griffiths) country house. And for another example of the way Shakespeare signifies gayness in American popular culture, see *Beverly Hills, 90210,* rebroadcast Dec. 20, 1996. In a theater class, David as Juliet and Donna (Tori Spelling) as Romeo perform a cross-dressed version of the balcony scene; their teacher Chris chides them for taking a "total cop-out," and going for a "cheap laugh" (the students had giggled throughout the performance of the balcony scene). He tells them they have to do it again, seriously: "Next time do it straight." This scene is followed by one on the beach with Kelly and a guy who had made a pass at her the night before but didn't follow through. He explains to her that he hasn't slept with a girl. She says that's OK, but he replies, "No, you don't understand. I'm not sure if I want to." "So you're gay?" she asks. "No. I'm not sure," he replies. Also noteworthy is an episode of the television sit-com *Brotherly Love* (originally aired in 1995 and rebroadcast on the Disney Channel on May 4, 1998) involving a school production of *A Midsummer Night's Dream.* The series is about three brothers raised by a single mom who owns an auto shop. In this episode, Matt, the middle brother, cast as Oberon in a school play, gets over his stage fright about playing a faerie when Joe (his older brother) reassures him that he is not "a gutless faerie," but the "king of the faeries." The teacher then pulls Joe into the play as well, against his own wishes, and he reluctantly plays Peaseblossom, performing his role as "heterosexually" as possible (he wears jeans rather than tights and swaggers rather than prances, as the other faeries do). Despite numerous references to the embarrassment of boys playing faeries (brotherly love, indeed), the episode seems less interested in the gay reference (a cute girl asks Matt out to the cast party) than in the embarrassment of the young male body under the pressure of the single female gaze. The teacher is a spinster, and Joe ends up modelling nude for a woman friend's art class (of women only) in order to escape playing Peaseblossom again. The episode closes with the mother appearing as Peaseblossom but upstaging her son Matt (who is again playing Oberon) as she begins to do Juliet's part in the balcony scene of *Romeo and Juliet.*

24. In making this argument, I take issue with D. A. Miller (1991) and Doty (1993), for whom connotations of queerness constitute a homophobic practice, the consequence of a closeted homosexuality. For me, queerness is precisely what cannot be denoted.

25. To be sure, this kind of project risks turning out to be a version of gay identity. Though queer theory has made the notable contribution of making heterosexuality problematic, in practice this sometimes amounts to seeing a gay foundationalism everywhere. For an example of such an approach, see the essays in Burston 1995. For thoughtful accounts of queer visibility in mass culture, see Doty 1993 and Straayer 1996.

26. The allusion may be intentional, made possible by a retroactive reading of *Spartacus* as a gay film in light of recently restored scenes cut from the original.

27. It is worth noting that in the less directly homophobic *Fame* (dir. Alan Parker, 1980), Shakespeare is used in an equally normalizing way. The first shot of the film is of a poster of Olivier playing Othello. The camera moves down to give a close-up of a teen giving an audition. He is clearly coded as gay. Later, a particularly stupid male applicant reads Juliet's lines from the balcony scene. The teacher tells him as he leaves, "You were reading the girl's part."

28. I would like to thank Don Hedrick for drawing my attention to *Porky's 2* and for giving me a copy of his unpublished essay on the film.

29. Though Elliot's director maintains that his interpretation is innovative, it has a precursor in Laurence Olivier's *Richard III* (1955). Olivier's performance quietly codes Richard as gay in a number of ways: the dandyish, mincing character of his voice and accent; his fur-trimmed hat, apparently drawn from 1950s women's *haute couture;* a number of shots of Richard in shadow, particularly a tracking shot of Richard with his sword hilt protruding like an erection and his sword seemingly entering his behind, a shot that ends with Richard bending down over Edward (who is seated on his throne) as if kissing him; and Richard engaging in "pillow talk" with Tyrrel, their faces an inch apart: "say it is done, and I'll love thee . . . and prefer thee." Olivier himself described his Richard in female terms: Richard's "disproportioned gait, his big nose, his stiff black curls add meanness and power to his eyes, whose lids flutter and blink like a gossiping noblewoman's as he stands a foot or so from the camera and speaks in clear, crisp tones" (1986, 85).

30. Williams returned to a gay Shakespeare in a skit entitled "Shakespeare in the Slums" during an episode of *Saturday Night Live* that he hosted (original airdate, November 22, 1986). Williams played an improvisational actor in the first production of Shakespeare's *Hamlet*. He goes on about the "Queen" to a transvestite actor dressed as Gertrude, and after Shakespeare objects, he is told by another actor to "cut the fag shit."

31. In this respect, the film stages a problem already present in marriage as represented in screwball comedies. As Stanley Cavell (1981) has noted, these films represent falling in love as an experience that has to be repeated.

32. Evidence for a reading of Neal as gay may be buttressed by a comparison of the film release with a radically different cut released for television (airing on USA in 1995). The television cut contains seven additional scenes, one of which involves Shakespeare and all of which serve to heterosexualize both Neal and theater in general. In one scene, Neal recites Hamlet's line "To be or not to be" and then invites Todd to act in the play because girls will be there; a subplot (entirely missing from the film version) involves a shy sister of Chip, Chris's boyfriend, played by Lara Flynn Boyle, whom Chris invites to try out for *A Midsummer Night's Dream*. The *Hamlet* reference, made in a scene that immediately precedes Neal's encounter with his irate father in Neal's room, suggests that the conflict between son and father (and father figure, Keating) is just an average Oedipal conflict.

33. Significantly, Jack never sees Bobby's ass. In the primal scene where Jack sees Lira and Bobby having sex, Lira's on top.

34. Love triangles are everywhere in this film. Even the other professors get off on Bobby's sexual escapades. The other assistant professor even asks to borrow Fine's office for the evening so he can have sex with one of his students.

35. Men go out of control when gazing at the spectacle of women with exposed rear ends. One man with a phallic jackhammer hits a waterline, for example, when looking at a young woman walking by in the jeans.

36. To be sure, *Four Weddings* does close off this utopian space by killing off the gay character who cites Shakespeare. On Hollywood's gay love affair since Mike Nichols's *The Birdcage,* see Isherwood 1997.

37. The relation between Kline and Hamlet was noticed by Blum (1997) and Corliss (1997).

38. The film thus makes explicit an ambivalence about Shakespeare as romantic signifier that arguably runs throughout American popular films. If Shakespeare is often aligned with heterosexuality, a marker of a deep, lasting love, he also constitutes an obstacle to romantic love. In *Soapdish,* for example, Shakespeare obstructs heterosexuality. Kevin Kline plays a former soap-opera actor who has left the soaps to do a dinner-theater production of *Death of a Salesman* in Florida. He has a bust of Shakespeare in his dressing room and hopes to do a one-man *Hamlet* on Broadway. When he reunites with his wife (Sally Fields) at the end of the film, he leaves Shakespeare and dinner theater behind. Shakespeare could similarly be construed as the obstacle that blocks a romantic relation between Scott Favor and Mike Rivers in *My Own Private Idaho.* even as it enables a heterosexual relation and marriage between Scott and his Italian wife.

39. Similarly, when, in *The Object of My Affection,* the elderly english critic Rodney Fraser totally trashes the modern-dress production of *Romeo and Juliet* within earshot of the director at the cast party, the director identifies himself and retaliates by decking Rodney.

40. The writer of the *People Magazine* article quips in conclusion: "scholars may never know for certain whether, romantically speaking, Shakespeare went both thisaway *and* Hathaway."

41. Knowledge of homosexuality by gays or lesbians may lead in a variety of directions, including criticizing closeted directors whose films were less queer than those of contemporary straight directors, as well as simply dismissing knowledge about directors as beside the point (identifications with gay or lesbian stars being the point). See Doty 1993, 19-21.

Chapter 2

1. The exception is Laurie Osborne (1993), who discusses the *Playboy Twelfth Night.* On *Othello,* see Lynda Boose 1997, Patricia Parker 1994, and Pechter

1996; on obscene Shakespeare, see Don Hedrick 1994. Susie Bright (1997, 18) cites *Richard III* in her analysis of contemporary sex practices in the U.S.

2. The film is also known as *Juliet's Desire* and won the Cannes Film Festival award for best erotic picture in 1969. I have not had the chance to examine silent pornography to see if stag films, for example, made use of Shakespeare. Barbara Freedman tells me there were a number of loops entitled *Romeo* and *Cleo* that had nothing else to do with Shakespeare.

3. There is also nudity in a number of films: Titania appears bare-breasted in Peter Hall's *A Midsummer Night's Dream* (1968); Romeo and Juliet first appear in the nude in Franco Zeffirelli's *Romeo and Juliet* (1968); in his *Tempest* (1979), Derek Jarman shows a bare-breasted Miranda bathing, a naked Ariel chained by Sycorax, a naked Ferdinand swimming ashore, and an adult Caliban suckling at Sycorax's breast; a character based on Miranda (Molly Ringwald) swims in the nude in Paul Mazursky's adaptation, *Tempest* (1989); and Kenneth Branagh shows some nudity in the opening of his *Much Ado About Nothing* (1993).

4. Greenaway suggests that Pornocrates may have been Caliban's father. He also notes "a blindfolded figure of pornography" in section 37 of the film. See Greenaway 1991, 83 and 82. See also anon. 1991, 127. In a television review on *Sneak Previews* in 1991, Michael Medved called *Prospero's Books* "kiddie porn." The French magazine *New Look,* a mix of *Playboy* and *Sports Illustrated,* did a spread on the film (anon. 1991).

5. Baz Luhrmann's *William Shakespeare's Romeo and Juliet* (1996) names a number of stripclubs in the Verona Beach "Sycamore Grove" after Shakespeare characters, including the "*Midnight Hags.*"

6. I have not seen the bondage *Midsummer's* (it is apparently no longer available because the production company is no longer in business), but information on it may be gleaned from the *Adult Video News* 1998 *Adult Entertainment Guide* (408) and Riley, 1996, 468. In one scene of *Censored* (Michael Zen, dir. 1996), T. T. Boy appears as Romeo and has sex with Lady Godiva (Jenteal). There is also a film called *The Tempest* (with Sunset Thomas, Lana Sands, and Rebecca Bardoux), though it has nothing to with Shakespeare's play. *A Mid-Slumber Night's Dream* has less to do with Shakespeare's play than Woody Allen's *A Midsummer's Sex Comedy* does. This porn video is about a woman who is advised by a girlfriend to explore her sexual fantasies and to cheat on her husband when he leaves on business. She appears to do just this. At the film's end, however, it turns out she's been fantasizing what appeared to be adulterous sex while having great sex with her husband. Well satisfied by his wife, the husband decides not to leave on business the next day after all. Finally, Douglas Lanier tells me he once saw a copy of a video entitled *A Midsummer Night's Wet Dream,* probably made in the 1980s, about the sexual exploits of the actors who perform the play. Unfortunately, he did not note the year of release, the director, or the production company when he saw the copy, and I have been unable to find a copy or mention of it anywhere. More tangentially, there is a film that cites *Romeo and Juliet* entitled *Star-crossed* (dir. Michael Spenelli, 1996), with Crystal Wilder and Jake Williams in the leads.

7. See the Introduction, note three, for the full references. Although these videos (and comics) are not pornographic, they are sold as adult products by Excalibur Films (there is some occasional, brief nudity, particularly when Ranma changes from a boy into a girl).

8. Also of interest is a video from Independent Edge entitled *Live Nude Shakespeare: To Bare or Not to Bare* (dir. Michael D. Fox and Dave Evans, 1997), in which men and women actors perform Shakespeare while stripping, and a website entitled "Attractive Nude Models Performing Shakespeare," in which photos of men and women with pictures of Shakespeare's face functioning as fig leaves are placed next to passages from the plays and sonnets (http://www.mediashower.com/zug/scrawl/nudebard/). A striptease is performed by Laurence Harvey while doing the "to be or not to be" soliloquy in the *Magic Christian* (dir. Joseph McCarthy, 1969). Shakespeare porn seems to be going mainstream. The December 1997 issue of *Penthouse* (vol. 29, no. 4) compares the issue's pet-of-the-month to Shakespeare's Juliet (p. 84), and the Houston Grand Opera mailed out a flier for Verdi's *Macbeth* that showed on its cover a photo of a woman bare from the shoulders up and that read "Dominant Scottish female seeks willing partner for ultimate power trip. Inquiries kept confidential." My thanks to Becky Kershman for providing me with a copy of this ad. There is also a distributor of porn videos in Boulder Creek, California, named *As You Like It Productions* (408 338-1990), and Wicked Pictures cites the second witch's line "something wicked this way comes" from *Macbeth* (4.1. 62) as the tag line in ads featuring two of their leading contract stars, Jenna Jameson and Serenity. For examples, see the January 1998 and March 1998 issues of *Adult Video News*, pp. 321 and 104, respectively. Along similar lines, Melissa Butler, an Oxford student who also strips in London, says she does "occasional naked performances of Hamlet" and does a splendid Ophelia, running about the stage ripping [her] clothes off and screaming" (1998,80). Her novel *Bluestocking* (due out in 1999) is a fictional account of her experiences. See also Robert Nye's novel *Mrs. Shakespeare: The Collected Works* (1993), in which a bisexual Shakespeare has anal sex with Anne Hathaway (and she likes it) in the second-best bed. I have not canvassed pornographic fiction, but Shakespeare does make an appearance in an s&m pornographic, novelistic adaptation of Oscar Wilde's *The Picture of Dorian Gray* by Amarantha Knight (1996). Knight rewrites Wilde's production of *Romeo and Juliet* with Sybil Vane as Juliet into a master/slave whipping fest pantomimed by (apparent) mutes. First, Romeo binds Juliet and whips her ass; then they change roles and Juliet whips him (pp. 58-63; 202-3). Dorianne Grey, Vane, and the actor playing Romeo then have sex together backstage after the show finishes. (Dorianne is a woman passing as a gay man in this adaptation.) Later in the novel, Knight also adds a spin-off (without Sybil Vane) called *The Taming of the Screw* in which Petruchio spanks Kate (pp. 131, 140). For Wilde's use of Shakespeare in *The Picture of Dorian Gray*, see Wilde 1891, 44-47; 65-68; 81-82; 93. And for two contemporary s&m porn rewritings of *The Taming of the Shrew* in which Kate is a mistress, see Chet Rothwell 19 and Winslow 19 . Shakespeare also

came up at the obscenity trial of 2 Live Crew's CD *Nasty As They Wanna Be*. Henry Louis Gates, Jr. defended the rap group in part by comparing them to Shakespeare. When pressed by the prosecutor, Gates backed off (see Campbell 1992, 153, 157).

9. *Romeo and Julian* won the AVN 1993 award for best gay musical score and best gay sex scene and was the lead article in the February 1994 issue of AVN. It was released in two versions, one X-rated, the other unrated. For more information, go to www.forumstudios.com. *Romeo and Julian* represents homosexuality in terms of heterosexuality, apparently invoking Romeo and Juliet as eternal lovers who can even get over affairs. As in standard heterosexual soap operas, Romeo cheats on Julian and lies about it. After Julian walks out of a party-turned-orgy (Romeo stays), the two lovers reunite for a happy ending. Romeo can't get it up for the orgy because he loves Julian after all. By contrast, *Le Voyage a Venise* does contain thematic parallels to Shakespeare's tragedy. In this case, the lovers are star-crossed because Romeo thinks he is straight (he's a ladies man and is engaged to be married in three days) and Julien's parents disapprove. But the film ends happily: after an orgy, Romeo decides he's not straight and Julien's parents go home to France, leaving him to settle down with Romeo in Venice. I saw these videos only after this book was in press, but will discuss them, along with *Eve's Bayou* (dir. Kasi Lemmons, 1997) and the off-broadway play *Shakespeare's R and J*, directed and adapted by Joe Calarco, in an article tentatively entitled "Masked Balls: Homonormativity, Romance Fiction, and Queer *Romeo and Juliet* Adaptations." Far from mimicking heteronormative norms in order to resignify and possibly subvert them, these films use Romeo and Juliet, I argue, to give expression to a gay utopian fantasy (with roots in earlier gay versions of the play like George Cukor's) whereby gay sex is normalized and heterosexualized according to the conventions of a now "feminine" genre, namely, the romance. Inverting the suggestion made by some feminist critics that the female-centered genre of romance may be read as softcore pornography for women, I maintain that gay male Shakespeare pornography may be read as romance for gay men.

10. Though this video is aimed primarily at children and is certainly not intended to be viewed as pornographic, it may be prosecutable under existing child pornography law (see Bernstein 1997 and Kernes 1997a). It's not clear that its being a Shakespeare play could save it from prosecution, not because the sex is softcore but because the characters, especially Juliet, "appear to be" in their mid-teens. (2.6) (See note 21) A Japanese spin-off animated adult version called Ranma 1/2 Anything Goes Series: Ranma and Juliet is perhaps also a vulnerable version, as it portrays Japanese high school students (who act the parts of Romeo and Juliet in a school production of the play), one of whom (Ranma) changes from a boy to a girl and then back. Though this video has only brief nudity, it is marketed in the United States as an adult title. Even if Japanese animated film were actually explicit, whether it would be child pornography in the American sense remains unclear, since it, like all Japanese pornography, is heavily censored in ways United States and European porn is not: pubic hair and penises can't

be shown in Japan (both are airbrushed out of photos or not drawn in comic books and cartoons [see Buckley 1991]). By American standards, what is a far less pornographic (because less explicit) version of *Romeo and Juliet* may nevertheless count under current U.S. law as child pornography.

11. This point indirectly received confirmation a month after this chapter was drafted when *Lingua Franca* ran a story on feminist pro-porn criticism (Lord, 1997).

12. Similarly, they are for sale through mail order and adult video stores, not in general audience video stores.

13. This is not the case in pornographic literature, however. As Laurie Osborne has pointed out to me, Shakespeare does have sex with a female character (Jessica, Shylock's daughter, who is also a movie star in the present and the narrator) in Erica Jong's novel, *Shylock's Daughter: a Novel of Love in Venice* (1995), originally published as *Serenissima* in 1986. Yet even Jong stops short of going in a fully pornographic direction. Initially, Jessica "sleep[s] with Shakespeare" (p.33), meaning his books, because she is celibate. And when she does actually have sex with Shakespeare the man, she refuses to narrate the sex scene:

> And here I confess I am torn—whether to break off . . . or whether, indeed, to describe our carnal amour as he himself, that most carnal of poets, would have done. Shall we pause and let the readers vote? . . . To detail organs, motions, sheets, wet spots, would be too gross, too literal, too finally deflating! It is quite one thing to imagine the poet abed with his convent Juliet or his bisexual earl—but for a mere player like myself to go back in time, bed him, and then tell tales out of school? Fie on't! Was Will Shakespeare good in bed? Let the reader judge! (191).

14. Russell Miller writes: "Hefner was thrilled at the prospect of becoming a movie producer, particularly in such illustrious company and on such a serious project. Here was *Playboy* proving it had come a long way from the days of tits and ass: bankrolling *Shakespeare*. Perfect." (1984, 240). For *Playboy* coverage of the film in production, with Hefner on site, see Anon. 1972.

15. To be sure, some states make access more difficult such that distributors will not mail porn to residents. For a detailed, funny, and rather disquieting account of the male porn star's low status in porn, see Heath 1996.

16. The Shakespeare porn films apparently have sold well. Excalibur Films, a mail-order company that stocks over 40,000 adult movies, showed for March, 1997, that *Hamlet: For the Love of Ophelia, Part Two* was number 7 of their 100 best-selling new releases, was 62, and *Hamlet: For the Love of Ophelia* was 73. See Excalibur's website at http//:excalibur.prtcl.com:80/html/excal/notnew.htm. In 1996 and early 1997, the now defunct Sarah Young homepage (http://members.aol.com/youngsarah/homepage.htm) featured an "Album of *Hamlet*" and advertised a CD-ROM based on *Hamlet: For The Love of Ophelia* "filled with facts, films and pictures from

this high-class erotic-movie." *Juliet and Romeo, Hamlet: For the Love of Ophelia,* and *The Taming of the Screw* all made it into *AVN*'s 1998 *Adult Entertainment Guide*'s "Top 2,000 Videos" list, and *Hamlet: For the Love of Ophelia* made it onto the more selective "Best of 1996" list in the 1997 *AVN* guide. In April 1998, *Juliet and Romeo* aired on a softcore adult network, The Spice Channel

17. The boxcovers of the film and its sequel boast that the budgets for each were $500,000.

18. See also Žižek 1997.

19. For an analysis on pornography in the context of feminist performance art, see Schneider (1996).

20. It is significant that Žižek leaves adaptations out of his account. Indeed, the example he gives of how a straight film can't have a pornographic sequence added to it without "undermining the consistency of the diegetic reality" (111) is the *Out of Africa* porn remake called, unsurprisingly, *In and Out of Africa* (dir. F. J. Lincoln, 1986)

21. Perhaps the most extreme example in recent porn is Joe D'Amato's *Othello: Dangerous Desire.* Early on Othello tells Desdemona, "You know, life is pretty strange, you know. As we were walking, you told me your name's Desdemona. And of course you know my name's Othello. Not to say that it has anything to do with Shakespeare. Thought it was funny. Thought it was wierd." The film indeed has next to nothing to do with Shakespeare. There is a character named Iago, but he tells Othello at the end of the film that he will not try to seduce Desdemona because he knows how much she means to Othello. (The film ends happily.) And for another measure of Shakespeare's exteriority to pornography, consider the place of *Romeo and Juliet* in recent American child pornography legislation. See note 10. This legislation, the 1997 Child Pornography Prevention Act (CPPA), makes some animated versions of *Romeo and Juliet* (one with nonpornographic sex, the other with pornographic) made outside the United States potentially liable to prosecution and confiscation as child porn. On August 13, 1997, Judge Samuel Conti ruled the law constitutional after a challenge from the Free Speech Coalition. In his opinion, Conti mentions *Romeo and Juliet:* "It is highly unlikely that the types of valuable works plaintiffs fear will be outlawed under the CPPA—depictions used by the medical profession to treat adolescent disorders, adaptations of sexual works like *Romeo and Juliet,* and artistically valued drawings and sketches of young adults engaging in passionate behavior—will be treated as 'criminal contraband'" (Kernes 1997a, 270). The law has led Judge Jeffrey Douglas in Oklahoma to order the confiscation of all copies of *The Tin Drum,* and thus far discouraged U.S. movie distributors from carrying Adrian Lyne's 1997 remake of *Lolita* (see Abramovitz 1997). What is new about this legislation is that it outlaws images (sketches as well as photographs) that simulate sex between minors by pasting the faces of minors onto the bodies of adults or by using actors who "appear to be" minors. Conti apparently assumes that *Romeo and Juliet* remains on the far side of pornography even though it is a "sexual work." It would seem that existing pornographic versions of the play are in no danger

of being confiscated under the CPPA since the actors are all over eighteen years of age and since no attempt is made to make them appear underage. Ironically, it's the less overtly pornographic versions that may be prosecutable. (Pornographic adaptations of *Romeo and Juliet* using minors are prosecutable under the CPPA.) Zeffirelli's film version seems open to confiscation, given that the actors were fourteen at the time the film was made. Two animated versions of *Romeo and Juliet* are perhaps on even shakier legal ground even though they are not meant to be regarded as pornographic.

22. The "money shot" in which the man's orgasm is displayed literalizes this outside position.

23. This is precisely what happens in *The Best of Christy Canyon*. Ron Jeremy holds a camcorder while having sex with Canyon. Some of the sex is seen through the camera, but the point-of-view is mostly of him having sex and recording it. Jeremy's *John Wayne Bobbitt: Uncut* (1994) also explores the topic of castration. In addition to showing Bobbitt's erect penis, Jeremy enters the scene and has sex with the women having sex with Bobbitt. Rather than see Jeremy's performance as a critique of Bobbitt as failed lover (Penley 1996, 107-09), I would argue that Jeremy enters the scene because Bobbitt's erect, surgically restored penis does not fully allay potential castration anxiety in Jeremy or among male viewers. Jeremy's erect penis acts as a supplement to Bobbitt's.

24. In a performance of "Hardcore from the Heart: My Film Diary of 25 Years as a Metamorphosexual," Pearl Street, Northampton, Massachusetts, March 8, 1997.

25. To be sure, Romeo too is loose. He has sex with Lady Capulet and, during the balcony scene, receives oral sex from a maid.

26. I would like to thank Kristine Ring for first suggesting to me a relation between Lacan's reading of *Hamlet* and this film.

27. *Part Two* does take a Freudian turn when Gertrude is vindicated from complicity in Old Hamlet's murder. In this version, she discovers that Claudius murdered Old Hamlet by putting poison on her labia. Old Hamlet dies after going down on her.

28. Courtney Love's band, Hole, is the most well-known riot grrrl group and the one the video cites. See also the CDs of Bikini Kill, the Red Aunts, and Babes in Toyland (the band whose lead singer, Kat Bejelland, Love heavily ripped-off).

29. See Hosoda 1995, 417-18 on Wilson as a male to female transsexual.

30. Perhaps we are to regard mermaids as oral specialists; Disney's "littlest mermaid" is punished by losing her voice.

31. Williams compares the recording of sound in porn to its recording in the musical, which postdubs the songs and places the mike next to the singer's body, sacrificing realism in order to create "greater clarity in the music and sung lyrics" (1989, 123). Porn, she says, seeks to produce "an effect of closeness and intimacy, rather than spatial reality. In hearing the sounds of pleasure with greater clarity and from closer up, auditors of hardcore sacrifice the ability to gauge the distances between bodies and their

situation in space for a sense of connectedness with the sounds they hear"
(123).

32. According to Williams, scenes involving homosexuality, children, or ani-
mals, are all taboo in heterosexual porn (1989, 128).

33. Cyberporn also directly complicates Butler's notion of social reality. See
Springer 1996.

34. To be sure, the theater as a social institution could be viewed as a "market
of bawdry," in Stephen Gosson's phrase. Shakespeare's plays were eventually
read as being full of obscene matter, but not until well into the eighteenth
century. See Marder 1963. Fineman (1991, 228) also discusses what he calls
Shakespeare's "pornographic ear."

35. This is true of props as well. In *Hamlet: For the Love of Ophelia*, Hamlet
constantly carries a skull around with him. Instead of eroticizing it along the
lines of Vindice in *The Revenger's Tragedy*, however, this film suggests it is
like a child's security blanket for Hamlet.

36. For a longer discussion of the complex relation between castration and
censorship, see Burt (forthcoming).

37. Pornographic and nonpornographic representations of Shakespeare as an
author are in this respect continuous. The Richard Loncraine/Ian McKellen
screenplay of *Richard III* has a cartoon of Shakespeare at the end with the
caption "What the hell do you think you're doing to my play?" (1996, 288).
Similarly, an actor playing Shakespeare shakes his head in dismay at the end
of Al Pacino's *Looking for Richard*. For another example of Shakespeare as
author, see the *William Shakespeare's Romeo and Juliet* website, Romeo-
Juliet@movie.com. Under the heading "The Author," we first see the
Chandos portrait of Shakespeare. After clicking on that, we then see "Meet
Bill," with the portrait modified: Shakespeare now wears dark glasses and a
backward red baseball cap with "Bill" printed on it. The ad copy for *Juliet
and Romeo* (dir. Joe D'Amato, 1996) says: "Somewhere Shakespeare is
smiling and spinning." See also the representation of Shakespeare as the
author of *The Taming of the Shrew* in the *Moonlighting* adaptation of the play.
The book on the screen lists William "Budd" Shakespeare as the author.

38. As Mark Cummings writes: "It may seem that Shakespeare would protest a
film which mixes in body-piercing, lesbianism, car crashes, and the Manhattan alternative underground with his concept of impossible love, but on
second thought, it seems absolutely appropriate. Didn't Shakespeare himself
appeal to those with the higher seats at the back as well as to the unruly
crowd down in front?" (1996, 1).

39. For an image of the pornographic author (the author is shown masturbating
with one hand while writing with the other) see Hunt 1993, 17. The image
is from the Frontispiece to *Histoire de Dom B——, portier des Chartreux*
(Frankfurt edition, 1748).

40. This is also true of *Taming of the Screw* and *Romeo and Juliet*. In the former,
the biggest star, Leanna Heart, is one of the two unnamed lesbians who have
sex with Kate. In the latter, Kim Alexis, the actress playing Juliet, is a relative
unknown who lasted about a year in the industry. The big porn stars get
smaller roles. Nina Hartley plays the wife of the director and Keisha plays a

nonspeaking part as a groupie of the actor who is supposed to play Romeo (Jerry Butler).

41. Polanski's relationship with *Playboy* was extensive. It began before the filming of *Macbeth*. Polanski had taken nude stills of his wife Sharon Tate and then sent them to *Playboy* to promote her (she appeared in a 1967 issue), and the two were married at the *Playboy* club in London. Polanski later met Hugh Hefner at the Playboy Mansion West where they discussed the making of *Macbeth*. Though the film went overbudget and past schedule, Polanski managed to get rushes of the opening sent to Hefner in time for a birthday party, with the sisters turning to the camera and singing "Happy Birthday" to Hefner (see Miller 1984, 218). From January 1971 to February 1972, three successive issues of *Playboy* promoted Polanski's *Macbeth*.

42. Moreover, Polanski makes Lady Macbeth a more equal character, dramatically speaking, than she is in the play. The letter from Macbeth she reads in act I scene 5 is transposed to an interpolated scene after Macbeth's "My life is fallen into the sere" and after her sleepwalking scene. The film also lingers over Lady Macbeth's corpse after her suicide. Macbeth sees her corpse on the ground as he walks down into the courtyard while delivering the "Tomorrow, and tomorrow, and tomorrow" soliloquy. We see it again with a blanket over most of it when Macbeth's soldiers are deserting, and then again when Macduff pulls off the blanket while speaking of revenging his wife and children, thereby ironically confirming a parallel with Macbeth's loss of his wife and his childlessness.

43. For a review linking Polanski's life to the film, see Kael 1972. And for press coverage of the Tate murders, see Bugliosi 1974, 26-32.

44. Polanski was something of a scapegoat, serving to keep similar criticism of Hefner (for not sleeping with any women over twenty) in a strictly comic register (Russell 1984, 313-14).

45. In late 1997, Polanski was rumored to be thinking of returning to the United States. See Patterson 1997.

46. The figures in the film depart from the screenplay description such that it is hard to tell that it is a pornographic book. Apart from a very brief sequence with a buffalo penetrating a woman, all the interactions between couples (hetero and homo) look more like wrestling than attempts to initiate sexual intercourse.

47. *Hyapatia Lee's Ribald Tales of Canterbury* (dir. Bud Lee, 1985) is also worth mentioning. Hyapatia Lee wrote the screenplay and stars as the Hostess. There is no Chaucer character. The Hostess has much more power in regulating the order of the tales than in the original. In this version, the Miller does not go first, but he is made to go after the Carpenter. The Lady of Bath [sic] is played by porn star Colleen Brennan, who makes her a sexy, dignified character. Lee's husband, Bud Lee, directs. Hyapatia Lee does one lesbian number with the Lady of Bath and the male pilgrims are allowed to watch but not to touch. To a large extent, Hyapatia Lee has the phallus. That does not translate into a claim for authorship, however, but an invitation to

the viewer "to be a part of" what he/she sees, as the opening song twice states.

48. As I write, Guccione is reportedly producing and directing an X-rated film about Catherine the Great with a twenty-million-dollar budget. It will not have any porn stars in it, however, but "real actors." See Kernes 1997.

49. I take it any such expectation of porn would derive from the way queer theorists have embraced Foucault's critique of normalization.

50. Ambiguities in copyright laws about what constitutes legitimate parody may also have contributed to the making of classics. In 1992, the producers of *Splatman,* a *Batman* parody complete with superheroes in black rubber outfits, were sued by Warner Bros., and since then the number of parody titles of contemporary films has noticeably dropped. Classics are of course in the public domain and hence can be parodied and adapted with impunity. See Svetkey 1997.

51. With its usual flair for the crude, *Hustler*'s film reviews are evaluated not in terms of the number of stars given but in terms of whether a penis is fully erect, three quarters, half, or one quarter erect, or just limp. And before that, *Screw* magazine used a "penis meter" to determine how arousing a porno film was.

52. This is the move Constance Penley, among others, has made in her study of pornographic rewritings of *Star Trek*. See Penley 1993 and 1997a.

53. Porno interpretations quickly spring to mind. How about a lesbian *Ass You Like It* with an all-female cast in which the women dress up as "men" to have the "women" (played as baby dykes)? (The production would aim to liberate the anus from gay/heterosexual porn for lesbian purposes.) Or what about a transsexual production of *The Merchant of Anus* in which Nerissa's "ring" would signify her anus rather than her vagina, suggesting that it had been the Clerk who had really been turning Gratiano on all along. (I owe this reading of Nerissa's "ring" to Donald Cheney. He has, of course, nothing whatsoever to do with the use I make of his reading here.)

54. From an academic point of view, making a porn classic may be a way of degrading a high-culture icon. But from the porn industry perspective, making a porn classic may be about cleaning up porn, making it more respectable. The examples of possible Shakespeare porn I list in note 53 show that pornographic rewritings of Shakespeare go in one direction, toward textual interpretation, while porn goes in the opposite direction.

55. Put another way, it might fail at failing as porn, most obviously because it might fail to arouse its viewers and instead turn them off.

56. The days of academies of pornography are of course long past. For an analysis of these, see Findlen 1994, 86-88, 92-93, 102-03.

57. This seems to be particularly true of the money shot. If it operates fetishistically to show the man's pleasure, the moment of the money shot also means that the average male viewer will not identify with the man onscreen since the average male viewer does not pull out before ejaculating precisely because it is generally less pleasurable to do so.

58. Private conversation with William Margold, March 18, 1997. To be inducted into *Legends of Erotica*, the performer has to have been in the business at

least ten years. In an essay on gay porn stars, Robert Hofler notes bemusedly that no one is ever just a porn actor; everyone is always a porn star (1998, 65). On gay porn stardom, see also La Rue 1997 and Hofler 1997.

59. Probably nowhere else either. On this point, see Culver 1994.

60. The *Lingua Franca* piece on feminist pro-porn scholarship, for example, singles out Joanna Frueh for criticism because she doesn't just talk about porn but also generates it. Apparently, good girls talk about porn and bad girls do porn. Frueh says her porn performances are "politically calculated," however. (See Lord 1997, 46)

61. For a rather predictable view of semen as waste in porn, one that does not conceive of theory itself as a waste product, see Thomas 1996, 22-23.

Chapter 3

1. There is a British spoof called *King Lear II*, but it deliberately pokes fun at itself. See MacKernan 1994, 88.

2. See also Fred Schepisi's *Roxanne* (1987), an adaptation of *Cyrano de Bergerac* in which Martin stars as the Cyrano character.

3. For a very different take on Shakespeare as the cultural property of New York rather than L.A., see the following exchange in Woody Allen's *Annie Hall* (1977):

> ALVIE: You're an actor, Max. You should be doing Shakespeare in the park.
> MAX: Oh, I did Shakespeare in the park. I got mugged. I was playing Richard the Second and two guys in leather jackets stole my leotard.

4. On *Star Trek* and Shakespeare, see the essays by Buhler, Dutta, Houlahan, and Pendergast in the 1995 special issue of *Extrapolations* devoted to Shakespeare's invocation in the series.

5. One might add that Shakespeare is the unconscious of this debate. Kutzinski mentions Caliban at the end of her essay and objects strenuously to Buell's attempt to reconceive canonical American authors of the nineteenth century as oppositional by showing that Caliban was for Central American writers originally a figure of the monstrosity of American imperialism. *The Tempest* also structures Eric Cheyfitz's (1991) account of American imperialism (he does not discuss America as postcolonial at all). See also Amy Kaplan's (1997) use of the play in her discussion of American domestic and foreign spheres in nineteenth-century American literature. On Shakespeare and Lincoln's assassination, see Furtwang, 1991. On Shakespeare and character assasination, see Garber 1992b.

6. This return of the foreign can't be written off as political timidity on the part of the director and/or screenwriter. *The Naked Gun Thirty-three and a Third* metes out punishment to President and Mrs. Bush lookalikes.

7. On Shakespeare in America, see Webb 1964, Garber 1987, Bristol 1989, and Levine 1988. See also Sepstrup 1989, Tracey 1985, and Roach, 1990. For an analysis of the role gender plays in Shakespeare's reception in American popular culture, see Dionne 1995.

8. As Neal Gabler puts it, "The paradox is that the American film industry... 'the quintessence of what we mean by "America",' was founded and for more than thirty years operated by Eastern European Jews who themselves seemed to be anything but American" (Gabler 1988, 1).

9. On silent Shakespeare films and American culture, see Uricchio and Pearson 1993, 3-4 and 59-99.

10. In 1986, total revenues for audiovisual products (film, pay cable, TV, and video) came to an estimated $2.5 billion. That amount grew to $11.5 billion by 1991 (Wasko 1994, 222). For movies alone, revenues grew from $2.43 billion to $3.13 billion in 1989.

11. Sequels marked as such began in the 1970s with *Friday the Thirteenth, The Godfather,* and *Rocky. Star Wars* led a rash of planned sequels in the 1980s, some consciously modeled, as were the *Indiana Jones* films, on 1930s and 40s movie-matinee serials and comic books.

12. Despite a massive ad campaign, including a tie-in show with MTV's "The Big Picture" at *Jack Slater IV's* premiere, *Last Action Hero* was a huge box-office flop in the United States, though it may have recouped its losses in foreign sales. Wildman and Siweck note that "foreign sales and rentals in some years account for half of the industry's revenues" (1988, 35).

13. On these developments, see Philips 1982, Wildman 1988, and Wasko 1994. For American film exports at an earlier historical moment, see Thompson 1993. To my knowledge, no one has yet written the history of the rise of the sequel in the 1980s and 1990s.

14. *Star Trek IV* also cites *Hamlet.* McCoy cites Hamlet addressing the ghost in 1.4. 40-57.

15. It may come more from lesbianism than from male homosexuality: the homoerotic female bonding of *Outrageous Fortune* (1987), which parodies the male buddy road picture and which revives a cross-gendered *Hamlet,* no longer seems possible in the all-male action Shakespeare of the 1990s. See chapter 1, note 16.

16. Without endorsing Frederic Jameson's (1992) account of mass culture as a dialectic of reification and utopia, I want to read these films in relation to his analysis of genre and mass culture. Jameson introduces the concept of repetition into his account of mass culture and distinguishes the function of genre in precapitalist and capitalist societies. In the former, he says, genre functions as a stable contract. In capitalist societies, however, the function is radically different:

> The survival of genre in emergent mass culture can ... in no way
> be taken as a return to the stability of the publics of pre-capitalist

societies: on the contrary, the generic forms and signals of mass culture are very specifically to be understood as the historical reappropriation and displacement of older structures in the service of the qualitatively very different situation of repetition the atomized or serial "public" of mass culture wants to see again and again: hence, the urgency of the generic structure and the generic signal. (1992, 17)

17. In an analysis of genre films, Jameson (1992, 83) suggests that a given genre becomes most vital at the moment of its eclipse. As a given genre ends, a "metageneric" (84) film is produced. This film uses "the pregiven structure of inherited genres as a pretext for production which is no longer personal or stylistic in the older sense of modernism" (84). Unlike modernist films, which were self-reflexive, these films, according to Jameson, are intertextual, opposed as well to the nonreflexive nostalgia film.

18. Of course, Smith's plastic surgery and weight gain complicate this opposition, since her breasts are the one hard part of her body.

19. See Abraham and Torok 1994 and Butler 1993 on Freud's distinction between melancholia and mourning. Perhaps a rejection of the mother is implied in these films as well in the act of trying to get close to Shakespeare.

20. In a Stratford, Ontario production of *Julius Caesar* (starring Lorne Greene), William Shatner played a boy. In 1968, Shatner released an unintentionally hilarious record album entitled *The Transformed Man* (MCA Records) on which he performed selections from *Henry V, Hamlet,* and *Romeo and Juliet* interspersed with covers of "Mr. Tambourine Man," "It Was a Very Good Year," and "Lucy in the Sky with Diamonds." He was billed as "William Shatner, Captain Kirk of Star Trek." The one serious exception from *Star Trek VI* is fellow Canadian actor Christopher Plummer, who had performed as Hamlet in a 1964 television production called *Hamlet of Elsinore* and as Iago in an American production of *Othello* the year before. In 1997, he did the one-man show *Barrymore* on Broadway, focusing on John Barrymore's Richard III.

21. Both films are also linked by the presence of a character who is a Vietnam veteran.

22. It's worth noting that in the President Clinton "Fornigate" scandal of 1998, it came out that Monica Lewinsky had taken out a personal ad for Valentine's Day (addressed to "Handsome") in which she cited Romeo's lines from the balcony scene (2.2) of *Romeo and Juliet:* "With love's light wings did I o'erperch these walls, / For stony limits cannot hold love out, / And what love can do, that dares love attempt." (She signed the ad "M.") See Isikoff and Thomas 1998, 47. Shakespeare continues to figure in American discussions of American foreign policy as well. See Friedman, 1998 for a rewriting of Hamlet's "To be or not to be?" as "2-b or not 2-b?" in the context of Clinton's then yet unmade decision not to bomb Iraq.

23. For other Shakespeare Westerns, see, among others, *Broken Lance,* dir. Edward Dmytryk, 1954, a spin-off of *King Lear,* and *Yellow Sky* (dir. William Wellman, 1948), a spin-off of *The Tempest.*

24. The gesture of burning is repeated later by Abby when she burns the cabin. The fact that Abby is already married before she meets "Shakespeare" and becomes pregnant by him further erodes the distinction between "Shakespeare" and Bethelem, who tries to rape her and beats her when he fails to get an erection.

25. In 1997, NBC aired a two part mini-series entitled *Mafia Wives* (released on video as *Bella Mafia*) in which a first murdered son reads *Hamlet* before going off to college in the U.S., and his avenger cites lines from the same play as well as from *Romeo and Juliet*.

Chapter 4

1. A reading of the film as gay could garner extradiegetic support from knowledge that DiCaprio, who plays Romeo, played gay characters in *Basketball Diaries* (dir. Scott Kalvert, 1995) and *Total Eclipse* (dir. Agniezka Holland, 1995). *William Shakespeare's Romeo and Juliet* arguably goes the furthest in a long line of critical and cinematic interpretations of Mercutio in implying that he is gay (though without yet knowing it). There is no attempt to make Mercutio pass as a woman: His beard makes his gender clear. More significantly, the medium shots of Mercutio show the butts of four male dancers at the "bottom" of the frame. On bisexuality, see Dollimore 1996.

2. At this point, Mercutio is in diminished drag, minus the sleeves and cape, wearing a shoulder holster and gun, a smaller wig, and only lipstick as make-up, registered in the soundtrack in terms of lip-synching.

3. The film produces a number of bisexual effects. The Capulet drag ball sequence raises questions about Romeo's sexuality, even though it is always clear that he is attracted to Juliet, not to Mercutio or to Old Capulet. If the ball is meant to be read as Romeo's hallucination, what does that suggest about Romeo's sexual fantasy life? Unlike in Franco Zeffirelli's version, in which Juliet appears at the ball from behind Rosaline, here Rosaline is absent and Mercutio is in her position. Mercutio is the first person Romeo sees at the ball. When Romeo looks in the mirror after washing up in the men's room, is he seeing himself reflected in Mercutio? Romeo's hallucination could be said to feminize Mercutio in that it strips him of his gun (worn in the fireworks scene but not at the ball; he has left it at the hat check). Perhaps it is Juliet's very boyishness that attracts Romeo to her. Wearing a white angel costume that makes her so flat-chested as to appear prepubescent, Juliet (Claire Danes) appears in the ball as Mercutio's apposite rather than opposite number. She is, after all, the daughter of a transvestite, at least in Romeo's hallucination, and she does not imitate her femme mother (who is strapped into her Cleopatra costume by her servants, and who is having an affair with the more masculine Tybalt, dressed at the ball as a devil). As a black man, Mercutio's interracial love for Romeo is just as taboo as a

heterosexual relationship between members of the two feuding families. Moreover, the shots of Romeo and Juliet meeting outside the ballroom by the huge saltwater fishtank separating the men's and women's rooms are themselves distorted. Less a wall than a membrane seems to separate the sexes.

Shots of Romeo and Juliet together invert the usual gendering of male and female placement. In this version, Romeo, not Juliet, is the sun. In the first shot of we see of him, Romeo is backlit by the sun. A similar shot is even more pronounced when Romeo yells out "Juliet" in his *A Street Car Named Desire* (dir. Elias Kazan, 1954) "Stella" moment. Here we actually see the sun in the frame. Romeo and Juliet are cast, in short, as bisexual lovers.

4. The film further disturbs a full synchronization of sound and image in a number of ways. The soundtrack both constructs and deconstructs a thematic opposition between the carnivalesque orgy and illicit sexuality of the ball and the romantic coupling of Romeo and Juliet, opposing "Young Hearts" to their theme song, a piano ballad. After Romeo leaves the ball room and first encounters Juliet by the magnificent fishtank separating the men's and women's rooms, the theme is heard, the piano marking a radical tonal shift. The music opposes Romeo's hallucination to the sober, and the queer and illicit to the heterosexual and the licit. But the clarity of this tonal shift is disturbed by a dynamic movement in which the music is alternately background and foreground. At first, we hear the singer Des'ree as if in the background and then the film cuts to Des'ree actually performing the theme song in the ballroom. The song is continuous in both locations. Only when we see Des'ree can we retrospectively surmise that Romeo hallucinated her as Mercutio in drag.

5. Renaissance critics and queer theorists tend to discuss transvestism in terms of male transvestism. While often celebrating drag as a potentially subversive resignification of gender norms, these critics nevertheless fear that the male transvestite recirculates the very misogyny and homophobia his transvestism would seem to subvert. In an essay comparing *Twelfth Night* and *The Crying Game,* Jonathan Crewe questions whether the latter makes any progress over the former: "the suspension of [the enforced marriage] plot as the dominant one for organizing and policing the sex-gender field seems less unequivocally emancipatory in *The Crying Game* than progressivist assumptions might lead us to expect. . . . The suspension of that plot . . . allows no polymorphous destructuring of the sex-gender field. If anything, its suspension allows that field to be restructured in male-universal terms anticipated in *Twelfth Night*" (1995, 102).

6. See Callaghan's (1996, 344-46) interesting essay on the voice and castration in the English Renaissance theater that ends, perhaps predictably, by criticizing Lacan's notion of the phallus for excluding women from the symbolic, even as it disavows doing so.

7. I am not suggesting, then, that women too can have the phallus, that they can deconstruct gender difference by appropriating the penis as the dildo or as flaccid penile implants (Straayer 1996, 147 and 159), or that women too can be men, if they wish.

8. See Gallop 1993 and Bernheimer 1993.

9. For example, in an essay on the transvestite early modern theater, Peter Stallybrass suggests, in a bawdy pun, that the boy actor's "part," his penis, "has been peculiarly distorted and enlarged by being thought of as the phallus, as if a boy's small parts weren't peculiarly—and interestingly—at variance with the symbolic weight of THE phallus" (1992, 68). Yet by calling the relation between a boy's parts and the phallus "peculiarly distorted," Stallybrass uncritically assumes, in an even more peculiarly distorted way, that someone else's (bigger?) parts, presumably those of a grown man, are not at variance with the symbolic weight of the phallus. In contrast, I would argue that the phallus always puts pressure on the male gender by calling into question the size of the penis. See Bernhemier 1993 for a reading that parallels my own but that stops short of considering penis size. It might be thought that a large penis would mean that size wasn't an issue. Yet some female porn stars won't have sex with generously endowed male actors such as John Holmes.

10. I borrow the term "classic cinema" from Silverman 1988, ix.

11. Penis size jokes throw into relief a certain lack of clarity about just what castration involves: just the testicles? part of the penis? Do the jokes involve a fantasy of surviving castration? Having something left over that exceeds what others are still feared to have (not yet lost)?

12. This question is raised not only by Mercutio's performance but later when a boy soprano covers "When Doves Cry," by the sexually ambiguous performer formerly known as Prince.

13. This is precisely Kaja Silverman's (1988) aim.

14. It is telling that Kaja Silverman (1988) and Joke Dame (1994) gender the castrato oppositely in discussions of Roland Barthes's reading of Honore Balzac's *Sarrasine* in *S/Z*. Silverman writes: "The castration which Zambinella [the castrato] undergoes not only 'unmans' him, making it impossible for him to speak any longer from a masculine position, but it produces a *female* singing voice" (1988, 193). In contrast, Joke Dame says: "When musicologists describe the features of the castrato's voice, the qualifications they deem appropriate are male connotated. As a result it seems justifiable to regard the voice of the castrato as a male voice, a high male voice to be precise; a male treble, or a male alto" (1994, 144). Dame reads Zambinella and Sarrasine as gay: "baroque operas gave rise to what might be called aural homosexuality" (147). It is also noteworthy that the film *Farinelli*, about the famous castrato, uses both male and female singers to dub Farinelli's voice. For an account of the way the castrato singer occupied both genders, see Keyser 1987/1988, 55. See also Abel, 1996.

15. In a special issue of *Yale French Studies* (1980: 3) a number of theorists show that recorded sound always alters the sound being recorded. See also Silverman 1988.

16. Butler shows a marked blind spot in her account of "reading." Though she qualifies her account of the unreadable performance with the words "appears to be," she doesn't rule out the possibility that a performance might actually be unreadable. Nor does she put any critical pressure on this

fantasy. Why, we might ask, would one want to be unreadable not only to outsiders but, more crucially, to other insiders as well? I take this blind spot to be symptomatic of the political critic's unconscious identification with the drag contestant. Far from being in a position to criticize the fantasies about stardom of the transvestites as so much false consciousness about what it means to be a woman (particularly a woman of color), the political critic enacts that very fantasy in terms of academic celebrity: the critic is the transvestite figure who can cross over from one space to another, the star who can read others but who can't be read. But the drag ball calls this fantasy of academic stardom as transvestism into question, for it shows that any attempt to evade being read fails. After all, the ball is there precisely because realness has to be judged. Even among insiders, there are insiders and *insiders*. Moreover, the ball must necessarily enforce its own point of view. The audience and/or some contestants may contest a judgment and make their own. And there is no way to assess the political status of this contestation by appealing to a position like the judge's since that is precisely what would in turn have to be judged again. One might ask, for example: Whose judgment can legitimately establish who is most "real"? Would a contested judgment be the result of envious misreading or a more discriminating reading? Would a dissenting judgment be subversive? Would a consenting judgment merely be subservient, caving into an established authority that may already be over-the-hill?

17. On noise, see Attali 1985, Rose 1994, and Russo and Warner 1989 / 90.

18. In an interview about her work on transvestism, Marjorie Garber affirms Shakespeare's centrality on a number of fronts: "Shakespeare is the unconscious of all literature—and a kind of cultural norm against which we measure certain kinds of personality types and individual gestures. Obviously, the cross-dressing element in Shakespearean drama became a starting point for *Vested Interests* [1992a]" (1995, 30). Shakespeare is apparently a cultural transvestite insofar as he can recycle Ben Jonson's view of him as a man who was "not of an age, but for all time": he is the one who can cross over from his own time to any subsequent historical moment. Shakespeare remains just as foundational in Jonathan Crewe's (1994) account of transvestism, even if Shakespeare is associated with a historically specific cultural form and narrative, the heteronormative marriage plot.

19. This is not to say that *The Taming of the Shrew* is by any means straightforward, just that the problems opened up as Kate openly gives her consent to Petruchio in the play (by the length of her submission speech, the fact that a boy actor played the part, and so on) are even more overt in the musical.

20. See Hodgdon 1992.

21. The body may be the grotesque body, but it's heterosexual.

22. My attention to the film's opening scene, as well as the scenes with Caesario and Orsino, is deeply indebted to a wonderful paper Kate Lemons wrote in a graduate seminar I taught on Shakespeare and American popular culture.

23. The gesture of removing the moustache is completed at the end of the film when Sebastian and Viola are reunited.

24. The conservatism of the film is marked also in the film's ending sequence. As the credits roll, we see various characters leaving Olivia's estate and finally the two couples and their guests dancing. Viola is dressed now as a lady.

25. There is one shot in which Olivia looks briefly as if she were about to kiss Caesario. Nunn can keep the Viola/Caesario distinction straight only by giving Olivia and Caesario exclusive rights to the use of voice-over. After Cesario leaves Olivia the first time he visits to woo her on Orsino's behalf, Olivia speaks her last lines in voice-over. When reflecting on Olivia's response to her, Viola has a visual flashback of Olivia's gestures, and later uses a voice-over. Women here are given the interior diegetic space usually assigned to men.

26. Of course, sisterly love can be read as lesbian. See Castle 1993. But the film tries to suggest otherwise.

27. As Périsson (1980) comments: "The phrase takes a height when the soprano joins her voice to the alto's in order to divide what follows in parallel thirds. Let us note that the "Barcarolle" was written to be sung by Giulietta . . . and by Nicklausse! It's not a matter, then, of an amorous duo in which the partners remain separate. Yet this confirms the necessity of giving Nicklausse a (cross-gendered) disguise ["travesti" means both "disguise" and a feminine role played by a man]. It's a question here of thirds, not of tenths, which would be an insupportable heresy! It's especially evident that when Nicklausse's role is performed by a man that the part is given to a mezzo-soprano specially engaged for it" (55) (my translation).

28. It may be a stretch to read this episode in terms of Shakespeare as symptom of U.S. postcolonialism, but given that Carmen's "Hanabera" aria refers to Havana, it seems possible that the island may be read as a version of Communist Cuba, permanently cut off from the United States. This episode, like so many others, inverts the social standing of the Howells. Mr. Howell at one point appears dressed as a butler and serves drinks to the Skipper, Gilligan, and the Professor.

29. This process of adaptation threatened Bizet as the author of his version. Of Escamadillio's "Toreador" aria Bizet is reported to have said "If they want trash, I'll give them trash!" (McClary 1992, 34).

30. Kuhn (1995, 8-9) reviews the question of whether Lupino can be considered an auteur.

31. The "Barcarolle" is repeated twice in Offenbach's opera, once at the end of Act Two and again as the finale of Act Three, when it is performed without singers.

32. This musical does notable things with sound and with the female voice. The white opera singer Marilyn Horne postdubs the songs over the black actress Dorothy Dandridge (who plays Carmen Jones) in an odd way. As Susan McClary notes, the adaptation of Bizet's music to a new context was "uncomfortable. . . . In many instances . . . the characters sing straight opera" (1992, 133). McClary points out that Horne, "who was brought in to do a part presumably beyond the capabilities of the black actress, was trying to produce a sound quality she identified with untrained singers, so as to

give the audience the illusion of authenticity. Horne's run in the 'Seguidilla' sounds suspiciously sloppy" (1992, 133).

33. John Storey, Telluride publicist.

34. Peter Donaldson (1997, 176) similarly stresses that Prospero's power in this film is increased through Greenaway's use of Gielgud in voice-overs.

35. In contrast to the actors playing Ariel, the actresses playing Iris, Juno, and Ceres all sing their parts.

Chapter 5

1. This is perhaps the latest version of a long tradition still very much visible in which a myth about Shakespeare as the voice of the popular gets taken up by an educated elite to legitimate its own critical authority.

2. Dick Hebdige's influential *Subcultures* (1979), for example, focuses entirely on British youth culture. And as I mentioned in the Introduction, one middle-aged, influential cultural critic graced the pages of *New York* magazine wearing hip-hop garb (Mead, 1995).

3. See, for example, the CD-ROM designed by Mark Rose for the *Norton Shakespeare* (Greenblatt 1997) and Al Braunmuler's excellent CD-ROM *Voyager* edition of *Macbeth*. The latter contains scenes from various films, full audio transmission, introductory information on Shakespeare's theater, and an annotated bibliography. But transmission here has its problems. *Voyager* couldn't buy the rights to the RSC video so they only have the actors' voices. And the amount of memory needed poses a problem as well, as does the expense. A recent CD-ROM version of *Romeo and Juliet* (Attica Cybernetics) sells for $49.00. It contains clips from a BBC production and a commentary by Germaine Greer.

4. A contradiction is that Ozzie quotes Hamlet at the breakfast table but never recites Hamlet's lines when his family, friends, and guest perform parts of the play.

5. Even in terms of the narrative resolution, there is a comically registered disturbance through a double ending. After Whitfield leaves, Ozzie and Harriet still try to make sense of his appearance until Dave brings in a sign Ricky put up earlier advertising the play and charging 25¢ for admission (he gets to keep the money, and his sense that the play is not commercial is thereby disproved). But, in a brief epilogue, Whitfield shows up at the poker game and is clearly not an innocent travelling actor but a card shark and con-man as well. Apart from the narrative and character contradictions, there are also disturbances in terms of the medium. This is a television episode that produces Shakespeare as an alternative to television. The only reason the family performs Shakespeare is that their television set is broken. Similarly, the casting of John Carradine betrays another contradiction. Carradine was an appropriate actor because of his experience doing Shakespeare on television: he had appeared as Malvolio in an NBC Philco

Television Playhouse hour-long production of *Twelfth Night* in 1949 and as Macbeth in an hour-long *Macbeth* broadcast on CBS in 1951. Carradine thought of himself as the successor to John Barrymore, whom he considered to be the greatest American actor of Shakespeare. Carradine had to pay for the Shakespeare plays he managed to do in the theater by (over)acting in trashy, low-budget horror films such as *Revenge of the Zombies* (1943), *Voodoo Man* (1944), *Bluebeard* (1944), and *House of Dracula* (1945). See Carradine 1995, 11-12; 47-50; and especially 54.

6. The film is also marked by Reagan's anticommunism. A subplot from the 1940 play on which the film was based, *The Male Animal,* about a sympathetically represented communist, was cut from the film. (The intact play was made into a film with the same name starring Henry Fonda in 1942.)

7. The recycling of *The Brady Bunch* episode as camp in the *MTV Romeo and Juliet Special* is another symptom of a U.S. postpatriarchal culture.

   One exception to the role of teacher of Shakespeare as loser might be an episode of the television spin-off *Dangerous Minds* (see note 10, this chapter). In the beginning of the episode, the teacher discusses a Shakespeare sonnet. While the teacher is not exactly a loser, she is a quitter (we know from the movie that she will leave the students after a year). Yet see also "Principal Takes a Holiday" (first broadcast on ABC's *Wonderful World of Disney,* January 4, 1998), in which two conniving students reject a ham actor doing *Hamlet* as a self-help musical ("I choose to be. I choose to be. I choose me!") in favor of a homeless rock drummer to impersonate their principal.

8. The same historical shift toward the loser can be registered as well in the difference between the Shakespeare tragedy most often cited now versus in the 1970s. Whereas *Hamlet* predominates in recent films, *King Lear* was the referent of the 1974 film about a Shakespeare-citing teacher, *Harry and Tonto* (dir. Paul Mazursky).

9. See Gates 1993 and the movie *Falling Down* (dir. Joel Schumacher, 1993) about a recently fired, divorced middle-aged white male defense worker in L. A. who loses it and goes on a murderous rampage (ethnic and racial minorities and his wife are his targets).

10. On April 27, 1997, ABC's *Prime Time* aired a show about former soldiers turned high school teachers. *Dangerous Minds* is about a young woman and former marine who becomes a high school teacher at an inner city school. On the military and education, see Noble 1989.

11. For another instance of Shakespeare harnessed to U.S. multiculturalism, see the episode of *Kung Fu: The Legend Continues* rebroadcast April 28, 1998, in which three immigrant entrepreneurs (from Japan, France, and Nairobi) taking an English as a second language class cite lines from their Signet editions of *Love's Labor's Lost*:

> JAPANESE MAN / KING: Proceeded well, to stop all good proceeding.

FRENCH WOMAN / LONGAVILLE: He weeds the corn and still lets
grow the weeding.
NAIROBI MAN / BIRON: The spring is near when geese are a
breeding. (1. 1. 95-97)

After Kane's police detective son interrupts the class, Shakespeare's play is
identified: "Where did we leave off?," the teacher asks. "*Love's Labor's Lost*,"
answers the French woman. The class is taught by Colleen Cameron, a
woman who identifies herself as the granddaughter of Irish immigrants.
According to her, Shakespeare is a hedge against the Balkanization of the
United States and the enabler of a "multicultural mosaic." In addition to the
kung fu skills of Kane and the three immigrants, Shakespeare (as a
metonymy for fluency in English) is a means to defeat the villain, Lee Sun's
(and his Young Luck Development Corporation's) attempt to force these
people out of business so he can retain control of Chinatown. At the
episode's conclusion, a "Chinese Business Revitalization" is celebrated
(complete with a shot of the American flag). By a rather strange logic, the
Chinese are removed from control of Chinatown in order to make way for a
more presumably progressive form of ethnic, entrepreneurial integration in
which English is the universal language among people of diverse races and
genders. The lines from *Love's Labor's Lost*, however, suggest a problem with
using Shakespeare in this way in that they are precisely about what does not
follow, as the rest of the passage makes clear:

DUMAINE. How follows that?
BIRON. Fit in his time and place.
DUMAINE. In reason nothing. (1. 1. 98-99)

12. For a contemporary example, see the *William Shakespeare's Romeo and Juliet*
screenplay published along with the play. It advertises itself on the cover as
"the classic play, the contemporary film."
13. For a valuable account of the new in relation to the avant-garde, see Groys
1991.
14. My account of the loser here emerged out of a discussion with Elizabeth
Power.
15. For an analysis of the shift in the word "culture," see Readings 1996.
16. Of course, this is just a fantasy, since computers are subject to crashing,
viruses, and hacking. Moreover, webpages have to be updated and maintained. There are also notable losses for book culture as books and journals
are put online. See Nunberg 1993.
17. The children are set up as losers also. Two dinner scenes at the eldest son's
show the family to be a complete mess; the daughter has been divorced four
times; and the youngest is recently divorced and flat broke.
18. *High School High* offers an interesting counterpoint to *Renaissance Man*.
Marketed as a spoof of films like *Dangerous Minds* and produced by "the
makers of *The Naked Gun*," the film is about an idealizing upper-class white
man named Mr. Clark (Jon Lovitz) who leaves a job at his father's elite all-

white prep school to teach history at an inner-city school (at one point, a student holds up a cake in front of Clark with the word "Loser" written on it). Shakespeare enters as a sign of Clark's victorious struggle to reach his students (which generates renewal of the school and the inner city). Two African American students (Mekhi Phifer and Malinda Williams) in his class have hooked up and the woman tells the man "we could both end up at the same school [college]" just before they enter a strip-club-turned-theater above which the male student lives, and the marquee announces "Girls! Girls! Girls! Hot! Hot! Hot! Live! Live! Live! *Macbeth* on stage" (see figure 5.2). The student says, "Mr. Clark has taken this place on as a special project." A stripper who had earlier decked Clark now performs as Lady Macbeth and does part of the sleepwalking scene, forgetting her lines at one point but receiving applause from the audience anyway as she makes her usual stripper moves. This low-brow porno adaptation of Shakespeare (as the stripper bows, we see a sign announcing "Next week, nude Ibsen") effectively compromises any claim for progress, however, and threatens to confirm the racist view of African Americans as failures due to their own stupidity articulated by the school's principal (Louis Fletcher) (and, as it turns out, the city's major drug dealer).

Though it focuses on the academic as scholar rather than as pedagogue, the video *Live Nude Shakespeare* (dir. Michael D. Fox and Dave Evans, 1997) also positions the academic as loser. The video borrows from Dan Ackroyd's skits on *Saturday Night Live* when he posed as a critic reviewing "really bad" plays, framing stripping with Shakespeare recitations in interviews of the strippers conducted by an academic named Dr. Waldorf ("Stinky") Emerson-Biggins. While he is turned on by the strippers, they remain utterly indifferent to him.

19. Given that Mark compares Charles to Christ (Charles is thirty-three, the age Christ was when he was crucified), the film could be said to recycle the most anti-Semitic right-wing Christian account of the crucifixion: here the "bad" untelegenic Jew kills Christ.

20. It's worth noting that in *Harry and Tonto,* a native American character heals Harry on his way to L. A.

21. In her essay "Camille Paglia" (1994), bell hooks makes a similar point: "progressive critical thinkers, especially feminists, who are concerned only with exchanging ideas within academic circles, concede the space of popular debate to those individuals who are eager to have a turn at stardom. This concession helps promote the rise of individuals like Paglia" (90).

22. On book cover colors, see the essay "Coloration" by Jane Gallop (1992).

23. In *Clueless,* Cher manipulates a romance between two loser teachers. Her position as loser yields various kinds of success, as when she gets higher grades by arguing well rather than doing extra work.

24. So the model of expertise here is belied by Baker's own rehearsal of an outdated and facile reading of *Henry V,* a text he celebrates as a "classic of Shakespearean creation" in a way no self-respecting critic doing Shakespeare criticism would. London working-class youth culture didn't need to wait for Baker to teach them how to recode Shakespeare's warrior monarch

in pop media terms. John Lydon, a.k.a. Johnny Rotten, the lead singer of the 1976-77 punk rock band *The Sex Pistols*, incorporated a rather different Shakespearean monarch, namely, Richard III, into his performances. As Lydon explains in his autobiography:

> Best of all I loved the way Laurence Olivier played Richard III. He portrayed the character as so utterly vile, it was great. . . . Johnny Rotten definitely has tinges of Richard III in him. I saw it long before conceiving Rotten. No redeeming qualities. Hunchback, nasty, evil, conniving, selfish. The worst of everything to excess. Having seen it aeons ago, I took influences from Olivier's performance. I had never seen a pop singer present himself quite that way. It wasn't the norm. You're supposed to be a nice pretty boy, sing lovely songs, and coo at the girlies. Richard III would have none of that. He got the girls in other ways. Occasionally, I think of Richard III when I do interviews with journalists I don't like. (1994, 54)

Lydon also gives an appreciation of Shakespeare, particularly *Macbeth*, which he terms "a gorgeous piece of nastiness" (1994, 62-63). And, according to Nancy Spungen's mother, Deborah, the "press portrayed Sid and Nancy as Romeo and Juliet in black leather" (1983, 273).

25. An interesting analogue is *The Madness of King George*. After King George passes through Lear on his way to recovering his sanity, he abandons the doctor who helped him, positioning himself as Henry V and the doctor as the spurned Falstaff.

26. If academia has relative autonomy from the cinematic and popular means of cultural reproduction, the reverse is also the case.

27. The teachers in *Clueless* and *Last Action Hero* are seen as uncool by the students. To improve her grades, Cher manipulates the love lives of two of her teachers, partly through the use of *Cliffs Notes*.

28. The Olivier movie is consistently linked to its teacher's female gender. Students giggle at Claudius's opening words, "Oh this black bosom," presumably because they take the word "bosom" to mean female breast.

29. Much of what follows in my discussion of these films is indebted to Kristin Brenna.

30. In this respect, it might be opposed to the use of *Romeo and Juliet* in the all-too-instructional antimarijuana film *Reefer Madness* (dir. Louis Gasnier, 1936). The two young lovers, Bill and Mary, are established in their first scene as innocent by their exchange of quotations from Shakespeare's tragedy. They kiss, but Mary's mother, who has been watching them, walks in on them before things can go any further.

31. Kaufman's identification of the 1934 Cukor film version in distinction to the Zeffirelli as his precursor may also betray a symptomatic identification with actors who are far too old for their parts, perhaps as out-of-place as he is.

32. *Shakespeare, the Animated Tales,* produced by an English and Russian team and distributed in the United States by HBO, is also addressed both to adults and to children. These cartoon retellings are meant to be appreciated by adults as art and are defined against Disney animation techniques. See Kendall 1996 and Osborne 1997a.
33. Transcripts of the shows are available online at http://www2.cruzio.com/~keeper/Shakespeare.html. There is also an episode entitled "The Taming of the Screwy," which has nothing to do with Shakespeare's comedy, and an episode of *Pinky and the Brain,* an offshoot of *Animaniacs,* entitled "TV or not TV?" That episode has nothing to do with *Hamlet.*
34. *Wishbone, Sesame Street,* and the *Muppets* shows all have merchandise based on characters in the shows (all are available online).
35. For the *Wishbone* version of *The Tempest,* entitled "Shakespaw," see Vaughn, 1995.
36. In contrast, the *Animated Tales* version of *Romeo and Juliet* does include the aubade and does briefly show the lovers nude.
37. To be sure, the similarity between plots isn't as strong as it could be. Though Rosie lives, she and Wishbone remain separated, their love unconsummated.

Conclusion

1. Something like this position was argued by Richard Wilson at a conference called "After the New Historicism," March 13-14, 1998. See also Wilson 1996.
2. There is a great deal of this material. See Gordon 1982 and Nye 1993 and the stories by Gregory Feeley, Barbara Denz, and Laura Resnick in Kerr 1994 and the anthology by O'Sullivan 1997.
3. I should note that Rooke is Canadian.
4. See Introduction, note 8, for the references.
5. Similarly, the "Midsummer Night's Dream" episode ends recording the death of Shakespeare's son, Hamnet.
6. And one wouldn't have to argue that they do so intentionally. The strong version of Bourdieu's argument is that this would be an effect, intentional or not, of a literary strategy.
7. For an opposed view of Shakespeare as a means of legitimating Gaiman's *Sandman* series, see Laura Wilson's (1998) fine essay.
8. According to Susan Buck-Morss (1991, 265), Benjamin saw the child as becoming adult and in need of education. In an analysis of Benjamin's scripts for a children's radio show, Jeffrey Mehlman (1993) reads them as a psychoanalysis of Benjamin and his own generation's writings as fulfilling the failed promise of Benjamin's intended immigration to America. Given the absence of the kind of childhood Benjamin celebrated, Mehlman's model no longer works, except perhaps for Mehlman's own generation or Mehl-

man himself (he collapses his generation and himself). Mehlman thus might be considered a loser in that he doesn't know he's a loser. For a different attempt to recuperate Benjamin as a figure of mourning in relation to *Hamlet,* see Derrida 1994 and Jameson 1995. On Benjamin's interest in the obsolete, see Foster 1993.

9. Even if children's television programs such as *Wishbone* were an exception to the rule of unspeakable ShaXXXspeares, Shakespeare could serve only as a diminished G-rated cultural icon for American children.

10. This hope is bound to be disappointed, of course. As Frederic Jameson writes: "mourning also wants to get rid of the past, to exorcise it albeit under the guise of respectful commemoration. To forget the dead altogether is impious in ways that prepare their own retribution, but to remember the dead is neurotic and obsessive and merely feeds a sterile repetition. There is no 'proper' way of relating to the dead and the past" (1995, 103).

Works Cited

Abel, Sam. 1996. *Opera in the Flesh: Sexuality in Operatic Performance*. Boulder, Co: Westview Press.

Abraham, Nicolas and Maria Torok. 1994. *The Shell and the Kernel: Renewals of Psychoanalysis*. Trans. Nicholas T. Rand. Chicago: University of Chicago Press.

Abramowitz, Rachel. 1997. "How Do You Solve a Problem Like Lolita?" *Premiere* 11 (1): 80-85, 97-99.

Anon. A. 1996. "Shakespeare: The Old Jane Austen." *Time,* September 9 (148): 16, 63.

Anon. B 1996. "Living Will." *People Magazine,* January 7.

Anon. 1971. "*Playboy* Interview: Roman Polanski." *Playboy,* December 18: 12, 93-119.

Anon. 1972. "The Making of *Macbeth*." *Playboy,* February 19: 2, 77-82.

Anon. 1991. "Les Orgies Greenaway." *New Look,* Mai 94: 120-25.

Aronson, Billy. 1996. *Wishbone Classics: Romeo and Juliet by William Shakespeare*. New York: Harper Paperbacks.

Attali, Jacques. 1985. *Noise: The Political Economy of Music*. Trans. Brian Massumi. Minneapolis: University of Minnesota Press.

Baker, Jr., Houston A. 1993. *Black Studies, Rap, and the Academy*. Chicago: University of Chicago Press.

Bate, Jonathan. 1989. *Shakespearean Constitutions: Politics, Theatre, Criticism, 1730-1830*. Oxford: Clarendon Press.

Baxter, John. 1976. *The Hollywood Exiles*. New York: Taplinger.

Benjamin, Walter. 1974. "Unpacking My Library." In *Illuminations*. Hannah Arendt, ed. Harry Zohn, trans. New York: Schocken, 59-68. Originally published 1931.

——. 1974a. "Left-wing Melancholy." *Green Magazine* (September) 15: 2, 28-32. Originally published 1931.

Bennett, Alan. 1995. *The Madness of King George*. New York: Random House.

Bernhard, Thomas. 1983/1991. *The Loser.* Trans. Jack Dawson. Chicago: University of Chicago Press.

Bernheimer, Charles, 1992. "Penile Reference in Phallic Theory." *differences*. (Spring) 4: 4, 116-33.

Bernstein, Jill. 1997. "Tin Conundrum." *Premiere* 11 (1): 23-24.

Bersani, Leo. 1995. *Homos*. Cambridge: Harvard University Press.

Bérubé, Michael. 1994. "Pop Goes the Academy: Cult Studs Fight the Power." In *Public Access: Literary Theory and American Politics*. New York: Routledge, 137-60.

Bhabha, Homi. 1984. "Of Mimicry and Man: Ambivalence in Colonial Discourse." *October* 28: 125-33.

Blum, David. 1997. "Closet Hamlet." *Time*. September 22 (150): 12, 88-90.

Boose, Lynda. 1997. "Grossly Gaping Viewers and Jonathan Miller's *Othello*." In *Shakespeare, the Movie: Popularizing the Plays on Film, TV, and Video*. Lynda E. Boose and Richard Burt, eds. New York and London: Routledge, 210-25.

Boose, Lynda and Richard Burt. 1997. "Totally Clueless? Shakespeare Goes Hollywood in the 1990s." In *Shakespeare, the Movie: Popularizing the Plays on Film, TV, and Video*. Lynda E. Boose and Richard Burt, eds. New York and London: Routledge, 5-25.

Booth, Stephen, ed. 1977. *Shakespeare's Sonnets*. New Haven: Yale University Press.

Bourdieu, Pierre. 1996. *The Rules of Art: Genesis and Structure of the Literary Field*. Trans. Susan Emanuel. Stanford: Stanford University Press.

Breskin, David. 1992. *Inner Views: Filmmakers in Conversation*. Boston and London: Faber and Faber.

Brett, Philip et al., eds. 1994. *Queering the Pitch: The New Gay and Lesbian Musicology*. New York: Routledge.

Bright, Susie. 1997. *The Sexual State of the Union*. New York: Touchstone.

Brin, David. 1985. *The Postman*. New York: Bantam Books.

Bristol, Michael. 1985. *Shakespeare's America/American Shakespeare*. New York and London: Routledge.

Buck-Morss, Susan. 1991. *The Dialectics of Seeing: Walter Benjamin and the Arcades Project*. Cambridge, MA: MIT Press.

Buckley, Sandra. 1991. "'Penguin in Bondage': A Graphic Tale of Japanese Comic Books." In *Technoculture*. Constance Penley and Andrew Ross, eds. Minneapolis: University of Minnesota Press, 163-96.

Buell, Lawrence. 1992. "American Literary Emergence as a Postcolonial Phenomenon." *American Literary History*. 4 (3): 411-42.

Bugliosi, Vincent with Curt Gentry. 1974. *Helter Skelter: The True Story of the Manson Murders*. New York: Norton.

Buhler, Stephen M. 1995. "'Who Calls Me Villain?': Blank Verse and the Black Hat." *Extrapolations*. 36 (1): 18-27.

Burgess, Anthony. 1970. *Shakespeare's World*. New York: Alfred A. Knopf.

Burston, Paul and Colin Richardson. 1995. *A Queer Romance: Lesbians, Gay Men, and Popular Culture*. New York and London: Routledge.

Burt, Richard. 1993. "Baroque Down: the Trauma of Censorship in Psychoanalysis and Queer Film Revisions of Shakespeare and Marlowe." In *Shakespeare and the New Europe*. Michael Hattaway et al., eds. Sheffield: Sheffield Academic Press, 328-50.

—————. forthcoming. "Thomas Middleton, Uncut: Castration, Censorship, and the Early Modern Stage." In *Thomas Middleton and Early Modern Textual Culture*. Gary Taylor et al., eds. Oxford: Oxford University Press.

Butler, Judith. 1990. *Gender Trouble: Feminism and the Subversion of Identity*. New York and London: Routledge.

—————. 1993. *Bodies That Matter: On the Discursive Limits of Sex*. New York and London: Routledge.

———. 1994. "Gender as Performance: Interview with Judith Butler." *Radical Philosophy* 67 (Summer): 32-39.

———. 1997. *Excitable Speech: The Politics of the Performative*. New York and London: Routledge.

———. 1997a. "Merely Cultural," *Social Text*. 52/53, Vol. 15, (3 & 4), Fall/Winter, 265-77.

Butler, Melissa. 1998. "The Student Body." *Up Front. Vogue*. (June) 76; 80.

Callaghan, Dympna. 1996. "The Castrator's Song: Female Impersonation on the Early Modern Stage," *Journal of Medieval and Renaissance Studies* 26 (2): 321-54.

Campbell, Luther and John R. Miller. 1992. *As Nasty As They Wanna Be: The Uncensored Story of Luther Campbell of the 2 Live Crew*. Fort Lee, NJ: Barricade Books.

Carradine, David. 1995. *Endless Highway*. Boston: Journey Editions.

Cartnell, Deborah et al., eds. 1997. *Trash Aesthetics: Popular Culture and Its Audiences*. London: Pluto Press.

Castle, Terry. 1993. *The Apparitional Lesbian: Female Homosexuality and Modern Culture*. New York: Columbia University Press.

Catalano, Grace. 1997. *Leonardo DiCaprio: Modern-Day Romeo*. New York: Bantam Doubleday Dell.

Cavell, Stanley. 1981. *The Pursuit of Happiness: The Hollywood Comedy of Remarriage*. Cambridge: Harvard University Press.

Chapman, Graham. 1989. *The Complete Monty Python's Flying Circus: All the Words*. 2 vols. New York: Pantheon.

Chauncey, George. 1994. "The Fairy as Intermediate Sex." In *Gay New York: Gender, Urban Culture, and the Making of the Gay Male World, 1890-1940*. New York: Basic Books.

Cheyfitz, Eric. 1991. *The Poetics of Imperialism: Translation and Colonization from The Tempest to Tarzan*. New York and Oxford: Oxford University Press.

Chion, Michel. 1982. *La Voix au cinema*. Paris: Editions de L'Etoile.

Chunovic, Michael. 1991. "Tied Up in Knots." *The Advocate*, (November): 96.

Corliss, Richard. 1996. "Suddenly Shakespeare." *Time*. November 4 (148): 21, 88-90.

———. 1997. "Dancing Around the Gay Issue." *Time*. September 22, 150: 12.

Cowie, Peter. 1994. *Coppola: A Biography*. New York: Da Capo Press.

Crewe, Jonathan. 1995. "In the Field of Dreams: Transvestism in *Twelfth Night* and *The Crying Game*." *Representations* 50: 101-23.

Culver, Stuart. 1994. "*Whistler v. Ruskin*: The Courts, the Public, and Modern Art." In *The Administration of Aesthetics: Censorship, Political Criticism, and the Public Sphere*. Richard Burt, ed. Minneapolis: University of Minnesota Press, 149-67.

Cummings, Mark. 1996. "The Art of *Tromeo and Juliet*." http://www.troma.com.

Dame, Joke. 1994. "Unveiled Voices: Sexual Difference and the Castrato." In *Queering the Pitch: The New Gay and Lesbian Musicology*. Philip Brett et al. eds. New York and London: Routledge.

de Grazia, Edward. 1992. *Girls Lean Back Everywhere: The Law of Obscenity and the Assault on Genius*. New York: Random House.

Dechter, Joshua. 1994. "Stupidity as Destiny: American Idiot Culture." *Flash Art* 178 (October): 73-76.

Derrida, Jacques. 1995. *Spectres of Marx: the State of the Debt, the Work of Mourning, and the New International*. Trans. Peggy Kamuf. London and New York: Routledge.

———. 1996. *Archive Fever: A Freudian Impression*. Trans. Eric Penrowitz. Baltimore: Johns Hopkins University Press.

Dionne, Craig. 1995. "Shakespeare in Popular Culture: Gender and High-brow Culture in America." *Genre*. 38 (Winter): 385-412.

Doane, Mary Ann. 1980. "The Voice in the Cinema: The Articulation of Body and Space." *Yale French Studies* 60: 33-50.

Dobson, Michael. 1992. *The Making of the National Poet: Shakespeare, Adaptation, and Authorship, 1660-1769*. Oxford: Clarendon Press.

Dollimore, Jonathan. 1996. "Bi-sexuality, Heterosexuality, and Wishful Theory." *Textual Practice* 10 (4): 523-39.

Donaldson, Peter. 1990. *Shakespearean Films, Shakespearean Directors*. Boston: Unwin Hyman.

Doty, Alexander. 1993. *Making Things Perfectly Queer: Interpreting Mass Culture*. Minneapolis: University of Minnesota Press.

Dutta, Mary Buhl. 1995. "'Very bad poetry, Captain': Shakespeare in Star Trek." *Extrapolations* (Spring) 36: 1, 38-47.

Dyer, Richard. 1991. "Believing in Fairies: The Author and the Homosexual." In *Inside/Out: Lesbian Theories, Gay Theories*. Diana Fuss, ed. New York: Routledge, 185-201.

Edelman, Lee. 1994. *Homographesis: Essays in Gay Literary and Cultural Theory*. New York and London: Routledge.

Ferguson, Margaret. 1987. "Afterword." In *Shakespeare Reproduced: The Text in History and Ideology*. New York: Routledge, 273-83.

Findlen, Paula. 1993. "Humanism, Politics, and Pornography in Renaissance Italy." In *The Invention of Pornography: Obscenity and the Origins of Modernity, 1500-1900*. Lynn Hunt, ed. New York: Zone Books, 49-108.

Fineman, Joel. 1991. *The Subjectivity Effect in Western Literary Tradition: Essays Towards the Release of Shakespeare's Will*. Cambridge, MA: MIT Press.

Fink, Bruce. 1996. "Reading Hamlet with Lacan." In *Lacan, Aesthetics, and Politics*. Willy Apollon and Richard Feldstein, eds. New York: State University of New York Press.

Fish, Stanley. 1993. "The Unbearable Ugliness of Volvos." In *English Inside and Out: The Places of Literary Criticism*. Susan Gubar and Jonathan Kamhotz, eds. New York and London: Routledge, 102-08.

Fiske, John. 1992. "The Cultural Economy of Fandom." In *The Adoring Audience: Fan Culture and Popular Media*. London and New York: Routledge, 30-49.

Foster, Hal. 1993. "Outmoded Spaces." In *Compulsive Beauty*. Cambridge, MA: MIT Press, 157-92.

Foucault, Michel. 1969. *The Archaeology of Knowledge*. Trans. A. M. Sheridan Smith. New York: Pantheon Books.

————. 1989/1996. *Foucault Live: Interviews, 1961-1984.* Sylvere Lotringer, ed. New York: Semiotext(e).

Fraser, Nancy. 1997. "Heterosexism, Misrecognition, and Capitalism: A Response to Judith Butler," *Social Text.* 52/53, Vol. 15, (3 & 4), Fall/Winter, 265-77.

Friedman, Thomas L. 1998. "America's Multiple-Choice Quiz." *New York Times.* Saturday, January 31, A25.

Freud, Sigmund. 1922. "Medusa's Head." In *Sexuality and the Psychology of Love.* Philip Rieff, ed. New York: Collier, 1974, 212-213.

Furtwangler, Albert. 1991. *Assassin on Stage: Brutus, Hamlet, and the Death of Lincoln.* Urbana and Chicago: University of Illinois Press.

Gabler, Neal. 1988. *An Empire of Their Own: How the Jews Invented Hollywood.* New York: Crown Publishers.

Gaiman, Neil. 1990. *The Sandman: The Doll's House.* New York: DC Comics.

————. 1991. *The Sandman: Preludes and Nocturnes.* New York: DC Comics.

————. 1991a. *Dream Country.* New York: DC Comics.

————. 1996. "The Tempest." *The Sandman* (March) 75.

Gallop, Jane. 1992. *Around 1981: Academic Feminist Critical Theory.* New York: Routledge.

————. 1997. *Feminist Accused of Sexual Harassment.* Durham, NC: Duke University Press.

Garber, Marjorie. 1987. *Shakespeare's Ghost Writers: Literature as Uncanny Causality.* New York and London: Routledge.

————. 1992a. *Vested Interests: Cross-Dressing and Cultural Anxiety.* New York and London: Routledge.

————. 1992b. "Character Assassination: Shakespeare, Anita Hill, and JFK." In *Media Spectacles.* Marjorie Garber et al., eds. New York and London: Routledge, 22-39.

————. 1995. *Vice Versa: Bi-sexuality and the Eroticism of Everyday Life.* New York: Simon and Schuster.

Gates, David. 1993. "White Male Paranoia: New Victims or Just Bad Sports?" *Newsweek,* May 23: 48-52.

Goldberg, Jonathan. 1994. "*Romeo and Juliet's* Open Rs." In *Queering the Renaissance.* Jonathan Goldberg, ed. Baltimore: The Johns Hopkins University Press.

Gordon, Giles. 1982. *Shakespeare Stories.* London: Hamish Hamilton.

Gould, Evelyn. 1996. *The Fate of Carmen.* Baltimore: The Johns Hopkins University Press.

Graff, Gerald. 1993. "Preaching to the Converted." In *English Inside and Out: The Places of Literary Criticism.* Susan Gubar and Jonathan Kamhotz, eds. New York and London: Routledge, 109-21.

Greenaway, Peter. 1991. *Prospero's Books: A Film of Shakespeare's Tempest.* New York: Four Walls Eight Windows.

Greenblatt, Stephen, Gen. Ed. 1997. *The Norton Shakespeare.* New York: W. W. Norton & Co.

Grossberg, Lawrence, Cary Nelson, and Paula A. Treichler. 1992. *Cultural Studies.* New York and London: Routledge.

Groys, Boris. 1992. *Ueber das Neue: Versuch einer Kulturoekonomie.* Munchen: Carl Hanser Verlag.

Halberstam, Judith. 1993. "Queer Sites: Transgenderism—Coming to a Theatre Near You!" *On Our Backs* (September/October) 30: 1, 10-11.

Hapgood, Robert. 1997. "Popularizing Shakespeare: The Artistry of Franco Zeffirelli." In *Shakespeare, the Movie: Popularizing the Plays on Film, TV, and Video.* Lynda E. Boose and Richard Burt, eds. New York and London: Routledge, 80-94.

Heath, Chris. 1996. "A Hard Man is Good to Find." *Details* 15 (4): September, 96-112, 270-71.

Hebdige, Dick. 1979. *Subcultures: The Meaning of Style.* New York and London: Routledge.

Hedrick, Don. 1994. "Flower Power: Shakespearean Deep Bawdy and the Botanical Perverse." In *The Administration of Aesthetics: Censorship, Political Criticism, and the Public Sphere.* Richard Burt, ed. Minneapolis: University of Minnesota Press, 83-105.

Hirsch, E. D. 1987. *Cultural Literacy: What Every American Needs to Know.* Boston: Houghton Mifflin.

Hodgdon, Barbara. 1991. *The End Crowns All: Closure and Contradiction in Shakespeare's History.* Princeton: Princeton University Press.

———. 1992. "Katherina Bound: Or, Play(K)ating the Strictures of Everyday life." *PMLA* 107 (3): 538-53.

Hofler, Robert. 1998. "The Men of Koo Koo Roo." *Buzz* (January): 62-65, 78-79.

Honan, William H. 1996. "A Sleuth Gets His Suspect: Shakespeare." *New York Times,* January 14: 1, 20.

hooks, bell. 1994. *Outlaw Culture.* New York: Routledge.

Hosoda, Craig. 1995. *The Bare Facts Video Guide.* Santa Clara, CA: The Bare Facts.

Houlahan, Mark. 1995. "Cosmic Hamlets: Contesting Shakespeare in Federation Space." *Extrapolations* (Spring) 36: 1, 28-37.

Howard, Jean. 1988. "Cross-Dressing, the Theater, and Gender Struggle in Early Modern England." *Shakespeare Quarterly* 39 (4): 418-40.

Hulktrans, Andrew. 1994. "MTV Rules (for a Bunch of Wussies)." *Art Forum* (February) 32: 6, 7-9.

Hunt, Lynn, ed. 1993. *The Invention of Pornography: Obscenity and the Origins of Modernity, 1500-1900.* New York: Zone Books.

Huyssen, Andreas. 1995. *Twilight Memories: Marking Time in a Culture of Amnesia.* New York and London: Routledge.

Irigaray, Luce. 1985. "Commodities Among Themselves." In *The Sex Which Is Not One.* Trans. Catherine Porter with Carolyn Burke. Ithaca: New York: Cornell University Press, 192-97.

———. 1985a. *Speculum of the Other Woman.* Trans. Gillian G. Gill. Ithaca and London: Cornell University Press.

Isherwood, Charles. 1997. "Breaking Out of the Celluloid Closet." *The Advocate* (September 30) 743: 44-48.

Isikoff, Michael and Evan Thomas. 1998. "The Secret War." *Newsweek.* February 9, 131 (6): 37-47.

Jameson, Frederic. 1981. *The Political Unconscious: Essays on the Social Function of Symbolic Form*. Oxford: Oxford University Press.

——. 1992. *Signatures of the Visible*. New York and London: Routledge.

——. 1993. "On 'Cultural Studies.'" *Social Text* 34: 42.

——. 1995. "Marx's Purloined Letter." *New Left Review* 209 (January/February): 75-109.

Jarman, Derek. 1991. *Queer Edward II*. London: BFI Publishing.

Jeffords, Susan. 1989. *Hard Bodies: Hollywood Masculinity in the Reagan Era*. New Brunswick, NJ: Rutgers University Press.

Jenkins III, Henry. 1991. "Star Trek Rerun, Reread, Rewritten: Fan Writing as Textual Poaching." In *Close Encounters: Film, Feminism, and Science Fiction*. Constance Penley et al., eds. Minneapolis: University of Minnesota, 170-203.

——. 1992. *Textual Poaching: Television Fans and Participatory Culture*. New York and London: Routledge.

Jensen, Jane. 1992. "Fandom as Pathology: The Consequences of Characterization." In *The Adoring Audience: Fan Culture and Popular Media*. London and New York: Routledge, 9-29.

Jong, Erica. 1995. *Shylock's Daughter: A Novel of Love in Venice*. New York: Harper Paperbacks. First published as *Serenissima*, 1986.

Joyrich, Lynn. 1993. "Elvisophilia: Knowledge, Pleasure, and the Cult of Elvis," *differences* 5 (1): 82-92.

Kael, Pauline. 1972. "Killers and Thieves." *The New Yorker* 47 (February 5): 76.

Kaplan, Amy. 1990. "Romancing the Empire: The Embodiment of Masculinity in the Popular Historical Novel of the 1890s." *American Literary History* (Winter) 2 (4): 659-90.

——. 1997. "Manifest Domesticity." Unpublished paper presented at Oberlin College.

Kaplan, Amy and Donald Pease, eds. 1994. *Cultures of U.S. Imperialism*. Durham, NC: Duke University Press.

Kaurismaki, Aki. 1991. *I Hired a Contract Killer*. Zurich: Haffmans.

Kellner, Douglas. 1997. *"Beavis and Butt-Head:* No Future for Postmodern Youth." In *Kinder-Culture: The Corporate Construction of Childhood*. Shirley R. Steinberg and Joe L. Kincheloe, eds. New York: Westview Press.

Kendall, Roy. 1996. "Animating Shakespeare." Unpublished paper delivered at the University of Massachusetts.

Kernes, Mark. 1997. "Briefs." *Adult Video News* (May) 13 (5): 149.

——. 1997a. "New 'Kid Porn' Law Survives First Challenge." *Adult Video News* (May) 13 (10): 270.

Kerr, Katherine, and Martin H. Greenberg. 1994. *Weird Tales from Shakespeare*. New York, Daw Books.

Keyser, Dorothy. 1987/88. "Cross-Sexual Casting in Baroque Opera: Music and Theatrical Conventions." *Opera Quarterly* 5/4: 46-57.

Kipnis, Laura. 1996. *Bound and Gagged: Pornography and the Politics of Fantasy in America*. New York: Grove Press.

Knight, Amarantha. 1996. *The Darker Passions: the Picture of Dorian Gray*. New York: Masquerade Books, Inc.

Koestenbaum, Wayne. 1990. "Wilde's Hard Labor and the Birth of Gay Reading." In *Engendering Men: The Question of Male Feminist Criticism.* Joseph A. Boone and Michael Cadden, eds. New York and London: Routledge, 176-89.

———. 1993. *The Queen's Throat: Opera, Homosexuality, and the Mystery of Desire.* New York: Poseiden Press.

Kracauer, Siegfried. 1938. *Orpheus in Paris: Offenbach and the Paris of His Time.* Trans. Gwenda David and Eric Mosbacher. New York: Alfred A. Knopf.

Kuhn, Annette, ed. 1995. *Queen of the 'B's: Ida Lupino Behind the Camera.* Westport, CT: Greenwood Press.

Kutzinski, Vera M. 1992. "Commentary: American Literary History as a Spatial Practice." *American Literary History* (Fall) 4 (3): 550-57.

La Rue, Chi Chi. 1997. *Making it Big: Sex Stars, Porn Films, and Me.* New York: Alyson Publications.

Lacan, Jacques. 1966. "The Signification of the Phallus." In *Écrits.* Trans. Alan Sheridan, 1977. New York: Norton.

Lane, Anthony. 1996. "Tights! Action! Camera!: Why Shakespeare Became this Year's Jane Austen." *New Yorker* 128 (November 25): 36, 65-77.

Lanier, Douglas. 1996. "Drowning the Book." In *Shakespeare, Theory, and Performance.* James Bulman, ed. New York and London: Routledge Press, 187-209.

Levi, Antonia. 1996. *Samurai from Outer Space: Understanding Japanese Animation.* Chicago and La Salle, IL: Open Court.

Levin, Tom. 1984. "The Acoustic Dimension: Notes on Cinema and Sound." *Screen* 25: 3, 55-68.

Levine, Laura. 1994. *Men in Women's Clothing: Anti-Theatricality and Effeminization.* Cambridge: Cambridge University Press.

Levine, Lawrence. 1988. "Shakespeare in America." In *Highbrow/Lowbrow: The Emergence of Cultural Hierarchy in America.* Cambridge, MA: Harvard University Press, 11-81.

Lieberman, Rhonda. 1993. "The Loser Thing." *Art Forum* (September) 31 (1): 78-82.

Longhurst, Brian. 1995. "Fans, Production, and Consumption." In *Popular Music and Society.* Cambridge: Polity Press, 226-48.

Longhurst, Derek. 1988. "'You base football player!': Shakespeare in Contemporary Popular Culture." In *The Shakespeare Myth.* Graham Holderness, ed. Manchester: Manchester University Press, 59-73.

Lord, M. G. 1997. "Pornutopia: How Feminists Learned to Love Dirty Pictures." *Lingua Franca.* (April/May) 6 (3): 40-48.

Lupton, Julia Reinhard and Kenneth Reinhard. 1994. *After Oedipus: Shakespeare in Psychoanalysis.* Ithaca: Cornell University Press.

Lydon, John. 1994. *Rotten: No Irish. No Blacks. No Dogs.* New York: Picador.

Lytle, Pete. 1997. "Mila, Absolutely the Filthiest Girl in Porn . . . Ever." *Hustler Erotic Video* (September) 12 (9): 50-53.

Macrone, Michael. 1997. *Naughty Shakespeare.* London: Andrews and McNeill.

Magner, Denise E. 1997. "Top English Departments No Longer Require Courses on Shakespeare, a Study Finds." *The Chronicle of Higher Education,* January 10, A12.

Marder, Louis. 1963. *His Exits and His Entrances: The Story of Shakespeare's Reputation.* Philadelphia: J. B. Lippincott Co.

Maslin, Janet. 1996. "Soft! What Light? It's Flash, Romeo." *New York Times,* November 1: C1; C12.

Mathews, Anne. 1991. "Deciphering Victorian Underwear and Other Seminars." *New York Times Sunday Magazine,* February 10, 42-43, 57-59, 63.

Mayne, Judith. 1991. "Lesbian Looks: Dorothy Arzner and Female Authorship." In *How Do I Look? Queer Film and Video.* Bad Object-Choices, eds. Seattle, WA: Bay Press.

McCauley, Stephen. 1987. *The Object of My Affection.* New York: Washington Square Press.

McClary, Susan. 1991. *Feminine Endings: Music, Gender, and Sexuality.* Minneapolis: University of Minnesota Press.

———. 1992. *Georges Bizet: Carmen.* Cambridge: Cambridge University Press.

McClintock, Anne, ed. 1993. *Social Text.* Special issue on "The Sex Trade." (Winter) 37.

McKernan, Luke and Olwen Terris. 1994. *Walking Shadows: Shakespeare in the National Film and Television Archive.* London: British Film Institute.

Mead, Rebecca. 1994. "Yo, Professor." *New York Magazine,* November 14, 48-53.

Mehlman, Jeffrey. 1993. *Walter Benjamin for Children: An Essay on His Radio Years.* Chicago: University of Chicago Press.

Mellencamp, Patricia. 1990. *Logics of Television: Essays in Cultural Criticism.* Bloomington: Indiana University Press.

Miller, D. A. 1991. "Anal Rope." In *Inside/Out: Lesbian Theories, Gay Theories.* Diana Fuss, ed. New York: Routledge, 119-41.

———. 1992. *Bringing Out Roland Barthes.* Berkeley: University of California Press.

Miller, Russell. 1984. *Bunny, the True Story of* Playboy. New York: Holt, Rinehart and Winston.

Mulvey, Laura. 1989. *Visual and Other Pleasures.* Bloomington: University of Indiana Press.

Murray, Raymond. 1996. *Images in the Dark: An Encyclopedia of Gay and Lesbian Film and Video.* London: Dutton.

Musil, Robert. 1937/1990. "On Stupidity." In *Precision and Soul: Essays and Addresses.* Burton Pike and David S. Luft, trans. and eds. Chicago: University of Chicago Press, 268-86.

National Alumni Forum. 1996. *The Shakespeare File: What English Majors Are Really Studying.* Washington, D.C.

Noble, Douglas D. 1989. "Mental Materiel: The Militarization of Learning and Intelligence in U.S. Education." In *Cyborg Worlds: The Military Information Society.* Les Levidow and Kevin Robins, eds. London: Free Association Books, 13-42.

Nunberg, Geoffrey. 1994. "The Places of the Book in the Age of Electronic Reproduction." *Representations.* 49 (Spring) 13-37.

296 / Unspeakable ShaXXXspeares

Nye, Robert. 1993. *Mrs. Shakespeare: The Collected Works.* London: Sinclair-Stevenson.

Olivier, Laurence. 1986. *On Acting.* London: Weidenfeld and Nicolson.

Orgel, Stephen. 1996. *Impersonations: The Performance of Gender in Shakespeare's England.* Cambridge: Cambridge University Press.

Osborne, Laurie. 1996. *The Trick of Singularity: Twelfth Night and the Performance Texts.* Iowa City: University of Iowa Press.

———. 1997a. "Film and Pedagogy: 'To new-found methods and to compounds strange.'" Unpublished paper delivered at the Shakespeare Association of America, Washington, D.C.

———. 1997b. "Poetry in Motion: Animating Shakespeare." In *Shakespeare, the Movie: Popularizing the Plays on Film, TV, and Video.* Lynda E. Boose and Richard Burt, eds. New York and London: Routledge.

O'Sullivan, Maurice J. 1997. *Shakespeare's Other Lives: An Anthology of Fictional Depictions of the Bard.* Jefferson: McFarland.

Parker, Andrew, Mary Russo, Doris Sommer, and Patricia Yaeger, eds. 1992. *Nationalisms and Sexualities.* New York and London: Routledge.

Parker, Patricia. 1994. "Hamlet and Othello: Dilation, Spying, and the 'Secret Place' of Women." in *Shakespeare Reread: The Texts in New Contexts.* Russell McDonald, ed. Ithaca and London: Cornell University Press, 105-46.

Patterson, John. 1997. "Get Shorty: The Return of Roman Polanski." *Neon* 12 (December): 74-79.

Pearce, Craig and Baz Luhrmann. 1996. *William Shakespeare's Romeo and Juliet: The Contemporary Film, the Classic Play.* New York: Bantam Doubleday Dell.

Pearson, Roberta E. and William Uricchio. 1990. "How Many Times Shall Caesar Bleed in Sport? Shakespeare and the Cultural Debate About Moving Pictures." *Screen* 31: 3, 243-61.

Pechter, Edward. 1996. "'Have you not read some such thing?': Sex and Sexual Stories in *Othello.*" *Shakespeare Survey.* 49: 20-26.

Pendergast, John S. 1995. "A Nation of Hamlets: Shakespeare and Cultural Politics." *Extrapolation* (Spring) 36 (1): 10-17.

Penley, Constance. 1992. "Feminism, Psychoanalysis, and the Study of Popular Culture." In *The Cultural Studies Reader.* Larry Grossberg et al., eds. New York and London: Routledge, 479-93.

———. 1997a. *NASA/Trek: Popular Science and Sex in America.* London: Verso.

———. 1997b. "Crackers and Whackers: The White Trashing of Porn." In *White Trash: Race and Class in America.* Matt Wray and Annalee Newitz, eds. New York and London: Routledge, 89-112.

Périsson, Jean. 1980. "Commentaire litteraire et musical sur *Les Contes d'Hoffmann.*" *L'avant-scene opéra* (Janvier-Fevrier) 25: 21-91.

Philips, Joseph D. 1982. "Film Conglomerate Blockbusting: International Appeal and Product Homogenization." In *The American Motion Picture Industry.* Robert Allen, ed. Carbondale: Southern Illinois University Press.

Pinkerton, James P. 1997. "The Bard Is Useful Even in the Locker Room." *Newsday,* February 3, H6.

Poizat, Michel. 1992. *The Cry of Angels: Beyond the Pleasure Principle in Opera.* Trans. Arthur Denner. Ithaca and London: Cornell University Press.

Polan, Dana. 1991. "The Spectacle of Intellect in a Media Age: Cultural Representations and the David Abraham, Paul de Man, and Victor Farias Cases." In *Intellectuals: Aesthetics, Politics, Academics.* Bruce Robbins, ed. Minneapolis: University of Minnesota Press, 343-63.

Polanski, Roman. 1984. *Roman.* New York: Morrow.

Porter, Joseph A. 1988. *Shakespeare's Mercutio: His History and Drama.* Chapel Hill: University of North Carolina Press.

Power, Elizabeth. 1996. "Reeling off Romanticism: Nabokov's *Lolita* and the Cinematic Art of Nympholepsy." Unpublished paper.

Powers, Ann. 1993. "Young and Beautiful." *Art Forum* 31 (March): 7, 9-10.

Readings, Bill. 1996. *The University in Ruins.* Cambridge, MA: Harvard University Press.

Rice, Anne. 1998. *Pandora: New Tales of the Vampires.* New York: Alfred A. Knopf.

Rickels, Laurence A. 1991. *The Case of California.* Baltimore: The Johns Hopkins University Press.

Riley, Patrick. 1995. *The X-Rated Videotape Guide.* Vol. 5. New York: Prometheus Books.

Ring, Trudy. 1996. "McKellen's Career Took Off After Coming Out." *Outlines,* February. http://www.suba.com/-outlines/february96/mckellen.html

Roach, Colleen. 1990. "The Movement for a New World and Information Order: A Second Wave?" *Media, Culture, and Society* 12 (3): 283-308.

Rodman, Howard A. 1991. "Anatomy of a Wizard." *American Film Review* 16 (November/December): 34-39.

Ronell, Avitall. 1996. "The Uninterrogated Question of Stupidity." *differences* 8 (2): 1-22.

Rooke, Leon. 1983. *Shakespeare's Dog: A Novel.* New York: Knopf.

Rorty, Richard. 1991. "Intellectuals in Politics: Too Far In? Too Far Out?" *Dissent* 38 (4): 483-90.

Rose, Tricia. 1994. *Black Noise: Rap Music and Black Culture in Contemporary America.* Hanover, NH: Wesleyan University Press.

Rose, Tricia and Andrew Ross, eds. 1994. *Microphone Fiends: Youth Music and Youth Culture.* New York and London: Routledge.

Ross, Andrew. 1989. "The Popularity of Pornography." In *No Respect: Intellectuals and Popular Culture.* New York and London: Routledge, 171-208.

———. 1991. "Hacking Away at the Counterculture." In *Technoculture.* Constance Penley and Andrew Ross, eds. New York and London: Routledge, 107-34.

———. 1992. "On Intellectuals and Politics: A Response to Richard Rorty." *Dissent* 39 (2): 263-65.

———. 1994. "The New Smartness." *Culture on the Brink: Ideologies of Technology.* Gretchen Bender and Timothy Druckery, eds. Seattle: Bay Press, 329-41.

Rothwell, Kenneth S. and Annabelle Henkin Melzer. 1990. *Shakespeare on Screen: An International Filmography and Videography.* New York: Neal-Schuman Publishers, Inc.

Rothwell, Kenneth S. Forthcoming. *A Concise History of Shakespeare on Film.* Cambridge: Cambridge University Press.

Russo, Mary and Dan Warner. 1987/88. "Rough Music, Futurism, and Postpunk Industrial Noise Bands." *Discourse* (Fall/Winter) 12 (1): 55-77.

Savage, Jon. 1997. "Blank Generation: Beavis and Butt-Head." In *Time Travel from the Sex Pistols to Nirvana: Pop, Media, and Sexuality*. New York: Vintage, 395-403.

Schneider, Rebecca. 1996. *The Explicit Body in Performance*. New York and London: Routledge.

Schwartz, Sherwood. 1988. *Inside Gilligan's Island: From Creation to Syndication*. Jefferson, North Carolina: McFarland & Co., Inc.

Sepstrup, Preben. 1989. "Transnationalization of Television in Western Europe." In *Cultural Transfer or Electronic Imperialism?: The Impact of American Television Programs on European Television* Christian W. Thomson, ed. Heidelberg: Carl Winter Universistaetsverlag, 99-136.

Silverman, Kaja. 1988. *The Acoustic Mirror: The Female Voice in Psychoanalysis and Cinema*. Bloomington and Indianapolis: Indiana University Press.

———. 1993. *Masculinity at the Margins*. New York and London: Routledge Press.

Sinfield, Alan. 1985. "Shakespeare and Education." In *Political Shakespeare: New Essays in Cultural Materialism*. Ithaca and London: Cornell University Press, 134-57.

———. 1992 "Cultural Imperialism and the Primal Scene of U.S. Man." In *Faultlines: Cultural Materialism and the Politics of Dissident Reading*. Berkeley and Los Angeles: University of California Press, 254-302.

———. 1994. *Cultural Politics: Queer Readings*. Philadelphia: University of Pennsylvania Press.

Smith, Bruce. 1991. *Homosexual Desire in Shakespeare's England: A Cultural Poetics*. Chicago: Chicago University Press.

Springer, Claudia. 1996. *Electronic Eros: Body and Desire in the Post-Industrial Age*. Austin: University of Texas Press.

Spungen, Deborah. 1983. *And I Don't Want to Live this Life*. New York: Ballantine Books.

Steinberg, Shirley R. and Joe L. Kincheloe, eds. 1997. *Kinder-Culture: The Corporate Construction of Childhood*. New York: Westview Press.

Straayer, Chris. 1996. *Deviant Eyes, Deviant Bodies: Sexual Re-Orientation in Film and Video*. New York: Columbia University Press.

Svetky, Benjamin. 1997. "A Porny Issue." *Entertainment* 392 (August 15): 50.

Thomas, Calvin. 1996. *Male Matters*. Urbana: University of Illinois Press.

Thompson, Kristin. 1985. *Exporting Entertainment: America in the World Film Market, 1907-34*. London: British Film Institute.

Torpov, Brandon. 1997. *Shakespeare For Beginners*. Illus. Joe Lee. New York: Writers and Readers Publishing, Inc.

Tracey, Michael. 1985. "The Poisoned Chalice? International Television and the Idea of Dominance." *Daedalus* 114 (Fall): 17-56.

Traub, Valerie. 1992a. *Desire and Anxiety: Circulations of Sexuality in Shakespearean Drama*. New York and London: Routledge.

———. 1992b. "The (In)significance of Lesbian Desire in Early Modern England." In *Erotic Politics: Desire on the Renaissance Stage*. Susan Zimmerman, ed. New York and London: Routledge, 150-69.

Ulmer, Gregory. 1989. *Teletheory: Grammatology in the Age of Video*. New York and London: Routledge.

Urichhio, William and Roberta E. Pearson. 1993. *Reframing Culture: The Case of the Vitagraph Quality Films*. Princeton, NJ: Princeton University Press.

Van Watson, William. 1992. "Shakespeare, Zeffirelli, and the Homosexual Gaze." *Literature and Film Quarterly* 20 (4): 308-25.

Wallen, Jeffrey. 1999. "Crossing-Over: The Academic as Porn Star." In *Closed Encounters: Literary Politics and Public Culture*. Minneapolis: University of Minnesota Press, 96-112.

Warner, Michael. 1993. "Introduction." In *Fear of a Queer Planet: Queer Politics and Social Theory*. Minneapolis: University of Minnesota Press, vii-xxxi.

Wasko, Janet. 1994. *Hollywood in the Information Age: Beyond the Silver Screen*. Austin: University of Texas Press.

Webb, Nancy and Jean Francis Webb. 1964. *Will Shakespeare and His America*. New York: Viking Press.

Wicke, Jennifer. 1994. "Celebrity Material: Materialist Feminism and the Culture of Celebrity." *South Atlantic Quarterly* 93 (4): 751-78.

Wilde, Oscar. 1891. *The Picture of Dorian Gray*. Donald L. Lawler, ed. New York: W.W. Norton and Co., Inc., 1988.

Wildman, Steven S. and Stephen E. Siweck. 1988. *International Trade in Films and Television Programs*. Cambridge, MA: Ballinger.

Williams, Linda. 1989. *Hardcore: The Frenzy of the Visible*. Berkeley: University of California Press.

Wilson, Laura. 1998. "Layered Stories: Shakespeare, Reality, and Authorship in Neil Gaiman's *The Sandman*." Unpublished paper circulated in the seminar "Citing Shakespeare in American Popular Culture," Shakespeare Association of America, Cleveland.

Wilson, Richard. 1996. "The Kindly Ones: The Death of the Author in Shakespearean Athens." In *The New Casebook A Midsummer Night's Dream*. Richard Dutton, ed. London: Macmillan, 198-222.

Žižek, Slavoj. 1997. "From the Sublime to the Ridiculous: The Sexual Act in Cinema." In *The Plague of Fantasies*. London: Verso, 171-91.

———. 1991. "Pornography, Nostalgia, Montage: A Triad of the Gaze." In *Looking Awry: An Introduction to Jacques Lacan Through Popular Culture*. Cambridge, MA: MIT Press, 107-22.

Winslow, Don. 1996. *Katerina in Charge*. New York: Masquerade.

Films, Videos, and TV Episodes Discussed

Abdul, Sam, dir. 1993. *Romeo and Julian*. USA. Forum Studios. With Grant Larson and Johnny Rey. Sound, col., 120 mins.

Abrahams, Jim, David Zucker, and Jerry Zucker, dir. 1980. *Airplane!* USA. Sound, col., 87 mins.

Abrahams, Jim, dir. 1991. *Hot Shots!*. USA. 20th Century Fox. Sound, col., 85 mins.

———. 1993. *Hot Shots! Part Deux*. USA. 20th Century Fox. Sound, col., 89 mins.

Aldrich, Robert, dir. 1955. *Kiss Me Deadly*. USA. UA. Sound, col., 105 mins.

Allen, Woody, dir. 1977. *Annie Hall*. USA. MGM/UA. Sound, col., 99 mins.

———. 1982. *A Midsummer Night's Sex Comedy*. USA. Orion. Sound, col., 88 mins.

Allers, Roger, and Ron Mikoff, dir. 1994. *The Lion King*. USA. Disney. Sound, col., animated, 88 mins.

Anon., dir. 1998. "Principal Takes a Holiday." *Wonderful World of Disney*. ABC. Original airdate Jan. 4. 46 mins.

Anon., dir. 1996. *MTV Romeo and Juliet Special*. MTV. Original airdate October 30. 26 mins.

Anon., dir. 1986. "Shakespeare in the Slums." *Saturday Night Live*. With Robin Williams. Original airdate Nov. 22. 7 mins.

Araki, Greg, dir. 1992. *The Living End*. USA. Desperate. Sound, col., 84 mins.

———. 1993. *Totally F***ed Up*. USA. Strand. Sound, col., 80 mins.

———. 1995. *The Doom Generation*. Fr/USA. Trimark. Sound, col., 85 mins.

Arnold, Jack, dir. "Juliet is the Sun." *The Brady Bunch*. Episode 52. Original airdate October 29, 1971. 46 mins.

Bergman, Andrew, dir. 1981. *So Fine*. USA. Warner Bros. Sound, col., 91 mins.

Berkeley, Busby, dir. 1943. *The Gang's All Here*. USA. 20th Century Fox. Sound, col., mins.

Bill, Tony, dir. 1986. *My Bodyguard*. USA. 20th Century Fox. Sound, col., 96 mins.

Bochner, Hart, dir. 1997. *High School High*. USA. TriStar. Sound, col., 85 mins.

Boskovich, John, dir. 1990. *Without You, I'm Nothing*. USA. MCEG Productions. Sound, col., 89 mins.

Branagh, Kenneth, dir. 1989. *Henry V*. UK. Samuel Goldwyn. Sound, col., 138 mins.

———. 1991. *Peter's Friends*. UK. Samuel Goldwyn. Sound, col., 101 mins.

———. 1993. *Much Ado About Nothing*. USA. Columbia/TriStar. Sound, col., 111 mins.

———. 1996. *A Midwinter's Tale/In the Bleak Midwinter*. UK. Sound, b/w, 98 mins.

Brooks, Mel, dir. 1967. *The Producers*. USA. Crossbow. Sound, col., 88 mins.

Cameron, James, dir. 1984. *The Terminator*. USA. Cinema '84. Sound, col., 108 mins.

Cates, Michael, dir. 1988. *A Mid-Slumber Night's Dream*. With Heather Wayne, Christy Canyon, and Erica Boyer. USA. 4 Play Video. Sound, col., 89 mins.

Cadinot, Jean Daniel, dir. 1986. *Le Voyage a Venise*. Fr. Videomo. With Benjamin Fontenay and Yannick Baud. Sound, col., 90 mins; *Carnival in Venice* in its U.S. release, 1987.

Chechik, Jeremiah S., dir. 1998. *The Avengers*. USA. Warner Bros. Sound, col., mins.

Chubbock, Lyndon, dir. 1995. *Naked Souls*. USA. Warner Vision. Sound, col., 90 mins.

Clark, Bob, dir. 1986. *Porky's 2*. USA. 20th Century Fox. Sound, col., 98 mins.

Coen, Ethan and Joel, dir. 1994. *The Hudsucker Proxy*. USA. Warner Bros. Sound, col., 111 mins.

Coen, Joel, dir. 1998. *The Big Lebowski*. USA. Working Title Films. Sound, col., 120 mins.

Columbus, Chris, dir. 1993. *Mrs. Doubtfire*. USA. 20th Century Fox. Sound, col., 125 mins.

Coolidge, Martha, dir. 1983. *Valley Girl*. USA. Valley 9000. Sound, col., 96 mins.

Coppola, Francis Ford, dir. 1972. *The Godfather*. USA. Zoetrope Studios. Sound, col., 161 mins.

————. 1990. *The Godfather III*. USA. Paramount. Sound, col., 170 mins.

————. 1992. *Bram Stoker's Dracula*. USA. Columbia. Sound, col., 130 mins.

Corbiau, Gerard, dir. 1994. *Farinelli*. Fr/It. Studio Canal/SONY. Sound, col., 110 mins.

Coronado, Celestino, dir. 1976. *Hamlet*. UK. Dangerous to Know. Sound, col., 67 mins.

————. 1987. *Midsummer Night's Dream*. UK. Dangerous to Know. Sound, col., 85 mins.

Costner, Kevin, dir. 1997. *The Postman*. USA. Warner Bros. Sound, col., 177 mins.

Crow, Art, dir. 1993. *A Midsummer Night's Bondage*. USA. Arlo Productions. With Candy and Lady Simone. Sound, col.

Crowe, Cameron, dir. 1992. *Singles*. USA. Warner Bros. Sound, col., 99 mins.

Cukor, George, dir. 1936. *Romeo and Juliet*. USA. MGM/UA. Sound, col., 126 mins.

Cunningham, Sean S., dir. 1980. *Friday the 13th*. USA. Paramount. Sound, col., 95 mins.

Czinner, Paul, dir. 1939. *As You Like It*. UK. 20th Century Fox. Sound, b/w, 97 mins.

D'Amato, Joe, dir. 1996. *Juliet and Romeo*. It. Excel. With Stephania Satori and Mark Davis. Sound, col., 90 mins.

————. 1997. *Othello: Dangerous Desire*. USA. Moonlight. With Courtknee and Sean Michaels. Sound, col., 90 mins.

Damiano, Luca, dir. 1996. *Hamlet: For the Love of Ophelia*. It. In-X-cess. With Sarah Young and Christopher Clark. Sound, col., 90 mins.

————. 1996. *Hamlet: For the Love of Ophelia, Part Two*. It. In-X-cess. With Sarah Young and Christopher Clark. Sound, col., 90 mins.

Davis, Desmond, dir. 1981. *The Clash of the Titans*. USA. MGM. Sound, col., 118 mins.

Demme, Jonathan, dir. 1994. *Philadelphia*. USA. TriStar. Sound, col., 125 mins.

Douglas, Gordon, dir. 1936. "Pay as You Exit." USA. MGM. With Our Gang. Sound, b/w, 20 mins.

————. 1967. *In Like Flint*. USA. 20th Century Fox. Sound, col., 115 mins.

Du Chau, Frederick, dir. 1998. *Quest for Camelot*. USA. Warner Bros. Sound, col., 85 mins.

Eastwood, Clint, dir. 1996. *Absolute Power*. USA. Castle Rock Entertainment. Sound, col., 121 mins.

Edwards, Blake, dir. 1982. *Victor/Victoria*. UK. MGM/UA. Sound, col., 175 min.

Elliot, Stephan, dir. 1994. *The Adventures of Priscilla, Queen of the Desert*. Aust. PolyGram. Sound, col., 103 mins.

Emmerich, Roland, dir. 1992. *Universal Soldier*. USA. Carolco Productions. Sound, col., 99 mins.

————. 1996. *Independence Day*. USA. 20th Century Fox. Sound, col., 145 mins.

Enright, Jim, dir. 1995. *Romeo Syndrome*. USA. Sin City. With April and Steven St. Croix. Sound, col., 86 mins.

Farrelly, Peter, dir. 1994. *Dumb and Dumber*. USA. New Line. Sound, col., 110 mins.

Ferrara, Abel, dir. 1986. *China Girl*. USA. Vestron Pictures. Sound, col., 90 mins.

Fishman, Bill, dir. 1988. *Tapeheads*. USA. Pacific Arts. Sound, col., 97 mins.

Fletcher, Mandie, dir. 1986. *The Black Adder II*. UK. BBC. Sound, col., 89 mins.

Ford, John, dir. 1949. *She Wore a Yellow Ribbon*. USA. RKO. Sound, col., 103 mins.

Fox, Michael D. and Dave Evans, dir. 1997. *Live Nude Shakespeare: To Bare or Not to Bare*. USA. Independent Edge. Sound, col., 65 mins.

Gambourg, Efim, dir. 1992. *Romeo and Juliet: Shakespeare, the Animated Tales*. Shakespeare Animated Films, Ltd., Christmas Films, and Soyuzmultfilm. 30 mins.

Gasnier, Louis, dir. 1936. *Reefer Madness*. USA. G&H. Sound, b/w, 67 mins.

Godard, Jean-Luc, dir. 1987. *King Lear*. USA. Cannon. Sound, col., 90 mins.

Goulding, Edmund, dir. 1932. *Grand Hotel*. MGM. Sound, b/w, 112 mins.

Greenaway, Peter, dir. 1991. *Prospero's Books*. Neth/Fr/It. 20th Century Fox. Sound, col., 126 mins.

Guccione, Bob, dir. Forthcoming. *Catherine the Great*. USA. Penthouse. Sound, col.

Haines, Richard and Samuel Weil, dir. 1986. *Class of Nuke 'Em High*. Troma Entertainment. Sound, col., 85 mins.

Haynes, Todd, dir. 1991. *Poison*. USA. Zeitgeist. Sound, col., 85 mins.

Heckerling, Amy, dir. 1995. *Clueless*. USA. Paramount. Sound, col., 97 mins.

Herek, Stephen, dir. 1988. *Bill and Ted's Excellent Adventure*. USA. Orion. Sound, col., 90 mins.

Herz, Michael, and Samuel Weil, dir. 1984. *The Toxic Avenger*. USA. Troma Entertainment. Sound, col., 100 mins.

Hickox, Douglas, dir. 1973. *Theatre of Blood*. UK. Cineman. Sound, col., 102 mins.

Hiller, Arthur, dir. 1987. *Outrageous Fortune*. USA. Touchstone. Sound, col., 91 mins.

Hoffman, Michael, dir. 1991. *Soapdish*. USA. Paramount. Sound, col., 97 mins.

Hogan, David, dir. 1996. *Barbwire*. USA. PolyGram. Sound, col., 109 mins.

Hogan, P. J., dir. 1996. *My Best Friend's Wedding*. USA. TriStar. Sound, col., 105 mins.

Holland, Agnieszka, dir. 1995. *Total Eclipse*. Fr/UK/Bel. New Line. Sound, col., 111 mins.

Hughes, Terry, dir. 1997. *The Third Rock from the Sun*.

Humberstone, H. Bruce, dir. 1952. *She's Working Her Way Through College*. USA. Warner Bros. Sound, col., 104 mins.

Hytner, Nicholas, dir. 1994. *The Madness of King George*. UK. Samuel Goldwyn. Sound, col., 110 mins.

———. 1998. *The Object of My Affection*. USA. 20th Century Fox. Sound, col., 112 mins.

Ippoliti, Silvano, dir. 1980. *Caligula*. Italy, USA. Penthouse Films. Sound, col., 115 mins.

Jacks, Peter, dir. 1994. *Heavenly Creatures*. NZ. Miramax. Sound, col., 98 mins.

Jackson, Mick, dir. 1991. *L. A. Story*. USA. Carico. Sound. col., 98 mins.

Jarman, Derek, dir. 1991. *Edward II*. UK. New Line. Sound, col., 90 mins.

————. 1986. *The Tempest*. UK. Boyd's Company. Sound, col., 95 mins.

Jeremy, Ron, dir. 1991. *John Wayne Bobbitt: Uncut*. USA. Leisure Time. Sound, col., 110 mins.

Jernigan, Richard, dir. 1995. "Rosie, O Rosie, Oh." *Wishbone*. Big Feats! Entertainment. 30 mins.

Jordan, Neil, dir. 1994. *The Crying Game*. USA. Miramax. Sound, col., 112 mins.

Judge, Mike, dir. 1996. *Beavis and Butt-Head Do America*. USA. Paramount. Sound, col., animated, 81 mins.

Kalin, Tom, dir. 1991. *Swoon*. USA. Argos. Sound, b/w, 94 mins.

Kalvert, Scott, dir. 1995. *Basketball Diaries*. USA. PolyGram. Sound, col., 102 mins.

Kaufman, Lloyd, dir. 1996. *Tromeo and Juliet*. USA. Troma Entertainment. Sound, col., 102 mins.

Kazan, Elia, dir. 1951. *A Streetcar Named Desire*. USA. Sound, b/w, 122 mins.

Kidron, Beeban, dir. 1994. *To Wong Foo: Thanks for Everything Julie Newmar*. USA. Universal. Sound, col., 109 mins.

Kleiser, Randall, dir. 1995. *It's My Party*. USA. UA. Sound, col., 110 mins.

Kotcheff, Ted, dir. 1984. *Rambo*. USA. Thorn EMI. Sound, col., 96 mins.

Kubrick, Stanley, dir. 1960. *Spartacus*. USA. Universal. Sound, col., 196 mins.

Kurismaki, Aki, dir. 1987. *Hamlet Goes Business*. FIN. Sound, b/w, mins.

Kuzui, Fran Rubel, dir. 1992. *Buffy the Vampire Slayer*. USA. 20th Century Fox. Sound, col., 86 mins.

Kwietniowski, Richard, dir. 1998. *Love and Death on Long Island*. Canada/UK. BBC/Nova Scotia Films. Sound, col., 93 min.

Lee, Bud, dir. 1986. *Hyapatia Lee's Ribald Tales of Canterbury*. USA. Caballero. Sound, col., 100 mins.

Lehmann, Michael, dir. 1994. *Airheads*. USA. 20th Century Fox. Sound, col., 92 mins.

Lemmons, Kasi, dir. 1997. *Eve's Bayou*. USA. Trimark. Sound, col., 108 mins.

Leslie, John, dir. 1989. *Slick Honey*. USA. VCA. With Selena Steele. Sound, col., 88 mins.

Levant, Brian, dir. 1994. *The Flintstones*. USA. Universal. Sound, col., 92 mins.

Levinson, Barry, dir. 1997. *Wag the Dog*. USA. Tribecca Productions/New Line Cinema. Sound, col., 126 mins.

Levitow, Abe, dir. 1959. *A Witch's Tangled Hare*. USA. Warner Bros. Sound, col., 7 mins.

Lincoln, F. J., dir. 1986. *In and Out of Africa*. USA. Penguin. With Nina Hartley and Angel Kelly. Sound, col., 90 mins.

Linklater, Richard, dir. 1993. *Slacker*. USA. Orion. Sound, col., 97 mins.

Little, Dwight H., dir. 1997. *Murder at 1600*. USA. Warner. Sound, col., 107 mins.

Livingstone, Jenny, dir. 1990. *Paris Is Burning*. USA. ICA/OffWhite. Sound, col., 71 mins.

Loncraine, Richard, dir. 1995. *Richard III*. USA. MGM/UA. Sound, col., 104 mins.

Luhrmann, Baz, dir. 1996. *William Shakespeare's Romeo and Juliet*. USA. 20th Century Fox. Sound, col., 120 mins.

————. 1995. *Strictly Ballroom*. Aust. Miramax. Sound, col., 94 mins.

Lupino, Ida and George M. Cahan, dir. 1964. "The Producer." *Gilligan's Island*. Sound, col., 46 mins.

Lyne, Adrian, dir. 1997. *Lolita*. France. Guild/Pathe. Sound, col., 137 mins.

McCarthy, Joseph, dir. 1969. *The Magic Christian*. GB. Republic. Sound, col., 88 mins.

McGrath, Douglas, dir. 1996. *Emma*. UK/USA. Miramax. Sound, col., 120 mins.

McKenzie, Will. 1986. *Moonlighting*. ABC. 46 mins.

McTiernan, John, dir. 1988. *Die Hard*. USA. 20th Century Fox. Sound, col., 132 mins.

———. 1991. *Last Action Hero*. USA. Columbia/TriStar. Sound, col., 90 mins.

———. 1995. *Die Hard With a Vengeance*. USA. 20th Century Fox. Sound, col., 128 mins.

MacKinnon, Gillies, dir. 1992. *The Playboys*. USA. Samuel Goldwyn. Sound, col., 113 mins.

Mack, Anthony, dir. 1929. "Shivering Shakespeare." With the Little Rascals. USA. MGM. Sound, b/w, 20 mins.

Marshall, Penny, dir. 1994. *Renaissance Man*. USA. Touchstone. Sound, col., 128 mins.

Martino, Raymond, dir. 1994. *Skyscraper*. USA. PM Entertainment. Sound, col., mins.

———. 1995. *To the Limit*. USA. PM Entertainment. Sound, col., mins.

Mazursky, Paul, dir. 1977. *Harry and Tonto*. USA. 20th Century Fox. Sound, col., 115 mins.

———. 1986. *Tempest*. USA. Columbia. Sound, col., 143 mins.

Meyer, Nicolas, dir. 1982. *Star Trek II: The Wrath of Khan*. USA. Paramount. Sound, col., 114 mins.

———. 1986. *The Voyage Home: Star Trek IV*. USA. Paramount. Sound, col., 119 mins.

———. 1991. *Star Trek VI: The Undiscovered Country*. USA. Paramount. Sound, col., 110 mins.

Mirkin, David, dir. 1997. *Romy and Michele's High School Reunion*. USA. Touchstone. Sound, col., 92 mins.

Moorhouse, Jocelyn, dir. 1997. *A Thousand Acres*. USA. Via Rosa. Sound, col., 120 mins.

Mulcahy, Russell. 1990. *Highlander 2: The Quickening*. USA. Republic. Sound, col., 90 mins.

Nakajima, Atsuko, dir. 1995. *Ranma 1/2: Ranma and Juliet*. USA. Kitty TV. Sound, col., animated, 52 mins.

Nelson, Ozzie, dir. 1952. "An Evening with Hamlet." *Ozzie and Harriet*.

Newell, Mike, dir. 1995. *Four Weddings and a Funeral*. UK. PolyGram. Sound, col., 117 mins.

Nichols, Mike, dir. 1996. *The Birdcage*. USA. MGM/UA. Sound, col., 119 mins.

Noble, Adrian, dir. 1996. *A Midsummer Night's Dream*. UK. Capitol. Sound, Col., 100 mins.

Nunn, Trevor, dir. 1996. *Twelfth Night*. UK. New Line. Sound, col., 133 mins.

Olivier, Laurence, dir. 1955. *Richard III*. UK. London Films. Sound, col., 161 mins.

Oz, Frank, dir. 1997. *In and Out*. USA. Paramount. Sound, col., 92 mins.

Pacino, Al, dir. 1996. *Looking for Richard*. USA. 20th Century Fox. Sound, col., 112 mins.

Parker, Oliver, dir. 1995. *Othello*. UK/US. Castle Rock. Sound, col., 123 mins.

Pasolini, Pier Paolo, dir. 1970. *The Decameron*. It/Fr/WGer. Waterbearer Films. Sound, col., 111 mins.

———. 1971. *The Canterbury Tales*. It/Fr. Waterbearer Films. Sound, col., 109 mins.

———. 1974. *The Arabian Nights*. It/Fr. Waterbearer Film. Sound, col., 130 mins.

Petersen, Wolfgang, dir. 1997. *Air Force One*. USA. Columbia. Sound, col., 125 mins.

Polanski, Roman, dir. 1972. *Macbeth*. USA. Playboy. Sound, col., 139 mins.

———. 1966. *The Fearless Vampire Killers*. USA. MGM. Sound, col., 107 mins.

———. 1968. *Rosemary's Baby*. USA. Paramount. Sound, col., 137 mins.

Potter, Sally, dir. 1992. *Orlando*. UK. SONY. Sound, col., 93 mins.

Powers, Jim, dir. 1997. *Taming of the Screw*. Notorious. Sound, col., 90 mins.

Preminger, Otto, dir. 1954. *Carmen Jones*. USA. 20th Century Fox. Sound, col., 105 mins.

Redford, Robert, dir. 1994. *Quiz Show*. USA. Hollywood. Sound, col., 133 mins.

Reiner, Rob, dir. 1989. *When Harry Met Sally*. USA. Columbia. Sound, col., 107 mins.

Robinson, Bruce, dir. 1985. *Withnail and I*. UK. Paragon. Sound, col., 104 mins.

Ross, Herbert, dir. 1977. *The Goodbye Girl*. USA. MGM/UA. Sound, col., mins.

Rudolph, Alan, dir. 1997. *Afterglow*. USA. Columbia. Sound, col., 120 mins.

Scheerer, Robert, dir. 1990. "The Defector." *Star Trek: The Next Generation*. Episode 58. USA. Paramount. Sound, col., 46 mins.

Schepisi, Fred, dir. 1987. *Roxanne*. USA. Columbia Sound, col., 107 mins.

Schumacher, Joel, dir. 1993. *Falling Down*. USA. Sound, col., mins.

Scorsese, Martin, dir. 1983. *The King of Comedy*. USA. Warner Bros. Sound, col., 109 mins.

Segal, Peter, dir. 1994. *The Naked Gun Thirty-Three and a Third: The Final Insult*. USA. Paramount. Sound, col., 83 mins.

Senowski, Ron, dir. 1998. *Let's Kill All the Lawyers*. UK. Barrister Films, Ltd. Sound, col., 103 mins.

Shardlow, Martin. 1990. *The Black Adder I*. UK. BBC. Sound, col., 100 mins.

Sidney II, George, dir. 1953. *Kiss Me Kate*. USA. MGM. Sound, col., 110 mins.

Smith, John, dir. 1994. *Dangerous Minds*. USA. Hollywood. Sound, col., 99 mins.

Smith, Mel, dir. 1989. *The Tall Guy*. UK. Columbia. Sound, col., 92 mins.

Spenelli, Michael, dir. 1996. *Star-crossed*. USA. VCA. With Sunset Thomas. Sound, col., 110 mins.

Spielberg, Stephen, dir. 1991. *Hook*. USA. Columbia/Tristar. Sound, col., 144 mins.

Stiller, Ben, dir. 1994. *Reality Bites*. USA. Universal. Sound, col., 99 mins.

Stone, Oliver, dir. 1991. *JFK*. USA. Warner Bros. Sound, col., 206 mins.

———. 1994. *Natural Born Killers*. USA. Vidmark. Sound, col., 182 mins.

Stoppard, Tom, dir. 1991. *Rosencrantz and Guildenstern Are Dead*. USA. Cinecom. Sound, col., 117 mins.

Stootsberry, A. P., dir. 1968. *The Secret Sex Lives of Romeo and Juliet*. USA. Global Pictures. With Foreman Shane and Dierdre Nelson. Sound, col., 90 mins.

Takeshi, Honda, dir. 1996. *Oh My Goddess! 2: Midsummer Night's Dream*. Japan. Kodansha. Sound, col., animated, 29 mins.

Thomas, Dave and Rick Moranis, dir. 1991. *Strange Brew.* USA. MGM/UA. Sound, col., 91 mins.

Thomas, Paul, dir. 1987. *Romeo and Juliet.* USA. Western Visuals. With Kim Alexis, Jerry Butler, and Nina Hartley. Sound, col., 85 mins.

————. 1988. *Romeo and Juliet II.* USA. Western Visuals. With Nikki Randal and Jaquline Lorians. Sound, col., 88 mins.

Van Sant, Gus, dir. 1991. *My Own Private Idaho.* USA. New Line. Sound, col., 104 mins.

————. 1997. *Good Will Hunting.* USA. Miramax. Sound, col., 126 mins.

Vaughn, Ben, dir. 1995. "Shakespaw." *Wishbone.* Big Feats! Entertainment. 30 mins.

Wellman, William, dir. 1948. *Yellow Sky.* US. 20th Century Fox. Sound, b/w, 98 mins.

Wertheim, Ron, dir. 1977. *Twelfth Night.* US/It. Playboy. Sound, col., 110 mins.

Wier, Peter, dir. 1987. *Dead Poets Society.* USA. Touchstone. Sound, col., 128 mins.

Wilcox, Fred McLeod, dir. 1956. *Forbidden Planet.* USA. MGM/UA. Sound, col., 99 mins.

Wilder, Billy, dir. 1959. *Some Like It Hot.* USA. UA. Sound, b/w, 121 mins.

Wise, Robert, dir. 1965. *The Sound of Music.* USA. 20th Century Fox. Sound, col., 174 mins.

Wise, Robert and Jerome Robbins, dir. 1953. *West Side Story.* MGM. Sound, col., 151 mins.

Yates, Peter, dir. 1983. *The Dresser.* UK. Columbia. Sound, col., 118 mins.

Zeffirelli, Franco, dir. 1966. *The Taming of the Shrew.* USA. Columbia. Sound, col., 122 mins.

————. 1968. *Romeo and Juliet.* It. Paramount. Sound, col., 152 mins.

————. 1986. *Otello.* It. Cannon. Sound, col., 123 mins.

————. 1991. *Hamlet.* USA. Warner Bros. Sound, col., 134 mins.

Zemeckis, Robert, dir. 1994. *Forrest Gump.* USA. Paramount. Sound, col., 142 mins.

Zen, Michael, dir. 1996. *Censored.* USA. Vivid. Sound, col., 75 mins.

Zucker, David, dir. 1988. *The Naked Gun: From the Files of Police Squad!.* USA. Paramount. Sound, col., 85 mins.

————. 1991. *The Naked Gun Two and a Half: The Smell of Fear.* USA. Paramount. Sound, col., 85 mins.

Index